The Palace A
2:
Where Eagles Fly

by

James Howland

ISBN: 1536846511
ISBN-13: 978-1536846515

CONTENTS

Chapter	Chapter Name	Page
	Before I begin…	4
-	**CPFC Sydney Supporters Club**	5
1	I've had Enough	7
2	Goodbye Selhurst. I'm going to miss you!	13
3	The Adventure Begins	22
4	Arriving in Sydney	28
5	Returning Faces and Gloom	46
6	It Never Rains	54
7	There's Only One Geoff Thomas	61
8	Supporters Clubs	65
9	Who do you sing for?	70
10	Playing for Palace	79
11	Football, Football Everywhere	84
12	The Robert Eaton Memorial Fund	94
13	Byron Bay	103
14	Disappointing Paradise	109
-	**A Hungarian Eagle – My journey to Addiction**	114
15	Brisbane	117
16	It Ain't All so Bad	122
17	Football, I'll pass.	126
18	We Can See You Puking Up!	128
19	Cairns	131
-	**Palace in South America**	135
20	Returning to Asia	136
21	Come Rain or Shine	140
22	The Jungle, an Island and Thailand	145
23	Crossing the Border	152
24	Oh Phuk-et	158
25	Over Land and Sea	164
26	Bangkok	171
27	The North Thailand Burnley Supporters Club	177
28	The Power of Football	183
-	**A Palace Fan in Namibia**	186
29	My Time in 'Nam	189
30	Christmas in Sydney	197
31	Focusing on Palace	205
32	The Asia Cup	213
33	Miserable	223
34	Newcastle, Twice.	228

35	Opposites at the Exhibition	235
36	The Losing Week	242
37	The Cricket World Cup	246
38	The Match Day Routine	251
39	Becoming a Film Star	253
-	**New York Eagles**	256
40	Canberra, Melbourne and The Great Ocean Road	260
41	Shaun Derry and The Bay of Islands.	266
42	Wellington Phoenix	270
43	South Island, West Coast	274
-	**Palace in South Africa – before worldwide coverage**	277
44	Queenstown and the Deep South	283
45	Palace up a Volcano	287
46	A Functioning Alcoholic	292
47	Preparing to Leave	295
48	The Last Game	301
49	Football in the Philippines	305
50	Reunited	310
-	**Hong Kong Eagles**	313
51	Same Old Palace	315

Before I begin...

Here we go again! My second book about my addiction – being a Palace fan! After releasing my first title, The Palace Addiction, in 2015, I couldn't believe its success. Not only in terms of sales figures and reviews, but also the opportunities that it has given me and people I've met.

Like with the first book, I couldn't afford a professional proof reader so I hope you can forgive the occasional mistake or typo and still enjoy the book.

As with my original book, I've tried to write as honestly and close to the truth as possible. Of course, writing after the events might have encouraged my mind to exaggerate some of them. However, I always tried to stay true to my emotions that I felt at the time – both in terms of my personal life and how I felt towards my beloved club.

I was delighted and touched by the contributions and time given to me Mile Jedinak and Steve Browett. Their enthusiastic response was excellent and really adds something special to my writing. I felt like a wide-eyed school boy as I had a phone conversation with one of my all time heroes, Mile Jedinak. I'd also like to credit and thank Palace's official photographer, Neil Everitt, for the photo of Mile on the front cover that the club kindly let me use.

I'd also like to thank the supporters and friends who contacted me to share their experiences of following Palace from all around the globe. Their insights again give the book something different and I hope you'll find them as fascinating as I did.

And finally, before you start to hear about a Palace Addict's adventures around the world, I'd like to say a few words of thanks to those who helped and advised me with the book.

Firstly, I'd like to say thank you to my Dad. Not only did he start my Palace Addiction by taking me along as a child, but he has always supported and encouraged me with this project. Secondly, I would also like to thank my friends Akos Kovach, Anthony Lock and Ryan Clarke for their proof reading and advice on the book. I'd also like to say a huge word of appreciation to Mark Grabowski for his proof reading support and advice. I'd also like to send my gratitude to my close friend Richard Sroka, who you will meet in this book, for his excellent job on the cover. Finally, I'd like to thank James Mitchell, despite having never met me, for his time, encouragement and advice on the book.

Tony King, Member of the Crystal Palace Sydney Supporters Club
- The journey of CPFC Sydney

I'd wanted to live in Australia for years, having been there on holiday I loved the weather and the lifestyle. But one thing always kept me home, my love of Palace.

I couldn't imagine a world where I didn't get up to go and watch Palace every weekend, a whole where I couldn't watch AJ score goals for fun, or watch Dougie bamboozle defenders with a single turn.

Then Peter Taylor took over.

And I suddenly realised, you know what, I've got better things to be doing that watching this s*** every week. So I packed up my bags and off I went to start a new life in Australia.

In those pre-facebook times, I just assumed I was the only Palace fan in Oz. Every Sunday morning (pre smart-phones) I'd wake up to see if my Dad had texted me the result, usually with a succinct summary of the game (along the lines of 'Lost 1-0, s*** game').

I met a couple of other guys down the pub when we lost the play off semi's to Bristol but with not much to cheer about, those games didn't really inspire us to meet up and do it again.

It all changed with that final game of the season at Hillsborough. By now the HOL had taken preference over the BBS for Palace info – and it was on there that I saw someone had arranged for a meet up to watch the game.

And it was there that the first seeds of CPFC SYDNEY were sown, where a stranger then, but good friend now, Jordo, went around and got people's numbers and email addresses. Obviously the game went our way and many beers were drunk, despite it being the early hours of Monday morning by the time the game finished. However, in our drunken state, it was agreed that we must do it again.

For a while, a few of us would meet at the Crystal Palace Hotel, great name but rather aptly, a total s***hole, and we'd sit around on match days with the BBC live updates on our phones, waiting for the results to come in from South London.

Luckily, the stars aligned for us Australian based Palace fans. Setanta Sports (RIP) started showing weekly Championship games and Palace signed a sometime Socceroo Mile Jedinak. Suddenly, there was interest in Australia about Palace, and every 6 weeks or so we could actually watch a live game. A *Facebook* page was started, Holmesdale Online was used to spread the word and before long 4 blokes sat around a phone at 2 in the morning became 30 blokes down the pub watching the red and blue on the big screen at our new home, The Royal Exhibition Hotel. This all coincided with an upturn in the club's fortunes, more success meant more coverage, which meant more people joining us on those late, late nights. And now we're in the Premier League, we get every single game broadcast over here, meaning we don't have to miss a minute of watching Palace.

It's not all good. We had to get up at 5am to go to the pub to watch the second leg of the Brighton Play off, knowing that we had to leave and go straight to work after, whilst we knew everyone back home was out celebrating. That was just one example of the harder side to watching Palace from another hemisphere.

However, I've met some of my best friends in Australia shouting at a blurry screen at 3 in the morning. I've had some of my best nights out dancing around that ropey pub and singing Glad All Over.

So it might not be the same as walking up the Holmesdale Road every week, but right now I wouldn't change a thing about being a Palace fan in Australia.

Apart from those 4am kick off times, they can 'root a boot' as they say in these parts.

The Palace Addiction 2: Where Eagles Fly.

Chapter 1 - I've had Enough – *Brighton, 17ᵗʰ March 2013*

Something had to change. I was miserable. And not just because of that moment.

We'd had the dreaded call on the Thursday night, Ofsted were coming. The year had been difficult throughout. I'd struggled with a lively class, consisting of children with various statements for autism, as well as other mental and emotional barriers to learning - before I even begin to think about the usual group of difficult strong minded boys and adolescent argumentative girls. I went home exhausted every evening and crashed on the sofa, too tired to do anything but throw a pizza in the oven. I began to get through days rather than relish them. I started to 'do' my job rather than embrace it. I began to cut corners and 'leave things for tomorrow'. I began to need long tea breaks to recover as productivity dropped out of the window. Work, and as I let it take me over, life, became a chore.

At least Saturday was an escape - to football, and for once, the football didn't disappoint. Top goal scorers in the entire football league - Crystal Palace Football Club. We'd even survived the wobble of losing our greedy bastard of a manager half way through the season as Dougie Freedman ended any last shred of belief that I had in football integrity. With us playing brilliant football, and having won six of the previous eight games, he walked out. Now, I suppose you could easily justify him going to a higher paid job, as he said, 'because he has kids to feed'.

However, this is a man who has spent nearly twenty years as a footballer and football manager earning presumably something like 5k-10k a week (or more at some points I'm sure) - mainly paid by our club. This is someone who was given extra playing contracts by our club because he was a legend in our corner of South London. This is someone who was given a chance in management because he was Dougie Freedman and we were Crystal Palace. This is someone who'd 'managed' us to two wins in eighteen league matches without so much as a murmur of discontent from the supporters because he was Dougie Freedman and we were Crystal Palace. In fact, the tune of winter wonderland with certain words replaced had echoed around the ground in all eighteen of those matches because it didn't matter that we were crap and playing defensive, turgid football. We were managed by someone we loved. We were managed by a club legend. We were part of something special. We were managed by one of us. We were managed by someone who after being linked to another club said that he'd *'never leave a job half done'*. Well he did leave, barely a quarter of the way though - and just two days after his loyal pledge.

Anyway, it taught me something. Support the club, support the badge, cheer the mercenaries, enjoy their skill, love their achievements, expect nothing. They'll be gone one day - and that day probably isn't far away. Rightly, pundits often point out that fans are just as quick to turn on a player as the players are to kiss a badge and leave, but with Dougie Freedman, it had been different. We'd appointed him and stuck by him purely out of loyalty and love for him. Thankfully, Ian Holloway came in and had taken the job on - in fact, he was doing a far better job for us than Greedman was in Bolton. Yet, I still wouldn't sing his name. The chant *'Manager's Name's Red'n'Blue Army'* had forever changed to *'South London's Red'n'Blue Army'* in my mind.

However, away from my occasional escape into the depths of football emotion, where nothing else matters outside of my own little red and blue bubble - sometimes games, but often rants such as the one above because being in a state of football outrage is when we're most comfortable as fans, I was miserable. Miserable about life.

I didn't really have any right to be either. I had so much going for me. Aged just twenty-five, I lived in a brilliant maisonette in Battersea with three of my best friends: Rob, Robin and Stagg. I had the job that I always dreamed of and a comfortable enough income to live pretty much as I wanted and a large enough group of friends to share life's journey with. However, with all three of my flatmates recently starting new relationships and me being single, I was fed up of feeling like a 'seventh wheel'. I would often opt to stay home alone on the sofa rather than make small talk with couples.

I don't think I'd realised how much work was getting me down until the entire school workforce were called into the staffroom on the Thursday lunchtime and met with the words *'they're coming'* and a list of jobs to do before *they* arrived: folders to update, classroom displays to be refreshed, scores to be monitored, targets to be recited, marking to be checked. As well as that, I knew I needed to keep my lively class focussed in the build up, producing top quality behaviour and learning.

For Ofsted, I was getting to school at 7am and leaving at 9pm. My folders weren't up to date, my books weren't marked, my displays were falling down. I hadn't been lazy, I'd previously been putting all that I had in terms of effort, emotion and time into the job but it wasn't enough. I'd lost focus in my own stress. I'd been failing. I'd been simply getting through each day. I'd been worried about Child X having a breakdown, Child Y ripping up Child Z's school shirt (and their inevitable retaliation) or Child R having family crisis, or Child O smashing a door, or Child B having lower levels than the average reception student. I was exhausting myself by fire fighting and frankly, I was containing issues rather than moving forward and letting other less prominent things, such as folders, or displays, or marking, or even personal sanity fall by the wayside. I was putting everything into giving the kids what they needed emotionally and their academic needs had gone out of the window. Academically, I was failing the kids and emotionally, they were relying on me. I hadn't been sleeping, I was barely eating; frankly, life was s*** and I hadn't even noticed.

Saturdays were all I lived for - Saturdays were my support group. They were a chance to meet my older Palace mates in The Selhurst Railwayman's Club prematch, watch Palace win (amazingly, we'd only lost one home game all season - the opening match), then head to Crystal Palace for post match celebrations with my mates Pavel, his girlfriend and adopted Palace fan, Georgina, Cliff, Neil and Dan - who I had a season ticket next to in Block C of the Holmesdale Road Lower Tier. Even if this routine usually did result in a 'Recovery Sunday' of lying on the sofa with a headache ahead of another long week.

Anyway, that was the plan. Football cleared my mind and focussed my week. It gave me something to look forward to throughout it and a reward at the end. I wasn't a struggling teacher on the Saturday, I was a Crystal Palace fan. I drank. I sang. I cheered. I ranted. I laughed. I stated geeky facts. I made bad jokes. I ate pies. I rolled my eyes at the idiotic comments from behind. I called the referee some rude words. I jumped. I sulked. I hugged. I despaired. I made terrible predictions. I made awful puns. I repeatedly stated how good Glenn Murray's movement was. I became an expert in everything. I moaned at subs. I saw friends. I saw family. I nodded at familiar faces. I joined the crush for a half time pee. I checked the live league table on my iPhone. I enquired as to what Dougie Freedman had done. I forgot life *and* I even smiled occasionally.

Football even helped in the classroom. Being the school football coach and wowing kids by telling them that you go to matches at the weekend makes any little football lovers in the class absolutely idolise their teacher. I'm not sure what's a bigger shock to them. The fact that their teacher has any sort of life outside of school or the even stranger fact that he likes something that they consider 'cool'. Even if the fact that I went to Crystal Palace was a little less cool than going to Chelsea (in their naive little eyes anyway).

On the 'Ofsted Saturday', I didn't go to football. I went to work. Only for seven hours that day but it was still far longer than I desired to spend of my weekend in school. I was behind on everything and needed to catch up. The next day, I woke up early to get some more work done before going to the football. Despite getting one of the few precious tickets, I had told my Dad that I couldn't go. However, he persuaded me to give myself a break and come anyway.

I supplied the beers on the train for Colin, Sunningdale Dan, Jonathan, Pavel, his girlfriend, Georgina, and the other Dan, who was passed out in the corner after a over drinking the night before, but I didn't have any booze myself. I knew that I had work to do that evening. To be honest, it was a good excuse to rid our flat of the unwanted array of crap lagers that had been left behind by various visitors.

The game should have been the biggest of the season. We were away at *them*. Our arch rivals, Brighton and Hove Albion. Throughout my life, they've been nobody. They've been lower league Brighton. I've known I hate them because we hate them and that's what we do. However, between 1997, when I began my Palace love affair, and 2011, it had always felt a bit like having a personal vendetta against a fly. While it's annoying, you know you're bigger and better and if you really want to, you can squash it with ease. But now, shiny new stadium in hand, Brighton were back. The fly had evolved and the b******s had actually finished above us in the previous season.

Still, normal service had been resumed and despite them being in the playoff positions, we were going for automatic promotion - a win would put us second, touching distance from promotion with eight games left. The train down was light-hearted, confident even - for the others, not for me as my mind returned to work with every gap in conversation. We had every right to be confident too - we'd won five and drawn two of our previous eight games. Glenn Murray, Brighton's nemesis, had already scored thirty goals for us in the season, including two in the home game against his former club. A brief exchange with a Brighton father and teenage son on the train brought a slight tenseness to the journey but although neither side would back down, everyone there was intelligent enough to realise that a few football insults was as far as it needed to go.

We met my Dad at Falmer station as we strode up to the away end and I finally began to forget about Ofsted and think about the match. In the ground, I even allowed myself a beer as they were selling 'Palace Ale' in the away end. For all their faults, they do look after away fans well down there: padded seats, projected pictures of past heroes, welcome messages and serving local beer. However, it all feels a bit strange to be made welcome in your surroundings in every way, except for the fact that twenty-seven thousand home fans want to inflict as much pain and misery as is humanely possible on you in the next ninety minutes - and in some cases, probably afterwards too.

The first half was lively and passionate. Not even the police moving it to midday on a Sunday could dampen the mood. Homophobic, aggressive, ardent, historical, abusive and derisory chants were thrown from one stand to the other. They sang about us burning our own town in reference to the Croydon Riots; we sang about them holding hands. They sang about us living in caravans. We enquired as to where their support was in the days before padded seats, when they couldn't sell 8,000 tickets at the Withdean Stadium. We both sang about Boxing Day. We hate them. They hate us. It's mutual.

The hordes of Police both inside and outside the stadium lined up to keep us apart (and probably counted their overtime pay too - the only Palace/Brighton trouble I've seen was before our 3-1 win in the previous season and had been instigated by the police leading us through the main home fans' pub. I ducked for cover from flying coins, bottles and aggression while thinking *'I was in a classroom and teaching a couple of hours ago!'*) Both fans and police need to remember that we don't live in the eighties anymore. Ten foot metal walls should not be required.

Just before half time, things began to go downhill. Despite dominating the first period, we conceded. Twice! Half time was sober, miserable and angry too. I was unusually quiet. In normal circumstances, I'd be the first to let everyone know what I think - especially when we're losing. But I doubt anyone cared for my thoughts. The fact that my APP (Assessing Pupil Progress) folder needed updating and my numeracy books required marking wasn't really relevant to most fans' present predicament.

The second half was one of the longest experiences of my life. They scored again early on. The game was over. They took the piss. Their fans took the piss in the crowd. Their players took the piss on the pitch. Even the weather and their bloody stadium took the piss as it started to rain and our seats in the fifth row were uncovered from the downpour. I wasn't even annoyed, I was just distracted. I needed to get home and get on with my job. I suppose it was a kind of weird payback for all the times that I'd been distracted from school by football that I was now distracted from football by school.

After the game, it was just as bad. The police had put an extra 16 carriage train on to get us all back to Croydon safe and sound. Although they ignored the fact that not all of us lived in Croydon, at least it started to address the issue that had been completely neglected in the planning stages of our rivals new home - one tiny station is totally inadequate for any sort of crowd, let alone regular twenty-something thousand gates. Maybe they were only expecting the six thousand who turned up before promotions and padded seats to attend? Anyway, the extra train wasn't due to leave until forty-five minutes after the final whistle so we were left trapped in the away concourse after the bitterest of losses. To be fair to Brighton, they continued to serve beer after the final whistle - not that I was partaking in any drinking. I had work to do and wanted to get home.

Perhaps it shows that my addiction was not as strong as it once was, or more likely, the amount of stress that I was under, that I'd have grudgingly accepted losing that match so painfully in a trade to get Ofsted out of the way. To get that week done. However, it showed me the larger problem. Once Ofsted had been and gone, I'd still have a class I was struggling with, I'd still have no energy, I'd still rely on Palace to pick me up, I'd still come home every night unsatisfied from doing an average job, I'd still know the children's levels weren't where they needed to be. I'd still be miserable and now, those few days had now shown me just how miserable I was.

Ofsted came and went - and we did well as a school. None of the books or folders or displays that I'd spent hours working on were actually looked at and I wasn't even observed but surprisingly, that didn't bother me. The miserable process had highlighted to me what I was doing wrong. I wasn't happy and if you're not happy, you can't possibly do a good job. Something needed to change.

Before I'd got into the everyday rut of adult life where you work first and live later, I'd had dreams and ambitions. There were things that I'd wanted to do; places I'd wanted to visit. However, I'd gone straight from school to university and before my twenty-first birthday, I'd taken a teaching job - which I'd stayed at for the four following years. I'd never been out of education. In fact, being in education and supporting Crystal Palace Football Club were the two most consistent things in my life to date. I still liked both. I still loved both. As difficult as they were, I loved my class and every single child in it. I guess that explains my love of Palace - I clearly love the things that get me down and cause me stress. However, I wanted something else. I wanted something different.

I'd had a nag in the back of my mind since I was eighteen. My brother had suggested moving to Australia with him for a year and it was one of the few ideas in my life that I hadn't followed through. Essentially, we'd both bottled it. I'm usually very driven when I get a plan - completing a whole set of toys or videos as a kid, going to every Palace game in a season, going to all ninety-two football league grounds (I was currently on 81), becoming a teacher, living in London, going to a specific holiday destination. When I get an idea, I obsess over it and I usually make it happen and to hell with the consequences along the way.

However, the Australia dream hadn't happened but it could. In fact, why shouldn't it? I had the money, I had no commitments, I had no girlfriend, no mortgage and a job that didn't require any long term obligation to stay. The more I thought about it, the more I realised that if I didn't go to Australia, I'd regret it forever. Even if that meant missing a whole season of Crystal Palace games.

Brighton...3 Crystal Palace...0
Amex Stadium, 17/03/13
Championship

Brighton: Tomasz Kuszczak, Gordon Greer, Andrea Orlandi, Inigo Caldero, Leonardo Ulloa, Matthew Upson, David Lopez, Kazenga LuaLua, Liam Bridcutt, Wayne Bridge, Will Buckley
Subs: Rodriguez Vicente, Marcos Painter, Dean Hammond, Lewis Dunk, Andrew Crofts, Casper Ankergren, George Barker

Palace: Julian Speroni, Jonathan Parr, Yannick Bolasie, Kagisho Dikgacoi, Mile Jedinak, Wilfried Zaha, Glenn Murray, Jonathan Williams, Damian Delaney, Peter Ramage.
Subs: Lewis Price, Jacob Butterfield, Kevin Phillips, Aaron Wilbraham, Danny Gabbidon, Dean Moxey, Andre Moritz.

Chapter 2 – Goodbye Selhurst. I'm going to miss you! – *Selhurst Park, 5th May 2014*

I don't think I've ever felt less stressed before a Palace game. The outcome was entirely irrelevant. Lose, and we'd had an amazing season, been on an outrageous journey and the game would be forever irrelevant. Win, and it would be a great big cherry, plonked on top of a rather unnecessarily large dollop of icing, which had been smeared all over a quite fabulous looking cake. The baker and ingredients had changed many times in the four years that it had been rising in the oven but it seemed nothing could stop it. Here it was. Displayed perfectly in the shop window. The Premier League shop, with the eyes of the world watching. It couldn't have been any further from the Sheffield Wednesday game four years earlier that had saved our club from liquidation and had got the ball rolling (well, cake baking).

In fact, the only emotion that I felt for the final home game of the 2013/14 season was personal. The football side was done and dusted. We'd finished mid-table and there was a sheer pride in the team. Since that Wednesday game, we'd rebuilt the club from top to bottom. We'd gone from Nike owning our club shop to having our own bespoke kits. We'd gone from flat lager in the terraces to having our own craft beer brewed for the club. We'd gone from sold out food kiosks to rebranded facilities named after former club legends. We'd gone from a chairman despising the fans to four (very rich) supporters owning the club. And probably most notably to the outside world, we'd gone from the bottom of the Championship to the middle of the Premier League.

While it was our status in the football placings that was probably most noted outside of South London, it was the small details that made us proud of our club. It was the fact that the owners were on the forums, posting as fans, that made the journey special. It was the fact that Steve Browett, one of the co-chairman, is more likely to be seen supping an ale, even advertising where he'll be beforehand, casually chatting about Mel Blythe or Vince Hilaire in the pub, rather than eating a prawn sandwich in a boardroom somewhere. It was that we'd done it as one and that was special.

And when you are doing things as one, they become much easier. Freedman walking out, Holloway being out of his depth and resigning, losing ten of our first eleven Premier League games, Zaha moving to Manchester United, Glenn Murray breaking his leg, none of it had beaten us. We just kept on plodding along - and we had come back stronger each time.

After surviving liquidation in 2010, we'd had another torturous year, with the low point being a 3-0 loss at Millwall and the high point being a 1-0 win over Leeds to keep us up. George Burley had come and gone as manager without it ever really working out, and numerous players were signed to fill a highly depleted squad. That first season had been all about recovery and building the foundations - and I must say that it had almost happened in the

background for me as I engrossed my life in my first year of teaching. In fact, the personal highlight was probably a 5-0 defeat to Derby County.
*"Why the f*** are we still here?"* had been the Palace chant that day to respond to the home fans asking us the same question. Well, the answer was simple. The football isn't always the most important part of following a football club. I made two very good friends that day - Dom and Ameer – who, like myself and Pavel, were using alcohol and humour to recover from the game. Football, thankfully, is about so much more than the players and results on the pitch. To be honest, after the stress of the year before, I was simply happy to have a club to support, have friends to go with and enjoyed everything that goes with it.

The following season (2011/12) had improved marginally in the league and despite an appalling end of season run, it had one real highlight. A favourable league cup draw gave us home games (and wins) against Crawley, Middlesbrough, Wigan and Southampton before a quarter final draw away at Old Trafford. Now, I must admit, it was around this time that I began to expand the after-work side of my work/life balance. While I was often meeting friends for dinners, or going on dates after work in a calmer, less-boozy side of life, I also discovered a love of playing five-a-side football. Since giving up being a goalkeeper as a teenager, I'd barely played the game that I love to watch, or done much exercise at all to be honest. However, I started playing twice a week which was great, even if one was organised by a part Middlesbrough, part Ch*rlton fan.

Meanwhile, I was also enjoying all the extra midweek league cup games. Palace being repeatedly drawn at home allowed me to leave work thirty minutes early, drive to the game, appreciate a pre-match pint in the ground, see us win and still be able to get back home to Southfields, where I was living, at a reasonable time. It was much calmer than the days of all afternoon student drinking that I'd experienced while at uni for midweek matches, but I was loving it just as much. Thankfully, things fitted into my life even better when the Manchester United away game was arranged for the day of the 2011 teacher strikes, thus allowing me to drive up with my Dad. After winning that game with a Darren Ambrose strike from just outside the Manchester ring road, the semi-final at Cardiff was a must. Luckily, an understanding Teaching Assistant took my class for the final fifteen minutes of the day to allow me to dash off down the M4 in time for kickoff. Unfortunately, that penalty shootout defeat in February pretty much ended our season.

The third year of the new era (2013/14) saw us lose our opening three matches, become favourites for relegation, sign a few players on free transfers, fly to the top of the league, watch Freedman depart, have a ridiculous wobble after *that* Brighton defeat, crumble into the play offs and get drawn against our arch rivals again. After a tense 0-0 draw at Selhurst Park, we had a magical night on the South Coast, with our England international, Wilfried Zaha, stealing the show in a glorious 2-0 win. Made all the sweeter by the 150 page thread on Brighton's message board discussing how s*** he is.

Surprisingly, I might be the only Palace fan in the world who actually has a small amount of sadness and regret when reflecting on that match. It will always remind me that for the only time in my life, I decided not to go to a big Palace game. Partly, because of the trauma of the league game and our form heading into the match, but mainly, because I had the most important head teacher observation of my life in the morning after it. As you know, until Ofsted that year, I'd been struggling. However, after that wake-up, and my decision that I was going to move onto new things, I had really focussed myself on my teaching and values in the classroom. Luckily for me, Palace's performance (despite only observing it from a pub - something that I would have to get used to) had left me walking on air and nothing could have stopped me in the days after that. I aced the observation and restored my own and the head teacher's faith in my ability.

From then on, the journey got better than better. Both for me and Palace. Damian Delaney, our aging Irish centre half had been close to retiring from football after being released by Ipswich and was in tears on the Wembley staircase after our 1-0 win against Watford to gain promotion. Despite our horrendous start to life in the Premier League, I was feeling surprisingly carefree towards our results.

I'd moved to teach a different year group at work and my new immediate colleagues were my close friend, Paul, and one of the leading teachers in the borough, who I also got on well with. I felt confident, valued and supported. I learnt a lot and feel that I offered a lot too. I was happy in my job again. I'd also got a new teaching assistant who was outstanding. Together, we worked brilliantly as a team to support the children and I'm confident that they all had a good year both emotionally and academically. Perhaps the difference in the children's attitude could be best summed up by their feelings towards my team. My difficult class from the year before had decided that they would support whoever Crystal Palace were playing against to tease me. While it was a light-hearted joke, it was noticeable that my new class decided that they all loved Crystal Palace as I did.

It would be a lie to suggest our arrival in the Premier League had been easy. Millions of pounds were spent on seventeen new signings with little impact and I decided that I didn't like the damn league anyway. We lost every week, we didn't have a Saturday 3pm home game until December 7th, we had fewer games to go to, I couldn't pre-book cheap travel as I was waiting for Sky TV to decide if they were going to show us or not, while the match tickets became harder to get and more expensive to buy. However, Tony Pulis came in and changed all that. Well, technically, he didn't, but he changed the fact that we lost every week and that made the other things seem less important. At the same time as Pulis entering Selhurst Park to change things for the better, a lady entered my life and showed me a love outside of SE25 - who'd have known it was possible?

Leading up to this game against Liverpool, we'd won five on the trot, beating Chelsea and Villa at home, as well as West Ham, Cardiff and Everton away. Even the loss in our previous game against Manchester City had hurt our opponents for this match more than it hurt us as it swung likely destination of the title away from Liverpool, yet meant very little to us. My life, and Palace's, had suddenly become brilliant. I loved my job and colleagues, I loved my flat and flatmates, I had a lively and varied social life, I had a great girl that I was dating, I was fitter than I'd ever been before and to top it all off, Palace had their best season in my living memory - we'd even beaten those b******s from the Bridge thanks to a John Terry own goal. I couldn't have scripted anyone better to be 'scoring goals for Palace'. Yet, as always, I'd made a plan and I was going to stick to it. I was going to Australia.

So to be honest, I wasn't going to this game out of expectation, or wanting to win, or with a feeling of nerves. I was going to the game to say thank you to my club and goodbye for now - I had my visa for Oz sorted and knew that this would be my final visit to Selhurst Park for over a year. This game wasn't actually anything to do with Liverpool from our point of view (although a heavy win would give them a chance of a nineteenth league title). This game was a celebration of how far we'd come and everything we'd achieved. This game was for me to let go and give up my addiction - my final live match.

I arrived at the Railway Club on the bank holiday Monday with enough time for a quick beer and a reflection on the season. It was a strange time for me. Obviously, I'd given up my season ticket for the following season so Dan was going to relocate to the Arthur Wait stand; I'd given up my flat and my flatmates were looking around London for new living arrangements. I'd resigned from my job with an amazing amount of goodwill coming my way. Not only had they suggested that there might be an opening to return after my travels, but they'd rejected my early resignation.

As well as going to Australia, I'd had another lifelong dream. Ever since they'd decided where it would be held, I'd wanted to go to the World Cup in Brazil. The fact that FIFA awarded the following competitions to Russia and Qutar made me even more determined to make it to Brazil and with FIFA inconsiderately scheduling the competition in term time, I'd had to resign for the Easter Holidays in April. However, I was asked to stay on until the end of the year and given unpaid leave to go to South America for three weeks. I guess us teachers don't get enough holiday usually...

All in all, life had changed for the better and despite no longer feeling the need for change that I'd felt a year earlier, there really was no backing out now. I'd given up everything to go abroad. I'd wanted something and nothing was going to stop me getting it - not even risking my job and four months' pay.

This was like my dream of attending a game at all ninety-two football league grounds. The day before the Liverpool match, my Dad and I had travelled all the way to Morecambe's Globe Arena to see them 0-0 draw against Bury to complete my challenge of going to every single league ground in England. Seventy of them were with Palace and most of the others were Brentford games that I'd attended with friends when Palace weren't playing. A few other grounds had fitted nicely into my Palace schedule, such as Accrington playing at home the day before we faced Liverpool, and Fleetwood having a suitable game before we took on Blackpool. However, I'd needed to go on a few strange, long trips to finish off the challenge. Luckily, for someone planning to move to Australia, travel has never bothered me. So triumphantly, nine years after first having the desire, I'd fulfilled my challenge of going to every ground. As always, I'd been dedicated to the end and to hell with anything else.

Back at Selhurst and the Liverpool match, I loved the early evening walk to the ground, warmed by the May sunshine. Its moments such as these, being surrounded immediately by your friends and family, in the middle of a mass of red and blue, that make live football so special. The collective love that allows men and women with little else in common to share something so gripping.

I met Dan in the ground by our season ticket seats for the final time and the atmosphere was already rocking. The red and blue masses were enjoying ourselves - together. The Holmesdale Fanatics had made a huge, two-tiered 'Fortress Selhurst' display, which while I don't think looked as good as some of their other spectacles, I was impressed by their effort and commitment for it nonetheless. I think we're the only club in the Premier League that has displays of this kind made for and paid for by the fans. The ultras group even turned down financial support when it was offered by the club's sponsors.

I don't think my voiced lasted the eighteen minutes that it took Liverpool to take the lead. It was croaking by then but it certainly didn't stop after that.
"South London's Red and Blue Army!"
"South London's Red and Blue Army!"
"South London's Red and Blue Army!"
"South London's Red and Blue Army!"
"South London's Red and Blue Army!"
The chant continued. The match didn't matter. We were having a party; celebrating the rise and rise of Crystal Palace Football Club over the previous four years. I almost felt sorry for any young fans who'd only started to follow the club in the last two seasons as they only knew success. That's not the Palace way. That's just not what we do. However, what we had done ever since falling into administration in 2010, was to create a racket and support the team one hundred percent.

I think it's fair to say that I attend matches as much for the crowd and atmosphere as I do for the results. All season, I'd claimed that I wouldn't be that fussed about returning from Oz to support a Championship side, but we had to stay up in our first season so that I could still watch the games while I was away. It would be bad enough not being in the ground for games, but I couldn't bear the thought of not being able to watch them at all. Every Premier League match is shown live on tele in Australia. Unfortunately, they didn't come with a twenty thousand strong crowd for me to watch the games with. Part of me wondered if it would even be worth watching the games in a pub or at home on tv?

The singing barely stopped for half-time and Liverpool's second or third goals couldn't dent it either. We were 3-0 down at home but we were singing 'Glad All Over' without the smallest hint of insincerity. After few chants about Steven Gerrard's infamous slip in his previous game, we then moved onto one of the most generic football chants in English football, but one that is saved for only the most special moments. One that is sung from the heart.

"We're proud of you, we're proud of you, we're proud of you, we're proud!"

As I said before the game, we didn't care that we were playing Liverpool or that we were being stuffed. We were just proud of what our team had achieved across the season. We were all happy to be there, over twenty thousand of us singing together, riding the CPFC rollercoaster.

Near the end, Dan and I began to discuss who our Player of the Year had been. We decided between us that we would give it to Damian Delaney for his commitment and the way that he'd risen to the challenge of playing in a higher league, so it was fitting that he scored the consolation goal which sent Selhurst wild. We'd jumped and hugged and danced and sang as if we'd won the World Cup. We'd wanted a party and now we had something to celebrate - no matter how insignificant it was with just eleven minutes left.

But before we'd had a chance to acknowledge how silly and over-the-top we'd been in our celebrations, Yannick Bolasie, the Bristol City reserve player we'd signed a couple of years previously, danced around the Liverpool defence before passing it to Dwight Gayle, the man who'd been a non-league player just two years earlier. Suddenly, it was 3-2.

After that, it became inevitable. No one in the ground was in any doubts as to whether we'd equalise. We could sense it. I think it was at this moment that my Dad, who'd been unable to get a ticket, began to really get jealous. He'd forever regret not being there. Radio or television couldn't do that night justice. Only being there live would do. Millions were watching across the globe and although I didn't quite realise just how big a worldwide impact our eleven minutes were having at the time, I knew that there were thousands of people desperate to be stood (yes, despite all seater stadiums, it does happen) where I was, experiencing what I was.

I have a friend who lives five miles away from Selhurst Park and he is convinced that he heard the cheer when Dwight Gayle equalised. The scenes were incredible. Bodies piled up. Men, woman and children lost control. We hugged, kissed, fell over, danced - and by we, I mean everyone. It was the greatest possible way to sign off from Selhurst Park and bizarrely, it was a meaningless end of season match for us!

I wasn't exactly close to tears (I left them to Luis Suarez) as the players did their end of season lap of honour, but I was past delirium. It was as if I was drunk and looking back it's a bit of a blur. At random moments, I'd punch the air, or grab someone near me and scream. It was one of the moments that us football fans live for. It was the epitome of our rise. It was the reward for all the owners' hard work. It's what I'd be missing for a whole year. We could win 5-0 at Old Trafford next season but it wouldn't come close to the collective emotion of that moment because with me watching on TV, I would see it but I wouldn't live it. I wouldn't be a part of it.

Coming out of the ground, someone grabbed me in elation. I recognised him but I couldn't picture where I knew him from. I stumbled as I moved forward to embrace him while I tried to figure it out. Such was my excited state, I couldn't get any words out and I was still shaking from the physical excitement of the recovery. We flung our arms around each other and jumped up and down, trying to find suitable words to express our feeling. I must have appeared hammered and it suddenly dawned on me who this guy was. He was a parent from my class. He grinned at me as he said *"Don't worry, I'll get my daughter to be quiet in class tomorrow!"*

With a huge grin and a deep breath, I took one last emotional look at my spiritual home and left. Little over a year earlier, going to the other side of the world had seemed such an easy decision to make but now, I suddenly had multiple reasons to stay. My support of Palace was going to be very different for the next year or so. After refusing to lose the club four years previously and protesting on the streets of London as business men in offices threatened to liquidate my love, I was now choosing to sit out of a whole season of Palace. Was I finally beginning to recover from my addiction?

The table below indicates just how much of a change it was going to be.

Year	Games Attended	Games Missed
2005/06	49	6
2006/07	45	4
2007/08	47	3
2008/09	46	5
2009/10	53	0
2010/11	36	13
2011/12	39	15
2012/13	37	13
2013/14	30	10

While I had seriously cut down (try explaining that to a partner), I was still going a lot. If I wasn't over the addiction, I was going to need to deal with the consequences from nearly seventeen thousand kilometres away - without a Saturday afternoon fix to look forward to.

Crystal Palace...3 Liverpool...3
Selhurst Park, 05/05/14
Premier League

Palace: Julian Speroni, Adrian Mariappa, Scott Dann, Damian Delaney, Joel Ward, Kagisho Dikgacoi (Thomas Ince 84), Mile Jedinak, Joe Ledley, Yannick Bolasie, Jason Puncheon (Dwight Gayle 64), Marouane Chamakh (Glenn Murray 71).
Subs not used: Wayne Hennessey, Danny Gabbidon, Jonathan Parr, Stuart O'Keefe.

Liverpool: Mignolet, Johnson, Flanagan, Skrtel, Sakho, Gerrard, Allen, Lucas, Sterling (Coutinho 78), Sturridge (Moses 86), Suarez.
Subs not used: Jones, Toure, Agger, Aspas, Cissokho.

"The 3-3 was a strange one. We were really on the ropes at 0-3 and there was only one team in it. We just said 'Look, we'll limit what's going to happen as they'll keep pushing and we'll stay strong, then see if we can get a goal. And funnily enough, we got two in quick succession before Gayley popped up in the last minutes to get another goal. Those are the kind of nights you don't forget because of how loud it was in the ground and you ruin their title hopes as well in the grand scheme of things.

It was a special night for us all."

Mile Jedinak

Chapter 3 - The Adventure Begins – *Singapore and Indonesia, 9-14th August 2014*

As these things often do, the date came around quicker than I'd expected. My time in Brazil had been and gone, with the experience lasting slightly longer for me than it had for the England team. And as I was back in work less than twelve hours after returning home, it soon slipped to the back of my mind as a distant memory.

The weekend before I left for Australia, I had a surprisingly good turnout for my leaving drinks, although many people commented that they'd only come to make sure I was really going. I'll let you decide if they were joking or not. However, what I did notice during a thoroughly enjoyable evening was that my group of Palace mates were the largest faction of attendees over groups from school, five-a-side, work, university and family. And I don't just mean largest in terms of having eaten the most half-time pies and drunk the most post-match pints. Although noticeably, the girl that I'd been dating had decided that me moving to the other side of the world wasn't conducive to our relationship and therefore did not attend.

The next day, I gingerly (due to the intake of alcohol from the day before) made my way to our pre-season defeat at Brentford, which was to be my only Palace game of the season. As always, the club couldn't let me sign off on the high of the previous season (losing 3-2 to the lower league side) but the enjoyment of one last game with my Dad and the chance to see my Brentford mates more than made up for the result.

After a few emotional goodbyes, I made my way to Gatwick Airport with a huge, green rucksack on my back and a second smaller one over my front on Saturday 9th August 2014. Ready to leave the country for a whole year and say goodbye to England, goodbye to my teaching job, goodbye to my friends, goodbye to my family and goodbye to Palace.

In order to break up the flight, I'd decided to have a stopover in Singapore. It seemed logical as a vaguely halfway point anyway but my friend, Tom (or Jesus in my first book), now lived there so it was almost rude not to. After a day's travel (changing at Vietnam to ensure a cheaper, if longer, flight), I arrived at the first point of call of my travels and my first venture into Asia. Now, I'll be honest enough to admit that I knew very little about the country before arriving – aside from the repeated sentiment that '*It is very clean*'.

Upon arrival, having sold my iPhone with the intention of buying a new smart phone compatible with an Australian network, I had a dilemma. How would I find out the Palace score of our friendly against the German side, Augsburg? Thanks to the wonders of the internet and modern technology, watching our 13-1 win against GAK Graz, a lower league Austrian team, and games against Columbus Crew and Richmond Kickers in the USA had not been a problem. The games had been streamed live. However, there has yet to be a wizz kid anywhere in the world who's managed to enable us to get internet reception or use our phones while thousands of feet up in the air (without paying exorbitant prices) so I'd been unable to follow the club's latest international adventure.

It almost seems ridiculous to be writing about Palace having games across various countries and continents as part of our pre-season regime. What's wrong with local games like the Brentford one? However, as the Premier League team that we now are, with all of our games shown across the world, increasing our 'brand' name has become vital for the club and games against Whyteleaf are unlikely to do this. It is also exciting for the privileged few fans who are wealthy enough, commitment-free and willing to travel across the globe to see us in another country. With Palace unlikely to be in Europe any time soon despite the ever-increasing amount of spaces allocated to each country (thus making us even more bitter about 1990 when our third place finish wasn't enough, despite Liverpool, who were banned from Europe at the time, being one of only two teams better than us in the entire country), pre-season jolly-ups abroad are about as close to the real thing as we're likely to get.

The size of our ever growing 'brand' (and no, I don't mean Palace fan and comedian, Jo) and the power of the Premier League had been emphasised to me in Brazil when my Palace shirt had been recognised by fans from all corners of the globe. The new fame wasn't for our South London identity, nor for our outrageous overachievement of finishing eleventh in the previous season. It wasn't even for our atmosphere (other than one enthusiastic Brazilian blogger) or the style of our play. We were mainly recognised as *'3-3! You're the team that f***ed up Liverpool!"*
Palace fans could make many cases for more important results in our history, but I doubt we've ever had a result that has had a bigger worldwide impact than that spectacular night in May 2014.

Anyway, I didn't travel half way around the world to worry about results of Palace pre-season friendlies. With Tom at work, in what was now the Sunday morning, I dropped my bags and went to see the famous Merlion Statue at the impressive Marina Bay. I wondered around the bay in the scorching heat, before heading to China Town for some food. Unsurprisingly, after my many previous warnings, I found the city to be very clean. Most noticeably, there seemed to be very little traffic (something that would become even more noticeable when compared to the rest of South-East Asia). I later found out that this was because of a 'Certificate of Entitlement ' being required to purchase a car, which costs between s$50-70,000 (roughly half that to find the English value). This is before you've even got to the showroom to consider which model you want.

Although some of the country's other laws, while they made for a nice place to live, were stricter than Tony Pulis' disciplined approach to management. Chewing gum is illegal for fear of people spitting it on the street.

In fact, spitting of any kind in public is strictly forbidden, heavy fines are issued for littering and failing to flush a public toilet can get you a large fine too. You can be physically caned for graffiti, bringing drugs into the country is punishable by death, even having a personal amount of usage in your blood stream, and it is illegal to bring any alcohol across the border. While the punishments seem a little heavy handed, I can understand the thinking behind banning the above.

However, I'm unsure of the logic and reasoning behind a two year prison sentence for being gay. Especially in a country that seems to promote multiculturalism in so many other ways. I spotted mosques and churches, as well as Buddhist and Hindu temples as quickly as I noticed the array of European football shirts, both on locals and in shops. Unfortunately, I didn't spot any Palace shirts but I did need a second glance at a red and blue Bayern Munich one.

In the evening, I met up with Tom and his girlfriend, Kresta, at a micro-brewery bar by Clark Quay, where we sat outside by the river, eating and drinking, catching up on each other's lives; making sure that we didn't spit anything out or buy any gum. I always flushed the toilet too - I didn't want to get arrested.

Me being me, I asked Tom if he was able to watch much of the football out there, and he said that although he saw the occasional game in the pub, he didn't really go out of his way for it. However, he said that he could watch games if he wanted to as they are all televised. He did tell me that he'd once walked into a bar showing our game against Manchester United in the previous season and his friends immediately enquired as to who this other non-famous team was. It was the perfect opportunity for him to step up and amaze them all by saying that not only had he heard of Crystal Palace, but he'd actually been to see them play - and win. Saying that, I doubt he felt the need to go into the glorious details of our 4-2 win at Reading in the obsessive manner that I would have. After a great catch up with Tom, I went to sleep to the familiar hostel sound of other people snoring that night.

As I'd had warnings from Tom and my friend Pavel that the four days I'd booked in Singapore would be too long, Tom and I had booked a ferry to Batam, a small Indonesian Island for the next morning. For our two day trip, I'd finally realised a lifelong dream. This time that day, I was a millionaire Rodders. The exchange rate allowing my £64 to be swapped for one million rupiah. For once, I could worry about spending a million notes as casually as a Premier League football team splashing out on a new signing and unlike a Premier League team, I got great value for money.

Tom and I went go-karting, rifle-shooting, had massages, ate a meal on the top floor of the tallest building on the island, watched a fire-breathing/glass eating show, ate out, drank out and stayed in an excellent hotel for our limited money. I also had a look in the shops, which were more like jumble sales or cheap markets than the western-style malls of Singapore, for a Bayern Munich shirt. While all the fakes and in fact most clothing cost just a couple of pounds to make them accessible to the locals, football shirts, like all genuine designer clothing, seem to have a universal price tag and being in a cheaper country does not translate to cheaper football shirts.

One of the things that I'd loved so much about Brazil in the previous June was how different it had been to anything that I'd ever seen before; the culture, the architecture, the food, the atmosphere. I'm incredibly lucky in the sense that I have travelled quite a bit in Europe and North America but after experiencing Brazil, it all seemed rather same-y. While Singapore could easily be in Europe, I again loved how different Indonesia was to my comfort zone. However, there was one difference that really made me feel uncomfortable and no, it wasn't the hole in the ground toilets - they're far harder to deal with for ladies than us men.

Our problem was that in every bar we went to, Tom and I were instantly approached by girls. Now, far be it from me to usually complain about such a problem but unless we'd suddenly turned into a couple of extremely desirable young men, who females found it impossible to resist, we made an educated guess that the girls were in fact, prostitutes. This made for an uncomfortable evening at certain points. Innocently, we simply wanted to have a beer and a good old catch up but the regular interruptions made this nearly impossible. It was embarrassing that the colour of our skin and accent of our voice made the girls assume that's what we were after. It was my first introduction to the huge problem of prostitution in South-East Asia as white males often only go to that part of the world with one intention.

Although, it did allow for one comical moment when one of the girls told us that as well as hoping we'd pay her for sex, she was also looking for someone to be her husband. She was very concerned that the man she found to walk her up the isle should be catholic and have strong morals. Especially as they'd need to financially support both her and her child. She was obviously slightly more liberal with her catholic morals than some. Anyway, it took us a couple of minutes to realise that she was entirely serious.

The next day, after a last look around the bargain basement shops, we got the ferry back to Singapore and I was met by another friend there. My former teaching colleague, Michaela, now worked in Malaysia and had flown down to visit me and see Singapore. Tom and I met her for some curry in one of the excellent hawker centres and then went for some drinks in Chinatown (free of prostitutes this time). There, we had had a lovely evening catching up. The three of us also took the opportunity to have a Singapore Sling cocktail in the World Famous Raffles Hotel. Although, with the weather so nice outside, we opted against going to the inside bar where you can throw your nutshells on the floor – and not be slapped with a hefty fine.

With Tom at work the following day, Michaela and I had a busy time being tourists. The pair of us visited various temples and marvelled at the detail in them, got food from Little India, went up the spectacular Marina Bay Sands (three skyscrapers are joined at the top by an enormous boat and luxury hotel), toured the city on a bus trip, and finally went on the Night Safari in the evening. The beauty of Singapore is that it is so small that you can do most of it in a couple of days. In the evening, we met Tom and Kresta to have a final drink and say our goodbyes.

At three AM the next morning, my alarm went off and I jumped in a taxi to the airport for my flight to Sydney. Singapore Airport is one of the most luxurious in the world and I made the most of their free wifi to catch up on some Palace news. What I hadn't previously realised was that England was still in 'yesterday' as I started my 'today' and when I sat down by the boarding gate, it was actually time for the League Cup draw. Palace's season hadn't started yet but the football league was already underway. Palace were pitted against Walsall in the second round (we received a bye in the first round as a huge, big, important Premier League team) and something dawned on me. While I'd be able to watch our Premier League games in Oz, there is no way that I'd be able to follow this game, which would kick off at 4am.

As I sat at the airport, waiting for my plane, I began to think about Australia. What did I want out of it? What was the purpose of my journey? Why had I given everything up to come out to the other side of the world? The few days in Asia had been amazing; I'd seen old friends, seen new cultures, tanned my skin and learned new things. Everything I wanted out of a short holiday (although some football would have been nice!) but that was different. That was a short holiday. In Australia, I'd have to work, and make friends, and forge a life from nothing. It was only at this point that I realised I hadn't really thought about expectations for the coming year, or even what I wanted to get out of it. It had just seemed like a good thing to do when I'd been down the previous year and I'd stuck by it religiously, without trying to unpick exactly why.

As well as that, I'd have to start watching Palace on TV, rather than in the stadium. After years of lambasting armchair supporters, that's exactly what I was set to become and armed with the knowledge that we had Tony Pulis in charge, I was also in a rare and dangerous territory of having expectations for Palace in the coming season. Despite realising that we'd over achieved in the previous year, I had no fears of relegation. There was enough rubbish in the league to ensure that Pulis would have no problems in keeping us up. Our signings of Fraizer Campbell and Brede Hangeland had been solid if unspectacular and as has been the general trend since finally getting a committee of sane owners, things were looking up. Our owner was talking positively about making new signings and with Pulis' reputation for deadline day deals, I was confident that we'd get the right players in before the end of the transfer window.

Just before boarding my plane, I started a thread about our opening game on the Palace forum, the BBS. I'd seen similar threads before and knew there were plenty of Eagles based out in Sydney so I was hopeful of having some companions for the match.

Title: Watching the Arsenal game in Sydney

Hi Aussie Eagles. Can anyone recommend anywhere to watch the game on Saturday?

Brentford...3 Crystal Palace...2
Griffin Park, 02/08/14
Friendly

Brentford: Button; McCormack, Tarkowski (Yennaris 72), Craig, Bidwell; Tebar (Dean 72), Douglas, Judge; Odubajo, Gray, Dallas (Smith 60)
Subs not used: Lee, Moore, Reeves, Diagouraga

Palace: Wayne Hennessey (Julian Speroni 46); Joel Ward, Scott Dann, Damian Delaney, Adrian Mariappa; Yannick Bolasie, Mile Jedinak, Joe Ledley, Jason Puncheon; Marouane Chamakh, Glenn Murray
Subs not used: Jake Gray, Jerome Boateng, Ryan Inniss, Sulley Kaikai

FC Augsburg...0 Crystal Palace...0
Augsburg Arena, 09/08/14
Friendly

FC Augsburg: Hitz, Verhaegh (Reinhardt 46), Callsen-Bracker (Framberger 82), Klavan, de Jong (Djurdjic 75), Baier, Thommy (Parker 46), Moravek (Kohr 46), Altintop, Werner (Caiuby 60), Matavz (Bobadilla 46, Molders 75)
Subs Not Used: Manninger, Fetsch.

Crystal Palace: Julian Speroni (Wayne Hennessey 46), Joel Ward, Scott Dann (Paddy McCarthy 82), Brede Hangeland, Jerome Williams, Jason Puncheon (Dwight Gayle 65), Mile Jedinak, Joe Ledley, Yannick Bolasie (Barry Bannan 65), Marouane Chamakh (Adeline Guedioura 72), Fraizer Campbell (Glenn Murray 65).
Subs Not Used: Mariappa.

Chapter 4 - Arriving in Sydney – *14th-23rd August 2014*

I stepped out of Sydney Airport at around 8pm after the surprisingly long flight (via Malaysia to once again save on the pennies - or should that be cents now?) ready to start my new life. There was drizzle in their air and a strong wind. This wasn't what I'd come for. Although my minimal research had told me that it was winter in Australia, I hadn't thought to change from the shorts and t-shirt that I was wearing in Asia. Shivering, I was the only muppet stood outside Kingston Sydney Airport in such inappropriate dress.

Rather than getting the train into town, I had to get a cab as I hadn't prepared anything to tell me how to get from the station to the hostel that I was staying in, called Bounce. Luckily, I had a few dollars given to me as a leaving present from my old colleagues. After paying the extortionate fare, including tolls that I later found out were entirely unnecessary, the cab pulled up alongside Central Station, where The Bounce Hostel was. I checked in and went to get my first Australian meal, a subway sandwich.

The hostel itself was nice; cleaner than I expected – certainly when compared to the one in Singapore where there'd been a procession of ants joining me in the shower. Additionally, it had a huge living room/drinking area, a very well stocked DVD/TV room, a clean and functioning kitchen and large, comfortable beds. Exhausted from my early start, I certainly made good use of my one that night.

I was surprisingly organised on my first morning in Oz, maybe even pushing the boundaries of productive. I had a list of things to do and was rattling through them: open a bank account, tick. Buy a new smart phone, tick. Get my Tax File Number, tick. Learn about Super Annuation (a required pension needed to take work in Oz), tick. Have my first beer, tick (in a Pub called The Palace Hotel on George Street, the main road through Central Sydney, and it was there that I learned about the Australian measurements of 'middies' ($1/_2$ a pint) and 'schooners' (425ml). Being English, I opted for a pint. Although, maybe in the confusion of having 'dollars' in my pocket, I ordered an *American*-hopped IPA. Talking of dollars, that was another ten (roughly £6) gone on my first expensive footsteps into Australian alcohol.

One thing that I noticed immediately was the amount of people who wanted to talk to me in the street. No, I hadn't suddenly become incredibly popular and gained film star attractiveness (you may find it hard to belive), but there was just an enormous amount of charity workers and product sellers out on the pavements. In Asia, the colour of my skin had highlighted me as a tourist. Here, it was my optimistic dress sense. I was in Australia and Australia is supposed to be hot. I had to resign myself to jeans, but I wasn't going to be lowering myself to wearing a coat. I was on holiday after all!

Rewarding myself for my morning of productivity, I logged onto the BBS to see if anyone had replied to my message about the Arsenal game overnight, which meant through the day in England. They hadn't. However, I had a brief look around the website to see if there was any other news. It was only two days until the season started and I was eager to see if we'd made any new signings. Our chairman, Steve Parish, had said some were imminent. I then clicked on a thread that I'd seen before, but hadn't bothered to look into called *'Pulis' odds drop on being the next Prem boss to go'.*

Naturally, in the free-speech and highly communicative world that we live in, any rumour of any sort is discussed in depth on the internet so I'd assumed that like most things in red-top papers and football supporters' forums, it was a mixture of wild guesses, trolling teenagers and people with little else to do but panic about football - not me of course, I'm far too busy and intelligent to be dragged into anything like that. However, I turned a few heads in the hostel reception room when I let out a *"What?!"*, which although it was politer than it might have been, was still too loud to be considered socially acceptable.

Tony Pulis had left Crystal Palace Football Club by mutual consent.

Suddenly, the next three hours were gone as I read every thread and article on the shocking events. Productivity was back to my usual lazy and distracted rate. I couldn't believe it. Our saviour from the year before had gone. The reason that I felt comfortable in the Premier League had left us. There were all sorts of emotions and conspiracies thrown around the message boards as people tried to get their head around it. Some were fuming at Pulis. Some were fuming at Parish. I just felt sad. Suddenly, in one depressing swoop, my confidence and expectation for the season had gone.

It seemed to me that we had two determined and strong-minded personalities who would not back down on certain issues - presumably in this case, transfer targets and/or budgets. When that is the case, the one higher up in the organisation is always going to stay and the other, either backs down or walks out. Pulis had decided to walk. Without knowing the details, I found it impossible to judge or criticise either of the men who had both saved our club in different ways. However, I felt Parish had more to gain than Pulis by backing down. Pulis kept his reputation while Parish lost his manager.

I guess the unfortunate truth is that whether Parish or Pulis was right is impossible to know. If Pulis was demanding that he should have more money than the agreed budget to spend on players, then of course Parish should not back down. We have been too close to losing our beloved club, not once, but twice, in recent history by overspending on players to risk it again. However, if the disagreements were about how the budget should be spent then I've got to say that I agreed with Pulis. Call me old fashioned but surely the man who'd performed such miracles at our club the year before deserved to be trusted enough to pick his own players for the coming season?

Anyway, as always with football, my opinion, as a mere fan, was the loudest but least listened to. It didn't matter what I or any other devoted supporter thought of the events, we had to deal with them. Well, I suppose there were four devoted supporters who's opinion did matter, and they'd invested millions of pounds each in order to be allowed that opinion; our owners, CPFC 2010. In a sombre mood, I decided to head out in the late afternoon for a Free Walking Tour to get to know my new home.

On the tour, I met an English guy called Nick. As usual, after getting the travelling politeness out of the way of asking where he'd been and what were his plans, I spoke in the only fully international language... football. He was a Forest fan and spoke of how difficult it had been to follow the news of the summer while he was away. Obviously, this left me feeling scared. How would I cope if I too couldn't follow the news? I didn't want to have my head buried into a computer for a whole year while wishing I was closer to the action, but at the same time, I didn't want to completely miss the season.

The tour ended at Sydney Harbour, giving me a first glorious view of the World Famous Opera House and Harbour Bridge. There's something quite spine tingling about seeing something so recognisable first hand. Whether that's a renowned stadium or footballer, or well-known national landmarks such as these, I get the same excitement of seeing something for the first time. Nick and I took a variety of photos, including one that I edited to show me upside down for *Facebook* with the caption *'Just landed in Oz'*, before heading off for some well earned dinner.

After the subway the night before, I decided that I wanted to try some 'real' Australian delicacies so we listened to the tour guide's advice and went hunting for a 'Kangaroo and Emu pizza'. Well, hunting in a metaphoric sense anyway. We didn't charge around Sydney with spears and nets; we simply wondered around, following our phones rather than our noses. Food can't really get more Australian than Kangaroo and Emu, the two animals stand proudly on the Australian Coat of Arms because, as I found out on the tour, they're the only Australian animals that can't move backwards. The badge was obviously made before Mile Jedinak was born.

As Nick decided that the $20 pizza was out of his budget (he was at the end of his trip while I was at the start of mine), we agreed to go elsewhere. What seemed like hours later, and following a KFC snack, we ended up getting a pizza hut, with no Emu or 'roo in sight, leaving us a couple of McDonalds short of a campfire song and me still feeling short of culture.

In fact, I'd been fairly unimpressed with my first sights of Sydney throughout the tour. Admittedly, I may have been slightly distracted by the Pulis news from the morning. Football, as much as I don't want it to, still steals my mind as it did when I was a school boy. However, I found the city to be similar to London, but smaller and with less history. The light drizzle that had fallen throughout the tour didn't help either. Rain was to be a constant theme of my first few weeks down under, which very quickly ended my non-coat wearing enthusiasm.

The next day I was rudely awoken - by the room's cleaner. I'd taken the decision to stay in hostels at first as I thought they would be the easiest way to meet people and make new friends. Unfortunately, other than Nick, the people I'd met so far made me feel rather old. Most were in their early twenties and late teens, only wanting to spend their time in tacky clubs and drinking cheap alcohol. While I'm by no means anti-drinking, I'd been through that stage at university and had no desire to do it again. The slight age gap and huge difference in life experience meant that I found it quite difficult to have any form of stimulating conversation with my fellow hostel users. I wasn't about to give up though and I decided that I would start to cook in the hostel to try and socialise over meals.

And it was the desire to make new friends that meant I tolerated being woken by a vacuum cleaner to a scene of semi-dressed roommates. The other immediate lesson that I learnt about hostels was that having a shared bathroom area not only means that they might not be as clean as having a private one, but also you shouldn't leave your shower gel lying around. Mine was pinched within five minutes of leaving it behind. Not an issue that you have to consider when sharing a flat with your friends. The worst they'll do is steal a squirt.

Early on the Saturday morning, I checked the BBS and was disappointed to see that no one had responded to my message about meeting up for the opening game that evening. I'd seen plenty of previous threads about fans meeting in Australia's largest city so I was quite surprised that no one gave me a response to my call. I was both jealous and intrigued that the Hong Kong Eagles thread was in full flow of busy arrangements for their first piss up of the season and the New York Eagles had plans in place too, although their morning kick off ensured that calmer plans were afoot for them.

When Palace were promoted to the Premier League, the tabloids made huge headlines about how much money it was worth to the club. However, with the extra revenue came higher prices, for the club and the fans. Higher ticket prices, higher replica shirt prices, higher wages, higher cost of players. In Australia, I was soon to find out that the wages were considerably higher than England for just about everyone but footballers. Unfortunately, when I went to the supermarket for the first time, the wage hike and lack of recession was reflected and I was shocked by the high price of food. I spent $50 on the mere basics and began to fret about how I would ever be able to afford to live in this country. A bit like Palace's panicked signings after our promotion, I ended up looking at the price rather than the quality of the products I was buying.

Once again, it rained all day and I ended up wasting most of it; I was far more focussed on Palace's 2am kickoff. In the evening, I played cards and drank beers with Nick and some Scandinavians on the rooftop of the hostel. As my fellow backpackers headed out to Darling Harbour, a popular area of the city, I sneaked away from the group and made my way to *Cheers* bar. Cheers is a sports bar and as I arrived at around half past midnight. The Premier League was already underway.

The pub was packed with a mixture of English expats and Australian football fans. There were shirts from Sunderland, QPR, Everton, Leicester, Tottenham, West Ham, Arsenal and Villa. There was singing and chanting, embracing and laughing - and even an aggressive edge. All the emotions you'd expect back home on a Saturday. However, the Australian TV deal allowed all five 3pm (or midnight in Oz) kickoffs to be shown live, while people discussed Manchester United's shock home defeat to Swansea in the 10pm kick off.

I squeezed my way through the crowd to the bar and ordered myself a pint. One thing that I had noticed and liked about Australia was that even in grotty, sticky floored, rough edged pubs like this one, they served drinkable Pale Ales on keg.

In order to provoke conversation and hopefully seek out other eagles, I'd worn my Palace shirt. As soon as I turned away from the bar, someone started to sing at me to the tune of *KC and the Sunshine Band*.
"NA NA NA NA NA NA NA NA... Mile Jedinak!"

The Arsenal shirt he was wearing told me he wasn't a Palace fan but it's clear that having the Aussie captain in our ranks made the locals appreciate us, which is quite a contrast to English football culture. I don't remember many English fans picking up supporting Real Madrid as a direct result of Beckham's time out there.

I got chatting to our captain's admirer and while Arsenal were his English team, he was adamant that Central Coast Mariners were his main love... Jedinak's first team. Like his time in South London, he'd had a slow start but as time went by, he grew and grew as a player into one that became the centre of their club. This supporter (and many other Mariners) had loved him ever since, even following him to Brazil for the World Cup - and he took great pride in showing me a video from the ground of Jedinak's goal against Holland.

Irrespective of our Mile love-in, I admired the fact that he supported his local team over his world-famous one. I could understand someone wanting to support a Premier League team and the truth is, there's no reason for that team to be anyone other than a top four side. Although, one of my favourite World Cup stories was meeting an American who'd decided to follow Bury and took great interest in asking me about Gigg Lane. However, a lot of people latch onto an 'EPL' team and ignore the chance of watching the live football on their doorstep. This is something I can't understand.

As well as liking Palace because of his favourite player, my new Aussie companion had a lower league team that he preferred to Palace but fell below Arsenal in his ever-increasing list of loves. His friend had taken him to watch this team when he'd visited England and he'd followed them ever since. I was horrified when I learnt that his third team was Charlton, even if it did allow me to be somewhat smug when he said he'd seen them lose 2-1 away at Palace in 2013.

After a long conversation about his many teams, he invited me to join him and his mates to watch the games. I loved the atmosphere. With so much going on, and two levels in the pub, it was impossible to follow everything. They'd be groans on one side of the pub, prompting a mass of eyes to turn to one screen, followed by cheers elsewhere and another switch of attention. While the atmosphere felt tense with all of the different allegiances spread around the venue, there was no trouble throughout the dramatic opening day.

Perhaps the most dramatic moment came in the final minute, as it often does with football, when the whole pub was fixed on QPR missing a last minute penalty and missed Tottenham snatching a dramatic winner at West Ham. However, the exaggerated cheers from the few Spurs fans in their corner of the bar gave us all the warning we needed as everyone turned to see the replays, upsetting the Arsenal fans in the pub.

The crowd in the bar did thin out between 2am when the main kick offs ended and 2:30am when Sky's selected match (Arsenal vs Palace) began. However, with Sydney's lock out rules meaning that there is strictly no re-entry into pubs in the CBD (Central Banking District) after 1:30am, lots of people stayed in the bar, knowing it was a choice of going home or watching our game.

Sky TV changing kick offs usually annoys me as anything other than 3pm on a Saturday upsets my routine. However, the one start time that I don't mind, as it gives me more time in the day and is easier to carry on drinking afterwards, is the Saturday evening games. Unfortunately, this 5:30pm kick off in England meant a rather anti-social start in Oz. As I stocked drinks from the bar (which had to close at 3), my friends back home sent me pictures of them enjoying the opening day in London. The most irrational envy went through me as I wished I wasn't in Australia for the chance of a lifetime, I wished I was in North London to watch a manager-less Palace take on Arsenal.

Finally, at 2:30am, the game kicked off. I love the start of the season. So much optimism and hope and excitement. With the news two days earlier, some of that had been taken away from us but once the game kicked off, it was back. Keith Millen, once again, had been asked to fill in while we searched for a new boss and as we always are when he's in charge, we were disciplined and organised. Ten minutes before half time, emotions and sounds and actions came to me that had been missing for months over the summer's football drought. Palace scored. I went mental. I turned away from the group of Gunners beside me and screamed out sheer joy.

As the game went on, the bar emptied. I think it was the time in the morning rather than my excited squeals but I couldn't be one hundred percent sure about that. You have to really love your team to follow them at three or four in the morning. The kick off times in Oz don't allow you to nip out for a sociable pint with your mate while you keep an eye on the game. In many ways, the people present were just as dedicated as those in the ground; simply watching the match in the pub is a huge commitment. Right on the stroke of half time, and after the last orders had been called and gone, Arsenal scored. Just as I had done, the Arsenal fans erupted.

In the second half, from all the way across the globe, I could hear the Palace fans loud and clear. As a supporter of a team that wins very little, (in the past I'd refer to us as a 'crap team' but with our recent success that term seems somewhat disrespectful) the noise that our crowd makes gives me an immense amount of pride. Non-football fans often claim that us supporters do nothing and are almost lying when we use the terms 'us' or 'we' but the amount of reports praising the Selhurst atmosphere and discussing the affect on the team suggests otherwise. And while it may not have given the players the desired lift, it was that feeling of pride that meant I felt it my duty to join in with the Palace fans singing, while I was alone in a pub full of Gunners on the other side of the world.

While it didn't provoke any trouble thankfully, it did irk the Arsenal fan who I'd met earlier, who was presumably further frustrated that his team didn't look like breaking down a well drilled Palace side. I assume the defence had been set up and prepared by Pulis before he left and they were showing the same discipline that he'd taught them in the previous season. By this stage, nearly four in the morning, the bar had almost completely emptied except ten or so Gunners – and me. The fact that a Spurs fan sided with the Arsenal fans suggested that either he didn't understand the rivalry or I was singing slightly more than necessary. Either way, it was a reality check that prompted me to cheer the team in a quieter manner. Well, that and the nerves I felt as I willed Palace to hold on for an impressive result. A task that got even harder when Jason Puncheon, one of our star players, was sent off with just seconds remaining (4:14am) for receiving a second yellow card. Then, a minute later, Arsenal scored again. We were beaten.

Their fans went mad. Jumping on me, screaming in my face. Celebrating their win. A mixture of the inevitable amount of alcohol consumed by that time in the morning and my previous singing had made it fair game in their eyes. I gritted my teeth, winced through my pain and clenched my hands. Anything to contain my anger. Seconds later, the referee blew for full time. Realising it was me who'd provoked their overreaction, I shook hands with the Jedinak fan who'd led the cheers against me and left. By the time I arrived home, having found most of the fast-food outlets closed, it was nearly 5am and I was soon to discover another pitfall of living in hostels.

When I went to clean my teeth, I stupidly left my key in the room. As I was locked out, wearing nothing but boxers, I couldn't think of another solution but to bang on the door to wake someone up so they could let me in. Unfortunately, it woke up a fair proportion of the room. After a German student let me in, I was suddenly faced with a voice in the darkness. A Columbian girl was screaming at me for being selfish and stupid. It did occur to me that if anyone wasn't awake before, they certainly were now. However, I simply mumbled an apology and clambered into my bed. If I hadn't made much of an impression in the room so far, I certainly had now.

Three hours later, I was woken again by the sound of South American anger (my new Columbian friend) coming in my direction. Good morning Oz and welcome to my first Australian hangover. I was also disappointed that Nick left the hostel that night. His tour was taking him quickly on to his next destination.

The following week was a mixture of settling in, trying to make friends, looking for work and being a tourist. I did things like going to the zoo, visiting the National Gallery, trying out different bars and taking wanders around the city. I couldn't believe how many places were named after English locations: Hyde Park, Oxford Street, Liverpool Street, Croydon, Kings Cross, The Crystal Palace Hotel etc. I guess it's only two hundred years ago that the people moved there to form a new settlement, pushing out the Aboriginal natives. There were lots of similarities: pubs were as close to an English style as I'd seen anywhere in the world, architecture was comparable to ours, but not as varied as London as there's so much less history, and football was everywhere.

With the games at such antisocial hours, they were repeated throughout the week and there would regularly be Premier League highlight programs showing when I walked into bars. In fact, I watched the entire repeat of the Burnley vs Chelsea game two days after it had been played as I realised that I didn't know the score. There were posters and banners everywhere, telling people of the games. 'EPL' is a huge pull for punters in a country that's traditionally had no interest in our beautiful game.

While familiarising myself with the city and being distracted by football, I also started to look for work. Wanting a break from the stresses of teaching (although I did get the ball rolling and applied for permission to teach in Oz), I set about getting a bar job, which means getting a RSA (Responsible Service of Alcohol) certificate. I paid for and sat through the whole-day course, listening to why alcohol is evil and learning about the strict laws of serving alcohol in New South Wales. There'd been a huge problem with alcohol related violence in Sydney, including 'one-hit-kills' and since then, strictly enforced laws on happy hours, prices, opening hours and serving already intoxicated people had been introduced.

As well as chatting to people in the hostel, there were a few people who I'd arranged to meet up with; the cousin of a previous colleague, the god-daughter of a friend of my Dad's and a girl that I'd met on the plane over. Each of them was welcoming and charming and I hoped to meet up with them all again. In the hostel, there was an Irish engineer, an eighteen year old English girl and very focussed female banker. Again, all of them were social but I had very little in common with them. I also made friends with a father and daughter from Barnsley, while I cooked a delicious kangaroo steak and they introduced some Swedish girls to Yorkshire puddings, mash potato, mushy peas and gravy. Needless to say, their Scandinavian friends were more than dubious of this brown sauce that they covered their food with. The northern pair were very welcoming until I announced my love of Palace. They were Sheffield Wednesday fans and refused to forgive me for Palace relegating them five years previously, or some of our fans running on their pitch afterwards.

Although there were people I could chat to, I decided that I couldn't justify staying in Bounce Hostel for longer than the week I'd booked as it was quite expensive and I was still unemployed. After chatting to a German in my room, I decided to book into the much cheaper Nomads Hostel. I should have been dubious as they wouldn't let me look at the rooms before moving in and was horrified at the grotty bathroom attached to the room, with a door separating the two that didn't close properly. I was also surprised to find no locker in the room and the kitchen was about as clean as the Selhurst Park pitch. My roommates were a rude Scottish girl, a shy non-English speaking Asian and a pleasant but simple big black guy from New Jersey. It was an interesting mix.

Once again, I'd posted on the BBS in the hope of finding a Palace fan to watch our game with me on the following Saturday against West Ham. While I'd liked the initial passion of *Cheers*, the atmosphere felt rough and the Arsenal fans' reaction to their win had annoyed me. I really wanted to watch the game with a Palace fan who I could share my match day emotion with.

In the hostels, I'd only met fans of 'top four' clubs, who's idea of discussing football is sharing who from the Chelsea squad is 'amazing' and who is 's***'. I've noticed that there seems to be very little middle ground with people who watch on TV. Whereas supporters of lower league teams can recognise that all players have faults and different players offer different strengths required for different matches. Fans who watch 'The Chels' on television can only say that Hazard is class and John Obi Mikel is '*absolute dogs*** and must have something on the manager'*. Well if he does, he should give up being a footballer and become a private detective as he's obviously had something on each of the last eight Chelsea managers. However, ironically, as much as I slagged off 'TV supporters', I was desperate to find one to watch a game with me... on TV!

Meanwhile, back in South London, Palace had moved swiftly to appoint

Malky Mackay as our new boss. I lay on my bed one evening reading about him as the rest of the room went out to a local club. Nomads was a 'party hostel' and they went to a different student-style club each night, with free goon offered beforehand. 'Goon' is a wine packaged in a bag-in-box. To give you an idea of the quality of this stuff, you can purchase five litres for about five dollars (£2.80ish). Having drunk things like a mixture of lambrini and white cider as a student, I decided that I was past this stage and always opted to buy decent alcohol to enjoy, rather than just get rat-arsed.

Anyway, on this night, with Palace due to appoint a new manager, I let my roommates go out while I stayed in, reading the BBS and starting to feel optimistic about our new boss. Wanting time to myself, I pretended to be asleep when the Scottish girl came in early. Unfortunately, having faked my state of unconsciousness, I didn't realise that she had a companion with her. It was only when the bed next to mine started to creek and stunted but definite noises began to come from her side of the room that I realised she wasn't alone. Not wanting to appear a peeping tom, I lay still, continuing to face the wall, and didn't say a word.

The next day I finally got to go on the Bondi to Coogee walk that I'd heard so much about. Despite it raining for the majority of the six kilometre coastal walk, it was spectacular throughout and it gave me a chance to chat to some people from my new hostel. There was a lovely German girl, whose English was far better than she believed it to be, an arrogant Aussie from Melbourne, an Irish musician, the American from my room and a Dutch girl he'd hooked up with, a tattoo covered guy from Belgium and a very simple Londoner. The odd mix made for a great variety of cultures but very little common ground. Even so, we all got along reasonably well despite our limited interest in each other's personal passions. It was a shame that the crap weather meant that at the end, rather than relaxing on the beach or going for a drink, everyone decided to go back to the hostel to dry off, where I had to sit through an almighty argument between my roommate and the girl he was with.

When I woke up the next day, I went straight to my phone to check the Palace news. I had nothing to get up for so it seemed pointless to force myself out of bed earlier than necessary. After the Pulis bolt from the blue, I wouldn't say that I was shocked by what I saw but it was yet another bizarre twist in the CPFC rollercoaster that I thought I knew so well. I simply rolled my eyes and sighed in resignation that nothing is ever simple. The only thing about my football club that can surprise me these days is that they continue to find new ways of shooting themselves in the foot. The previous year, we'd not only been caught 'spying' on Cardiff to find out their team sheet, but we'd also managed to text our top secret knowledge to our former manager, Dougie Freedman, who'd then grassed us up. Every story seems ludicrous yet original as we go from one disaster to the next.

Football rivalries tend to be natural; Tottenham and Arsenal, Manchester United and Manchester City, Liverpool and Everton, Sheffield United and Sheffield Wednesday, Bristol City and Bristol Rovers. But not Palace. Oh no. We have to be different. Not only do we have an intense and irrational share of loathing with Brighton, a team from another city. We'd somehow managed to build up a rivalry with Cardiff City, a team based 173 miles away. In the previous few years, the two teams had shared false allegations of racism, numerous red cards and bad tempered matches, a league cup semi-final, a promotion battle, being relegation rivals, had the aforementioned spygate incident, we'd appointed their sacked Director of Football, who'd then been banned from entering their ground upon his return with us, and now we were appointing their previous manager, who'd very publically fallen out with their Bond-style villain owner, Vincent Tan, who very publically didn't like us. All in all, there was already a lot of bad blood between the two clubs.

Hours before we appointed McKay, Vincent Tan made his own announcement. He'd been investigating both Malkay McKay and our Director of Football, Ian Moody, who'd been in the centre of the 'spygate' situation, as they'd both tried to sue their previous boss for wrongful dismissal. On company owned phones, they'd sent the following text messages that Tan had found.

'Fkn chinkys. Fk it. There's enough dogs in Cardiff for us all to go around.'
On the arrival of South Korean international Kim Bo-Kyung

'Go on, fat Phil. Nothing like a Jew that sees money slipping through his fingers'
On football agent Phil Smith

'He's a snake, a gay snake. Not to be trusted'
On an official of another club

'Not many white faces amongst that lot but worth considering.'
On a list of potential signings

'I hope she's looking after your needs. I bet you'd love a bounce on her falsies.'
On a player's female agent

A picture entitled Black Monopoly (where every square was a "Go to Jail" square)
Sent to members of Cardiff's staff

Sadly, the fact that someone involved in football was racist, homophobic and sexist was not really of any surprise at all. Although, some of his choices of phrase were as ridiculous as they were offensive. Of course, Tan's announcement meant that we withdrew the job offer. I found it sad that, along with a mumbled apology, Mackay said that he felt he'd done nothing wrong. At least Moody had the decency to resign over the incident. However, this left us with no manager, no Director of Football and a fast approaching transfer deadline. Nothing was really going right, for me or Palace.

After nearly two weeks of trying, in the hostel, I finally found someone who I actually got along quite well with. A German guy from Hamburg replaced the rampant Scottish girl from the night before. The pair of us shared a love of good beer and went exploring pubs in Surry Hills, an area of Sydney that endeared itself to me more than the rest thanks to its excellent drinking venues and less rowdy vibe. Unfortunately, as quickly as he entered my life, Morgan, the German, left it. He checked out the next morning and moved on. The hectic life of a backpacker.

Finally, the Saturday came and I got a response off the BBS. *'Ships is Back'* a poster from Brisbane put *'Palace Supporters Club are meeting at the Exhibition tonight. Should be about 30-50 Palace fans there tonight I'm told. Enjoy yourself. If you're up in Brisbane soon, let us know.'*
I couldn't believe it! 30-50 Palace fans. That sounded amazing. As we had a 'normal' 3pm kickoff, it meant a Sydney start at the much more sociable time of midnight. Enthusiastically, I turned up at about ten thirty to the suitably named Royal Exhibition Hotel but I didn't spot any Palace fans. I'd worn my evil sash away kit to make myself instantly recognisable and I displayed it proudly as I bought myself a schooner of ale. Straight away, I noticed that the pub had a far better selection of beer than *Cheers Bar* had offered the week before. Despite the lack of Palace fans, there were a few Hammers and some Newcastle fans watching their 10pm kick off against Aston Villa so I sat down with my beer to follow the early game.

Immediately, a bald chap, around average height and with a noticeable Aussie accent came over and introduced himself. He wore a white Palace polo shirt and his name was Jordo; founder of the Crystal Palace FC Sydney Supporters Club. He'd lived in London in 2004 and fallen in love with the club then, cumulating in our playoff win against West Ham in Cardiff. He showed me the group's badge, where our eagle was perched proudly on the Opera House, which I noticed was on both his shirt and his beer cooler. After introducing himself, he took me over to some more Palace fans: Paul, a bald, older chap from Bromley, Dale, a black guy in his thirties, also from Bromley and Jimmy, another Londoner in his mid-twenties.

The first thing they wanted to know was *"Do you play as well?"* to which I replied *"I try to..."*, reflecting on the fact that despite my highly limited ability, I was a willing worker. They explained that they have yearly fixtures against both West Ham and Brighton's Sydney Supporters groups, and were looking for more games too, as well as talented players. I felt I could fit into the 'players' category, if not the 'talented'.

Soon, while it was closer to twenty than the 30-50 predicted on the BBS, the bar began to fill up with ever-more red and blue shirts, but even more ones of claret and blue. What I hadn't realised was that *we* shared the pub with the West Ham Supporters Group. On the other side of the world, this was our own rivalry and there'd been a big push to get people to come to *this* match. I'd fluked that my first game was to be the biggest of the season. Well, in that pub anyway!

It was little wonder that when I'd phoned up the pub in the day to check if they'd be showing the Crystal Palace vs West Ham game, my request was met with a laugh before giving me an answer. I bet the landlord couldn't believe his luck on that night and was praying for as many cup games as possible between the two. Just before kick-off, I was urged to move forward and take the central table in front of the main screen, as we decorated as much of the pub in red and blue as possible and our opponents did the same in claret and blue.

Once the game started, it was like being there live. Songs were exchanged in both directions as the fans 16,983km away from the action sang about the game, put down each other's team and proclaimed that *'This is our pub!'* Singing wasn't about cheering the boys on, it was about outdoing our opponents. We couldn't help the team win the battle of the match so we were desperate to win our battle of the pub. However, unlike such occurrences in England, the battle involved no threats, fists or weapons. Merely the clapping of hands and proud raising of voices. Although, it's a shame that the players couldn't hear us as it might have inspired them to do better than fall 2-0 down in the first half.

The second half was little better and I began to get worked up as the West Ham fans enjoyed their victory and sang in our direction. When losing, the last thing I want is to be around gleeful opponents, something that I was experiencing for the second week in a row. Not that I'd be any different myself of course. I felt my blood pressure rise and once again, I was forced to bite my tongue and grit my teeth, not wanting to show my true emotion. I watched the game glumly with two Palace fans, who I could chat to easily, called Russ and Nick. While Russ was another South Londoner from Croydon, Nick had been born in the Midlands and found Palace later than in childhood. However, his love was still strong enough to turn up and watch us in the middle of the night from the other side of the world.

They explained that when we were in the Championship, everyone would make a huge effort to see us every time we were on telly but now we were on every week, it was really easy to take it for granted. Although Nick expressed the difference in reaction that he got from when he'd first moved over. Originally, people would simply look at him blankly if he said he supported Palace but as football got a wider following, Palace did better on the pitch and with the ever widening reach of the Premier League brand, people started to know of us. Unfortunately, this usually prompted a laugh and a snide comment. However, even that was an improvement on people being blissfully unaware of our existence. Amazingly, with our recent success, especially that magical night against Liverpool, people would now look at him with a respectful nod of acceptance and even be able to enter a brief conversation about our beloved South London club.

In the end, Palace deservedly lost 3-1 to a surprisingly good West Ham side. Only Marouane Chamakh came out of the game with any credibility, putting in a hardworking performance and scoring our goal. But for once, the score didn't really matter to me. For the first time in the ten days that I'd been in Oz, I really felt at home. I'd been surrounded by Palace fans who I could chat, drink and moan with, in the usual enthusiastic tone that follows me around the subject of Palace.

As soon as the whistle went for full time, the Hammers came straight over. I shook their hand with a mixture of dignity and insincerity to congratulate them on their deserved victory. B******s. Or so I thought. The longer we chatted, the more I realised there was no gloating or taunting from our opponents as there had been from the Arsenal fans the week before. Just football chat. The kind that happens in pubs and grounds, on trains and busses, and in living rooms or work offices, up and down the country every week. Except I was fast finding out that the 'EPL' wasn't just discussed up and down our country. It was discussed up and down, left and right, this way and that way, all around the globe.

Any anger or bitterness that I'd felt during the match soon left me. I was faced with gracious, well humoured and generous opposition, who loved their club and drinking and singing and socialising. I identified just as much with the expats from East London as I did with those from Croydon. We were all grabbing the part of home that we missed the most and recreating it thousands of miles away. I'd always pitied 'TV supporters' but suddenly I got it. We'd all invested just as much into the match as we would have done in the ground. We all felt the same Saturday afternoon (well, Sunday morning) emotions that football fans crave for so much. We all got the atmosphere and intensity of singing across a barrier to support and offend. We all felt the pain of the loss as *they* felt the joy of victory. And most importantly, we spent it with friends.

Well, everyone else did. I would be lying if I claimed that I had an instant close friendship with anyone there but for the first time since stepping foot on foreign soil, I was confident that I'd found people who could become just that. And it was all because of football. Or more specifically, Crystal Palace Football Club. There again, what is friendship? If I think of my best mates back home, I think of a deep rooted history of shared stories and tribulations. With Palace fans, I have that as soon as I meet them. Even if they've experienced the same stories, highs and traumas from a different angle – or in this case, a different hemisphere.

After spending until the pub closed at five in the morning happily sharing stories and getting to know both Palace and Hammers fans in the pub, I finally made my way home for some much needed sleep. Except, despite the alcohol, I couldn't nod off. I was excited. This is what it was all about. Meeting people, sharing experiences, having fun, ignoring the pit falls. Both travelling and football were summed up in one night, a 3-1 home defeat gone well.

Arsenal...2 Crystal Palace...1
Emirates Stadium, 16/08/14
Premier League

Arsenal: Szczesny, Debuchy, Koscielny, Chambers, Gibbs (Monreal 53), Arteta, Wilshere (Oxlade-Chamberlain 69), Ramsey, Cazorla, Sanchez, Sanogo (Giroud 61).
Subs not used: Martinez, Coquelin, Rosicky, Campbell.

Crystal Palace: Julian Speroni, Martin Kelly, Scott Dann (Damian Delaney 75), Brede Hangeland, Joel Ward, Jason Puncheon, Mile Jedinak, Joe Ledley, Yannick Bolasie (Stuart O'Keefe 90), Marouane Chamakh, Fraizer Campbell (Dwight Gayle 85).
Subs not used: Wayne Hennessey, Paddy McCarthy, Barry Bannan, Glenn Murray.

Crystal Palace...1 West Ham United...3
Selhurst Park, 23/08/14
Premier League

Crystal Palace: Julian Speroni, Martin Kelly, Brede Hangeland, Damian Delaney, Joel Ward, Barry Bannan (JohnnyWilliams 70), Mile Jedinak, Stuart O'Keefe (Glenn Murray 83), Yannick Bolasie, Marouane Chamakh, Fraizer Campbell (Dwight Gayle 70).
Subs Not Used: Wayne Hennessey, Adrian Mariappa, Paddy McCarthy, Adeline Guedioura,.

West Ham United: Adrian, O'Brien, Reid, Tomkins, Cresswell, Downing (Diame 89), Kouyate, Noble, Vaz Te, Zarate (Poyet 82), Cole (Sakho 67).
Subs Not Used: Jaaskelainen, Demel, Morrison, Valencia.

"At that point of time and having been around and seen that group grow –with only a few additions coming in – it made me feel really proud of being able to lead them on a regular basis and knowing that we were all in it together, trying to get us home in the league and really kick on.

On the eve of the season, we didn't have a manager in place but we'd done the preparation and we knew each other so well, we knew each others strengths so we knew what our best game plan would be, and we'd worked on that. So we just went about out business. The Arsenal game wasn't anything out of the ordinary for us. Nothing we were asked to do by Keith was foreign and part of that was the significance of having a tight group. I felt that we put in a pretty good performance against Arsenal. Although, we were narrow losers at the end of the day, we walked away from that, having been manager-less, thinking "y'know what, we're still in with a very good chance as long as we keep doing the right things by each other. Whatever decisions are made, we just have to continue to do the things that we're doing. That was our mentality from the get-go."

Mile Jedinak

Chapter 5 – Returning Faces and Gloom – *Sydney, 24ᵗ August-29th August 2014*

Buoyed with optimism from the night before, I decided to head out and around some of the pubs that I'd frequented in Surry Hills with Morgan to look for a job. Each pub ebbed away slowly at my enthusiasm as they took a lack of interest in my offer of work and seemed almost annoyed as they had to go through the effort of accepting my CV. Presumably to discard it as quickly as Palace ditched the seventeen new signings that we'd made on our arrival to the Premier League.

After a long and fruitless walk, I made my way back to the Hostel, where I planned to once again try a different organised pub crawl and club that evening in an attempt to make friends. I'd specifically looked for craft beer bars to work in as I wanted to not only earn money, but to also learn about something I'm passionate about. While I wasn't ready to start teaching, I didn't want to just take on any old job. However, although I had a small amount of savings to see me through the opening few weeks of my adventure, I was very disheartened after my unsuccessful stroll. With hostel companionship and social life hardly endearing itself to me, I was keen to get work to help me make new friends as much as anything else.

The Palace crowd from the night before had been a rare glimpse into recognisable social circles in Australia. Most of the hostel users were either just passing through Sydney and the 'long-termers' seemed to be school drop outs, who'd come over to Oz for a yearlong party, having missed out on the university experience. I'd been on a few nights out and enjoyed them but with clubbing not really my scene, excessive drinking games being a thing of the past and mainstream, thumping music seeming tacky and repetitive, I wasn't exactly thrilled at the prospect of a whole year of them.

People in hostels seemed to be very happy living a simple life. The sad thing was, in my late teens and early twenties, it's a simple life that I'd have loved. However, now, with me feeling old for the first time in my life, I knew that I wanted people to go to nicer bars with, and go out for meals, and to not worry about penny pinching with at every possible moment. Not simply go to foam parties with 2-4-1 cheap drinks.

Anyway, starting to feel desperate for a job, I decided to go into a bar in the centre of Sydney by the hostel. It was a grotty looking Irish bar called Scruffy Murphys. Its logo was the pub's name written in gold on a green sign, with a ginger Irishman playing a violin above it. Outside, there were a few lads in bright orange jackets after a day of construction work and I instantly noticed a variety of large adverts by the entrance: *'Every Manchester United Game Shown Here'*, *'$6 Guinness Pints!'* and *'2-4-1 house beers and spirits!'*. Inside, the pub had the predictable range of poor quality lagers lined up on the bar and plenty of brightly coloured spirits stocked up behind it. It wasn't exactly my kind of pub.

However, I did notice something in the corner. The pub was showing a rerun of our game against West Ham. I hoped it was a sign. A sign of friendship and enjoyment rather than a sign of the knowledge that I was heading towards an inevitable defeat. Anyway, I made my way to the bar and asked the girl who was serving about a job. She told me to wait for the manager. I didn't want to. I wasn't even sure if I wanted a job there as I listened to the barely comprehensible ramblings of the old Irishman next to me, probably called Paddy. I wasn't sure how he, or indeed most of the clientele, fitted into Responsible Service of Alcohol.

Eventually, a young bloke appeared and after checking I had an RSA and some sort of experience, he offered me a trial for that evening. I nipped to K-mart (the Australian alternative to Primark) to buy some suitable clothes for my shift and headed into work about eight. The manager was busy when I arrived and I was left for thirty minutes to sit and wait. After checking with the bouncer, it turned out that they'd simply forgotten I was there. When he finally did arrive, he asked one of the girls behind the bar to show me how to use the till and then I was off. It was a strange feeling to be working in a pub again after four years of teaching. I got plenty of abuse for daring to be English and the inevitable following question for the '*locals*' was "*Who do you support?*"

Although, it was an interesting interview style from my new customers. Rather than asking who I *did* support, upon discovering my English roots, they enquired who I didn't support.

"*Aye laddie, you don't support Arsenal/Man You/Liverpool do you?*"
I did find it ironic that it was the fact that I was English that prompted those questions as it seemed to me that being Irish ensured football fans had to follow one of the bigger teams. My answer of '*No, Crystal Palace*' was inoffensive to anyone and was reasonably well received. However, I wasn't sure sure how I felt about this. While I liked the fact that it avoided aggro, in some ways it would be nice for other people to care about your team, rather than for them be 'little old Palace'. Still, I suspect Liverpool fans were slightly more wary of me.

As time went on, I began to get twitchy, unsure if I was being paid or simply being used for free labour. The clientele got drunker and ruder, leaving me confused as to who to serve and who to avoid with the RSA rules still fresh in my mind. Each time I checked, I was told not to worry and simply serve them anyway.

"*Oh Darragh's fine. He's always like that! He just likes a drink, so he does!*" or "*Don't worry about Siobhan, she can never stand up in the wee hours!*"
While it was comforting to get a second opinion, the fact that the $1100 fine would be on my shoulders rang loud in my ears.

Each hour seemed to bring in a new law too. No jugs of beer allowed after eleven. Four drinks per transaction after twelve. No bombs, doubles, special deals or shots after midnight. Two drinks per transaction after two. The bar strictly shuts, including to bar staff, between three and five am. Drinks must be poured, paid for, and passed over the bar by 3am or it is illegal to serve it. CCTV may be checked. At the end of the seven hour trial, unable to have a drink as I hadn't poured my 'staff one' before three in the morning, I was shown how to sign in and out, and told to come back in the week to ask for more shifts. I briefly chatted to my new workmates, who had been savvy enough to pour their own drinks in time, and then left, ready for bed. While it was hardly a dream job, it was handy to have some income and hopefully I'd make some new friends. The expensive cost of living was digging deep into my savings.

The next day, I finally found an area of Sydney that I liked – Manly. Originally, I had been supposed to go with some people that I'd met in the hostel but their hangover dictated that they couldn't be bothered. Not wanting to waste the day, I got the ferry from Circular Quay (Sydney Harbour) to North Sydney's pretty seaside village. On the way, I saw dolphins playing in the water by the boat. The majestic and intelligent creatures impress me in all ways but one: being Brighton's original nickname before they changed to seagulls to mimic our own eagle.

While Manly boasts beautiful beaches, cycle paths, walks and nature reserves, as well as fantastic fish and chips, perhaps the largest influence in my favourable reaction to the area was spotting the Four Pines microbrewery and pub, overlooking the ferry port and beach. It was a shame that I was alone or I would have happily stayed in there all afternoon. As it was, I had a quick schooner and checked the odds on the next Palace manager. It was a pretty uninspiring list: Keith Millen, Steve Clarke, Tim Sherwood and Neil Lennon were the front runners. The former West Brom manager, Clarke, seemed the best fit to me.

While I'd enjoyed the day, it was a shame to be experiencing these places alone. Hostel life, especially in the dirty Nomads, was pretty depressing, particularly having come from a comfortable flat in London, living with my best friends, and if I wasn't finding anyone I was fussed about in the hostels, what was the point of staying in them? On the ferry back 'home', I sent some messages out to the friends of friends that I'd met in the first week to try and arrange to meet up again. Trying to take on the loneliness issue head on, I also vowed to talk to anyone and everyone that night.

After discovering camel burgers in the supermarket, I decided to give them a try that evening in the hostel. While cooking, I tried to start up a conversation with a typical traveller girl. She had frizzy curly hair, wore a chequered shirt over a vest-top and a pair of scruffy jeans. To be fair, other than the vest top, it's a look that wouldn't be too dis-similar to my own. Unfortunately, with the best will in the world, it's very difficult to begin a conversation with someone who doesn't speak the same language as yourself.

Armed with my camel burger and home (well, hostel) made chips, I then chatted to a couple of guys from Brisbane, who soon left as they were meeting their girlfriends. After they'd gone, I chatted to some teenagers who were there on holiday, but they were keen to sleep after a heavy night the day before. I then had a brief chat with an arsehole who was boasting about stealing food from people and his mate putting rohypnol in drinks of mates for a laugh, but I decided to leave that conversation. With the brief exception of before certain miserable Palace games, I have no intention of letting my drink be spiked by the blackout drug. I had a few more conversations with people trying to outdo each other with their own traveller bull s*** and eventually gave up – retreating to my room.

Back in London, I'd started to organise a weekly five-a-side kick about. When the original organiser had moved to New Zealand, I took over and added some of my own friends to the list, enabling us to have some excellent 'Palace vs Non-Palace' matches. Thankfully, some of the other Palace supporters were better at football than me and we had a favourable record. While I realised that re-creating a Palace vs Non-Palace weekly fixture was unlikely, I was keen to start playing again and try to not only regain my fitness, but to hopefully make some new friends. That evening, I googled *"5-a-side in Sydney!"* and looked for a team or kick about to join.

I found a couple of websites where you could sign up to be a ringer for teams short of players and a couple of adverts for trials but nothing concrete. However, I did find an advert on Gumtree where someone who'd recently moved to Sydney from Perth was asking for friends and five a side so I messaged him to see if he fancied going for a drink. It did occur to me that perhaps we could try and start a team so we could join a five-a-side league if we got on, maybe even inviting some of the Palace Supporters' Club to join us.

Over the following few rain soaked days, I achieved very little other than filling out forms for my new job, and being charged $50 for the uniform. The weather and company were hardly conducive for productivity and neither was my disheartened mood if I'm being completely honest. Alone, I simply mulled about really, chatting to people here and there, spending time reading, and listening to traveller woes about money or petty fallings out. Trying to fit in, I went for a couple of nights out with 'The Nomads Crew', but I was already pretty bored of them, often leaving early with other cynical folk, who felt too old for the crowd.

On the Tuesday evening, despite going to bed late after visiting *World Bar*, I didn't quite make it until five am when Palace kicked off against Walsall. There was no free way of following the game by a stream – or even on the radio. Believe me, I tried my best to find one. Briefly, I did consider paying for 'Palace World' so that I could listen to it, but my previous experience was that the online, club owned facility was rubbish quality and I'd only use it on rare occasions anyway. So, for the first time since Ipswich away on the opening day of the 2006/07 season, when we won 2-1 with goals from new signings Jobi McAnuff and Jamie Scowcroft, and I was on my brother's stag do with no phone reception, I wasn't going to even follow the score of a Palace game. No text updates, no BBS, no twitter, no teletext, no Sky Sports News, no TV, no radio. I was going to be sleeping, dreaming of a Glenn Murray hat-trick.

I woke in the morning and my phone had received plenty of messages to my Palace WhatsApp Group named 'Alan Wilbraham is Allah' and no, I can't really explain why. The first message was from Pavel and simply read *'Boom Boom Boom... lemmie hear you say Gayle'*

It was easy to infer that he'd scored but I still didn't know the actual result. The rest of the comments in the group were from Dan and Ameer saying that our goalscorer had to start the next match against Newcastle. Quickly, I redirected myself to the BBC website and found that we'd won 3-0 with a Gayle hat trick. Filled by a feeling of glee, I replied to the group but I instantly realised that it was now the middle of the night back home and my friends were all asleep. Using a mixture of Twitter and Youtube, I soon found a video clip of all three goals and agreed with my mates' sentiments. This goal machine had to start.

Later that day, I met up with Mark from Gumtree. Like me, he was also new to the city and hunting for friends. I was surprised to find out that he supported Middlesbrough. At school in Perth, Western Australia, all of his friends had supported Manchester United or Liverpool or Arsenal but he'd decided to pick a different Premier League team. Unfortunately for him, not all top flight games were shown live at the time and since Fox Sports' deal to show every game had come into play, 'Boro had dropped out of the league, meaning that he'd very rarely actually seen his team play – even on TV. However, he was clued up on the fact that they'd won three of their opening four games of the season.

While the pair of us got on and could happily chat, we didn't really click and were very different. However, when we shook hands and said bye, we were both keen to meet up again. He did suggest going to watch some AFL (Australian Football League) together as he usually went alone. This sounded good to me. While I was keen to see Western Sydney Wanderers FC play, as they were managed by former Palace captain, Tony Popovic, I hadn't really thought about watching other sport out there, except possibly catching some of the cricket World Cup in January, so the idea of learning about a new sport was appealing to me.

As we were saying our goodbyes, I received a WhatsApp message, and a few more instantly after that. Being polite, I left my phone buzzing in my pocket until Mark had gone. When I looked at it, I couldn't believe what I'd read. Neil Warnock, the man who'd deserted us when we needed him most, was set to be appointed as our new manager in the next couple of hours. All my previous positivity and *even streaks of expectancy* left my body and mind instantly and the words that followed out of my mouth were far from polite.

The fall out on our message boards and WhatsApp group went long into the night. Some people, like me, simply couldn't forgive Warnock for walking out during his previous stint as manager. He'd repeatedly claimed that he was up for the fight, until QPR offered him a way out and a larger pay cheque, leaving our club facing oblivion. It's widely accepted that if we'd been relegated that season, CPFC 2010 would not have been unable to save the club. Plenty of people claimed that it was understandable to walk away from a team in administration but for me, that's what made it so unacceptable. As a football creditor, he legally had to have his contract paid in full – a contract that he said he was able to retire on.

However, faced with the biggest challenge of his career, he'd told the administrator that he didn't have the stomach for the fight and asked to leave for one of our relegation rivals. Now that we were in the Premier League, he was back, and desperate for the job. When we needed him, he was nowhere to be seen but now he needed us, we were giving him a final, undeserved crack at the Premier League. What made it worse was that he made it out as if he was doing us some kind of favour! This was a man who'd been relegated or sacked in all of his previous attempts to keep a team in the top flight.

Regardless of the manner in which Warnock had left at the end of his first stint, there was a lot of debate over whether or not he was a good choice in order to keep us in the league. To be honest, I didn't think he was the worst name that we'd been linked with in terms of managerial ability, but he was hardly a top manager, whose performance would leave me staring in awe, wondering how he'd achieved so much. After having Tony Pulis in charge the year before, the Premier League Manager of the Year, it felt like a huge step down in quality. While Warnock had done a great job in his first spell at Palace (until he bottled it), Pulis had amazed me with the detail of his decisions and ability to see things before they happened. However, for me, it wasn't about his ability. I didn't like Warnock, I didn't trust him and I didn't want him anywhere near my club.

No sooner had he returned, and we had had another returning face. It's fair to say that this one was welcomed back more warmly than 'Colin Wanker' (an anagram of Neil Warnock for anyone that's somehow lived under a stone for the last ten years and missed that).Wilfried Zaha returned on loan for the season. While I was delighted that one of my favourite ever Palace players had come home, I was a little concerned that this supported the rumours that Parish was forcing signings on Pulis, resulting in his resignation.

I can't imagine why any manager wouldn't want to sign Zaha. As Alex Ferguson knew, he can do tricks with the ball that no one else in England can do and while his end product is hit and miss, I've seen enough to believe that it will come good. All interviews and evidence from his time at Palace suggested he was a shy lad who needs an arm around his shoulder, something he hadn't received at Manchester United after the man who signed him left before Wilf actually arrived. However, I don't believe that any manager should have decisions forced on him that he has to live and die by.

Like Zaha in Manchester, I'd failed to settle in my new environment too. Although for me, that was one of the cheapest hostels in Sydney, rather than one of the world's most famous football teams. I decided not renew my weekly rent and tried a third different hostel in as many weeks. 790 on George Street. Depressed from the news, I arrived in my new six-person bedroom, which was empty except for an Irish bloke, who seemed keen to communicate as little as possible.

Later, long termers Richard and Chaz came into the room after their days at work and seemed uninterested in expanding their friendship group. I joined in with a bit of their banter but once again, I didn't really feel part of it. Immediately, I felt lonely as I had done in the previous two hostels. Lost in life, I clambered up to my top bunk, which may well give you status in the nick, but is a right pain in the arse in terms of practicality. With the Warnock debate raging on, not even the BBS could give me solace from my nightmare and I escaped into the empowering distraction of the fictional world of Football Manager.

Trying to distract myself further from the struggles of my life and club, I took myself to visit the spectacular Blue Mountains, seventy miles west of Sydney. The name comes from the layer of blue haze that sits above the rainforest and is created by dispersed droplets of Eucalypt oil combining with dust particles and water vapour to scatter refracted mystical rays of blue light. After getting off the train at Katoomba, I went to visit the famous Three Sisters rock formation to get a spectacular view of the whole area, and when the sun briefly poked its nose out from behind the clouds, I got a beautiful view of the blue mist reflecting in the sunlight.

From there, I walked along the dramatic cliff top to the skyway cable car, which takes tourists past Katoomba Falls, the stunning 244m water drop. After my suspended sky ride, I dropped down from the cliff top to the rainforest floor on the World's Steepest Railway, which has a 64% incline for the 310 meter track. To be honest, going down it did remind me of Palace's season so far, a near-vertical descending trail, leaving me staring down in horror. At the bottom, I had a short trek through the rainforest, before getting a cable car back up to the top. I hoped Palace would find their own cable car soon enough, even if I doubted Warnock was to be just that.

I went to work on the Friday night and was disappointed to be put on the small nightclub bar, as opposed to the main one upstairs. This meant that I was alone again. So much for making new friends through work! The nightclub was largely empty, with an overenthusiastic DJ, who might as well have been a CD player, and customers who were ridiculously drunk, staggering around an empty dance floor. When they came to me, they were rude or racist, asking why JP (the manager) had employed an Englishman. Well, that's the polite version. It was usually an English p**** or t*** or c***. Eventually, I decided to stop serving someone who could barely stand, worried about my RSA certificate and a potential fine. The bouncer overruled me and claimed they were a regular. There's nothing quite like support for colleagues. Finally, the bar shut at 1am, two hours before the main bar upstairs, where I was relocated to.

At the end of the shift, myself and the other bloke on duty, Tom, had to clear the bar as the girls got to clock off and start having drinks. Apparently, restocking fridges and wiping the bar down were jobs beyond any female's ability and men were only employed to either manage or close down the bar. I finally finished at about five am and, after walking back to the hostel in heavy rain, slept through most of the next day. Once again, I was working the following night, while Palace were away at Newcastle.

Walsall...0 Crystal Palace...3
The Bescot Stadium, 26/08/14~
League Cup R2

Walsall: O'Donnell, Kinsella, Holden, Downing, Taylor, Chambers, Clifford (Flanagan 61), Forde (Benning 75), Sawyers (Baxendale 61) Grimes, Bradshaw.
Subs not used: MacGillivray, O'Connor, Morris, Bakayoko.

Crystal Palace: Wayne Hennessey, Adrian Mariappa, Paddy McCarthy, Damian Delaney (Brede Hangeland 46), Jerome Binnom-Williams, Johnny Williams (Owen Garvan 75), Adeline Guedioura, Barry Bannan, Jerome Thomas, Glenn Murray, Dwight Gayle (Jake Gray 61).
Subs not used: Chris Kettings, Jerome Boateng, Jason Puncheon, Sulley Kaikai.

Chapter 6 – It Never Rains – *30th August – 15th September 2014, Sydney*

Jealously is a strange thing. As a kid, I remember being incredibly bitter and angry that Matthew Wade had managed to complete the entire set of Western Lego models before me. I knew that I was going to be able to spend my Christmas money the following weekend on the final kit that I needed, but in that moment, I would have done anything to have had that Lego – now. It wasn't about needing it; it was about wanting it, and feeling that someone else had what I wanted. I'd been happy enough playing with my own Lego until that moment when he smugly informed me that he'd won, I raged inside and lied to his face.

Once again, jealousy was rushing through my body and I couldn't even blame smugness this time. I probably wouldn't have gone to Newcastle. In fact, a few months earlier, I'd had the chance to go to Newcastle in the previous season and decided not to. A rather good decision in hindsight as we lost 1-0 to a last minute Cisse goal. So it was a bit rich that I'd have done anything to have been back home and be able to give an answer to Pavel's WhatsApp message. A message that filled me with bitterness and envy, and to be honest, my reply would have probably been *"I'd love to but I can't afford it."*

Pavel had found some flights from London to Newcastle and had decided to go to our game at the last minute. I hated that I didn't have the choice and to make it worse, I wasn't even going to be watching the game on TV at The Exhibition with the other Palace fans, as I was at work. Optimistically, I hoped I'd be in the main bar so that at least it would be on one of the screens around the pub but, alas, no. I was back on my own in the downstairs club, which seemed to become busy just after the midnight kick off.

Before the rush, I did receive a message from Pavel. Palace had taken the lead after 29 seconds through Dwight Gayle who, thankfully after his goals in the week, had been given a rare start. I let out a yelp and poured the next few pints with a huge grin on my face, even dancing a bit to the booming, tasteless music. By the time that I managed to organise cover for a loo break, Palace were 2-1 up. After Newcastle had equalised, Jason Puncheon had scored in the forty-eighth minute to regain our lead with what was apparently a fabulous volley. Just after that, the nightclub was closed and I was then moved to the main bar, which was very busy and not with a view of the Palace game either. The screen had been switched over to show West Ham against Southampton. Around three in the morning, after the bar had finally shut and the game had been finished for an hour or so, I looked up the score.

Three all! It's fair to say that I didn't expect that! Newcastle had equalised on 73 minutes and taken the lead with two minutes left. Thankfully, the prodigal son rode into town and true to the script, there was a party. However, rather than the proud father, as Warnock was stealing the role of, it was the son who hosted the party – Wilfried Zaha. He snatched a last gasp equaliser on his second debut, giving us the fairytale that we were craving. Although, having gone from leaving us in a winning position, to finding us snatching a draw, I couldn't help but feel a little downhearted. I'd been deprived of that last minute goal feeling by my job. Regretfully, I could only imagine the scenes in The Royal Exhibition Hotel, let alone those in Newcastle.

I finished around five am, having still had little or no chance to get to know my new colleagues, and lay on my top bunk, reading about the game on the BBS and watching the match highlights on my phone without sound, while strangers snored around me. Pavel shared pictures of himself throughout the day: he'd found a craft beer bar in Newcastle, met our chairman and then shared a flight back to London with the Newcastle centre back, Fabricio Coloccini. He'd had a great time. Whereas I'd worked, been abused and missed the game. Football is all about following the highs and lows of the club, and enjoying the ride. Out in Australia, I felt like I was stuck in a queue watching the rollercoaster go round.

In August 2014, Facebook exploded into a frenzy of the ice bucket challenge to raise awareness for Motor Neurone Disease. Dan and John, two of my Palace mates, had completed the task and nominated me to be the next one to take part. I had a plan. A very cunning one if I do say so myself. I was going to perform the challenge in front of the Sydney Opera House. Where better to do it? I bought some ice from the supermarket, Woolworths, and made my way down to the Opera House on a rare sunny Sydney day. It was beautiful, and the restaurants and bars were buzzing with activity, one of which kindly gave me an ice bucket and water that I could top up with my frozen cubes. Unfortunately, after asking a tourist to film, a bouncer swooped in and confiscated my tools for health and safety reasons. After yet another Australian failure, I was beaten and resigned to the nearby Botanical Gardens, where I noticed the revolting sounding 'Charlton Swimming Pool'. In the park, but no where near the pool, I lay in the sun, reading the fallout from the previous day's game on the BBS.

Regrettably, I also realised that none of the people I'd messaged about meeting up had got back to me: my Dad's friend's daughter, the girl from the plane or my colleague's family. I hadn't exactly had a mind blowing time with any of them, but I'd enjoyed their company and had hoped they'd support me in moving to a completely new country. Not wanting to nag, I decided against giving any of them a prod, despite them all saying that they'd be keen in the future but were currently busy.

Eventually, I gained the motivation to get myself up and have some dinner before working in the evening. Work was once again lonely and abusive. I'd been scheduled to close the bar alone, meaning that I'd finish at 6am. Scruffys was packed and we unable to have any meaningful conversation behind the bar until it closed at three am. When it emptied, the rest of the staff slipped off home, while I was left alone to close down until it reopened at six.

I found myself once again sleeping through another day, only rising to grab a quick KFC. I had planned to do one of the North Sydney walks in the week but the constant drizzle persuaded me to wait for the summer, or at least spring, before trying to take in some of Sydney's beauty. Additionally, I had hoped to get the Saturday off work so that I could join the Palace contingent in The Royal Exhibition Hotel for our game against Burnley the following week, but I was once again only given three shifts: Friday, Saturday and Sunday. I could hardly turn them down and expect to get more.

For the first time, I decided to extend my stay in a hostel to a second week. Richard, one of my roommates, an English born lad who'd grown up in Florida and had a thick American accent, was the same age as me and seemed to have a bit more about him than the average hostel user. He worked in advertising and was easy to chat to. As well as that, he seemed keener to find decent bars, suitable for daring to engage in conversation with people, rather than soulless nightclubs. I even forgave him for being a glory-hunting Manchester City fan. Chaz, his friend in the room, was ok too. He was only nineteen and incredibly naive but I could chat to him happily. While I wouldn't have exactly classed them as friends, there was a respect between us and a comfortable living environment.

The hostel, while not as clean as Bounce, was kept reasonably liveable, unlike Nomads. The people seemed slightly friendlier and there was more of a buzz in the huge, shared kitchen area. Again, it had a TV room, which wasn't as well kept or stocked as Bounce, but it had a selection of films. All be it with a larger selection of empty DVD cases. With the unrelenting drizzle outside, I found I could fill time easily by watching films, especially when people brought their hard drives into the area. There seemed to be a real community feeling between the backpackers of sharing and helping each other out. I liked it and wanted to be a part of it.

We briefly had a scouser in the room, who was starting his second year in Oz after finishing his three months farm work. The pair of us spent a whole day playing football manager, slowly building our clubs to be the best in the world. It was exactly what I needed as it created a homely and familiar feeling. In the evening, we dressed up and headed out for drinks in the city. Although, as I'd found before, no sooner had I began to build some friendship, he left the hostel and I had to restart the process all over again.

Quickly, the weekend came and it was time to work once more. Friday was uneventful, as I heard the same songs from the previous week. I later found out that the 2009/10 Palace team used the song 'I would walk 500 miles' to motivate them pre-match and I wish I'd been privy to this information at the time. I think it would have motivated me, by linking it to my Selhurst heroes, rather than killing me a bit inside as I watched a mass of green go crazy for the tacky pop song.

The other song that got to me every time it was roared out was 'All about the Bass' by Meghan Trainor. It wasn't even really her song that I didn't like. It was the words in the chorus.

"Because you know I'm all about that bass,
'Bout that bass, no treble
I'm all 'bout that bass, 'bout that bass, no treble
I'm all 'bout that bass, 'bout that bass, no treble
I'm all 'bout that bass, 'bout that bass"

Through most of the night I heard meaningless songs, where the thumping background came shattering through over the top of sounds like the words or tune and I hated it. Whatever I'm doing; socialising, watching football, teaching, listening to music, I like to identify with it. I simply couldn't get my head around how people were enjoying this stuff.

On the Saturday, I actually got a half hour break for the first time. Despite them being legally required for shifts over four hours, I actually didn't mind not receiving them. When your break starts at 1:10am, there's only so much you can do with it. Well, in usual circumstances, there wouldn't be much at all, but when it's a Saturday night/Sunday morning in Australia, the second half of the 3pm Premier League fixtures have just kicked off.

I did ask the duty manager if he would put our fixture on one of the screens. However, they had Southampton vs Newcastle, Chelsea vs Swansea and Tottenham vs West Brom on. He cruelly laughed when I suggested that Palace vs Burnley might bring in more customers. With the Exhibition too far away, I ran up George Street to *Cheers Bar,* which was once again packed with supporters of all clubs. Although there was one less Spurs fan in there when I arrived as he was being dragged out by the bouncers. As always, Cheers were showing every game. Ours was being shown on a small screen in the corner. For 25 minutes, I watched alone as we struggled to break down an organised Burnley side.

I loved seeing Zaha back in red and blue, although he was bizarrely dragged off soon after I arrived. During a break of play, they showed replays of our first half chances which we'd missed. However, in the time I watched, we failed to create a single opportunity against the side that were strong favourites for the drop. Painfully, with just over ten minutes left, I had to leave the pub and go back to work.

Scruffy Murphys was busy when I returned. I had no time to look at my phone as I felt it buzz away in my pocket. Had we scored? Surely we hadn't conceded? I hated it. I slipped off 'to get ice' as soon as it vaguely needed replacing and looked at my phone.

Dad – This has been rubbish.
Dad – and now it's a penalty
Pavel - Oh God

At this point, I knew the game was over but I still didn't know quite what had happened. I'm not sure they realised that as they happily messaged away.

Dad – saved.

I still didn't know who'd been awarded the bloody penalty.

Dan – YES DO DO DO...
Neil - ...Julian Speroni!
Dom – phew

That was a more positive sign. At least we'd been let off with that and hadn't contrived to *lose* the game.

Dad – Full time. 0-0. Rubbish.

Part of what makes the key incidents of following a football team so special is that as fans, we take ownership over them. Dwight Gayle didn't fire us back from 3-0 down against Liverpool, *we* did it. We're part of it; we celebrate it and embrace it. I was once following a Friday night game away at Derby on Twitter, while in The Grape and Grain pub in Crystal Palace with some of my fellow eagle mates. We won 1-0 and Speroni saved a last minute penalty. The fact that we weren't there and couldn't see it didn't matter. As Palace fans, we shared the anguish of conceding the penalty and the euphoria of our save. It was still our moment. However, with this dramatic moment, hearing about the incident after the event had taken place, took all that away from me. For one of the first times in my life, it felt like Palace weren't part of me, just something I liked. I was simply following *their* results in the same way that I'd look out for Brentford's or Dumbarton's or Bromley's.

At the end of my shift, learning from previous mistakes, I remembered to pour myself a beer before 3 so that I could drown my sorrows as I watched Villa win at Anfield. The Sunday shift was horrendous. It was the busiest yet and after a rare hot August day, we had an onslaught of sunburnt and drunken customers arriving from Bondi Beach. I was exhausted from a lack of sleep and three consecutive night shifts, so when I finally finished at 6am, I was in no mood for a pint.

As I went to leave, I discovered that my coat had gone from our cloakroom, which was shared with customer belongings. One of the other bar staff had allowed someone into the area to find their jacket and they'd stolen mine. I walked home in the rain, as the first glimmers of daylight were starting to show, and for the rest of the day, I slept, only stirring to eat.

After a wasted 24 hours feeling sorry for myself, I decided to fix the wrongs. I'd hastily vowed to quit the job, fed up with the drunken and rude customers, unsupportive management and lack of socialising opportunities, not to mention the loss of my coat. However, I soon realised that would be foolish and leave me once again needing money so I decided that I'd look elsewhere and also work on pursuing teaching down under. Blimey, I've just realised how dirty 'teaching down under sounds'. Anyway, I also decided to buy a new coat.

Of course, sometimes, no matter how positive you try to be, things just go wrong. For a start, when going out to replace a stolen coat, the universe decides that it's the perfect opportunity to start to rain. Heavily. I put my head down and squinted my eyes to block out the falling missiles, each one determined to add to my misery. I marched as quickly as I could towards Westfields, not stopping for anything; the beggars, the sellers, the free sample offers. I was a (wet) man on a mission. I eased my way past the crowd of people waiting for a light to change and stormed over the one lane, one way street. It was at this point that a large, intimidating man approached me with a tablet. I tried to avoid eye contact and keep on going. I was fed up with people asking me to do surveys or give to charity, as there seemed to be on every corner of every street in Sydney.

It was only just before I passed him that I noticed his police badge and I stopped.

"Have you got any ID, Sir?" he asked.

Confused as to why the police would want to speak to me, I handed over my UK driving licence. As soon as he had it, he began to fill out a form.

"Are you aware that you just crossed a red light, Sir?" he started, in the continuing rain. "By crossing the road in full view of a red pedestrian light, you have infringed Regulation 231 of the Australian Road Laws. This offense comes with a $79 fine and you have thirty one days to pay it or are liable to be taken to court, or for foreign citizens, deported."

I couldn't believe it. I froze. I wanted to argue, but I knew I was 'guilty'. I had indeed crossed the single lane, one way, empty road on a red pedestrian light. I stood in the rain, without a coat, as he read the jargon and filled out my form.

As the enormous officer strutted off, I quickly sneaked off into a small alleyway, hiding from the world and cowering from the rain. The downpour wasn't only coming from the skies, but from my sunken eyes too. I'd chosen to lose everything. My flat, my friends, my football, my girlfriend. Not content with what I'd given away to come to Australia, Sydney had taken away my coat, my confidence and my dignity.

Newcastle United...3 Crystal Palace...3
St. James' Park, 30/08/14
Premier League

Newcastle United: Krul, Janmaat (Anita 79), Coloccini, Williamson, Haidara, Colback, Sissoko, Cabella, de Jong (Perez 79), Gouffran (Aarons 67), Riviere.
Subs not used: Elliot, Dummett, S.Taylor, Obertan.

Palace: Julian Speroni, Adrian Mariappa, Scott Dann, Damian Delaney, Martin Kelly, Jason Puncheon, Mile Jedinak, Joel Ward, Yannick Bolasie (Glenn Murray 83), Marouane Chamakh (Fraizer Campbell 52), Dwight Gayle (Wilfried Zaha 70).
Subs not used: Wayne Hennessey, Brede Hangeland, Barry Bannan, Johnny Williams.

Crystal Palace...0 Burnley...0
Selhurst Park, 13/09/14
Premier League

Palace: Julian Speroni, Joel Ward, Damian Delaney, Scott Dann, Adrian Mariappa, Mile Jedinak, James McArthur, Jason Puncheon, Wilfried Zaha (Yannick Bolasie 70), Fraizer Campbell (Kevin Doyle 61), Dwight Gayle (Johnny Williams 73).
Subs Not Used: Wayne Hennessey, Zeki Fryers, Martin Kelly, Joe Ledley,

Burnley; Heaton, Trippier, Duff Shackell, Mee, Arfield, Marney, Jones, Boyd, Jutkiewicz, Ings (Sordell 42).
Subs Not Used: Gilks, Reid, Ward, Wallace, Long, Barnes.

Chapter 7 - There's Only One Geoff Thomas – *Sydney, 16th–18th September 2014*

Throughout my life, ever since I can remember, football has always been there for me. Whether that was in the guise of having my three older brothers whack a ball at me in the garden as we made a goal between two trees, just in front of my Dad's greenhouse, or whether that is discussing the game at the pub, or playing five a side, or wasting my spare time on computer games, or watching Palace, or collecting stickers, or writing a book. It's always been there. It's been an identity. It's been me.

My mother believes in guardian angels that look out for us, keeping us safe and giving us a lift when required. Football has been my guardian angel. It's always there for me, lighting my passion, supplying special moments and making me friends. Football protects me. Protects me from loneliness, distracts me from difficult times, focuses my emotions and channels my aggression. Football picks me up when I fall down. Past Palace wins have masked the pain of a girlfriend heartache, or taken the edge off the stress of work. However, since my arrival in Australia, I'd lost that. Football had tried; the Palace fans at the Exhibition had been brilliant and given me a truly happy night, despite the loss, but I was forcing myself to be cut out, missing games because of a s**tty job.

As well as feeling regretful and lonely, I felt empty, as I knew this wasn't what I wanted from my experience. The lack of football was exaggerating that. I was absent from friends, losing my team and neglected by the world. I was wallowing in my own self pity. I'd spent time trying to be positive, I really had, but every time I renewed my optimism, something else battered me down.

In the hostels, I had little interest in joining in with the football chat that usually centred around the big clubs. They don't interest me and I can't identify with them. The fact that Fabregas was looking 'class' for Chelsea and Alexis Sanchez looked 'unreal' for Arsenal was irrelevant to my life or interests. To be honest, hearing about them meant about as much to me as hearing about a race horse or a rugby team. The big clubs are shoved down our throats by the TV companies so much that it's almost impossible to not have an opinion on most of their players, no matter how large or small your football addiction is. However, when I talk about football, I like to learn something new, whether that's a different view point or a ground or player that I know little about.

I know what I want to know about the big clubs and already have my opinions on them. I don't need to hear what others think. Which lets be fair, is usually pretty much the same all round. It's hard not to admire the footballing ability of Rooney or Ronaldo or Costa. Just like it is hard not to dislike their human being abilities. There's no debate. Supporters of lower clubs have to choose between their favoured strengths of players. Supporters of Palace have to decide whether they worship a player like Mile Jedinak because of his strength, tackling and leadership, or whether they want to drop him because his lack of passing ability infuriates them. There are people who would prefer to give up strength in our midfield and try someone weaker but more skilful, such as Johnny Williams or José Campaña. We have to search for a players' strengths and adapt to them, ignoring their weaknesses. Whereas, midfielders at the top clubs have it all. If they have a real weakness, they don't stay long!

Lacking motivation and stuck in a rut, I started to hide in the TV room at the hostel. Content in my own little world, I could vaguely be sociable in there between films but most of the time, the light was off, a film was on and I could escape into a fantasy world. A bit like I do at Palace. As one film ended around 9pm one evening, I was hoping to get another one on quickly so I could finish it before the room closed at eleven, when I could realistically go to bed. However, before anyone had a chance to change the disk over, a group of lads burst into the room. I'd seen them about before and hadn't particularly taken to them. One of them was a small guy, maybe only 5"5 or so and obviously worked out at the gym a lot, his arms were enormous. In our previous meeting, he had grinned at me with an annoyingly big smile as he shaved his chest while standing next to me in the shower rooms. The other two were a tall black guy with an afro and an Irish lad.

It was the small guy who started to talk, mainly about his irrational dislike of someone who'd used the lift ahead of him. They then moved on to Transfer Deadline Day, although I doubt they cared much for our transfer business of signing Zeki Fryers from Spurs or James McArthur from Wigan. The loud trio were far more interested in Falcao signing for Manchester United, City letting Negredo go and Javier Hernandez moving to Real Madrid. I tried to switch off and buried my head in my phone as I read about further possible signings for Palace. We knew we needed a striker.

However, there was one comment that caught my attention.
"...and we burst in like..." started Pete, the afro donning black guy, who I noticed had a strange accent that I later found out was Norwegian.
"...like Geoff Thomas busting through from midfield..?" quipped in Rich, the smaller guy with giant arms, before his friend could finish. I'm not sure that's quite how the sentence was originally going to be completed but I loved how it had been. I looked up straight away. Could it be? Had I found another eagle?

I didn't want to make assumptions and dive in straight away. I'd been given false hopes before so I simply asked him why he picked that player. He wasn't a Palace fan; he supported Crewe Alexandra but that didn't matter. He knew what supporting a crap football team is all about. He said that not being able to watch his team was the worst thing about being in Oz, but at least he could see the Premier League games. He'd also been able to watch Crewe win what he called 'The Cup Final', purposely neglecting to mention that it was the Johnson's Paint Trophy. However, that mattered little to him. All that mattered was that his team had won at Wembley and even more importantly, the game had been shown live in Australia.

We talked about Geoff Thomas, we talked about the lack of cover from the weather at Blackpool, we talked about Dean Ashton and Gresty Road. We talked about following your team while away from home and a dislike of Simon Jordan. We shared stories of skiving school for away trips and finding bizarre ways to travel the country. We discussed the awful away facilities at Kenilworth Road and shared our thoughts on the worst grounds out of the 92. Unsurprisingly, he mentioned Port Vale and I remembered my visit to The Withdean Stadium, Brighton's old ground. The fact that he didn't support Palace didn't matter, we shared the same experiences and passion for our club.

We'd been chatting for well over an hour when he said he needed to go bed as he had work the next day. Out of mere politeness I enquired what he did for a living, especially when he mentioned that he had a 'pretty sweet job'. *"I'm a teacher,"* he replied.

His answer provoked a further thirty minutes of shared passionate discussion, mainly in regards to him giving me advice on how to move forward with teaching in Australia. I thanked him and for the first time since the West Ham game two weeks earlier, I went to bed feeling content and optimistic. Football had done it again. It had hovered over me and helped to take me from my misery. Although, it reminded me the next day that it can be a right pain in the arse too when I woke up to news that Warnock had loaned out Glenn Murray and brought in Kevin Doyle.

Over the next few days, I continued to talk to Richard around the hostel, as well as the Richard from my room. To avoid confusion, I will now call them 'American Rich' and 'Crewe Rich', or as they referred to themselves 'The Two Dicks'. Through them, I began to meet more and more people around the hostel: Emma, a girl from Macclesfield, Pete, the Norwegian, Teun (pronounced Tony), a Dutch guy, John, an Irish lad, Kate, a Scottish lass and Saskia, a German girl.

I started to do every day things that I enjoyed from back home, such as going out for dinners, going to the cinema and having barbeques at the park (ok I can't do that back home in winter). I was also introduced to 'Trampoline World', which was not only good fun but also a surprisingly good work out. The weather even picked up and I could sample Sydney's famous beach life.

At work, I finally had a chance to get to know my new colleagues when the management gave the staff a free $500 tab behind the bar one night as a thank you. I had a great evening and really felt relaxed for the first time in 'Scruffys'. It certainly made me look forward to my shifts more than I had been.

Football had got the ball rolling and given me confidence when I was feeling down, and it helped me further when I could use my knowledge of the country to shock people by telling them that I'd visited their home town of Chesterfield or Morecombe or any other of the many far reaching and random places that I'd gone for the beautiful game. However, as I began to feel more at ease with the people around me, I missed the football less and less. Even so, I had another search for five-a-side and found more luck this time. On Gumtree,

I found an advert asking for players 'of all abilities' for a Saturday Morning kick about.

Unsure what to expect, I turned up on at 8:30am for the game, while messaging friends back home who were still out for their Friday night drinks. The organiser, Matt, had rented an outdoor Astroturf pitch and with numbers dwindling, placed the advert to keep it going. The standard was low, even compared to my limited ability, but it was great to be playing again. I had a nice surprise when I turned up as Mark, who I'd met on the night that Warnock had been appointed, was also playing, having responded to the advert. At the end of the game, one of the better players, George, said there was another kick about organised for Wednesday night at the Rocks, an area of Sydney that used to be where the criminals were dumped but is now highly trendy. Suddenly, I was playing twice a week. Even if I was embarrassed by my ability and fitness in the first Wednesday session.

Unfortunately, the teaching wasn't going so well. I was informed that as I'd only spent three years at university rather than four, I wasn't qualified to teach in Australia. Although, I later received a letter suggesting that I might be able to do some supply work. This sounded good to me, especially when I heard that the pay was over $300 a day.

Having said that, now that I'd started to receive payments from Scruffy Murphys, I was enjoying a decent amount of dollar, making the job a lot more bearable. I was on $26/hour, $28 on Saturdays and $33 on a Sunday, with tips on top. Watching my bank balance rise has never been so easy. For one of the first times in my life, I didn't have any money worries. I could pretty much do everything that I wanted to, and I was still saving money, while working part time. The bosses were obviously pleased with my work as my hours were increased each week, edging me closer to full time, which suited me just fine. It was still far less hours and stress than I'd had when teaching in England.

As I was walking home after my second Wednesday five-a-side, I noticed something in a pub window. They were showing the first leg of the Asian Champion's League semi-final. Korean side, FC Seoul vs Western Sydney Wanderers. It was the football that pulled me into the establishment but as soon as I stepped into Harts Pub I loved it. They had an outstanding selection of ten craft beers and a reasonable selection of bottles to boot. While I enjoyed an expensive ($13/pint) beer, I took in the football. I'd already booked a ticket for the second leg in two weeks time but was keen to see the action from this game. Not that there was much drama, it finished 0-0 and I can't say that anything about the game really got my heart rate rising. Tony Popovic, the former Palace captain, was pleased with the team that he now managed and had plenty of reasons to be optimistic ahead of the second leg back in Sydney.

Chapter 8 - Supporters Clubs – *Sydney, 21st September 2014*

The following Sunday I found myself in a position that I had never envisaged. I was in a bar (*normal so far*), watching the football *(still not out of the norm)* with The Manchester United Sydney Supporters Group *(send me to hell – or was I already there?)*. I have no great love for the red half of Manchester, and Surrey, and Asia, and America. In fact, it's fair to say that I have a fair amount of irrational hatred. However, I was chosen to be the sole bar tender for the group as their match against Leicester City was shown in the basement of Scruffy Murphys. It was the day of the All Ireland Hurling Finals and both the bar and restaurant were crammed full upstairs. However, Manchester United, Heineken and certain pubs, including ours, have a deal where every United game must be shown live and Heineken be offered at $5 a pint to people wearing the vile badge.

The group couldn't have been further from our Palace one in any way. It had been set up by worldwide organisations and had official club memberships, whereas ours was made for and run by exiled supporters. While we were a mixture of South Londoners and the odd Aussie, not one of the thirty or so fans that they had turn up used a Manchester accent. We drank craft ales and had a selection of interesting beers, whereas they lapped up Heineken, a flavourless brand. They drank their crap beer in a mainstream pub, with no link or connection to their club, owned by a Spurs fan, simply using it because it made sense financially. There was no passion or heart in it, unlike our supporters led group in a pub named after the building that gave us our name.

Sure, they clapped and high fived as United eased their way into a 3-1 lead and I must admit, even I gasped in astonishment as their new fifty-seven million pound winger, Angel Di Maria, scored a sublime chip with exquisite technique. However, there was no thrill in it for them. It was just a routine, every week, Premier League away victory. How I dreamed of away games being like that.

I've seen 193 Palace away games, mainly in the Championship, and we've lost 79, drawn 61 and won a mere 53 – just over one in four. In fact, in sixteen live Premier League away games, I'd only seen one win, which was against Everton in the previous year, who ironically, we were playing that night. And I was incredibly lucky to have made it to that one. I'd booked transport to rush up to Liverpool after work for the game, totally neglecting to notice that it was in fact parents evening. When I realised, I decided that it would be frowned upon to not turn up to parents evening (as the teacher) and had to miss out. Fortunately for me, if not the fans who did go, the game was called off forty-five minutes before kickoff and rearranged for the Easter Holidays, meaning I got to go to the game, tick off ground number ninety and see Palace win.

Anyway, unlike me, these Man United fans had probably seen hundreds of Premier League away victories (on TV). In fact (at the time, thankfully not now!), I'd actually seen more Manchester United away Premier League victories myself than I have Palace ones thanks to their wins at Selhurst in 1998 and 2014. This win was neither a surprise nor special. It wasn't theirs in the way that felt I owned Palace wins, as it was expected. They demanded a win from the team they supported as a gift wrapped present, whereas I was begging mine for one in the sanguine hope. Almost wishing Santa was real, knowing he's not.

But on that night, something different happened. The original script was thrown out and a comedy was penned. Leicester scored four goals in twenty-one minutes to steam roll United aside and take a 5-3 victory. It was beautiful. I didn't care that a relegation rival had got an unlikely three points as I knew how every Leicester fan was feeling and it took my mind back to the 3-3 game with Liverpool. Even the referee was against United, gifting Leicester a soft penalty for the strike that gave them the lead. I'd hated having my bar draped in red flags and having to argue with my manager about wearing a United shirt. There was no chance in hell of that happening. I would honestly have rather walked out of the job there and then, sooner than don that shi(r)t. However, I was surprised at how easy it was to refrain myself from dancing about behind the bar as each of the home side's goals stunned the pub further.

Sure, it was lovely to watch their reaction of disbelief as each goal flew in, and feel the anger in the room growing. Oh, how I laughed at their disgust at Leicester's soft penalty as I thought back to the one's they'd got against Palace the year before. But overall, as they moped over to the bar for their discounted Heineken, I actually felt a bit sorry for them, through empathy, and in a really strange way, pleased for them. For one night, Manchester United fans learnt a lesson. They found out what it was like to follow other teams. To follow a team that shoots itself in the foot and manages to lose in the most astonishing circumstances. And when they won the following week, as they inevitably would, that result would be slightly more special than if they'd beaten Leicester. Because they following week, they'd be approaching the game with fear, rather than expectancy.

After the United game, which ended just before one, the fans went home and the big screen was replaced with a DJ. However, it took a while for people to realise that my downstairs bar was open, which gave me the chance to look at my phone as I got text updates about our game. The weekend's other results had left us bottom of the table with two points and no wins from four games.

My Dad, Pavel and Dom were all watching at home on streams and commenting on how bad Palace were playing. Everton took a deserved lead through Lukaku and my joy from the United game turned to anger at Warnock. I'd seen us deservedly win at Goodison just five months earlier and from what I was seeing by text, Everton could hit us for four or five. My phone continued to buzz as the bar got busier and busier. However, unlike the Newcastle and Burnley games, I managed to check the messages as they came through.

After half an hour, in seemingly our first attack, we got a penalty. Jedinak scored it and to be honest, my mood changed very little. From what I'd heard, we had simply been lucky after our opponents had battered us all game. Although, after our goal, Dan, Dad, Pavel and Dom all commented that we'd massively improved. The psychology of a goal is enormous. I bet the Everton players couldn't believe their hard luck.

In the second half, Palace actually had the audacity to not only score once, but twice. First, Fraizer Campbell scored his maiden goal for the club with a header that looped over the keeper and trickled into the net. Then, Yannick Bolassie, our smiling winger, got his first Premier League goal for the club. With Palace winning, it became harder and harder to concentrate on pouring drinks as my heart and mind were in Liverpool. I might not have been watching the game live, but at least I was following the emotion and excitement of it. That was enough for me.

My task, of concentrating on the job in hand, tipped over from difficult to impossible as Everton scored with seven minutes left. Luckily, a couple of minutes later, just after half past two in the morning, the manager came down and asked me to shut the nightclub. He even allowed me to watch the end of our game upstairs in the main bar before I washed down the bar and cleared the stock away.

I saw a tense final two minutes and an even tenser six minutes of stoppage time as Everton, armed with four strikers on the pitch, assaulted our goal with wave after wave of attack. However, just as we had done in the previous April, we held firm for a 3-2 away victory at Goodison Park and moved up the table to fifteenth, level on points with Manchester United. The rest of the shift was unsurprisingly upbeat. I definitely felt involved enough to count this as 'our' victory, rather than Palace's.

In my first few shifts, the only person who I'd spent any time with was a guy called Tom. However, without warning, he'd not turned up to work that night and was never seen again. This meant that I did more and more shifts in the week. Amazingly, when I got five days of work a week, I was earning just as much as I was teaching back in London. The midweek shifts were great too, as I had more time to chat with the other staff and get to know them. A Manchester United fan named Paul was the only other barman and we were good at helping each other out when closing down the bar, enabling us to get away slightly earlier than usual. The girls were great too. More and more I was nipping into the pub when I wasn't working to go for drinks with my colleagues, as well as going out for dinners and spending time at the beach.

Life was stress free. I also started swimming every day. As part of Sydney's Olympic legacy, there are a variety of 50m outdoor pools available to use cheaply around the city. One thing that I did notice is that Australia seems to stop for bad weather. In England, we're so used to it being unreliable that we carry on regardless, whereas Aussies know that the next day or weekend is likely to be more suitable and put things on hold.

I'd arrived in Oz at the worst time of year for the weather, but as we entered September and spring time, it quickly improved. Temperatures were regularly 25-35 degrees and the outdoor pools would be packed. However, if it dropped to 20-22 degrees, which was still a pleasant temperature for me, I'd pretty much be swimming alone. Likewise, if it rained in the evening, the pub was pretty much empty as people couldn't be bothered to venture out in the wet. I enjoyed an empty pub one rainy night as the Everton game was replayed in full on Fox Sports, allowing me to see all that I'd missed.

The swimming was brilliant as it gave me routine. I've always found myself happier when I'm in a good routine, at work, for football, for sport. Everywhere really. As a teacher, I've seen first-hand the positive effects of children having and knowing a set routine that leaves few surprises and brings familiarity. Like with many things, what's helpful for kids, is also helpful for me. Each day, I would wake around mid-day, head to the pool for a swim, buy some lunch with my tips, do a bit of work on my first book in the afternoon, spend the rest of my tips on a healthy dinner, socialise in the evening with either the hostel long termers, like The Two Dicks, or some of my work colleagues, and then finally go into work, starting somewhere between eight and twelve.

While it was simple, it suited me as I began to readjust my expectations for the year. Easy as life was proving, I knew I needed something to look forward to so I booked a three week trip to travel up the East Coast of Australia from Sydney to Cairns. It caused the Canadian travel agent a lot of amusement that I booked things around the two weekends so that I didn't miss either of our games against, Manchester United or Sunderland. His colleague was less than impressed. Having grown up in Brighton, she hated Palace, not because of any love for her hometown club but because of how much she was inconvenienced by the police shutting down half the town each time Palace play down there.

I also booked a flight to Kuala Lumpur to visit Michaela, and a flight back from Ho Chi Minh in Vietnam, leaving myself five weeks to get from A to B.

Over time, I also started to gain confidence and take control over the things that I wanted. I requested four of the next five Saturdays off (the other was an international break) so that I could watch our games against Leicester, Hull, Chelsea and West Brom in The Royal Exhibition Hotel. I may have hated Warnock, but I still wanted to watch us and be part of the games. As settled as I was now feeling in Sydney, I still hated the idea of missing Palace.

Everton...2 Crystal Palace...3
Goodison Park, 21/09/14
Premier League

Everton: Howard, Baines, Jagielka, Distin (Gibson 84), Stones (Mirallas 64), Barry, McCarthy, Osman, Atsu (Naismith 64), Eto'o, Lukaku.
Subs not used: Robles, McGeady, Besic, Alcaraz.

Palace: Julian Speroni, Martin Kelly, Scott Dann, Damian Delaney, Joel Ward, Jason Puncheon, James McArthur (Adeline Guedioura 84), Yannick Bolasie (Zeki Fryers 86), Fraizer Campbell (Kevin Doyle 86).
Subs not used: Wayne Hennessey, Adrian Mariappa, Wilfried Zaha, Dwight Gayle.

Chapter 9 - Who do you sing for? – *Sydney, 24th September- 1st October 2014*

One evening after work, at 5am, I paid for the hostel's rubbish and overpriced internet to try and stream our League Cup game against Newcastle United. Despite it not being on TV anywhere in the world, the BBC had chosen it to be one of the main games for their highlights programme and somehow, Palace fans had found a way of watching it. To be honest, the picture was blurred and lying in a hostel room in the middle of the night, headphones in, trying to watch us play on my 7" tablet, wasn't exactly much fun. Not even Dwight Gayle giving us the lead from the penalty spot could entice me to continue to follow the stop-start stream.

I gave up when I heard Newcastle had equalised before I'd seen the goal and found out we'd lost 3-2 in extra time when I woke the next day. Sullay Kaikai, the latest youth player to make his debut, had a dream start to his Palace career by scoring a last minute equaliser to extend the game by thirty minutes. Andy Johnson also made his second debut for the club after he'd been re-signed in what was an unlikely and nostalgic return. He never played again. Johnson's second coming was a strange one for me. He and Clinton Morrison are my all-time favourite players and I imagine it was pretty special for the people who went to the game to see him back in red and blue. However, being the sucker for the statistics that I am, I didn't want to see his incredible goal scoring ratio ruined!

It was during my third week in '790 on George' that the dynamics in my room sadly changed. Chaz and American Richard both moved out but with the wonders of modern technology, I wasn't worried about losing touch. For various communication requirements, we'd exchanged Facebook, mobile numbers and email addresses and on the following Wednesday, I had a Sydney first where I asked 'to bring a friend along' to join in with five-a-side. Despite his American education on football, Richard was surprisingly good. Having said that, the Americans that I'd encountered in Brazil for the World Cup had disappointed me. There were no loud-mouth 'defence/offense' shouting morons, who thought that offside meant the ball left the field of play at the side and 'Extra-Time Multi-ball' should be introduced for excitement. Instead I merely found fellow football fans, who were able to discuss the game with excellent knowledgeable detail, often putting the English fans that we met to shame.

Along with playing football weekly, Rich and I started to make visiting the Hart Pub a post-match a ritual too, undoing any of the good fitness work from the evening.

Having booked off the Saturday to watch Palace, I enjoyed an afternoon at the local Albert Park with a barbeque and people from the hostel. American Rich and I invented our own master piece in 'The Green Eyed Baceroo':

kangaroo burgers, bacon, cheese and guacamole for the green eyes. It was a delight. Unfortunately, as good as the bonding was, I couldn't persuade anyone to visit the Royal Exhibition that evening, even Crewe Rich, who I'd shared a long and detailed discussion with about all things Palace and Alexandra.

At around 10pm, I made my way to the Palace pub for our match against Leicester City, with a large amount of fear after seeing them destroy United the week before, and began to build up for the game. Unfortunately, I couldn't spot any Palace fans – but it was packed with West Ham supporters who were there early and enjoying the Merseyside derby. As I recognised many of the Hammers from my first trip to the pub, I joined them and once again loved talking about all things football. Different allegiances mattered little in comparison to passion, memorable stories and respect. The real drama and excitement of an away day can often happen in the stands, trains or pubs around the ground, rather than on the pitch, which means a lot of us have been through the same things, no matter who we support.

By midnight, when our game began, the area of the pub in front of the main screen was packed with Hammers watching their team play against Manchester United, but there was still no sign of any other Palace fans. And even worse than that, they hadn't even put our game on the telly at the back of the pub. Maybe the United fans weren't doing it all wrong after all? At least they were guaranteed their air time.

I went to enquire at the bar and was assured they'd put it on. Eventually, from looking at our Supporters Group's Facebook page, I discovered that it was being shown on the red button, rather than one of Fox Sport's main channels. As our screen flicked between different matches, none of which were Palace, and the main screen occasionally jumped about too, briefly showing golf, someone tapped me on the shoulder.

"You're Palace aren't you?" asked a tall and lanky guy, who looked about my age, certainly in his twenties, and wore his hair spiked up at the front.

As I wasn't wearing any colours, I wasn't sure how to take this news.

"James isn't it?" he continued, slightly uncertainly.

I looked at him. I definitely didn't recognise him but he must have remembered me from the West Ham game.

"Yeah... Sorry mate, I don't remember your name. You're Palace, right?" I enquired, hoping I'd finally found a fellow eagle, even if I hadn't found the game.

"It's Sean, we met at Blackburn away... we were drinking in Preston after the game mate!"

I had no recollection of him but there were plenty of gaps in my memory from that particularly drunken away day in our promotion season. At least from his reaction, I didn't think I'd offended him.

The manager came back out from behind the bar and said he couldn't find it. Having heard that the game definitely could be shown, I wasn't going to give up that easily, particularly having given up both work and the chance of go out with my hostel mates in order to watch us play. He took me to the control room to try and find it. They had six Fox Sports boxes all lined up and he wasn't sure which control worked for each one, and some of them worked for multiple boxes, hence the interference with the Hammers game. Eventually, we got a blurred picture of the Palace game, which only took up about two thirds of the small screen. It was far from ideal but at least we had something – and he offered to go back to try and improve it. Unfortunately, all he managed to do was to lose our picture completely and once more upset the large group of West Ham fans by managing to switch their screen over. He returned rather sheepishly, stating that he wasn't going to risk distressing his customers any further and was now going to give up. He didn't even want to try and get our blurred picture back, which had been fine for Sean and I. Not even his offer of a free apology drink could entice us to stay. Choosing Palace over free alcohol, two disgruntled eagles headed out into the night to hunt for our game.

First, we tried The Crystal Palace Hotel, as I'd been told that they show all of our matches live by a colleague. Unfortunately, the truth was that it shuts at midnight so if they were showing our game, it was a secret viewing. After that, we once again made our way to *Cheers*, which was packed. We went to the bar and asked for the Palace game. Predictably, they hadn't previously found it, but using my 'red button knowledge' the bar manageress agreed to go and have a look.

For the second time in the evening, I found myself in a pub's TV control room, although this one was far more organised and, well, actually controlled. She found our game and had a monitor in the room to show what she was changing to before affecting any of the screens in the pub. As soon as she flicked onto our match, which was early in the second half by now, Scott Dann won a header from a corner and the slightest touch from Fraizer Campbell turned it in to the net. Palace were 1-0 up.

I punched the air, let out a whoop and ran downstairs to grab Sean and tell him the good news. Not only had we found the game, Palace had also taken the lead. Happily, he went to the bar and I skipped back upstairs to find the screen that had been blessed with our game. It was still a blurry picture that didn't cover the whole screen, but that bothered me very little. I had a Palace friend, I had our match and we had the lead.

As I got to the top of the stairs, the manageress was still in the control room, working out which screen to air our match on. She called me in to check that I didn't mind that it wasn't full screen and as I stuck my head into the cramped room, they were showing a replay of our goal, or so I thought. I quickly realised that it wasn't a replay as nobody was on the line to turn it in this time. It was in fact an immediate second goal, scored by our captain, Mile Jedinak, also from a corner. Once again, I leaped, danced, jumped and grinned as I went to find Sean, who still hadn't been served at the bar. I think my reaction was enough to tell her that I didn't mind at all.

The rest of the game was pretty dull. Palace were in control without ever really threatening and Leicester didn't look like repeating their comeback from the previous week at all. I guess they did have tougher opposition this time around.

Despite the two wins (and two draws) in Warnock's first four League games, my attitude to him didn't soften at all. While I could recognise that he'd made a decent start, I was still a little bit unsure that he could keep it up and was very sure that I couldn't forgive him for the way that he'd previously let us down. Of course I enjoyed our wins, but that didn't change my view of Colin. I wanted him out however he did. I guess that's the pig headedness of football fans for you. We not only want success, we want success our way. I couldn't cheer for someone who had harmed our club in a way that his actions could have killed it. Bitter? Quite possibly. Unproductive? Very definitely. Passionate? Absolutely.

Sean left at full time but I decided to stay and watch the North London derby. Soon enough, in the way football fans do, I got chatting to a Manchester City fan. Although he supported the reigning champions of England, our football experiences had actually been very similar. We'd both seen second tier relegation battles and had the unique emotion of a playoff win at Wembley. His first away game had been a 2-1 loss at Lincoln City in October 1998 and while I'd avoided Palace having that particular embarrassment, I had seen us lose at Crawley, Gillingham and Barnsley. It was almost a competition.

Yet now, in a very different world to Lincoln City, he loved supporting his club and he loved them winning things. Of course, he'd rather they'd done it without the money but realistically, is there any other way? Any City fan will tell you, that seeing Alex Ferguson turn around and hear of their two title winning goals in 2012 was worth every penny spent. Us football fans live for those moments and the emotion in Manchester that afternoon beamed out of him two years on, but no brighter or duller than him reliving the 1999 third tier playoff final. His team winning was his team winning, no matter how good or bad they were at the time.

Not long after that, we were joined by two Australian Liverpool fans. They'd never been to England, never mind Anfield, but were clearly passionate about their club. The year before, the pair of them had travelled 878km by coach to watch their heroes play against Melbourne Victory. Despite it only being a friendly, he retold the story with the passion and excitement of a child visiting their first match. 95,000 fans, all wearing red, passionately and collectively cheering on their side, singing 'You'll Never Walk Alone'. I got it, I really did. It was great that someone born so far away from our home, in a country that doesn't prioritise 'soccer', could love our game so much.

I thought back to the Manchester United fans in Scruffys on a work night at 1am for a match against Leicester City and I loved that too. They'd captured and understood and harnessed the thrill of live football and made it happen in a pub. How brilliant was it that these two Liverpool fans had been able to see their heroes live? Even if it was just a friendly. For one night, they experienced that collective feeling of infatuation that a football ground brings. Of course, I really loved the people I met who randomly chose to support a rubbish team, maybe even Palace, but why should they?

Geographically, while supporting Dover might be the closest option, it doesn't really make a difference when choosing a team on the other side of the world. Likewise, many of us ignore our geography and follow our heritage, our father's or grandfather's team, but in Australia, many people don't have that football role model. Often, football is picked up by adults in the pub, rather than kids in the school playground. So I got it. For Australians, picking the big team that jumped out to them for whatever reason made sense, whether that was colours, players, style, fans, songs, the first one they saw, their mates liking them or even simply that they won a lot. As long as they stuck to one team, I didn't mind.

However, what I ended up passionately debating, and not understanding, was that as well as supporting Liverpool, why didn't they support either Sydney FC or Western Sydney Wanderers? Their answer was because *"Those teams are s***!"*
And that is where it was handy to be with a Manchester City fan. While Palace always have been, and probably always will be 'a bit s***' in their eyes, Manchester City had previously been s***er than Palace but were now better than Liverpool. Both scenarios mattered little to Dan, my Mancunian companion.

These two Liverpool fans had experienced the thrill of live football, and the passion of the ground, and the collectiveness in the stands, and the abuse of the referee, and the pre match drinks, and after match moan. Yet, despite there being some genuine live football on their doorstep, they ignored it because of the quality on the pitch. I can't relate to that at all. Surely, if they supported their local team, and raised the profile of the sport in their country, the quality would soon improve as more people got involved, more money was invested, more overseas players came to play and the media became more intrigued. Besides, Western Sydney couldn't be that bad, they were hoping to get into the Asian Champions League Final and become champions of an entire continent later that week.

At around five in the morning, with the sun starting to rise outside, and Arsenal pushing Spurs for an equaliser at the Emirates, I gave up on the football and made my way home to the hostel.

Over the next few days, I tried to build up my swimming ability, setting daily targets to improve on distance and time. Work became busier with the Sydney University Games challenging students to participate in as much binge drinking as possible. The room dynamics changed as I finally got a bottom bunk and three Estonian lads moved in, loudly, as I tried to recover from an overnight shift at work. The room became dingy as they regularly drank booze and smoked pot, while leaning out of the fifth story window. However, they were always pleasant enough to me and offered me drinks so I didn't mind them. They were always considerate enough of my obscure sleeping hours which were enforced by my job, and they also respected my stuff, which unfortunately isn't always a given in hostels. The only real complaint I had was their snoring, which wasn't exactly their fault.

On the Wednesday, I was finally going to see some live football. I made my way to the suburb of Parramatta, home of Western Sydney Wanderers, for around six o'clock as it was the day of their Asian Champions League Semi-Final. Australia are a bit like the MK Dons of International football and confused by their own geography. While Australia is clearly not in Asia, both the national and club sides compete in the Asian competitions. In order to have more competitive games and improve their chances of World Cup qualification, Australia left the Oceania Football Confederation in 2006 for a new life in Asia. I wonder if England would be more successful if we joined the North America confederation?

While the westbound train out of central Sydney had been quiet and sombre in mood, possibly thanks to the strictly enforced ban on drinking alcohol on trains, the streets of Parramatta were buzzing when I arrived. The town hall had been draped in Red and Black, the colours of Western Sydney, and had a huge banner saying 'We sing for Wanderers'. Everyone, and I mean everyone, was wearing a shirt and heading to the ground. All of the pubs were packed, as were the restaurants. There was singing, clapping, chanting, shouting, beeping, buzzing and a whiff of anticipation in the air. This was an exciting time. Parramatta was alive.

When I got nearer the ground, I felt the usual senses tingling; the smell of burgers, the sound of merchandise sellers, the warmth in the cool evening air as an un-natural amount of bodies made their way to an enclosed area. I was slightly disappointed that match day programmes don't seem to have made their way out of Europe yet and as with the World Cup, I was unable to find one. Inside the ground, I queued for a beer and safe in the knowledge that I was going to be trusted to watch the game without starting a fight, I got two to take out to my open aired seat, avoiding having to queue again. Soon after sitting down, it became fairly apparent that although I was in the 'drinking allowed' section, it was still the family stand and much calmer than the other three boisterous areas of the ground.

The players came out to an enormous roar and instant singing from the packed stand opposite me, behind the goal at the far end. They linked arms, and bounced, and sang and most of the ground joined in but it was clear they were leading it. I've been to all 92 grounds in England, I've followed a team who is widely regarded as having some of the best fans in the country, I've been to a World Cup and seen friendlies overseas, but I have never seen an atmosphere like it. It was loud, and consistent, and coordinated, and passionate. The stand must have been holding two or three thousand and to a man, they were jumping and proudly waving their arms or clapping, all wearing colours. It was like the ultras group at Palace, The Holmesdale Fanatics, but instead of a hundred or so in the corner, there was an entire stand of them.

While I was sure that this was a special atmosphere for the biggest game in the club's short history, there was no way it was a one off. Something as coordinated as that simply couldn't be. I guessed the added enthusiasm from the two side stands, which were also packed, was probably heightened for the occasion but the RBB (Red and Black Block) were unrelenting for the entire evening. My favourite song was one where everyone sang a verse together that I couldn't catch the words of, then the RBB would point at a different stand and chant 'Who do you sing for?', to which the other stand would point back and scream 'We sing for Wanderers!', explaining the message on the town hall.

The game itself was of low quality. In fact, despite being supposedly two of the best teams in a continent (plus Australia), it wouldn't have been out of place in League 1 or 2 in England, but that mattered little to anyone in the ground. Western Sydney won 2-0 with goals in the fourth and sixty-fourth minute. I would tell you who scored but that meant very little to me. I hadn't fallen in love with the team's players. Sure, I already loved their manager, Tony Popovic, from his time at Palace but I'd fallen in love with the Western Sydney Wanderers fans that night. I had something to support and I wanted to be a part of it. The Liverpool fans from *Cheers* were more than missing out. This was what football is all about for me. Who do I sing for? I sing for Wanderers! I was desperate for a ticket for the final and wanted to share the electric atmosphere with my friends.

Crystal Palace...2 Newcastle...3
Selhurst Park, 24/09/14
League Cup R3

Palace: Wayne Hennessey, Adrian Mariappa, Paddy McCarthy (Jake Gray 89), Brede Hangeland, Zeki Fryers, Wilfried Zaha, Adeline Guedioura, Johnny Williams (Sulley Kaikai 79), Barry Bannan, Kevin Doyle (Andy Johnson 71), Dwight Gayle.
Subs not used: Lewis Price, Joel Ward, Peter Ramage, Martin Kelly.

Newcastle: Elliot, Janmaat (Haidara 46), Taylor, Coloccini, Dummett, Colback, Abeid, Ameobi (Sissoko 66), Obertan, Armstrong, Riviere (Perez 80).
Subs not used: Alnwick, Anita, Cabella, Ferreyra.

Crystal Palace...2 Leicester City...0
Selhurst Park, 27/09/14
Premier League

Palace: Julian Speroni, Joel Ward, Damian Delaney, Scott Dann, Martin Kelly, Mile Jedinak, Joe Ledley, James McArthur, Yannick Bolasie (Adeline Guedioura 90), Jason Puncheon, Fraizer Campbell (Marouane Chamakh 71).
Subs Not Used: Wayne Hennessey, Adrian Mariappa, Kevin Doyle, Wilfried Zaha, Dwight Gayle.

Leicester: Schmeichel, De Laet (Simpson 64), Konchesky, Drinkwater, Morgan, Hammond (James 69), Vardy, Moore, Cambiasso (Mahrez 64), Ulloa, Nugent.
Subs Not Used: Hamer, King, Schlupp, Wasilewski.

"Y'know there's a passion out in Australia for football. There's no doubt about that. How big can it get? I personally think that the sky is the limit. Obviously, there needs to be things put into place to improve in the form of the competitiveness of the league, such as having relegations and promotions. When adding that criteria happens, I don't know, but all the ingredients are ready. The support that most A-League clubs receive is quite significant and they're able to generate really big crowds for derbies, which is really encouraging.

Every time we go back with the national side, especially on the back of the success of the Asia Cup, the support and the passion for the game and the audience that we're getting is on the up. Hopefully that will continue. As much as we'd love it to be, that trend doesn't have to be a rapid rise but it would be great even if it was slow and steady progression."

Mile Jedinak

Chapter 10 - Playing for Palace – *Sydney, 4th–11th October 2014*

As time went on, my sleeping habits became more and more obscure as I started to socialise after work with my colleagues. We had a good routine, where we could pour a couple of drinks before 3am to see us through to five and then after five, the bar reopened and we could buy one or two more. While I was keen not to drink too much, I loved the social side of it and we had some real laughs in the pub. As I gained experience, I was used on the main bar more and more, and was given small tokens of responsibility, such as restocking the tills with change and organising breaks for everyone. While it might seem like a small thing, I appreciated the trust in handling the business' money and responsibility of managing time for others. To be honest, it was more about the change in attitude towards me from managers and punters alike. I'd clearly earnt my stripes, which as an Englishman, wasn't the easiest thing to do in an Irish bar.

The other staff were great too. Emily was a fun loving girl who was saving to go travelling around Oz with her partner, Sarah was a bit of a moaner but always fun to work with, Paul was so laid back and sociable that I forgave him being a Manchester United fan, Amy-lea was a loveable but ditsy blonde and Shannon was great fun too. Even the managers grew on me as I realised they were generally up for a laugh and enjoying the relaxed style of Australian life. They were all Irish so they were all pissheads and keen to inform me of how England had failed to control them for 800 years. The other thing I found with the Irish was that while they seem to have an incredible ability to sniff each other out around the world and stick together, often being rude to anyone who isn't Irish, especially us English, once you're in their trusted group, they treat you as their own.

On the Saturday, I once again went to the Royal Exhibition Hotel for the Palace game. This time we were away at Hull City. I'd learnt from my previous lesson against Leicester and had checked on the group's facebook page who else was going to be there beforehand for the midnight kick off. It was to be the last one for a while as the Australian clocks were due to go forward at 2am that night, meaning that from now on, there would be a ten hour time difference, resulting in 1am kickoffs for most matches.

I was joined in the pub by Jordo, the organiser of our group, Russ, one of the regulars who I'd sat with in the first game, a small bald chap named Will and two others. Most of the talk was about the upcoming Football Fans Down Under 5-a-side tournament.

The match itself was dull as Palace deservedly lost a tame affair 2-0 and after the incredible atmosphere I'd experienced in the week, watching Palace lose in the early hours with just a handful of strangers, was a bit of an anticlimax. I wandered home at two in the morning, which suddenly jumped to three in the morning on my phone as I texted my Dad, thoroughly pissed off with what I'd seen.

When American Rich had moved out of the hostel, Crewe Rich had also taken himself away for the school holidays to tour the East Coast of Australia and the double disappointment had left me worried that I'd be lonely. The reality was, that the time actually passed quite quickly and strengthened other friendships I'd made, especially at Scruffys.

The day after the Hull game was the final day of the Australian Rugby Premier League Season. South Sydney Rabbitohs won the Grand Final and became the new champions. Not only were their fans celebrating that, the Monday was to be a bank-holiday, allowing their supporters to party all night long. Scruffys was heaving and it felt amazing to be part of the team that held it all together behind the bar. Despite only being in the job for about seven weeks, I felt like one of the more experienced there as we took on the onslaught of customers.

A Northern Irish lad named Reece started that night and we instantly formed a strong friendship. While he was a bit younger than myself and quite naive, he was a great guy. One of those people who everyone loves for their enthusiasm, kindness and honesty. As well as meeting Reece, the other highlight of the night was discovering that I was on double pay of $52/hour for the bank holiday. Despite living a busy, healthy and comfortable lifestyle, my saving for the trips I'd planned was coming along well. Not every shift was as busy as that though. A couple of times, the club was so dead that the DJ stormed out! Still, the pay was good no matter how busy or dead it was.

By this stage, early October, the weather was constantly hot, unlike Palace's performances, and I was loving my daily swim. I would complete two kilometres each day and tried to shave a minute or two off my time. The following weekend was an international break back home so I'd agreed to work, but I swapped shifts with Reece on the Saturday night to allow me to leave at four, rather than six am as I was set to fulfil one of my biggest life ambitions.

As I was a goalkeeper as a kid, my dream lasted slightly longer than most, and it was only when I hit my mid-twenties that I began to accept that I wouldn't play for my beloved Palace as a living. However, having vented at Ade Akinbiyi, and Shefki Kuqi, and Calvin Andrew, and Wayne Andrews, and Amir Karic, and Scott Flinders, and many more useless recruits, while they attempted to play football for the club, I'd had to concede that *even they* were better equipped than me to don the shirt. Mind you, Johnny, who plays on the wing for the Dog and Duck Third XI, is better than me, and by some distance too.

However, I was going to finally do what I'd dreamed of through most of my literacy lessons at school, what I'd pretended to do in the garden as a kid, what I'd imitated doing on the play station as a teenager and what I never believed would ever actually come true. I was going to play for Palace.

Sure, it wasn't the first team at Selhurst Park, but I was going to pull on a red and blue shirt with the famous badge for the Crystal Palace Sydney

Supporters Club in the Football Fans Down Under 5-a-side tournament. The draw looked like this.

Group 1	Group 2	Group 3
Tottenham Hotspur	Chelsea 'A'	Blackpool
Arsenal	West Ham 'A'	Liverpool
Sydney FC (Cove 22)	Northern Ireland	Crystal Palace
West Ham 'B'	Sydney FC (Cove 23)	Brighton
Leicester City	Swansea City	Chelsea 'B'

The top two teams from each group progressed through to the Quarter Finals, along with the two best runners up. As I'm sure you've guessed, there was only one match on everybody's lips. We had another chance to play against *them*. I turned up as an older Brighton fan was tying a giant seagull flag to the high fence that ran around the perimeter of the Group 3 astroturf pitch. *"What league are you lot from? It's great to see lower league teams represented too!"* I asked with a grin.

He looked down at me in dismay and simply asked *"Pardon?"*

After my first friendly exchange with the enemy, I went to find my own type. Not wanting to be outdone by the almost professional looking camp that Brighton had set up, Jordo was trying to assemble a gazebo to cover us from the scorching and punishing hot sun. Armed with a barbeque and an array of meat, we knew it would be a good day regardless.

Our first match was the one we wanted, Brighton. Unfortunately, we knew they were a strong side. Certainly comparably stronger than their first team back home. While most teams had a mixture of reasonable footballers and pot-bellied piss heads, Brighton's team starred Paul Reid, a thirty-five year old former Australian International and Albion midfielder, along with his semi-professional brother.

Jordo led our starting five out for our first match. Regrettably, we weren't accompanied by Dave Clark Five ringing out, and even more disappointingly, the scantily dressed Crystals were nowhere to be seen. Mind you, we didn't even have a matching kit as we each used our own various Palace shirts ranging from early nineties Virgin shirts to the current one. As it's rare that I ever have an up to date shirt, I was wearing the 2012-13 promotion season's offering. You know, the one where we beat Brighton in the playoff semi-final. I hoped it would be a lucky omen.

The game began at a frantic and unmanageable pace in the baking conditions. I lined up alongside our five replacements, who would all be used in a rolling system so no one had to run for too long. As we kicked off, we realised that Brighton had another star amongst their ranks. Lloyd Owusu, who'd scored 128 league goals in England (only 7 of which were for Brighton), who was still only 37 and was built like a tank, lined up against us.

Amazingly, despite playing against three former professionals, we took the lead early on. Unfortunately, it didn't last and Owusu soon equalised. In the searing temperatures, no one could play for too long and after ten minutes or so, I was subbed on for a quick cameo. Now, as a kid I played as a goalkeeper. In kick abouts and friendly five-a-side, I scored the odd goal but I usually stuck to a trusty defensive position, where I was allowed extra time to control the ball. So despite being aged twenty-five, I'd only ever scored one 'competitive' goal – the fifteenth in a 15-0 win when I was taken out of our own net and allowed to goal hang for the final five minutes of a "league" five-a-side game.

So when the ball immediately fell to me on the volley, just outside the Brighton penalty-d that was marked out on the small sided pitch, I was shocked that I didn't panic. I swung my foot at it and connected well enough to guide the ball into the top corner of the net. I let out a huge cheer and punched the air. I had no idea how to celebrate. I'd never needed to before. Never mind celebrate a goal that had put us ahead against an all-star Brighton side (those are words that I never thought I'd write!).

Unfortunately, my joy was short lived. Apparently there was a ridiculous law against subs coming on and scoring immediately to stop people taking advantage of the rolling subs rule. I couldn't believe it. I'd been robbed. Palace had been robbed. The scum had got off lightly. Without a programme to check, I could only assume that Rob Shoebridge, the ref who'd ignored Freddy Sears' goal at Bristol in 2009, had taken up refereeing in Oz.

By the time I left the field exhausted, we were 3-1 down thanks to two more goals by the former players and it finished 5-1. Brighton had cruised to victory, knowing the referee was on their side. Not that I'm bitter about it. Hopefully, in fifteen or so years' time, Wilfried Zaha and Yannick Bolassie will turn up at a similar event and torture some Brighton fans in the same manner. One thing I will say, is that everyone, including Owusu and Reid, played the game in a great spirit and there was no danger of trouble between the two sets of rival fans.

Still, we couldn't dwell on our loss and recovered well to beat Liverpool 3-1 and Blackpool 2-1. In the Blackpool game, despite generally running around chasing shadows, I managed to make the key pass to set up Jordo for the decisive winning goal. Although the most surprising thing about the match was that it was the Brighton fans at the side of the pitch who persuaded the referee that a late Blackpool shot hadn't crossed the line after he originally gave a goal. Maybe he (and they) weren't so bad after all.

Our final game was against a useless looking Chelsea 'B', who'd been stuffed in every match thus far, so we were confident of getting the win that we needed to secure second place in the group and automatic qualification to the Quarter Final. Unfortunately, things are never that simple. Chelsea 'A' loaned their mates a couple of players and we had a much tougher match than we'd anticipated. However, we won 2-1 and once again, despite doing little else, I set up the winner as we marched on to the quarter-finals in second place. I think it demonstrates the professional nature of our team that some of us, myself included, were gutted that this meant we had to delay our barbeque.

The quarter final was against Sydney FC (Cove 23). Cove 22 and 23 are the two main blocks behind their goal at home games, who are dedicated to singing in the same way as the RBB at Western Sydney Wanderers. We felt we were the stronger team but unfortunately went down to a 2-1 defeat. On a personal note, I managed to miss two good chances to equalise and will be forever haunted by the second one, which even someone of my limited ability really should have done better with. It was even more gutting that we missed out on a very winnable semi-final against Blackpool, who eased past Sydney FC but were thrashed by Brighton in the final. Still, at least we got to have our barbeque, even if we didn't have any shrimps to throw on it. Only beef sausages (as is the norm out there) and ribs.

It was interesting that the only team I saw giving abuse to the referee or other teams throughout the entire day was the other Sydney team (not the one we played). All of the English based sides took the day in a relaxed and fun nature. I think that's the way that most exiled Brits live in Australia. Compared to life back home, it's so much easier and less stressful. There's been no credit crunch, jobs are better paid, expectations on workers are lower, the beach is nearby and the sun is shining. People don't need to take their anger at life out on a football pitch and can play for enjoyment.

And despite the disappointment of not winning, we certainly got the enjoyment out of it. It had been a brilliant day, where one of my biggest dreams had (kind of) come true.

Hull City...2 Crystal Palace...0
The KC Stadium, 4/10/14
Premier League

Hull City: Harper, Robertson (Rosenior 81), Davies, Dawson, Chester, Elmohamady (Bruce 90), Huddlestone, Diame, Livermore, Hernandez (Ramirez 75), Jelavic.
Subs Not Used: Jakupovic, Brady, Quinn, Ben Arfa.

Palace: Julian Speroni, Martin Kelly, Scott Dann (Adrian Mariappa 12), Damian Delaney, Joel Ward, Mile Jedinak, Joe Ledley, James McArthur (Dwight Gayle 70), Yannick Bolasie, Jason Puncheon, Fraizer Campbell (Marouane Chamakh 64).
Subs Not Used: Wayne Hennessey, Adeline Guedioura, Wilfried Zaha, Kevin Doyle.

Chapter 11 – Football, Football Everywhere – *Syndey, 14th-18th October 2014*

One Tuesday night, after my shift ended at 4am and I'd started supping on my post-work ale with Reece, England kicked off against Estonia. Now, I've never been a huge follower of the National Team to be honest. Although, it was beating Spain and losing to Germany on penalties in Euro 1996 that first captured my football addiction. In 1998, I vaguely remember the drama of Michael Owen's goal against Argentina, David Beckham's red card, Sol Campbell's disallowed header and David Batty's missed penalty as we returned home from France. However, I'd not really followed England away from major tournaments and had certainly never been tempted to go to Wembley to watch them play Macedonia or Andorra there. Although, I did enjoy watching us beat Germany 5-1 in Munich!

After an amazing season with Palace, I'd gone out to the World Cup in Brazil for a celebration and holiday more than I went to follow England. However, the way it worked out, it was easier to get England tickets than other matches so we ended up going to the games against Uruguay in Sao Paulo and Costa Rica in Belo Horizonte. I found the atmosphere flat, the players lacking in passion and the whole experience as disappointing as I'd imagined. Those two games had been the only England ones I'd watched since Euro 2012 and I certainly wasn't fussed by this one. In fact, the longer it went on, I focussed more and more on Scotland playing away at the World Champions, Germany. I was absolutely gutted for them, especially Palace midfielders Barry Bannan and James McCarthur, as they conceded a last minute goal to lose 2-1. Scruffy Murphys might have been a rough Irish Pub but at least it had multiple screens to surround me with football.

As time passed by and I had settled in Australia, I found that not only did I need to request time off to watch Palace, but there were more and more social events that I wanted to go to; birthdays, parties and other shenanigans. It was a balance though as my travels were fast approaching and I couldn't afford to miss out on too much work.

However, at the bar, the tips alone were amazing. I couldn't believe the generosity of the Irish. While it obviously helped that I worked alongside a lot of good looking girls, I would usually take home enough tips each night to buy lunch and dinner out the next day. Considering the main clientele were students and backpackers, I was staggered by how much they gave. If I wasn't eating out, I was cooking healthy and high quality food in the hostel, often sharing the cost and prep with Ali, a Turkish guy who moved into my room. Without wanting to add to stereotypes too much, I will explain that he did work in a kebab shop. Considering he got free food at work, I think he appreciated our health drive.

The following Saturday I was once again locked in football as I planned to go to the Sydney derby in the early evening and then watch Palace in the early hours. While it had been a relief at first and taken me out of the doldrums, it did worry me slightly that the majority of my social life was coming from football. Of course, while it ensured passionate debate, easy conversation and friendly banter, I couldn't help but feel that focussing on 'soccer' made me being on the other side of the world all rather pointless.

Yes, I was enjoying watching Western Sydney, cheering Palace on TV, playing five-a-side and making friends along the way. However, despite this, what was always on my mind was that in England, I could watch Palace live *and* play five-a-side with my closest friends. Admittedly, watching Western Sydney Wanderers might have proved more difficult. I wanted football to supplement my life down under, but not be the focus of it, like it had been for many years back home. I'd hoped to find a cure for my addiction. However, I seemed to be setting up a network of friends which was like a light version of my life back home, which in some ways represented Sydney quite well compared to London.

Both of the cities are similar in many ways as the majority of Australians arrived from England two hundred odd years ago. Now, I am aware that not *all* of them were criminals but I bet the bastard who stole my coat was a descendant of one. Anyway, regardless of being built by convicts, Sydney has some great points but if you take out the beaches and sun, I honestly believe that London comes across as a bigger and better place all round. Probably because, like myself back home, London's had longer to establish itself. It has more variety of things going on, a better selection of bars and beer, and more famous landmarks and history. The landmarks are spread out further in London too. You could walk around all of the main sights of Sydney in half a day, whereas going from Crystal Palace to Alexandra Palace in London would be bordering on a short hike.

Food is similar in both to be honest, other than Australians putting their non-poisonous native animals to good use. A lot of the Aussie traditions are similar to our own as they were brought over by the English; roast dinners, fish and chips, steaks, sausage and mash, regular pie shops. However, lamb and beef (but not cheese) were considerably cheaper than back home, meaning that I dined on steak and chops a lot more regularly than I would in England. However, London seemed more welcoming of foreign cuisine. Curry houses seemed to be confined to the same street, Chinese restaurants and take-aways were (predictably) kept in Chinatown and Thai food in the Thai area. Although, most streets seemed to have a western style Sushi chain, which was certainly a benefit over London. Overall, like with most things, while food wasn't in any way limited in Sydney, there seemed to be more options in London.

However, you can't discard the weather and beaches when comparing the two and it is them, along with the high pay, resulting in a comparative lower cost of living and less overcrowding, that makes Australian culture so much more relaxed than London life. The second biggest criticism of us Londoners from the rest of the world (after the weather naturally) is that, despite seemingly having everything we could possibly want or need in London, we never smile. Well, they should have gone to Selhurst Park in the 2013/14 season. There was plenty of smiling Londoners there, even if Neil Warnock's arrival had now somewhat glumly matched our faces with the rest of the capital city. Anyway, having experienced living abroad, I could certainly see where that stereotype came from. Sydney was a city of carefree smiles compared to London.

Still, back on track, the point that I was originally making is that life is easier in Sydney but there's more going on in London and that reflected my experiences of the two quite well. I had no stress from work or money, and I had friendship and locations I liked, but I still felt that I had more going on back home. I wanted to find something special that was unique to Sydney and while football had helped me settle in, it wasn't going to provide uniqueness. I had moved abroad in search of *something* and while I wasn't entirely sure what thing that was, I was fairly sure that I hadn't moved abroad to learn about and immerse myself in football.

And I think it was that attitude that allowed me to enjoy the Sydney derby so much. If I'd tried to recreate the pure passion and love that I get from watching Palace, then I'd have been disappointed. I wanted Western Sydney to win but I didn't *need* them to. It's not often that I can say this but I also knew that they weren't going to provide the quality on the pitch that Palace could offer either. However, I took so much out of the match in a different way. I wasn't trying to replace my Palace experience but I was trying to find something new. Often, at football, I refuse to accept that I am just an observer, having invested so much time, money and emotion into the game – but for this match, I was.

And not just an observer of the pitch. I was observing the fifteen thousand away fans that had come across the city in red and black. They'd invaded Sydney FC's Allianz Stadium, and the city centre. The pubs were awash with their colours and songs. It was the ultimate away day. The largest Palace away following that I'd been in was for Sheffield Wednesday in 2010, when we'd needed to win to survive. This number nearly trebled that!

Wanting to share the special atmosphere that I'd experienced for the Champions League semi-final, I went to the game with Mark from gumtree. In the pub beforehand, the songs were loud and long. I felt bad for not knowing them and tried to join in with the choruses. Now, I've attended plenty of games as a neutral and enjoyed them for various reasons; atmosphere, occasion, friendship, beer, visiting somewhere new. But this was an entirely different feeling because for the first time, and I include watching England in the World Cup in this, I wanted to cheat on Palace. I wanted to sing and cheer for another team.

I didn't know who any of the players were. I didn't know the words to their songs. I didn't know their club history or how they'd built up so many fans in a mere two years of existence. I didn't know their previous record in the derby or of any grudges between the two clubs. I didn't know who to look out for (former Palace player and Sydney FC midfielder Nicky Carle was injured and absent). I didn't know who owned the club or of any past players. I simply knew that they were managed by Tony Popovic, they were in the Asian Champions League Final and that their fans were incredible. I'd decided against FC Seoul that they were no longer 'they' but 'we' and I was going to stick to that.

I vindicated my mindset as if it was a page of an information book on me and my life. Under the heading 'Football Teams', there would be a huge section on Crystal Palace, detailing comprehensive facts, figures, stats and useless information, spread over multiple pages. Around the sides of the pages, there would be small fact boxes about other teams that I liked and looked out for the scores of, such as Dumbarton, the Scottish side that my Grandfather followed, Oldham, the team of my other Grandfather, Bahia, the Brazilian side from Salvador, who play in red and blue and I'd adopted out there, Bromley, as they link my family to South London, Truro, because I like the place, Basel, because they beat Manchester United and wear red and blue, and Brentford, because after Palace, I've seen them play the most.

However, I'd never gone out of my way to go to the stadium in order to sing and chant and embrace in any of those clubs so Western Sydney Wanderers deserved more than them in my book, but obviously far less than Palace. I doubted that I'd be up at 2am on a Sunday morning watching Western Sydney once I was back in England. Therefore, I decided that WSW would get their own single page and it would be fun to fill in the gaps as I learnt about my new Australian club. That way, I knew they were completely separate to Palace, despite being another football club to watch. Besides, I preferred Western Sydney's manager to our own anyway.

The following ninety minutes were exciting, bizarre and baffling in equal quantities. However, there was very little talent in terms of control, passing, dribbling or shooting, and the less said about the goalkeepers the better. There's no way that I could have enjoyed this match if it had involved Palace, yet I laughed the whole way through as I took in the action on the pitch, in the stands and even in the executive boxes!

Both ends of the ground were rocking in song and the stadium was a 45,000 sell out. Mark, who'd only previously been to see his home town team, Perth Glory, was in awe of the occasion and enthusiastically described it as 'The biggest match he'd ever been to!' I didn't have the heart to list of some of the higher profile games that I'd been to. However, once again, not many could match it for atmosphere. The RRB group made a great noise and we were right in the heart of it this time, behind the goal. Although, this did mean we couldn't see the opening moments as various flares were let off, which clouded our view. However, I did just about make out the impressive blue display that Cove 22 and 23 held up before kick-off.

_We_ started well. In five glorious minutes, midway through the first half, Western Sydney scored twice. The first was a decent volley from twelve yards out that bounced down and then up into the top corner. The second was punched ridiculously into his own net by the hapless Sydney FC goalkeeper, while under next to no pressure as the ball looped slowly towards him.

What I noticed about both goals was that the Western Sydney fans barely stopped to celebrate. I mean, sure, there was an original cheer and throwing of beer and letting off of flares, but they were soon back to the well oiled robot that was drilled to sing. Quite how everyone managed to sing the long tunes, I don't know. There was a man with a microphone at the front, conducting the thousands of away fans behind the goal but all of the songs, and there was about ten or so different ones, seemed to last for minutes with choruses and various verses to familiar tunes. It was almost impossible to join in with most of them but I waved my arms and clapped my hands to try and feel part of it all.

However, I did manage to join in with one simple song.

"You Can't Hear Sydney FC
You Can't Hear Sydney FC
You Can't Hear Sydney FC
We'll Sing On Our Own
Don't Wanna Go Home
Don't Wanna Go Hooooooooome
This Is The Best Trip, I've Ever Been On!"

This chant stood out to me for two reasons. For one thing, it was shorter than the others, and secondly, it was the only derogatory song that they sang. The passionate crowd seemed much keener to focus on singing positively about their team than putting the other side down, or even slating the referee. I did notice that there was less spontaneous chanting and humour in the way that there would be at an English ground but in terms of making noise and colour in a 'ultras' style of support, both sides seemed streets ahead of anyone back home.

One element of the atmosphere that I didn't like was that none of the players or managers had their own chants in the way that they would in England. Partly, this annoyed me because I was keen to sing 'Tony Popovic's Red and Black Army' to remind myself of my first and main love, but I was also disappointed as it made it very hard to learn the players' names. I often feel that I support the badge rather than individuals at Palace but this was even more evident here as I didn't know who any of the individuals were. I needed to look up after the game to find out who'd scored for 'us', which made it feel considerably less of an 'us'.

In order to feel closer to my new team and more like a fan, I really wanted to despise our city rivals. I wanted to dislike and criticise everything about them from their fans, to their badge, to their style, to their history, to their stadium. In the way that I would irrationally and hypocritically put down Brighton. However, despite being two nil down to their arch rivals, and having a third of their own stadium invaded by them, the Sydney FC fans in Cove 22 and 23 at the other end of the stadium continued to bounce, and sing, and support in the same passionate way that the RBB did in Parramatta, Western Syndey. Premier League clubs could certainly learn a lot from them. So despite them being the enemy, I actually had a begrudging respect for the sky blue side and just before half time, they got a goal back.

I think this is where I noticed that despite wanting to be a part of it, I wasn't watching *my* team. When our arch rivals scored, I was a bit disappointed, but I wasn't filled with unexplainable rage and resentment in the way that I would be if Brighton scored against Palace. However, being slightly detached from the intense emotion of the game allowed me to reflect on the moment and notice what I loved about my new club. Like the Sydney FC fans, the Western Sydney lot didn't seem to notice the fact that they'd conceded to their rivals and their singing remained undeterred.

After half time, another awful goalkeeping error levelled the scores. This time it was our keeper who'd feebly let the ball trickle past him. Still, as I now came to expect, the Western Sydney supporters didn't let the fact that the team had thrown away a lead stop them; they continued to sing. They refused to let the referee distract them either when he harshly sent off one of their players. I say harshly because it appeared that way at the time. With the benefit of replays, I would now describe it as either a 'full blooded derby-match challenge' or 'f***ing dirty' depending which side of the city you come from (or landed in).

With Popovic's army down to ten men, Sydney FC took control and soon enough found a break through to take the lead. Immediately, the masses behind the goal stormed onto the pitch to mob the goalscorer. Before the stewards could react, there was about fifty or so sky blue supporters on the field. Flares went off, players squared up to each other, the referee desperately blasted his whistle trying to gain order and stewards began to panic. Yet still, the Western Sydney fans ignored the mayhem happening all around them and continued to sing for the team, choreographed perfectly with bouncing and clapping above heads, and seated and standing bits of songs. They were a machine.

The game took minutes to re-start as flares had been thrown on the pitch and needed to be cleared. As well as finals, semi-finals, rivalled matches, grudge matches and last day show downs with Palace, I've also been to five World Cup games and a Champions League Semi-final between Liverpool and Chelsea, but none of those events had the intensity in the stands of this occasion. What the players lacked in ability, they made up for in passion and commitment. The tackles were flying in hard from both teams. I absolutely loved it. It made no sense. Western Sydney Wanderers were only in their third ever season but the numbers and passion of their support was incredible.

Soon, as I'd experienced at Brighton when we lost 3-0, the home fans in the private boxes above the away end began to goad the fans below. As I'd seen on the South Coast of England, a swarm of coins made their way towards the taunting target. However, in Sydney, it didn't stop there as some fans decided to try and climb up to get at them. The rich boys in the boxes got a bit of shock when they were suddenly faced with some swinging arms flying towards their grins as they showed three fingers on one hand, and two on the other.

Again, being slightly detached from the emotion, I was able to rather sensibly tut and shake my head. Despite not really approving, I did laugh at the absurdity of fans climbing up to start a fight with the prawn sandwich brigade. Whereas, had some Palace fans taken this course of action at the Amex I'd have probably moronically justified it by stating that it will teach them to try and mouth off. While I would not be climbing up or starting violence, I'd probably be sticking two fingers up at the taunting home fans and telling them in no uncertain terms where I wanted them to go.

As the police stepped in to arrest the invaders and move the home fans inside their box, the majority of the Western Sydney fans simply continued to sing and encourage the team, ignoring the disappointment that had happened before them on the pitch. I wish I could say that Palace fans would do the same at the Amex or the Den but I doubt we could. Speaking personally, I certainly wouldn't be able to hold in my anger and continue to chant proudly. I'd be too busy letting our centre back, or manager, or the home support exactly what I thought of them.

I'd probably feel that after everything I'd given Palace, I deserved better. When I used to go to every game, I felt no entitlement. I was simply happy to be there. However, now that I pick and choose my Palace away games a bit more, I feel that I've made more of an effort to go and have invested a larger proportion of my spare time in making the effort. As a result, I feel slightly more entitled to a good performance, especially when we play our rivals. Whereas Western Sydney owed me nothing. I'd invested very little into them so far so although disappointed by the outcome, I wasn't devastated.

In fact, I spent a lot of time chuckling in amusement at the events happening around the pitch and dare I say it, I enjoyed the whole experience. The match had over 40,000 fans, a record crowd for the derby, an electric atmosphere, five goals, a come-from-behind victory for the home side, goalkeeping blunders galore, blood and thunder challenges, a red card and a pitch invasion. What more could you ask for from a game? However, if it had involved Palace, I'd have traded it all in for a 1-0 scrappy victory, or even a 0-0 draw to deny our rivals. So, in a strange way, it upset me that I enjoyed the game so much, because how could I claim to be a fan when I took any sort of pleasure out of losing to our arch rivals?

Then I wondered what this said about me as a person. I was longing to feel devastated about a defeat and was annoyed with myself that I gained some enjoyment out of the event that I'd paid to see. Inevitably, the longer I stayed out in Sydney, and the more emotion, time and money that I invested into my enjoyment of the Wanderers, the misery would grow. I felt guilty that I'd latched onto their semi-final win as my own but their defeat couldn't harm me.

Even at the end, after an injury had reduced Western Sydney to nine men, I felt no anger, unlike some of the supporters outside the ground who were letting each other know exactly what they thought of their opponents and all connected to them. While I'm in no way a violent person, I do love the heightened emotion and heated football 'hate' of a derby game. I like the tenseness and the us vs them mentality.

I know myself, and when I watch Palace, a mixture of alcohol, loudness and passion might get me into trouble outside grounds. Over the years, I have had to learn when humorous (well, humorous in my humble opinion anyway, even if no one else in ear shot agrees) verbal assaults are appropriate and when they're not. However, male testosterone and pride has often left me not wanting to let anyone have the last word against my club, especially from our rivals, which can make me appear rather antagonistic. But outside the Allianz stadium, with other fans losing their head, it was my loudness and alcohol consumption that kept the peace.

With abusive fans to the left and right of me, I spotted gold Australian shirt up ahead – with the name 'Jedinak' on the back. Instinctively, spotting something Palace related prompted me to burst into song!

"NA NA NA NA NANANA MILE JEDINAK, JEDINAK, MILE JEDINAK!"

Both sets of supporters stopped shouting at each other and looked at me. They then looked at the shirt ahead. Suddenly, the sides were united. We all sang together.

As I often do in a football crowd, I enjoyed eaves dropping on other people's conversations and I heard the usual comments of blaming the referee, picking out individual performances, singing songs and looking at the table. The win had put Sydney FC top of the league after two games. Out of the excited voices, one comment from an Australian voice leapt out at me.

"I wish I'd worn my Palace shirt!"

Naturally, I made a b-line for the guy. He was in his twenties and had gone to the game with his girlfriend. He'd fallen in love with football as an adult when he started to go and watch Western Sydney.

Like most Australian soccer supporters, he'd realised that he wanted a European team too so he'd embarked on the task of selecting one. Inspired by Popovic and Jedinak, two former Aussie captains who'd both played for the same, small South London side, he realised that there could only be one team for him. Crystal Palace. The previous April, he'd visited England and managed to fulfil a dream by watching us win 1-0 away at West Ham. Jedinak had even scored the winning penalty. He'd loved it. However, he then said something to further justify me cheering Wanderers as my own. He explained that Palace were the English team for a lot of their fans as Popovic had given us fame and their club's formation had coincided with our footballing rise.

The football for the night didn't let up there either. I had the Palace game to look forward to that evening. Still worried that football was taking over my life down under, I decided to compromise for the evening. Rather than go to the Royal Exhibition Hotel, I agreed to go for a night out with friends, provided we went somewhere showing Palace vs Chelsea. After much debate and suggestion, we unbelievably ended up in Scruffy Murphys. At least I got cheap drinks in there. Before hitting the dance floor, we pre-drank while watching an incredible game at Manchester City. They stuffed Spurs 4-1 in a match where referee, Jonathan Moss, awarded four penalties. It was nearly as dramatic as the game I'd been to.

The match also gave me the chance to tell a disbelieving Crewe Rich about Kelvin Morton awarding five penalties in a Palace vs Brighton match in the late eighties. While City and Spurs were no doubt aggrieved at missing one each, it didn't compare to Palace missing three of their four on that occasion! Still, we won 2-1 regardless.

At one in the morning, I slipped off the dance floor and plonked myself in front of a large projector showing our game. Admittedly, watching a game at 1am made it very difficult to stay sober, especially having been to a live game in the early evening, which in turn, makes it very difficult to take in the details of the match. Further disorientating me was the fact that although my screen was showing our game, the sound was of the commentary for the Arsenal vs Hull game, making it very hard to follow if I looked down at my phone and very easy to miss moments when I was talking. To be honest, I had very little expectation for the game but I remember Fraizer Campbell causing Chelsea problems early on, which gave me some much needed encouragement. However, that was soon damped when we fell behind after just six minutes.

With it already being in the small hours of the morning, and having no confidence in Warnock, I'd pretty much accepted defeat from that point on. That was until midway through the first half when Chelsea had Cesar Azpilicueta sent off for an awful tackle on our Aussie legend and captain, Mile Jedinak. Suddenly, I had some hope. It didn't last. Damian Delaney was also sent off three minutes later. In my drunken, tired state, I was infuriated at the time. Much like Western Sydney fans earlier in the day and just like them, my complaints were unfounded. I even had the benefit of TV replays to show me exactly why he'd been sent off, but I still refused to accept it in the moment.

Chelsea scored a second just after half time and controlled the game from then on. As time approached three am, and the bar had nearly completely emptied, I decided to cut my losses. With the game entering stoppage time, I nipped off to empty my bladder and leave. I text my Dad saying *"We don't even look like scoring!"* as I moped down the stairs. My phone beeped almost instantly.

"Other than then you mean?"

Luckily, I hadn't quite left the building and found myself on the wrong side of the Sydney lock out laws so I went back upstairs and checked the screen. Palace had scored and I'd bloody missed it. I watched the last few minutes of stoppage time, where we didn't get an equaliser, and was almost relieved at the final whistle so I could finally make my way to bed.

The following week was fairly uneventful. I had a night out with my colleagues after being disappointed because the brewery tour that had been organised by Scruffys was cancelled. To be honest, the newness of being in Sydney had now worn off and it just felt like everyday life. I worked regularly, went swimming daily, knew the pubs I liked, met with friends frequently and had football all around me. At my Wednesday five-a-side, it was nice that people commented on my improving ability and decreasing waistline. At work, a new manager called Darren joined and we got on brilliantly. He was quick to tell me that they'd take me back on when I returned from my upcoming travels, which was excellent news.

The biggest disappointment of the week was that I didn't get a ticket for the home leg of the Champions League Final. Unlike the European competition, the final was to be played over two legs: the first in Sydney and the second in Saudi Arabia, home of Al-Hilal. After reaching the final, Western Sydney members had been able to vote on where they played the home leg of the tie.

The options were:
1) Parramatta Stadium – their home ground (20k)
2) Allianz Stadium – the home of Sydney FC (45k)
3) ANZ Stadium – the national Stadium (90k)

They voted to play it at their home ground and that meant tickets were incredibly limited. Only a few hundred made it on sale to the general public. Not realising this, I missed out after assuming I'd be able to log on around mid-day on the day that they were released to purchase one.

Although I was annoyed to miss out, I was pleased that they'd opted to play the game at their home ground. All of their season ticket holders and members would be able to get a ticket so no true fans would miss out and if Palace found themselves in a huge match of this ilk, I'd be gutted if we decided to move it to White Hart Lane or Wembley so we could sell more tickets. More people would mean more revenue but it don't think it would do much for the atmosphere. I highly doubt the Saudi Arabians would have ever played in an environment like the cauldron of noise and passion that I'd experienced for the semi-final. Playing in Parramatta was the right option and offered 'us' the best chance of winning.

Crystal Palace...1 Chelsea...2
Selhurst Park, 18/10/14
Premier League

Palace: Julian Speroni, Martin Kelly, Brede Hangeland, Damian Delaney, Joel Ward, Mile Jedinak, Joe Ledley (Adrian Mariappa 58), James McArthur (Adeline Guedioura 69), Jason Puncheon (Wilfried Zaha 69), Yannick Bolasie, Fraizer Campbell.
Subs not used: Wayne Hennessey, Zeki Fryers, Dwight Gayle, Marouane Chamakh.

Chelsea: Courtois, Ivanovic, Cahill, Terry, Azpilicueta, Matic, Fabregas, Willian (Luis 42), Oscar, Hazard (Salah 86), Remy (Drogba 90).
Subs not used: Cech, Zouma, Mikel, Solanke.

Chapter 12 - The Robert Eaton Memorial Fund (Australian Style) –
Sydney, 25th October 2015

Quickly enough, another Palace weekend was upon me. As usual, I used my day off to focus on the red and blue. Despite only getting an hour or so sleep, I made my way to Parramatta early on the Saturday morning to once again wear the famous red and blue for the REMF Charity Match: Crystal Palace Sydney Supporters vs Brighton Semi-Professionals (not that I'm bitter about them having some former players on their side for a "supporters' game"). Maybe a more productive response would have been to contact Craig Foster, Nicky Carle and Tony Popovic, who all lived locally.

REMF (Robert Eaten Memorial Fund) was set up in 2001 by Brighton fans after the cowardly attacks on the Twin Towers in New York. While the world was moved by the tragedy, Brighton fans were particularly touched by one of the day's casualties, Robert Eaton, who was a devoted Brighton fan living in New York. Having visited NYC in 2006 and 2007 as a teenager, when they were still clearing the mess left behind, I was moved beyond belief by the sheer size of the catastrophe. Terrorism is one of life's many ways of reminding us that football is actually so meaningless in the great scheme of things.

However, it is when football is given a perspective that it often brings out the best in us. Fans in England unite every year in memory of the Hillsborough and Bradford disasters, minute silences are impeccably observed around the country. Another recent example of football fan's response to sheer horror was the Sunderland fans raising money for supporters of their arch enemies, after Newcastle supporters died in the Ukraine plane crash. A smaller scale of pain, but no less of a gesture was made by Bournemouth fans when they raised £3000 for Burton Albion supporters after a game was cancelled an hour before kickoff, allowing the lower league fans to return for the re-match.

In the aftermath of New York's lowest moment, Palace and Brighton fans put our differences aside and hastily arranged a match to raise money in Robert Eaton's name. The match, observed by over 1000 supporters (and thankfully no police installed metal walls) raised thousands of pounds. That cash helped provide football equipment to Los Peladitos – a youth football team in Queens, New York, helping promote societal benefits of playing football, while supporting underprivileged Latino children gain soccer scholarships to US universities.

Since then, through a mixture of the original fixture becoming an annual match and other events (such as this one) being organised around it, hundreds of thousands of pounds have been raised, which is used to help deprived children as close to home as Sussex and Croydon, and as far reaching as Africa and North America. This is football at its powerful best.

Anyway, the venue was outstanding. A private school complete with Olympic standard swimming pools, cricket pitches, multiple football pitches and areas for other sports. It may have been a 9am kick off but the sun was already beating down hard. However, charity event or not, we were desperate to beat them. It may not have been as financially important as the 2013 play offs, where we won, although maybe the smaller fees were being put to better use, but it was just as passionate. Unlike the Sydney derby, I felt we had to win.

It was to be a tall order though. Brighton did have three former professionals. To be honest, we had a squad of about sixteen players and I was quite happy to be starting on the bench as I hadn't finished work until 6am the night before. I'd paid my $10 fee and was more than happy to simply have a short cameo at the end. The match started slowly as both teams were wary of the sun. I must admit, I loved the approach of our manager. He stood at the side of the pitch with a can of lager while he barked out instructions. With such hot conditions, I did feel tempted to join him.

The match was split into four twenty-two and a half minute quarters to allow for drinks breaks and in the opening session, we took an unlikely but deserved lead. The small section of ten or so Palace fans and subs went wild and even began to sing towards our rival's fans. However, that wasn't my highlight of the first session.

Unfortunately for him, our star striker and goal scorer, Sean, had to limp off. While that might sound like a cruel highlight, please bear with me. I don't have any sadistic tendencies or hated towards him. How could I? He's a Palace fan!

As he collapsed on the side, someone tended to his ankle and sprayed it with an icy squirt.

"Are you alright son?" came a concerned voice from above him.

"Yeah thanks..." grimaced Sean, briefly looking up, before wincing and turning back to his wound. Suddenly and quickly, he threw his head back up to look again.

"What the f*** are you doing here?" he enquired, bemused.

Unbeknown to him, his parents had not only flown into Australia from South London that morning, but they'd also got a taxi straight from the airport to the match. Unfortunately, Brighton equalised soon after. Predictably, one of their professionals, Paul Reid, got the goal.

Just before the end of the opening quarter, with our newly subbed on centre half struggling for position and pace, I was thrown on the pitch to release him far earlier than I'd expected. Now, my eleven a side football experience has been as a goalkeeper but as I'm a mere 5"10 (and a half, it's important to add), when the goals got bigger in my late teens, I didn't. Nowadays, my 'position' has generally been as a full back, where little is expected of me and no one else wants to play. So to suddenly be thrown on as a centre back, against taller and faster players, was terrifying and it got worse than that too...

As I was subbed on for Palace, so was Lloyd Owusu for Brighton. The beast of a man was twice the size of me, and would have been difficult to handle if he was useless. However, as previously discussed, he wasn't just huge – he was also a highly successful former international footballer. Ok, it was only one cap for Ghana, but still, I was proud of my two 'caps' for the Charters School team when I was twelve.

Immediately, the ball was played perfectly into his feet with his back to goal. I raced (as fast as I ever "race") up behind him, tackled him hard but fair, winning the ball. From there, I brought it forward five yards and passed it to a team mate ahead of me. It was by far the highlight of my footballing career so far. I turned to the bench, realising that it was likely that I'd peaked and called for them to sub me off.

"Just get in f***ing position!" came the reply from my gaffa, spitting out some lager in disbelief at my lack of professionalism.

The first break came and went, and I was shocked that the boss wanted me to remain in the centre of our defence. I assumed they must have been strong lagers he was drinking. At half time, with the scores still locked at one all, I was surprisingly moved to central midfield. My regular swims and newly found fitness were clearly impressing in the searing temperatures. Although, just before we actually kicked off, our right winger asked to swap positions with me and, as I was aware that I'm actually a pretty terrible footballer, I agreed.

Despite my initial reservations, I found the position quite fun. Although, without me holding the centre of our defence together (I say that with my tongue firmly tucked into my cheek), we did let the bastards take the lead. Owusu won a penalty, which our players claimed he dived for, and the rather large chested organiser of the Brighton group was allowed to take it and score. While I personally don't think that Owusu did exaggerate his tumble, it didn't stop me remonstrating to the referee with my team mates. Unfortunately, footballers were my role models as a kid and I'm sticking to blaming them. Mainly because I don't want to admit that it was a bit Neil Warnock-esk.

Despite the disappointment of falling behind and the searing intensity of the heat, I had the legs to get up and down the wing efficiently and managed to find myself in one or two decent crossing positions, even if my final delivery let me down. But that wasn't a problem, right? I mean, we've all seen Zaha and Bolasie struggle with that so it surely didn't matter that I found it hard?

My defining moment came from an attack down the our left wing. The cross came in and was half cleared by a Brighton defender, looping up and away from goal. It fell to me, unmarked and about 15 yards out. I had time let the ball drop, or even control it. Unfortunately, I reacted less like Glenn Murray and more like Aaron Wilbraham in front of goal. I panicked and threw my head at it. The ball looped harmlessly over the bar. I may have been seventeen thousand miles from Selhurst Park but I could hear the crowd groaning.

After they got a third from another soft penalty, we were deflated. Every time we switched the players about with our rolling subs, I looked towards the bench, hoping to be dragged off, but my name was never called. Eventually, after an injury to Dale, our strongest centre half, I was moved back to the centre of our defence. Almost immediately, my replacement right winger got the ball in the acres of space that I'd failed to exploit. He charged towards the penalty area and beat the two defenders who'd sprinted over to cover, before he played in the perfect cross for our striker, Louis, to tap into the net. With two minutes left, we were back in the game.

Sniffing out an unlikely draw, everyone charged forward. Except myself. I decided to make what I thought at the time was a sensible decision to stay at the back. However, as Brighton hit us on the counter attack, I was faced with both Lloyd Owusu and Paul Reid charging towards me. It's fair to say that their fitness and pace were stronger than mine. As they passed it around me and between each other at speed while running forward, I was chasing shadows. I wished I had charged forward and left them to it to be honest as my running was doing little to stop them anyway. With only the keeper to beat, and me about ten yards behind them, Reid unselfishly rolled the ball across for Owusu to convert it and kill the game at 4-2.

After the match, there was a fantastic ceremony of respect between the two groups and the organiser explained how the money we'd raised would be used, before both sets of fans tucked into a barbeque. Although, being true football fans, we spent most of it asking the Brighton lot how much they'd paid the referee for their two penalties. Together, everyone involved had done something good and had fun along the way. The whole event was played in a brilliant spirit and it was a thoroughly enjoyable morning, which is not something that I ever imagined I'd say about any defeat to them.

After the game, I crashed and slept for the rest of the day until 7:30pm, when I went to Scruffys for some food and watched the Melbourne derby on the TV. Another sell out crowd and a record A-league attendance of 43,729. Again, the game was low on quality but high on entertainment. Melbourne Victory beat Melbourne City (owned by Manchester City) 5-2 in an excellent match. After the game, I went to Harts pub for three reasons. Firstly, to meet American Rich, secondly, because it was Sydney Craft Beer week and they were hosting a tasting session, and thirdly, to watch the first leg of the Asian Champions League Final.

I deliberately didn't mention it at the start of this chapter as I wanted to focus on the brilliance and atmosphere of the charity game but I did discover something on the train out to Western Sydney for the Brighton match: Josh Harris, an American Billionaire, wanted to purchase my beloved club. Now, having been in administration twice in ten years, Palace fans are probably more wary than most about these matters. However, I felt a great deal of sadness when I heard the news.

I had no idea whether this billionaire would be good for the club or not. I also had no idea if the current owners wanted to sell or not. But what I did know, was that I'd loved everything about our club since the current four supporters had taken over: the beer, the football, the atmosphere, the togetherness, the bespoke kits, the communication. The fact that they were often on the terraces made them understand what we wanted as fans more than any American billionaire ever could. Indeed, when Steve Parish had been visiting Australia the year before, he'd nipped down to the Royal Exhibition to watch a game with the fans. Not as a gimmicky PR stunt ala Mike Ashley's early days at Newcastle, but simply because he was desperate to watch the club he loved with fellow fans.

Having said that, I couldn't blame the owners if they did want to sell. They purchased the club for around £5million each and the papers were suggesting that they could sell for £70-100million. Five years earlier, when they bought the distressed club, which even with their sensibly tight ownership was losing £5m a year, no one could have imagined that they'd make money out of it. They'd saved our club out of their own back pockets and now they'd more than earned their rewards.

But football fans are selfish. So even though I understood why they'd want to sell, I hoped they wouldn't. I hoped we'd still have four South Londoners controlling the club and an owner in the boozers, chatting about days and months and years gone by. I hoped we'd still have an owner on the message boards listening to ideas about catering, or sorting out a system to support regular away fans, or listening to ideas for the club's new badge. It wasn't a focus group or market research, it was simply helping the fans. What makes supporting a club so special isn't about moments on the pitch or winning trophies (but don't get me wrong, that would be nice), it's about being part of something bigger. I'd happily take feeling part of a Championship club over being a customer of a successful one. CPFC 2010 made me feel valued and important in a way that Simon Jordan or Ron Noades could never have done. For that reason alone, I wasn't anti-John Harris but it made me very sad to imagine a club without Parish, Browett, Long and Hoskins, our current owners and saviours.

After watching Western Sydney and Tony Popovic edge closer to their trophy by winning the first home leg of their final 1-0 in the pub, Richard and I made our way to Surry Hills and The Royal Exhibition Hotel. Palace were due to play West Brom that evening. We had invited the Brighton fans to join us but with the wonders of modern football, they were more than happy to stay at home and watch their impressive home draw with the mighty Rotherham United on a stream. It's just as well really. If I spent too long hanging out with them, people would begin to talk.

It was a strange game for me because for the first time since I was very young (a midweek 1-0 home loss to WBA in 2001, when Wayne Routledge, who was nearly as young as myself, made his debut), my Dad was going to go to a game without me. Through his work, he'd been offered a box for a West Bromwich Albion game of his choice.

"Manchester United, Chelsea, Arsenal, whoever you like!" he was told.

Well, obviously there was only one answer.

"Palace!"

Along with my Dad, all three of my brothers were going and from a selfish point of view, I was relieved that my six year old nephew wouldn't be joining them. It was decided that it would upset me too much if I wasn't present for his first Palace experience. Anyway, pre-match, they sent me pictures of a very expensive looking box, laid out for a three course lunch, and I replied with drunken and battered looking mob, drinking to lick the wounds of our morning defeat.

Like many fans from countries where our beautiful game isn't the primary sport, American Rich had got into football at an older age. Upon discovering the sport and the 'EPL' in 2006, he decided that he wanted to support a Premier League Club that went against the usual trail of United, Chelsea or Liverpool, so he selected Manchester City. Obviously, with everything that's happened to the blue side of the city since picking his team, when people hear his American accent, he's tarred with the brush of being a glory hunter. A sentiment that the Palace fans were keen to suggest.

What was even more unfortunate for Rich was that we shared the pub with West Ham, who were playing his side in the early kick off, and beating them. Comfortably. There must have been over thirty hammers in the boozer that night and he was soon identified as the enemy, but he took it well, acting far more graciously than I ever would in defeat.

When Richard briefly lived in England, he did manage to see City play live, in an FA Cup win over Chelsea. However, he also adopted Derby County as his local team and visited an array of Championship stadia with them, so his glum mood perked up a bit when he met a fellow Ram in the pub. The midlands fan was so shocked to discover an American Ram that he even invited Richard, previously a complete stranger, to his wedding. Once again demonstrating the love of football. I can just imagine the conversation with his fiancé the following morning.

"Oh yeah, I invited Rich to the wedding!"
"Who is Rich?"
"Ah, he's a Derby County supporter that I met last night in the pub."
"So why the hell have you invited him?"
"Well he's American and we don't get many Derby-loving yanks, especially not in Oz!"
"So what? You can be mates with him but he's not coming to the wedding!"
"But I've invited him now. I can't let down my fellow supporters!"
"I sometimes think you love that club more than you love me!"
"Of course not...."

With Rich ignoring the happy hammers and looking at suits on his phone for the big day, the game kicked off. I must admit, having been indulging in craft beer since waking in the early evening, combined with the English clocks moving back an hour, I was very drunk by the time that the 3pm game kicked off at 2am. That didn't stop me though. In fact, it encouraged me with my singing. Who cares whether the players can hear you or not? I was watching my team in our pub. It was time to be loud and proud and Palace.

The game started brilliantly. Brede Hangeland headed us in front early on and we controlled the rest of the half. Just before the break, we doubled our lead, with Jedinak scoring from the spot after Bolasie was fouled in the area. The ten or so tired Palace fans in the pub were so jubilant (or maybe drunk) at three am that not even the replaying showing that we should have had a second penalty could bring our mood down.

Early in the second half, the atmosphere changed. West Brom pulled a goal back after Speroni flapped at a corner. To make matters worse, our Argentine hero had to go off injured after conceding the goal as he was concussed. After letting one in, Palace sat deeper and deeper, allowing West Brom to take the initiative. We screamed at Warnock to make some subs but he waited and waited. Eventually, he took off our only striker for a midfielder, inviting more pressure on us. In stoppage time, with a final, regretful action, Jedinak made a foul and gifted Albion a penalty of their own and a last minute equaliser. Partly out of irrational hated of Warnock and partly out of large quantities of alcohol, I burst out.

"You f***ing useless t**** Warnock! You nearly killed our club last time and you're relegating us this time. Just f** off out of our club."

I hated him. Nothing would change that. I'd even considered writing a letter to him to ask him to explain his actions from his previous spell, not that it would particularly deserve a response. However, I didn't know what to do. As I explained with the Josh Harris rumour, supporting Palace is about more than results on the pitch for me and how could I fully support someone who's actions left me raging?

Jordo turned to me with a look of shock. Friends back home have seen my heated alcohol and Palace-fuelled outbursts on many occasions and are used to them. However, Jordo hadn't and could see that it wasn't appropriate for a group of mates meeting up for a drink. It was four in the morning in an emptying, friendly pub and he didn't want his group to have the image of an angry mob so he asked me to calm down, which to be honest, only left me stewing more. Agitated, I stomped over to the remaining Hammers to continue my rant about Warnock some more. Finding supporters of other clubs who share my hate of him was never a challenge.

By half five, when I left the pub, I'd began to relax again. It was to be my final game in Sydney before I went travelling for two months so I said some polite goodbyes in the pub and had an emotional moment with Richard outside. Admittedly, we may not have been hugging in the road if we hadn't been consuming an ill-advised amount of beer, but we would still have had the respect and enjoyment of each other's company. I knew, if nothing else, I had one true friend in Sydney. Hostel life had been worth it after all.

Quivering from the effects of a heavy intake of alcohol, I did notice a difference between Rich and I the next day too. As he had his own space, he hid under his covers, recovering from the night before all day. Yet, because I was in the hostel and lacked the privacy of a real home, I had to stir and even managed a swim. Something I certainly wouldn't have done after a heavy session back in London. Although, I did stare at my phone in disbelief the next morning when I went on Twitter. Speroni hadn't flapped at the corner, he'd been assaulted.

Craig Dawson, the West Brom defender thug had charged at him from a distance and elbowed him in the face. It was disgusting. Fox Sports hadn't shown a clear enough angle of the incident and I'd been oblivious to it at the time so I could hardly blame the referee. But after a crime like that, retrospective action must be taken. The FA hide behind a nonsense rule of not changing a decision if the referee has seen it, so they don't undermine him, but in my opinion, referees just need to be big enough to admit that they sometimes understandably get it wrong. It's not undermining them, its applying justice. If the referee had really seen what had happened clearly, then he'd have disallowed the goal and sent off the offender. Dawson's thugishness got his team an undeserved draw and could have seriously injured a fellow professional, yet there was no consequence for him. What kind of message does that give out about our sport? It is messages like that (and my foul mouthed outburst) which undo all of the good work of events like our charity match.

West Bromwich Albion…2 Crystal Palace…2
The Hawthorns, 25/10/14
Premier League

West Brom: Foster, Wisdom, Dawson, Lescott, Pocognoli, Brunt, Gardner, Dorrans (Blanco 83), Morrison, Sessegnon (Anichebe 46), Berahino.
Subs Not Used: Myhill, Gamboa, McAuley, Mulumbu, Ideye.

Palace: Julian Speroni (Wayne Hennessey 55), Joel Ward, Adrian Mariappa, Brede Hangeland, Martin Kelly, Mile Jedinak, Joe Ledley, Wilfried Zaha (Jason Puncheon 64), Yannick Bolasie, Marouane Chamakh (Adeline Guedioura 73), Fraizer Campbell.
Subs Not Used: Zeki Fryers, Barry Bannan, Kevin Doyle, Dwight Gayle.

Chapter 13 - Byron Bay – *29th October- 3rd November 2014*

The final few days in Sydney were frantic as I tried to tie up all my loose ends, while still taking on every shift that I could. Reece kindly gave me his shifts to allow me to earn a few extra cents for ice cream money on my travels, and rather appropriately, I had my final drink with him in The Crystal Palace Hotel on George Street.

I also had a good send off with The Two Dicks, and realised that Crewe Rich would be back home in Blighty, on the terraces at Gresty Road, by the time that I returned to Sydney for Christmas. As we joked about football, teaching, people from the hostel and discovered a mutual fondness of the TV show Red Dwarf, I realised something. I realised I was sad. I didn't want to leave. I was just getting to know a city really well and was even attacking the boarders of close friendship with a few people, but now it was time to go. Would I ever see Rich again? I certainly hoped so but I couldn't be sure. I wasn't due back in England until July 2015, a whole nine months away, and even then we'd be living hundreds of miles away from each other. It would take a lot of shared effort to keep our friendship but it was something I wanted to do. However, if Palace ever got Crewe away in the cup, I'd be a lot keener to go than I had been previously. That's the beauty of football based friendships, the game keeps them alive.

I also had a lovely send off from work. Once again, I went on the stunning cliff top walk from Coogee to Bondi. Compared to my first walk there was a notable difference, and I don't just mean the festival of art sculptures that we saw on the way. Firstly, the weather was scorching and gave a beautiful backdrop to the picturesque setting and secondly, I was surrounded by friends; Reece, Sarah, Jackie, Emelia, Amy, Megan and Shannon. While I was unsure how much I'd see of them in the future, they'd made my experience abroad come alive and I will cherish the feeling that I had on that walk forever. Relaxed and Happy.

After a unhappy and lonely start to my adventure, I was now sad to be leaving Sydney. I was sad to be walking away from the people I'd met and who'd welcomed me into their life. However, I knew not to be scared. I'd hidden in the early days of my trip and it had done me no favours what so ever. Now, I felt liked and wanted and I was going to throw myself into whatever experiences and challenges my trip brought up, as long as I could watch Palace around them...

I got on a coach at 11pm on the Wednesday night and began the first leg of the trip. A fourteen hour overnight journey to Byron Bay. I barely slept, but at least I had some movies to watch that American Rich had put on my tablet for me. It was only after I'd handed it over to him, I realised that I'd trusted someone who I'd only known for a couple of months to take my prized possession to a location that I didn't know. Fortunately, Rich, and the movie-filled tablet returned before I left.

Eventually, we arrived at the artsy and trendy hippie base that is Byron Bay. Surrounded by dreadlocks, regrettable tattoos and weed, I began to relax in the beautiful setting by chatting to fellow backpackers, going for walks, attempting to surf and sleeping in a hammock while listening to the gentle breaking of the waves. When discussing Byron Bay, the easiest response is to describe it as 'chilled' and as stereotypical as that is, it really is the most accurate portrayal of the place. I was certainly not going to be fined for crossing the road here – I don't think they even required pedestrian lights to contain order.

In the evening, everyone sat out in the middle of the hostel together, drinking, barbequing and listening to the live music supplied by the venue. Although the performance of acoustic covers was fairly average, I loved having live music. One thing that I'd noticed in Brazil was that there was live performers everywhere from cafes to night clubs and it made for a brilliant atmosphere. As well as avoiding the 'all you can drink sangria for $5', I spent the evening talking to people from all over Europe, and not once did I feel the need to revert to my easiest conversation. Football. Maybe I was finally learning that Crystal Palace simply don't impress the ladies?

Although, even if I'd wanted to follow the football, I wouldn't have been able to. All of the pubs shut at midnight, when the early game kicked off, and very few were advertising Fox Sports anyway. Mega rich corporations simply weren't the vibe that this place had to offer. I was glad that I would be in the highly commercialised Surfers Paradise by Tuesday morning when our 'Monday Night Football' match against Sunderland kicked off. As Palace bring out a highly organised side of me that seemed to be lacking in my everyday life, I'd already researched a 24 hour casino to watch the game in.

Mind you, I did manage to catch the second leg of the Asian Champions League Final. The game itself was tense and tedious as The Wanderers battled for an away 0-0 draw to win the match on aggregate. At full time, the eleven fanatical supporters who'd managed to make it out to Saudi Arabia for the final went crazy with delight. Whereas for me, it was a strange feeling. I'm not used to my club winning, let alone becoming the champions of an entire continent with the biggest trophy available! However, it was more than that. I'd missed the journey to become the best: their founding in 2012, The A-League titles in 2013 and 2014, and of course, even the majority of this incredible cup run. While I was truly delighted for them, I didn't feel that I could call the victory mine.

After briefly going to a distinctly average night club in the small town one night, I decided to head to the beach where I'd heard rumours of a Halloween party taking place. I loved it. Unlike the club, which was playing generic club music and serving generic drinks to suit the masses, the beach party had been made for and enjoyed by the same people. They'd set up a light system of flashing green lazers and had plugged their ipods into a huge amp to blast out the house music they were into. Although I'm not keen on this genre of music, I understood and related to the ownership they took of it. This was their party and their music and their fun.

It reminded me a bit of the Holmesdale Fanatics. They hadn't liked the vibe and atmosphere of the clubs in town so they'd gone against the grain of proscribed fun to do something about it. As a result, they make an atmosphere and displays that Palace want and they make them for us. At the beach party, I danced and partied and conversed into the night, stumbling on the perfectly soft sand as the booze began to take its toll. It was a brilliant night in a true Australian beach spirit.

While in Byron, I went to the bizarre hippie town of Nimbins. For some reason, this village of just 352 people is the Amsterdam of Australia, where drugs aren't quite legal but certain laws seem somewhat relaxed. Weed is openly bought and sold by little old ladies in the street to the hundreds of daily tourists. On the way to the hippie settlement that hosts 'MardiGrass' each year, a cannabis law reform rally, I'd been chatting to a blonde Canadian girl called Carla about the trip. Like me, she was somewhat inexperienced in the use of and purchasing of drugs.

Upon arrival, we committed an illegal offense in full open view and purchased some cookies, which the kind and frail lady, who must have been in her sixties, warned us were very strong. Although our lovely old dealer advised us to only have half of one each, she insisted that we had to buy them in packs of three so Carla and I decided to sell one of them off to a couple of girls who were on our tour. Nimbins had already changed me. Within ten minutes of arriving, I'd gone from having never bought drugs in my life to being a fully operational, buying and selling dealer.

Of course, the other thing that I learned was that if you decide to eat weed, it doesn't go straight into your blood stream and it faffs around for an hour before actually taking affect. A bit like Shefki Kuqi in front of goal really. This meant that after eating our half of a cookie, we had an hour to wonder around the village waiting to see what happened. There was a fairly boring low budget museum and a mountain of cannabis memorabilia ranging from towels to t-shirts to statues that weren't particularly exciting. Although, meeting a stumbling mess of a man who told us tales of meeting both Jesus and the devil was more interesting in both a comical and warning sense.

After killing time for roughly an hour, we headed back to where we'd agreed to meet the coach driver to move on to a lake for lunch and began to mingle with the other backpackers on the tour. Like us, some people had bought cookies and were still waiting to feel any changes in their body, while others had smoked their pot and were well and truly under the influence, leading to a hilarious two levelled conversation.

Suddenly, it hit me. A tingle on the nose turned and spread. My arms became heavy, as did my legs and head, so so heavy! It reminded me of a dream I often have. I'd be playing football, usually at Selhurst Park, and the ball would fall perfectly for me to score the winning strike but as I go to connect with it, my body seizes up and tenses. It becomes hard to move and the weights attached to my legs push them deep into the hallowed turf, leaving me unable to move. However, this wasn't a dream, this was the affects of drugs on someone who hasn't touched them before.

I felt sick. I wanted to pass out. Everyone was watching me, laughing at my predicament. I tried to say nothing; to hide and hope they wouldn't notice. But I couldn't help myself.

"I'll just go and sit over here," I justified to the piercing judgemental eyes. Everyone looked at me. Stared. Judged. I wanted to stand up, I needed to move my lungs, but I couldn't. My head became ever more blurred and I wanted help.

I needed drinks. My throat was dry and my head pounding. Someone gave me some lemonade and it helped. I wanted to down it but the strain on my brain wasn't enough to make me ignore all social etiquette like I do in the terraces, my other drug. Carla came and sat next to me. She leaned in and whispered *"Has it hit you too?"*

Thank god! She was feeling the same. It wasn't just me but soon, I had a new worry. Soon, I'd have to get back on the bus, the bumpy, bumpy, seatbelt-less bus. I already felt sick. Surely I wouldn't chunder or 'whitey' on the rainbow-striped vehicle in front of everyone? How embarrassing would that be?

Minutes rushed by as seconds and I had to get on. I delayed it as long as I could but soon there was no one to let in on in front of me. I held onto the sides as I made my way back to the seat, back to Carla. She represented safety. I needed a drink. As I released my muscles and collapsed next to her, I noticed something. I had a beer left, beer has suger, the suger in lemonade helped, I smiled. I knew how to balance myself out. I cracked it open with the bottle opener on my key ring and took a huge swig. It's not often you can say this with any sincerity but I genuinely think the beer helped.

However, once I was on the bus, my stomach calmed down. Although, my brain didn't. The headache went and ideas came. Despite the bumps, I felt good. Really good. I couldn't help but think of happy thoughts like ice cream, and writing, and Palace. Palace winning. Palace winning against Brighton, where there is ice cream, and flakes, like I used to have on holiday as a kid in Norfolk, when Dad bought us ice cream, and we used to listen to the opening day of the season on the beach, and Lombardo scored against Everton, and the Palace fans sang his name to the tune of a song about ice cream from It-a-leeeee!

My mind became happy. A huge inane smile stayed on my face until I physically removed it. I was excited by things: any things and all things. I was getting distracted and then distracted again from my distraction. My mind was faster than Yannick Bolasie running down the wing. I had so many ideas for writing to go into my first book that I was editing at the time and I frantically tried to scribble them all down. I could see why so many musicians, artists and writers indulge in weed to develop their creativity. There was no barriers to my brain. It was free. Everything was exciting

With a coach load of excitable conversation behind him, the driver began to have fun. He raced down a long, steep hill to make it seem like a roller coaster and fitted the music perfectly to it from start to finish for the four minute song. As we went down a slope, Carla threw her hands in the air and shouted 'weeeeeeee'. Our smiles were back. The driver had skilfully fitted all of the music to the roads and scenery. It was slow going up the hill and fast coming down, with random sounds like police sirens and cranks and bangs mixed in to confuse his suggestible passengers.

Suddenly, he threw the coach into a lay-by and ordered everyone off. He'd spotted a koala. High up in the sky, barely noticeable to the naked eye, there was a small bundle of grey fur. It barely moved and wasn't showing its face. Was it real? How could he have spotted it and how lucky was it that there was a place to pull up alongside it. Most Australians don't get to see a koala in the wild! They're rarer than Calvin Andrew goals. It had to be a well planned prank? Surely he couldn't have spotted it while driving; they was hard to find when looking for them.

After taking photos, just in case it was real, we went for lunch where I had more than my fair share of the beef sausages that were supplied. In fact, I had double the allocated food per person but only when I was absolutely sure it would be wasted otherwise, such was my paranoia about upsetting others.

Once lunch was over and we were back on the coach, where the atmosphere was more subdued. Like when I used to get the supporters' coach back from away games, everyone was tired and deep in thought. Whether they were happy or depressive, it didn't matter, no one spoke as we took in the background music rather than the five live phone-in that I would have done on the long trips back from Preston or Burnley.

Back at the hostel, my Swiss roommate, Freddy, invited me to go for a beer with him on the sea front. We sat in the huge open terrace of the beech hotel and chatted to an Aussie from Melbourne, along with two older women who were there for a long weekend. However, I couldn't concentrate. Each time I was talked to, I would give passionate and detailed answer, but when I wasn't directly addressed, I was staring out to sea. After a couple of schooners, I picked up a burrito and chips to eat on the way home and crashed on my pillow.

To be honest, I got the whole weed thing. Taking it was like an adventure, with many twists and turns, ups and downs, highs and lows. Compared to boozing, I certainly enjoyed the next morning when I woke without a hangover and a clear memory of the previous day's events. However, I wasn't rushing out to do it again. I like to think of football being my drug. I'm definitely addicted to it and it gives me a high in the same way that Nimbins had. A rush and adrenalin. The surge of thoughts and creativity was incredible but it's not healthy. I'd visited another world where there were no boundaries and imagination runs loose, but its fantasy. It's just another way of escaping reality with heightened unimportant emotion, like football does for me and thousands of others each week. So as much fun as I had with paranoia and F1 brain trails, I think I'll stick to following Palace for my highs. Not that we'd had many recently.

Chapter 14 - Disappointing Paradise – *Surfers Paradise, 3rd-4th November 2014*

Early the next morning, I left the tranquil hippie town of Byron Bay and got the coach to the high-rise jungle of Surfers Paradise on the Gold Coast of Australia. Is there a more pleasant sounding name anywhere in the world? Paradise in Gold! Other than Crystal Palace, I doubt it. However, unlike the array of pubs and restaurants on the triangle at our South London parade, Surfers Paradise doesn't live up to its name. Even the waves are disappointing. The whole place is superficial and tacky. The settlement was originally named Elston but was changed in 1933 by the owner of the biggest hotel to make it more marketable to tourists and it hasn't become any less fake since then.

In May 2013, after that fabulous weekend when we saw Palace win at Wembley to enter the world of international TV coverage, I went with some friends to Devon for the half term week. One sunny afternoon, we cycled along the River Ex and onto the coastline from Exeter to Teignmouth, where we discovered the tired and forgotten English seaside venues of the Victorian age. The fairgrounds were closed, the bright signposts faded and the pier was empty. Long gone are the days of us going for a sunburnt week by the sea in England, only Blackpool seems to survive, with even Margate and Southend struggling to pull in the summer numbers. Cheap deals to the Costa del Sewage and Greek Islands have put pay to us using our own shores.

However, after seeing the modern day version in Australia, where the sun had stayed and the holiday makers lingered, I was almost glad to have seen ours give up and stay in the sixties. The seafront was a line up of fast food chains: Pizza Hut, next to McDonalds, next to Hungry Jacks (Burger King without naming rights), next to Subway, next to KFC, next to Dominos, next to Wendys. The bars had offers of $4 happy hours of Tooheys New schooners plastered all over their walls. The town centre was entirely indefinable with thousands of empty bachelor pads towering over the sales reps offering trips to theme parks, whale watching cruises, skydives and waterskiing.

To be honest, tacky as it was, I'm sure that I could have had enjoyed it in the right company and weather but I didn't have either. The sky was overcast and I was alone. Being a Monday, the place was deserted too. It was a weekend venue for lads on the pull. My highlight was stepping out onto the beach and being able to look left and there being nothing but soft, yellow sand as far as the eye could see, before turning right to the same view. I guess that's why it's called the Gold Coast.

Once I'd got the measure of the place, I headed back to the hostel, which seemed deserted except a group of fat northern lads playing volleyball in the small pool at the front. In my room, there was a Boston-born American in his thirties called Sam so we agreed to go out that evening to try and make the most of our surroundings. I was glad that I only had one night there.

While roaming the town, I made the essential phone call to a nearby casino to ensure that they did in fact have Fox Sports 4 and would be showing our game the next morning. With Palace kicking off at 5:30am the next day, I had planned two options. If the night was going well, I was going to try and party through the night until kick off and then make my way to the casino, where I could watch the game. If I wasn't feeling it, as I suspected I wouldn't, I'd leave early and try and at least get a few hours sleep before seeing us take on Sunderland. A game that my Dad was going to as Pavel couldn't use his season ticket.

Before heading out, Sam and I bought some beers and headed to the kitchen to try and socialise with other guests. Other than a depressed Norwegian girl who cried into her pasta as she missed home and lacked money, we didn't see another soul in the shared area so we set off with little hopes for the evening. I noted how few of the lights in the multiple towers of bachelor pads were actually turned on and realised that the atmosphere would be more like the early rounds of the league cup than a bustling sell-out crowd.

The bar we'd been recommended was empty and had no resemblance to the 'German-Style-Beer-Bar' that we'd been sold it as. It was a huge sports bar. Complete with dozens of screens, pool tables, dart boards and very few people. We had a few games of pool and chatted to some locals but it was a tourist town out of season. Even the whales had left, which I'm reliably informed had been spotted heading up the coast every day of the month prior to the day of my arrival. I don't think it was personal but I could be wrong.

After briefly looking at some empty nightclubs, we decided to grab a kebab and call it a night around twelve. I can't say I was too disappointed. I had a match to watch.

The game kicked off at 8pm in England, which meant it was 6am the next day in this part of Australia. My alarm went off after my short sleep and I ordered a taxi to take me to Jupiter's Casino. I was shocked by the splendour of the venue when I arrived. As John Hammond would say, they'd "Spared no expense!" Thankfully, unlike the Jurassic Park creator or Mark Goldberg, they'd actually backed up their impressive intentions.

Barely awake, I sleepwalked through the glass-doored entrance and past a huge selection of bars and restaurants either side of the grand entrance hall. I noticed a sign by the entrance describing itself as 'A Vibrant Hub of Glamour, Style and Sophistication'. My Palace shirt and Topman shorts seemed more than fitting attire for the fancy venue to me, if not the security guard who swiftly moved across to ask me some questions.

As soon as he was content that I wasn't drunk, he let me past and I made my way straight to the 24-hour-casino's main games room. It was enormous. You could have fitted two or three football pitches in the space. There were 70 table games and over 1,600 gaming machines, most of which were winding down in the small hours. Untouched by my surroundings and focussed on Palace, I found my way to a bar with a TV screen. Behind the drinks counter, there was an old monitor with a fuzzy picture of some rugby, which flickered away unwatched by anyone but me in the background. I didn't look closely, but I guessed that it was European. As much as the Aussies love their rugby, I don't think they play TV worthy games at sunrise.

Politely, and with a small hint of South London desperation, I asked the barman to change the channel to find the football and he duly obliged. Unfortunately, we soon discovered a problem. While they had Fox Sports One, Two and Three, the casino didn't have Fox Sports Four, and therefore, couldn't show Crystal Palace vs Sunderland. Just when I thought that I couldn't dislike Surfers Paradise any more, it had reached a new low. Despondently, I got a tram back into town to continue my hunt as I followed the game using a mixture of the BBC website and twitter on my phone. However, ahead of the internet, my Dad text me the news first. It was 1-0 to Sunderland.

I rushed through the many bars that were starting to open up for breakfast and while some were more helpful than others, none of them managed to find the game for me. I was gutted. If we were going to lose, I wanted to at least be able to watch it. Especially after my early alarm call. Defeated, I trudged back to the hostel. As I sneaked back in, with the game having stopped for half time, I noticed something. Attached to the hostel, was an internet cafe. I bought an hours worth of time from reception and logged on.

Quickly, using Wiziwig, a host for online streaming, I managed to find the game and put the large headphones on. I could hear the roar of the Selhurst faithful. We may have still been losing but at least I felt close to the action. Just before the game restarted, they showed the first half highlights. I agreed with my Dad's assessment that it was a soft goal to concede and also saw he'd been right about the other key incident of the first half. Palace should have had a penalty in the opening minute.

To my surprise, Palace played really well. Zaha, who'd arrived to such a wave of excitement but was yet to deliver, was really getting at the unorganised Sunderland backline. Bolasie was doing great on the other wing too. However, it was disappointing not to see Puncheon or Gayle playing as they'd been our top two goalscorers in the previous season. After ten minutes of intense pressure, Palace did equalise. Fraizer Campbell backheeled the ball across goal and Wes Brown turned it into his own net. Amazingly, since Palace had returned to the Premiership in August 2013, Sunderland had managed to score ten Premier League own goals. No single Palace or Sunderland player had managed that many at the right end. Anyway, own goal or not, I let out a huge yelp of celebration in the empty room.

Football mentality is a bizarre thing. While it's obvious that confidence and the attitude of the crowd affects the players' brains, I don't understand how Palace scoring slowed them down so much. As soon as we got the goal that our performance had been demanding, we seemed to stop and let Sunderland back into the match. The game fell flat and was screaming out for a substitution. The manager's lack of ability to impact matches had been painful to watch in lots of our games so far. When things weren't going to plan, Warnock seemed to wait and wait and wait, before eventually making a change. It was only when Sunderland scored again that he threw on Jason Puncheon.

After that, our North-East opponents looked more than comfortable holding on for their win. Jedinak, our captain, who'd previously been the master of playing on a yellow card, kicked out at their player in the centre circle and was deservedly sent off. We seemed to run out of ideas. I was furious. I couldn't believe we were losing in such a lame manner to such a poor team. Other than a couple of magnificent victories/a draw that felt like a win at the end, Pulis had built our success of the previous season on beating the rubbish teams around us. Our record against the top nine was awful. However, this season, we'd already lost to West Ham, Sunderland, Hull and drawn at home to Burnley. That was ten points that we were down on compared to the year before.

With the match in stoppage time, the team looking lost and me getting angry, my hour of internet time cut out. I stormed back to my bedroom and threw myself onto my bed. Well, getting up early to watch Palace had been one let down after another. Should I be surprised? Not really. But I was furious. I did quickly use my phone to check that we hadn't scored a stoppage time equaliser. We hadn't. In fact, we'd conceded a third at the death.

I let out an ironic cheer and unleashed my fury on my Palace whatsapp group. I wanted to seethe with my mates. The game had been entirely unsatisfying alone. Even during our good spell at the start of the second half I was texting friends at the game. Football is about discussion and debate; sharing moments. The players, fans, manager and owners are as one in the ground. Cheer together, win together, lose together, laugh together and cry together. However, I wasn't with them. I was alone; cheering, then stewing, by myself. I wasn't as bitter about it like I had been earlier in the season because I was excited for my travels, and knew that I wanted to be touring – but it still didn't feel right.

However, I wasn't sure if that was because I wasn't surrounded by fellow eagles, or if it was because there was an obvious black sheep amongst our group. The manager. The manager I hated. The manager who I wanted nowhere near my club no matter how good a job he did. The fact that he was doing an awful job made me wince even more.

The players, who'd been so disciplined and organised during the previous year, just looked lost. They were clearly frustrated. Jedinak and Delaney are two of the strongest leaders that I've seen in football but they had both lost their cool and received stupid red cards for second yellow cards in recent weeks. They clearly weren't happy with the direction of the club and neither was I. Sunderland's goals had been good finishes and they'd deserved their win, but we wouldn't have allowed them to walk through our defence as easily in the previous season.

I spent twenty minutes or so venting on the forums, where after less than three months and just eight matches, the first 'Warnock Out' thread was started on the BBS. While the responses were mixed and hiding behind a keyboard makes these things easier to exaggerate, there were already plenty of people who wanted him gone. As usual, while the thread burst into passionate debate, Warnock began to blame the referee for our result for the third consecutive game.

Being a supporter, I'm happy to moan about referees and their general ineptness. However, I expect the manager to be capable of picking out ways of improving, rather than constantly droning. It wasn't going to get any easier either, we had Manchester United and Liverpool up next, where we were even less likely to receive any favours from the referee.

Rather than wind myself up further, I decided to haul myself out of bed for a second time and made my way down to the beach. It was only eight thirty but the sun was already quite high in the sky. Dan, who was drowning his sorrows in the Falcon at Clapham Junction, text me some anti-Warnock messages in his own unique and experienced manner, expressing that the dinosaur simply had to go. I sighed. I'd calmed down by now. It was impossible not to. I was having my first ever post-match sunbathe.

I can't think of a worse way to start the day to be honest. My whole experience of Surfers Paradise was summed up by anyone who turns up with a board. Disappointing. There was no surf to board on and that's exactly how our futile attacks had felt in our morning kick off, but I wasn't going to let that ruin my day. Early in the afternoon, I made my way to the bus stop to go to Brisbane. At least there I'd be greeted by three Warnock-free days!

Crystal Palace...1 Sunderland...3
Selhurst Park, 3/11/14
Premier League

Palace: Julian Speroni, Martin Kelly, Brede Hangeland (Dwight Gayle 84), Scott Dann, Joel Ward, Mile Jedinak, Joe Ledley, Wilfried Zaha, Yannick Bolasie, Marouane Chamakh (Jason Puncheon 76), Fraizer Campbell.
Subs Not Used: Wayne Hennessey, Adrian Mariappa, Barry Bannan, James McArthur, Kevin Doyle.

Sunderland: Pantilimon, Reveillere, Vergini, O'Shea, van Aanholt (Brown 37), Cattermole, Gomez, Buckley (Bridcutt 82), Larsson, Wickham (Altidore 78), Fletcher.
Subs Not Used: Mannone, Mavrias, Johnson, Graham.

<u>Ákos Kovách – A Hungarian Eagle – *My Journey to Addiction*</u>

I fell in love with English football in general in the 80's without having any affection for a specific club. There was a mystic atmosphere around English football. It was hard to get any news regularly for a boy growing up behind the iron curtain, but all I knew was that when English clubs came to play in Europe, they normally won as a rule. I fancied the Cup Winners Cup winning Everton team, then the legendary Liverpool side of the same era. A bit later, I respected the Arsenal back four, and also liked Clive Allen (an ex-Eagle but also an ex of six other London clubs!) scoring for fun for Spurs.

And then I did watch an FA Cup final on telly (the second televised final in Hungary) with a relatively unknown team with a classy name (perfect for a new romantic band!), a nice shirt and a funny sponsorship logo on it. My inner romantic obviously wanted the underdog win the cup, which almost happened thanks to two goals scored by their best player coming in as a substitute. I learnt a couple of days later that unfortunately they lost the replay, but for me the first step has already been taken to become an Eagle.

My connection with the club was just further reinforced by the signing of two Hungarian players in the mid 2000's, which also led to my first ever match in England: as a Christmas gift I could attend the game against Liverpool at Selhurst Park and even better, my ticket was handed over by Gábor Király (part of the Christmas gift!) in the players' car park! On the top of all that, Palace won the game thanks to a goal scored by AJ and a superb save by Király from Gerrard's shot at the end!

Since that time, I follow Palace regularly (or sometimes less regularly) and for a couple of seasons now I have been a member, can afford to fly over 2-3 times per season to watch Palace at Selhurst (or at Wembley if it happens!) and enjoy pre-match drinks with other Eagles I met thanks to Palace, who have since become good mates.

Before the Premier League years, I usually spent my Saturday afternoons with a headphone on the ears to listen to live radio coverage by BBC South London via Internet (at that time no subscription was required) which reminded me of my own early years, sat around a radio with my father and brother to listen to live commentary of the Hungarian Championship, when no live TV coverage was available back at that time. Many great moments were left to my own fantasy to imagine actions, dribbles, crosses and goals!

Luckily, I managed to watch some Palace games on telly, such as witnessing John Bostock's debut as the youngest ever player for the club, and the much hurting play off semi-final defeat against Bristol City.

Now, it is really easy to follow the club from Hungary: if the match is not televised, you can easily find a stream to watch it. You will need a bit of patience though to find a stream which is relatively stable, enjoyable and does not freeze or stop every minute.

Although, funnily enough, despite the coverage, I did not watch Crystanbul and probably I may be among very few Palace fans with that! It was a Monday

night game, Palace were already safe from relegation, I had some work to do, so I just followed it on BBC live score and did not believe to my eyes when they started scoring!

I am now used to watching Palace alone at home, behind a closed door to allow me to concentrate better on the game (and also to sort out quickly the dodgy stream if it is stopped). However, it is not always easy to convince family to spend Saturday afternoons at home, especially when the weather is nice out there!

Since the early 2000's when live Premier League games have been available in Hungary, most of the people follow the big (fat) clubs and no particular attention is turned to smaller teams like Palace. This has not been changed since the FA Cup final either but this is not a problem as I can keep a private connection with the club. I have a mate who is also a Palace fan but does not really follow Palace on a regular basis anymore and I am not sure that he would be able to list more than five players from the current squad!

One game that I will always remember is when I had a slipped disc surgery back in May 2013, so the play of semi final victory against Brighton particularly cheered me up (although I am too far to really feel the rivalry). I tried to watch the final on a stream in the hospital. Unfortunately, the stream that I found was so bad that I had to turn it off, but when I checked back for the extra time, I just witnessed one of the best taken penalties in my life (with my weirdest celebration ever lying almost motionless in a hospital bed!) which helped Palace to get to the Premier League and took me to the next level as a Palace fan.

Chapter 15 – Brisbane – *4-6th November 2014*

I arrived in Brisbane to a searing heat and a cheeky chappie taxi driver. He reminded me of an East London cabbie as he gave me a very proud verbal tour of his home city. During which, we passed the impressive 52,000 seater Suncorp Stadium, which is home to Brisbane City (the city rugby union team), Queensland Reds (the state rugby union team) and Brisbane Roar FC. I couldn't help but put on my Western Sydney hat and hum *"Your grounds too big for you!"* as I passed it. 'Roar' average just eleven thousand.

In England, gates tend to go up and down throughout the season for various reasons; form, rival games, large away followings, historically tense matches, etc. However, in Australia, the geography dictates that the away fans impact is minimal and local rivalries don't really exist. The closest club to Brisbane is Newcastle Jets, 800km away, and the furthest league match is Perth Glory, a short 4341 kilometres each way by car. That's the same driving distance as going from London to Kiev – and back! In some seasons, they'd have to go there twice! Maybe they should fly as its only a mere 3614km then.

In some ways, I think they should simply set up their own league. Brisbane has a population of 2.2million, which is the same as the West Midlands, which manages to host Birmingham City, Aston Villa, Coventry City, West Bromwich Albion, Wolverhampton Wanderers and Walsall. That league would be half the size of the A league on its own and would probably have more quality too.

As well as the geography meaning that away games need to be a short holiday, rather than a Saturday piss up, the relatively short history of the sport means that grudge matches haven't really built up. They only way to achieve swollen crowds is to bump them up with performances on the pitch. It made me appreciate Western Sydney's sell out crowds even more. However, it also showed the lack of interest in Brisbane compared to Sydney and Melbourne. Both of which host two clubs with larger average gates.

Anyway, once I'd paid the cab driver and checked into the hostel, where I received multiple tokens for drinks, breakfast and internet, as well as being sold day trips to here, there and everywhere, I decided to go and explore the city. I was directed to the main street by the river and loved it immediately. Eagle Street. I felt instantly at home and posed for various photos with Eagle Street signposts, Eagle House and Eagle Pier. I later found out that the street also hosted the Brisbane Crystal Palace FC Supporters' Group.

I'd heard it previously mentioned that this was the day of the Melbourne Cup but until I went out and discovered the bars, I didn't quite realise how big a deal it was. It is Australia's major thoroughbred horse race and marketed as *"The race that stops a nation!"*

So what I thought? I grew up in Ascot and routinely attended the Royal Race Week, attended by the Queen of England herself. The lady who smiled at me every time I handed over an Australian $5 note. What on earth could The

Melbourne Cup offer me that I hadn't seen before? I wasn't even in the same state.

Well, that mattered little. Although only the 5.83 million residents of Victoria, the state of Melbourne, receive the day as a public holiday, most of the country treats it as one. Men get out their best suits and bowler hats, while women spend months saving for and planning their outfits to simply go to the pub and watch it on the screen. Pubs advertise for weeks in advance and fill their bars with horse-styled scalextric races and giant fake trophies to collect bets. The whole country goes into meltdown. It's one of those things where you feel ridiculous all dressed up in an average pub for a horse race, which is happening thousands of miles away, but you simply put it down to the culture and go with it. I'm sure there are Aussies who've worn a red top, screamed at a TV and found the passion and pride of FA Cup Final day a bit absurd. While football is growing in Oz and catching aussie rules, rugby and cricket, I think all sport will always be secondary to betting out there.

From Eagle Pier, I got a free boat up along the river to the town centre, getting off at Southbank, where I found similar entertainment and vibe to what you'd find on London's Southbank. However, with the G20 summit due to be held in Brisbane the following week, there were plenty of special lights and beautiful lilacs up for decorations. Presumably there were some security measures too.

On the way back, I strolled through the gorgeous botanical gardens, which were much smaller than Sydney's offering, before I then wondered through the fairly unremarkable city centre. Which, to be honest, could have been any city centre in the western world, with the usual lists of fast food chains, clothes shops and banks.

That evening, I used my drinks tokens in the hostel bar and headed out into China town with a group of fellow backpackers. While I became jealous of some of their tales about riding around South East Asia on motorbikes, I became more and more uneasy as they discussed and boasted about their frequent use of Asian Prostitutes. As it turned out, I spent most of the evening talking to a girl from Darlington, County Durham.

Like many before her, she couldn't believe that I'd actually visited her home town and could vaguely discuss it. My trip to Darlington had been one of the more ridiculous away games that I'd been on. Although it was still not as crazy as a Brisbane Roar fan going to Perth Glory away. For my trip to Darlo, I was going to Middlesbrough with Palace and despite it being two-hundred and fifty odd miles north, I set off by travelling one hundred miles west to meet two of my Palace mates, who were studying at Bristol University. As the weekend continued, my decision making continued to tumble as much as Palace's form under George Burley was at the time.

Encouraged by spending one too many of our Wetherspoons discount vouchers on the Friday night, we decided that it would be a brilliant idea to go nightclubbing in our Palace shirts. Therefore, we hid them away under some more suitable attire and headed to Bristol's O2 Academy. Inside, local Bristol City fans continued to take exception, informing us that *"Neil Warnock's a wanker!"*

Considering that he'd recently done his deserting act from his first spell (Y'know, the time when we needed him), I would simply smile and agree, before smugly adding *"Steve Coppell's a legend!"*

Sir Steve had recently resigned from his post as Bristol City manager after less than four months in charge.

Anyway, relationships with the locals became more fractious as the evening went on and we suddenly found the three of us cornered in the corner of a grotty nightclub. I've never been so relieved to see a couple of oversized bouncers come and kick me out of a club! The next morning, with our tails between our legs and our heads pounding, we made the six hour train journey, changing at Darlington where we nipped out for a quick look and a pint. Palace lost 2-1 and I haven't returned to either Middlesbrough or Darlington since. Once should have been enough but me being me, thanks to my trip in the previous season, I'd gone twice in less than six months.

Although my female companion for the evening was impressed by my limited knowledge of Darlington, including one pub, one supermarket and the criminal mystery surrounding their unnecessarily large football stadium, I don't think she was so impressed by my clubbing or football exploits.

The following day, a group of us headed to the Lone Pine Koala Sanctuary, stopping at the top of Mount Coot-tha to take in the view over the whole of Brisbane. By now, I was beginning to adopt a regular pose. I've always been a bit awkward in photos and never know what to do with my hands so I decided to do a daft and inane wave. Needless to say, once it went on Facebook, it prompted fierce abuse from so-called friends back home. I assumed they were simply jealous. Anyway, after the initial hatred, people began to like it. Soon, 'The Howland Wave' was more divisive than a handful of Palace shirts in a Bristol nightclub.

The sanctuary was brilliant. I got to cuddle a koala and feed a kangaroo. What more could you wish for in an Australian zoo? It ticked all the boxes. Like seeing a kiwi in a New Zealand zoo, a panda in Chinese zoo, a lion on safari or Eric Cantona in a French zoo. However, there was one thing that I didn't like – snakes. The scaly, slithery creatures are just about the only thing on earth that have given me more nightmares than Ade Akinbiyi.

Like our over-priced flop of a centre forward, snakes scarred me from a young age. Firstly in the film Aladdin and secondly, watching my mother scream in panic as we came across one in a friend's garden when I was barely walking. No matter how irrational I accept my fear is, I can't help but shudder at the mere name of the horrible creatures. While I chose not to go to the talk on snakes, as I found a scouse girl who was a fellow wimp to sit outside with, I did hear one line.

"In one bite, this snake has enough poison to kill one-hundred and fifty men."

I'm sorry, but that's really not necessary – unless they're all Brighton fans of course.

While I avoided the snakes, I did take a lot of time observing the koalas. They're fascinatingly stupid animals really. Like me, they were desperate to avoid the snakes and other predators that roam the Australian land so they found the tallest tree and climbed it. The eucalyptus tree. Unfortunately, the leaves for it are poisonous but they didn't let this stop them. Just like us fans don't stop and consider the future consequences when daring to buy food in the ground at half time, koalas don't consider the future risks or consequences of their food either. However, while we rely on Peter Taylor's boring style of management to send us to sleep, it's the food that ensures koalas need 20 hours slumber a day as their stomach uses more energy to eat the leaf than it actually gets from the food.

Again, a bit like Peter Taylor's time in charge of Palace, eating the poisonous leaf has killed half of their brain, making them unable to function properly. Unless the eucalyptus leaf is actually on a branch, they can't recognise it as food. However, like any father who stopped dragging his son to Selhurst under the snore-fest of Taylor, Koalas are responsible parents. They recognise that their young can't handle the leaf whole, so they give them a diluted version. Just like Taylor, they serve up their own shit (to their own children).

On the way back from the sanctuary, I noticed something that I hadn't thought about since first arriving in Sydney. In the space of three minutes I saw Rotherham Street, a signpost for Ipswich and a sign to Everton Park. Considering I'd already found Liverpool Street, York Street, the Crystal Palace hotel and Preston in Sydney without trying, I wondered if there was a place in Australia for all ninety-two football league grounds? While I realised that actively searching for said locations might not be the best use of my time travelling*, I certainly wanted to see how many I could coincidently notice in Australia. I will include an appendix at the back with my findings.

That evening, I went out with the same guys from the hostel. It wasn't that I particularly loved them or they were that annoyingly regular backpacking phrase of 'The most amazing people' (as I'm sure they wouldn't describe me either) but they were there and they were friendly. I spent a long time chatting to a Mancunian called Tim. He was enjoying travelling but he was doing it on his terms. I.e. making the experience as similar to home as possible. He wanted the same food, drinks and company.

---

*Just to clear this up, by 'time travelling', I mean the period of time that I spent moving around. I didn't discover a machine to send me hurtling through time and space – but if I did, I know where I'd go: The 89th minute of the 1997 Play Off Final to relive my Palace-capturing moment as an old, long suffering and understanding supporter, rather than the fresh faced newbie that I was.

Mind you, I wasn't so different really. Just a bit more pretentious about it. I was insisting on only drinking good quality beer. Surprisingly, I'd even go without alcohol than drink crap, which was quite often the case in backpacker bars. However, I was shocked to discover that the recommended bar that evening, doing 'Trannie Bingo', had a wide selection of Australian Craft Beers. I was in heaven. Although, it would be a bit expensive to drink craft beer for eternity. Money would soon run out at $14 a pint and then I'd be very lost. It would be hell watching other people sup away at the drinks I wanted. Having said that, a combination of the price and me trying to watch my fitness meant that I didn't throw too much money down my throat.

Chapter 16 - It Ain't All so Bad – *Noosa, 6-8th November 2014*

The next morning I left Brisbane bright and early to get the coach 151km north, up the brilliantly sounding Sunshine Coast, to my next stop, Noosa. Along the way, both the village and street names continued to amuse me, which were a mixture of English imports and aboriginal heritage. We passed Mooloolaba and Wooloowin, which were either side of the awfully named 'Brighton' and swiftly followed by Mansfield Road, giving me two more of my 92 clubs. Naturally, I decided that the East Coast seaside village of Brighton must be a s*** hole, although I have since noticed that the sea-front road is called Flinders Parade. Presumably after the former Palace and Brighton keeper, Scott. A player who was horrendous for us but more than adequate for our lowly rivals.

On the coach, when I wasn't wondering if the Brighton beach resort's toilet floors were filled with faeces, I met a couple of people who I would be spending the next few days with. Paddy, a bar manager from Chichester, and Inge (pronounced Inga), a Dutch girl who was travelling while her boyfriend back home built their house. I can't help but feel she was getting life right. What I liked about both of them was that they had a complete freedom in their attitude. As cheesy as that sounds, the two of them had simply stopped their lives for two months and decided to go travelling alone. While I was alone, I fully expected for me to stay in places, like Sydney, for longer periods of time and establish friendships, whereas these two were moving from A to B to C so quickly that they relied on making new companions on a daily basis.

Once we arrived, the three of us, joined by a teenage German actress called Zoe, an Israelian guy named Matty and a Californian girl called Jessie, went to a small cafe for some lunch. It was the kind of place that you'd find on most busy streets in England but I noticed was largely absent in Oz. With the hot weather beating down and a desire to maintain some sort of fitness, I opted for a slightly healthier wrap than my usual Full English Breakfast, even if Australia is one of the few other nations that seem to be able to make decent bacon.

After lunch, we began to explore the picturesque town of Noosa. Its rolling rivers, golden beaches, local everglades, view-giving hills and peaceful vibe make it the perfect middle class weekend getaway. More than content, we all spent the afternoon lying on the beaches, taking in the sun and scenery. Australia is often seen as the tackier and uglier relation to New Zealand but the landscape and natural beauty of Noosa stands up to anything that the kiwi lands have to offer. However, even on the backpacker's trail, it was noticeably more expensive than other places we'd been.

That evening, we all attended the hostel's 'Mexican Night', which consisted of disappointing burritos and $5 coronas and tequila shots. Throughout the night, I was just as determined in avoiding the vile shots as I would be in avoiding home fans outside The New Den. Just like Millwall fans, they make me want to instantly throw up.

The next day we took in some true Australian culture and woke up early to go surfing. After the disappointment of Surfers Paradise, I wanted to make the most of the waves and spend a few hours praying that no sharks mistook me for a giant turtle, or more specifically, dinner. I am proud to be able to tell you that not only did I avoid being eaten by a shark, but I also managed to stand up on the board for a few short but magical (millie) seconds – before collapsing like Tommy Black in the Walsall penalty area.

After a long work out in the sea, we set off on a walk along the coast in the National Park to the rocky outcrop known as devils kitchen, where we were met with powerful crushing waves against the cliffs, sights of dolphins and even, high up in its poisonous tree, a wild koala. This time, I had no reason to doubt it was real. After our walk, we were taken by the hostel to the view point at the top of Noosa Heads. As the sun set gently over the everglades, I couldn't possibly decide where to look. In one direction was the sea and crystal clear water, in another was the National Park, in another was Sunrise Beach and in the distance, was the orange glow behind the everglades. I often joke about Selhurst Park being picturesque but this was the real deal.

In the evening, our ever widening group was joined by a Swedish guy and three Welsh lads from Wrexham. Although, I'm sure they were lured in more by the birthday cake that we'd bought for Paddy, rather than our great company. There was a lovely atmosphere that night as everyone worked hard to make the day special for someone we'd just met. In many ways, it reminded me of the atmosphere on the train to or from an away match. No one has much in common but everyone gets along thanks to one shared love. Football, or in this case, backpacking.

After some drinking games, which my reluctance to join in with made me feel very old, we headed out to a bar in the town. I'm not really a fan of having TV's in bars unless there's a specific reason. I.e. a big match or the Grand National. Naturally, the flashing light and moving pictures draw your eyes to a screen that you're not actually particularly interested in. In this bar, despite having a live band playing covers for the dance floor, they kept their TV screens on; showing a football match from India's newly formed ISL.

Being in Australia, I assume there was money being placed on it. Betting machines, fruit machines and even computer animated horse racing screens are almost standard in Australian pubs. I found it hilarious that more Aussies seemed to know of my hometown, Ascot, than Brits did. I must admit, other than the natural allure of the screen, I was interested in the match for two reasons. Firstly, I wanted to look out for Andre Moritz as the former Palace midfielder had recently joined Alessandro Del Piero, David Trezeguet, David James, Freddie Ljungberg , Robert Pires and Peter Taylor in earning a pension in India. Unfortunately, I had no idea which of India's eight Super League teams he played for. Secondly, grabbing my interest, one team was wearing red and blue so obviously, I wanted them to win.

Once I managed to pull my hooked eyes away from the football, I began to talk to the Wrexham fans. I quickly won favour with them by knowing their ground's name and also telling them of my 100% record of watching Wrexham, having seen them beat both Brentford and Bristol Rovers. They quite liked Palace too. Apparently we're popular in Wales thanks to having four current Welsh internationals: Wayne Hennessey, Lewis Price, Joe Ledley and Johnny Williams.

They'd spent eleven months working in Australia and were now enjoying a holiday at the end. With them not being fortunate enough to support a team currently in the global brand of the Premier League, they'd become more and more distanced from their club. Despite being season ticket holders for most of their lives, they were now at a point where they had little or no interest. Following a fifth tier side was too much to maintain from the other side of the world. Their team was out of sight and out of mind so much that they didn't even know who they were playing on the following weekend.

I must admit, now that I was travelling and not surrounded by fellow football addicts as I was back home and in Sydney, I was thinking less and less about Palace and certainly wasn't hooked to checking the BBS in the way that I have been since my mid teens when I discovered it. I could see that if I maintained that distance and distraction from my addiction then maybe one day, I too would be less obsessed. Having said that, I'm not quite there yet.

We moved onto an expensive yacht clubhouse on the seafront where there was another live band and certainly no flashing screens. Once the DJ came on, we danced the night away to a random selection of songs from 70s classics through to hip hop and grunge music, which arrived in no particular logical order. However, being the Palace Addict I am, there is only one song that I remember being played from that night. As soon as the opening beats of the tune came on, I was transported from Noosa to a 0-0 draw at Doncaster, which should have been quite a downfall.

But as always with football, depression brings out the best in us. Faced with the adversity of expected relegation and rubbish football in May 2011, when constant singing and a party atmosphere had failed to inspire the players to muster a single decent effort on goal in a crunch relegation battle, Palace fans did what we do best. We stayed behind after the players had long gone, stuck together in unity and sang a song.

> *"Singing, don't worry!*
> *About a thing,*
> *Cos every little thing,*
> *Is gunna be alright!"*

Bob Marley and Three Little Birds will no longer have any meaning to me other than 'Doncaster Away'.

The next day (In Oz, not Donny) we were taken about half an hour out of town to the top of Cooroy Mountain, where we could look over the rainforest, past the beaches and out to sea. Once again, it was stunning.

Scientists have long investigated the cognitive thinking behind the human brain taking things for granted. Why don't we stop and marvel at the ability to breathe? It's the most important thing we do, yet we give it little or no thought. Our brain's need to work effectively and efficiently dictates that we don't think about being able to walk, or being lucky enough to have a hot shower each day, or the fact that Palace are in the top two divisions of English Football.

In our one hundred and ten years of history, we've spent forty-eight in the top two leagues and sixty-two lower than that! In fact, it took us fifty-nine years before we even experienced the second division. Yet anyone my age (and most who are older) expect us to be in the second tier and pushing towards the top as a minimum. Indeed, if truth be told, one and a bit years in the Premier League was already beginning to change our subconscious state and what we'd take for granted. Wins against Leicester and Walsall were easily brushed aside as insignificant.

It was no longer a treat to simply be in the top division and playing against the big boys. For some, the enticement and excitement of playing at Old Trafford, where we were due to visit on the following Saturday, was already diminishing. We wanted more. We wanted results. Results that Neil Warnock certainly wasn't giving us. I dread to think what the atmosphere would be like at Selhurst if we lost ten games out of eleven as we had done at the start of our top flight adventure.

Maybe I was guilty of feeling this expectation and amnesia towards recent success but I don't think I was. Defeats didn't bother me. Losing under Warnock bothered me. I hated the man. Wins (rare as they were) felt hollow and defeats crushing. It was the irrationality of a football fan at its best.

And just like staying in the Premier League was being taken for granted in South London, I was starting to take being on a once-in-a-life-time, year-long holiday in Australia for granted. I no longer became stunned and stunted by the splendour of views such as this. I was simply muttering "wow" and posing for a quick waving photo. Every day was giving me unbelievable sights, which made them the norm, rather than the spectacular. Sometimes in life, it's important to sit back and think. 'Cos you know what, it's not a bad old life. Not in Australia, and not in the Premier League.

Chapter 17 - Football, I'll pass. – *Fraser Island, 8th-11th November 2014*

On the morning that I left Noosa, I was reminded of the bad side of hostels. I'd loved meeting people and making a range of friends from a variety of different countries, but I was less impressed to discover that some b**tard had stolen the breakfast that I'd bought the previous day. Gritting my teeth to hide my annoyance, I made my way to the coach park to move on to the magnificent sounding Rainbow Beach.

Once there, I had two main items on my itinerary; watch Palace play against Manchester United and head to Fraser Island, which would hopefully be better than Fraizer Campbell, who was proving to be a distinctly average signing. Arrogantly, and again taking things for granted, I'd assumed that I would be able to watch Manchester United play any match from anywhere in the world, such is their worldwide support. However, I arrived at Rainbow Beach to discover a tiny village, with little more than a convenience shop and a liquor store. It was simply a stopover for backpackers who wanted to go to Fraser.

Undeterred, before I'd even gone to the safety meeting required to drive a 4x4 on the world's largest sand island, I'd checked that the hostel's computer room would be open all night and purchased two hours worth of internet usage. I had my priorities.

In the safety meeting, we were given a hallowing warning and reminder that reckless driving had been responsible for the death of a young girl the week before. While the eye-witnesses that I'd met further down the coast had put less blame on the driver than the company organising the tours were keen to, it did get the point across loud and clear.

That evening, I headed to bed early as I set my alarm for 2am to get up and watch Palace play. However, when it sounded, well aware that I would have to get up at 7am for my trip the next morning, combined with a deep rooted acceptance of a defeat, I decided to switch it off and roll over. The next couple of hours were bizarre as I drifted in and out of consciousness, knowing that Palace were taking on Manchester United thousands of miles away.

My subconscious played tricks on me as I struggled to distinguish between the fiction and reality, dreaming of waking to texts telling me of goals for both teams. I wanted to sleep and my body was tired but my mind wouldn't leave the game alone. Eventually, I ended up using my phone to follow the final ten minutes of the match on the BBC's live text updates. Once we'd lost, my mind would let me rest again. I went back to the land of nod.

I would love to tell you of the amazing experiences that I had driving around Fraser Island, seeing wildlife such as snakes (to my horror), lizards and dingos, driving on the beach, swimming in picture perfect lakes and generally laughing, talking, dancing and eating in brilliant company, but to be honest, it adds little to my story of discovering Palace around the world, or about my addiction. I had no phone reception and learnt of no fallout from the United game. I'll be honest and admit, I thought very little of it. In fact, I don't think I had a single football related conversation during the entire three days. No one there knew me as James the Palace fan, as I had been defined all my life and to my surprise, I liked that. I didn't need football. It was simply something that I could turn to when I wanted it.

Manchester United...1 Crystal Palace...0
Old Trafford, 8/11/14
Premier League

Manchester United: De Gea, Valencia, Blind, McNair (Fletcher 90), Shaw, Carrick, Fellaini, Januzaj (Mata 63), Di Maria (Wilson 71), Rooney, van Persie.
Subs not used: Lindegaard, Vermijl, Blackett, Herrera.

Palace: Julian Speroni, Adrian Mariappa, Damian Delaney, Scott Dann, Joel Ward, Jason Puncheon, Joe Ledley, James McArthur, Yannick Bolasie (Dwight Gayle 80), Marouane Chamakh (Barry Bannan 80), Fraizer Campbell (Kevin Doyle 90).
Subs not used: Wayne Hennessey, Martin Kelly, Zeki Fryers, Paddy McCarthy.

Chapter 18 - We Can See You Puking Up! – *Whitsundays, 11th-14th*
November 2014

From Rainbow Beach, I got a coach to Hervey Bay, where I found a
sleeping town and joined a pensioner's quiz team, before I jumped on an
overnight coach to Airlee Beach. Once again, I barely slept on the twelve hour
journey as I struggled to find a comfortable temperature or sleeping position.
In Brazil, I'd got a luxurious sleeper coach from Rio to Belo Horizonte and slept
the entire trip. I didn't understand why Brazil could offer retractable and comfy
chairs but it was beyond Australia.

When I finally arrived, I discovered a wealthy seaside settlement, with a
harbour full of yachts and private boats. Thanks to the array of vessels, the
actual beach wasn't much to write home about but there was an incredible
lagoon on the seafront. Almost everyone in the hostels was there for one
reason only. To sail around the Whitsunday Islands.

My boat, Apollo, had been sold to me on the basis that it was not just a
'party boat', but it also offered the chance to go scuba diving, which had been a
lifelong dream of mine. As with Fraser Island, I found the team spirit and
general togetherness of everyone on the boat one the highlights. We'd been
thrown together with no prior meetings, but we all got on and enjoyed
relaxing, swimming, eating, drinking and sun bathing together. Although, once
again I felt like I should be carrying a walking stick as I opted out of the drinking
games by secretly using water instead of booze. Later in the night, when it
began to get excessively rowdy for a sober participant, I started to chat to a
scouse girl who was feeling under the weather and also steering clear of
alcohol.

Again, throughout the trip, there was limited football chat amongst the
crew but I only really noticed that when the sport was brought up by others.
Firstly, by people who were trying to find the England result using the limited
reception on their mobile phones. I wasn't particularly bothered to hear that
they'd beaten Slovenia 3-1. To be honest, I only knew they were playing that
weekend because Palace weren't and I had no idea which day the game was.
Secondly, I was drawn in by a Bristol Rovers FC beach towel.

I've always had a soft spot for Bristol's second club, mainly due to my
irrational hatred of their city rivals, coupled with the fact that they gave us
Nigel Martyn. However, the towel's owner was more interested in a different
link between the two clubs, his absolute footballing hero, Ian Holloway. He was
keen to find out why it hadn't worked out for 'Olly' at Palace. While I have little
belief in the man's management ability, I have a huge amount of admiration
and respect for him as a human being. The way that he resigned from his job
and carried his head high, living and dying by his own morals and principles
during his time in charge of our club made me very proud for him to represent
us. Despite it being doomed to failure. Yet I'd still rather him in charge than a

ranting and lying Neil Warnock, even if he was less out of his depth in the Premier League.

It was interesting to speak to a fellow addict about his feelings towards the club in their darkest hour. With the impending take over and Warnock in charge, the fact that we were actually doing the best we had done since I started supporting Palace in 1997 didn't really matter to me. I felt detached from the club. Martin, the Rover's fan, was saying how being relegated to the conference had brought everyone together at his club. Just like administration had dragged us to unity in 2010.

Dropping out of the football league for the first time since joining in 1920 hadn't made Rover's gates drop. In fact, they were planning a two-thousand-strong invasion of Dover over Christmas, via a booze run to France. What I'd give for a chance to go to a game like that. Conference football has always intrigued me. There may be smaller numbers attending but the passion is just the same as any other league in the country.

After two days of sailing, including scuba diving, visiting the world famous Whitehaven Beach, swimming with giant turtles and seeing both sharks and dolphins by the side of the boat, I woke to a horrible surprise on the third and final morning. With the sun still lurking under the sea, I had to charge up to deck and vomit over the side of the boat.

In 2011, we played Barnsley at home in a relegation six pointer. When Palace took the lead in the thirty seventh-minute through Darren Ambrose, I couldn't partake in my usual routine of excessive physical movements and highly raised heartbeat that involuntarily follows a Palace goal. Rather torturously, I found it hard to raise a cheer at all as my head was faced down into the basin of a toilet in the Holmesdale Upper Tier, and not because of a heavy night before as suggested by my mates at the time. I was ill. Seriously ill, and it was bloody horrible. I'd been fine in the morning but I became weaker and weaker on my route to the ground.

After the goal and my unfortunate incident, I left Selhurst and went back to my flat, only later finding out that we'd won 2-1. As much as I love our ground as a second home, I couldn't think of anywhere worse to be when you're not well. It's cold, its full of people and the game was teasing me as it was happening behind my back, yet right under my nose. I love the togetherness of watching our team but on that day, I've never felt so alone.

Back on the boat, that's exactly how I felt. People were lovely and supportive when they had no need to be. They were on holiday and had only just met me, but even so, I simply wanted to be back home in England, lying in my own bed. Unfortunately, unlike when I was at Palace, I couldn't make that happen. I'd known that the scouse girl had felt queasy but until I got the bug, I didn't realise quite how bad it was. Thankfully, after a day of sleeping and vomiting, the bug left as quickly as it arrived. Unfortunately, the other twenty or so people on the boat had it the next day. Typical, all it took was one scouser and we had an entire crew down with scurvy. They say that you should take your jabs when you're abroad, but no one mentioned the scouse one.

Chapter 19 – Cairns – *15th-20th November 2014*

Late in the evening, after returning to mainland, I made the final leg of my journey on an overnight coach from Airlie Beach to Cairns, which is some 620km, taking the total distance that I'd travelled up the East Coast to 2,419km. However, when this is put into the perspective of there being 35,876km of coastline on the main island of Australia, you begin to get a feeling for the size of the country. It certainly gives us some food for thought next time we complain about a 'long' journey to Preston or Sunderland.

I arrived in Cairns, after next to no sleep and still feeling under the weather, around six in the morning and had to wait around until midday before I could check into my seafront hostel. Like Airlie beach, the actual seafront of Cairns offered very little in terms of a beach, but this was again more than made up for by an excellent artificial lagoon. Although, just a short drive away, there are a selection of world class beaches with golden white sand, crystal clear water and an array of creatures able to kill you, lurking beneath the waves.

Cairns impressed me. It has an embarrassment of riches in terms of natural attraction. The sun is always shining, the rainforest is walking distance away and the Great Barrier Reef is a short, affordable boat trip from the seashore. Despite having so much to do, I simply crashed by the lagoon in the early morning heat with some of the other people who'd been on my Whitsundays boat. It was during the long wait and first real pause for thought moment I'd had in about a week that I considered going on the BBS.

With Palace not playing and me having the time of my life, I'd not really thought about the club and had little knowledge of what was happening back home. In some ways, I wanted to reach out to Palace as a comfort blanket while I was feeling ill but in others, I was enjoying the fact that I seemed to have found the cure to my other illness: My addiction. I reached the home page of the forums and stopped myself. Despite having six hours to kill, I didn't want to waste them by reading arguments and insults about who was to blame for our current winless run.

Football message boards have good intentions and can be a brilliant platform, full of information, debate and humour. However, they open up a whole world of faceless opinion. I've seen some horrendous comments on them that range from personal and direct abuse of our owners, to someone comparing us selling Zaha to a relative getting cancer. They infuriate me far more than they inform, yet since I discovered the BBS aged 14, I've been addicted to it. Like the rest of the world, I want tomorrow's news. Now. Hell, I'd even moved to a country eleven hours ahead of us to find it.

However, on holiday, in a town that I was likely to only spend four days of my life in, with people who I may never see again, I decided to keep all of the world's knowledge safely left in my pocket and enjoy the moment, sittting in the sun. And for once, I began to wonder if I was thinking like a normal person.

Enjoying my holiday was more important than knowing what other fans, who I'd never met, thought about Chamakh's injurey, Zaha's lack of form and Warnock's inability. In fact, I didn't really have an opinion on any of that (other than the fact that I wanted Warnock sacked), let alone care what others thought. It might not sound like much to a non-football fan, but for me, this was a dramatic change. Was this the 'growing up' that my mother had talked of?

After a rare and needed quiet day, the next one was to be anything but. I was to be flown fourteen thousand feet into the air, before being dropped out of the window and left to freefall back down to earth. And no, that's not a metaphor for Palace under Tony Pulis. This was actually happening and worse still, I was paying for the privilege! I was going to do a skydive.

To be honest, I wasn't actually that nervous. In fact, as I waited in the reception room for my flight, I was calmly chatting to the girls who were due to jump with me and casually eating my breakfast. I was excited and ready. Compared to the final twenty minutes against Chelsea after John Terry had put us 1-0 up, when I was a sweating, shaking mess of nibbled finger nails, twitching muscles, deep long breaths and covered eyes, preparing to jump out of an aeroplane was quite easy really.

In reality, jumping out on an aeroplane is safe. My instructor, who I was tightly tied to, had done 5-8 jumps nearly every day in the last twenty years. He'd done over ten thousand dives in his life – more than twenty times as many jumps as Palace games that I've been to. And there'd been more disasters at Palace than he'd had too. The odds of a parachute not working are over one million to one. The odds of two parachutes not working (they always dive with a spare) are basically impossible.

He did the safety checks, he knew when to jump and did it for us, he was in charge of pulling the parachute and he was going to guide us back down to earth. All I had to do was pay for it and enjoy the very expensive theme park ride. I was so relaxed that it was only when I was high above Cairns and taking in the stunning views of the rainforest, rivers, sea and Great Barrier Reef that I thought about what I was actually going to do. Jump out of this small, rickety plane.

With limited warning, the pilot announced the height, 14,000 feet, and the first person went. We all shuffled along the bench towards the open door and the instructor gave me one last reminder.
"Head back and arms crossed as we leave the plane!"
Bang, another one went and I was at the front of the line.
"Head back and arms crossed!"
I did as I was told. Before I knew what was happening, we were falling. There was no count down or warning. We'd gone. I was flying. He had told me that once we were moving I needed to push my legs back and arms out but that wasn't a problem. The wind did that for me. The plane was out of view within a second or two. We were hurtling down to earth.

We spun a bit as we left the plane as he'd asked me if I'd wanted to. He had control. We were doing loop the loop in the sky. I was free. The adrenalin was like nothing I'd ever felt before. Even Palace goals were pale compared to this. Not that I was thinking that at the time. I was simply loving it. The wind on my face. The freedom of falling. The rush of my heartbeat. The grandness of the view.

Escapism is the main reason that any of us have a hobby, whatever that may be. Football is an amazing form of forgetting life because it becomes so important to us that it takes over. For ninety minutes it takes all our emotions and passion and anxiety and pain and joy. Our jobs, our wives and girlfriends, our mates, our worries and money are forgotten. As one, we escape to the world of CPFC as we join the red and blue army in going to war. However, the skydive eclipsed even that. Occasionally in matches, not often but occasionally, my mind slips off to the world outside Selhurst Park. There was no way that my mind could ever be on anything but the adrenalin of freefalling towards earth in a skydive.

Whack! Without warning, after fifty seconds of freefall he pulled the chord. The parachute flew up and yanked me upwards. After the initial pain of the pull, we had a beautiful decent down to earth. The views became easier to take in and the movement became gentle but still my heart raced. The rollercoaster was over and I was on the lazy river down to earth. Looking down, I could just see my legs dangling, thousands of feet in the air above the world. It was magical.

Eventually, after five minutes of gliding, we reached the ground. I felt dizzy and queasy; probably not helped by the fact that I was still tired from my illness. The rest of a day is a blur. I hung out with my fellow divers at the lagoon and uploaded the video of my jump to facebook. The 'likes' rolled in as the world of social media that we live in dictates that we can't do anything without having the justification of sharing it and boasting about it to our absent friends and family.

Although my trip to Facebook did inform me of two things. Firstly, England had played a second match and more importantly, former Palace graduate, Nathanial Clyne had made his England debut. Another shining light to our academy. Although nothing will top 2013/14 for the pride in our youth system:

- Wilfried Zaha got an England call up and was signed by Sir Alex for £15m.
- Victor Moses won Player of the Tournament as he led Nigeria to win the African Cup of Nations.
- Moses scored in both legs of the semi-final and won the UEFA Cup.
- Ben Watson scored the winning goal in the FA Cup Final.
- Wayne Routledge won the League Cup.
- John Bostock did nothing.

The next couple of days in Cairns almost seemed like an afterthought to the jump. I took in a trip to the rainforest, where I went on numerous walks in the trees, swims in the lakes and plays in the waterfalls. It was there that I learned of the Amethystine Python, a snake that grows to an average length of five metres and can grow up to eight and a half metres. After acquiring this knowledge, as someone who has been terrified of snakes and even been known to run away from a small British grass snake, I can't say that I felt particularly comfortable with the rest of my day. I would put my uneasiness not only above my pre-skydive thoughts but also as worse than my long-established discomfort of a slender Palace lead.

The tour guide loved taunting us with nature. He played us a tune on the minibus called 'Deadly Animals (Visit Australia)', which was a strange Australian humour of a travel brochure; simply listing all of the animals that could kill you. The one that intrigued me the most was the little known cassowary. The vegetarian and flightless birds have less remaining in the world than Giant Pandas in China. However, what grabbed my attention was that Steven Speilberg studied these creatures when researching velociraptors for the Jurassic Park films because when threatened, they attack from the side, using their claws to pull out the victim's stomach.

To be honest, the whole rainforest felt like a set from Jurassic Park, with some of the world's oldest species of plants taking residence there. One plant named Gastrolobium Grandiflorum has heart shaped and furry leaves, which look perfect to give to your beloved. Unfortunately, the species has survived by having enough poison in it to be as deadly as Kevin Phillips from the penalty spot. Based on the local's pride on the danger of their wildlife, I'm surprised VisitAustralia doesn't use the tagline:
Australia, if the animals don't kill you, the plants will.

In the evening, I met up with Inge from Noosa and a couple of people from Fraser Island. One of the nice things about the entire East Coast was repeatedly bumping into people who I'd met earlier as everyone was doing the same route, either north to south or vice-versa. The next day, I flew back to Sydney, where I ended up staying on American Richard's sofa as the hostel was fully booked. From there, my next adventure was about to begin. I was flying to Asia.

A Scottish Palace fan, living in South America.

We live in Cuenca, Ecuador, and are able to watch Palace live every week via Direct TV from the US. We also get every EPL game live free of charge, as well as all of the rugby, four nations and tennis so as you can see: if you are couch lover, it's a great country for sport on the box.

Of course, seeing our Palace heroes play, hasn't always been this easy. When the Eagles were in the Championship, none of our matches were shown out here but with brilliant internet, we were able to stream important matches.

Our usual matchday routine is to get up around 6am and head down to the local market and buy all our fresh fruit, veggies and fish, before walking home and then settling down to enjoy breakfast and Palace for the rest of our Saturday morning.

There are only approximately 14 people from the UK living in Cuenca so finding fellow Eagles has been hard. However, unbelievably, there is one other Palace fan out here who I can scream, shout and swear at the television with. As for the locals, they don't really take much if any notice of our club. Interest is much more for Spanish teams, especially as many Ecuadorians have relocated to Spain.

One special Palace moment that we experienced from South America was the famous 3-3 game against Liverpool. We were seated and ready for Palace v Liverpool, complete with a full English breakfast! The sausage and bacon tasted even better that day! However, my fondest memory of watching Palace from a different hemisphere actually happened back in Oz. Me and my friend travelled to a pub in Brisbane that showed both the Scottish Cup (I'm from Glasgow originally and also a Rangers fan) followed by the FA Cup. A brilliant but long night with a disappointing finish at around 5am Sunday morning, but well worth the trip to be amongst fellow Palace fans.

Chapter 20 - Returning to Asia – *Kuala Lumpur (Malaysia) 21st-23rd November 2014*

I was excited. Truly excited. The East Coast had been good but this was the one that I was really looking forward to. Ever since my few days with Tom in Singapore and Indonesia, I'd been desperate to return. Return to the cheap cost of living, return to the amazing food, return to see Tom and Michaela, return to the relaxed way of life and eye-opening poverty, return to the varied cultures and I was looking forward to some jaw-dropping scenery.

Once I was over the disappointment that none of my friends from England would be joining me, I'd set about planning the trip. With the East Coast trip, the travel company had done all that for me, booking my accommodation, route, coaches and activities. Here, it was all on me. Although, that didn't bother me at all. I'm used to planning things. It was usually me who was in charge of booking away trips back home and I'd noticed that Pavel and Dan were yet to leave London to watch Palace this season without me to badger/organise them. I'd always taken charge of holidays away with my friends too. Besides, booking things yourself gives you control to do it your own way: going to the places you want to visit, picking the dates that you want to travel and most importantly, arranging the best way for you to fit Palace into your schedule.

Although, I made a conscious decision regarding watching Palace in the next five weeks. I wanted to watch the games and would if I could, but I was determined not to miss out on any opportunities in order to see Palace play.

I flew from Sydney to Kuala Lumpur, where I met Michaela, and the flight was long and painful. Not that I could complain really. Thanks to an administrative error by the booking company, which I twice alerted them about, my eight hour AirAsia flight cost just $9 rather than the $200 it was supposed to. On the foodless and entertainment-less flight, I briefly chatted to a Malaysian next to me. He asked me about English football and told me about the poorly supported Malaysian league. Unfortunately, when he asked me who my team were, he told me that he hadn't heard of Crystal Palace, which upset me deeply and ended the conversation.

As soon as I landed in Asia, I noticed 'EPL' advertising on the walls of the luggage rack. Rooney, Costa and Gerrard were thrown down mine and the local's throats. Locals who were covered in big club memorabilia. Unfortunately, I couldn't see any Palace promotions, despite the QPR poster in the corner. I guess having a Malaysian owner helps their brand. As I waited at the luggage reclaim, I felt a tap on the shoulder. It was the guy next to me from the plane. I smiled politely but it was nothing compared to the grin on his face. "Crystal Palace!" he started, "You broke Liverpool!"

I liked that. We certainly had; and the whole world knew it.

I met Michaela that evening and we dined out under the famous towers in the centre of the enormous city. As we ate our rice dishes, I watched the fountains in the front of the skyscrapers dancing to the music, a piece of choreography which would have made Western Sydney Wanderers fans proud. I loved the warm air on my already browned body and was excited about my trip ahead. Over a drink in one of the plush skybars opposite, I told Michaela about my plans. I'd decided to prepare a route as far as Bangkok, which should take about 2 and a half weeks and would give me the same amount of time to get from Bangkok, the Thai capital, to Ho Chi Minh in Vietnam, where I would fly back to Oz from.

The next day we went to watch the second ever Formula E race. It was a new initiative with electronic race cars and was going to take place over ten street races around the world, starting in China and ending in London. Through a work colleague, Michaela had managed to get us VIP seats overlooking the finish-line and 'access all area' tickets.

The race was actually held in Putrajaya, just south of Malaysia's capital and home to the government's immigration offices. The city was built in the late 1980s and planned as a 'Garden and intelligent city', where 38% of the area is reserved for green spaces by emphasising the enhancement of natural landscape. We couldn't help but notice the emphasis of the city on being 'green' and the large amount of solar panels covering just about every building, as well as the open spaces and wide boulevards.

After a dramatic race, won by the Brit, Sam Bird, we went to meet the drivers and look at the cars in the pit lanes, as well as indulge in some of the food from the VIP area. Although the cars were quieter and slower (their top speed is about 150mph) than F1 cars, the race was still exciting to watch and as always, I loved being in a stadia of any kind, even a temporary one such as this. The whole experience was enjoyable and made me keen to go and see the real deal of motorsport at some point, which I'm not sure was the purpose of the event designed to promote 'sustainable racing'.

In the evening, we went for dinner in an Asian cafe with some of Michaela's friends, where I experienced my first Asian downpour, which made us retire inside. As my trip fell in November, it coincided with the South-East Asian rainy season, which I was quick to discover put London and Sydney's constant drizzle to shame. When it rained in Malay, it meant it. Really meant it. It bordered on a monsoon, which wouldn't be ideal when you want to watch Palace as I was soon to find out.

Over our shared feast of rice, pork belly, chicken fish (the lack of comma is intentional), satay, sweet and sour chicken, garlic cabbage and seafood noodles, we discussed the difficulty of one of her ex-pat friends living in Asia. He couldn't eat spice, which severally limits your eating options. In a strange way, it summed up my relationship with Palace quite well at the time. He loved lots of Asian food but was wary of ordering anything as he was unsure how spicy it would be. Apparently, eating the wrong dish had made him physically sick. I loved Palace but knowing there was a key ingredient (the manager) who made me feel queasy, made them quite hard to stomach, especially when they lost – which happened a lot at the time.

After food, we went to an area of the city called Changkat, where we drank in an array of cocktail and rooftop bars, made possible by the storm clearing almost as quickly as it had descended upon us. I couldn't believe how easily an hour's worth of rain evaporated.

One thing that I did notice as we crawled from bar to bar was that come 10pm, each one had different EPL game showing. I was relieved that Palace weren't playing that night as I don't think it would have been socially acceptable to go and watch it, which would have been torture seeing as though I could see how easy that would have been.

However, on our way to Havana, the nightclub of our choice, as I glimpsed through one bar window, I was pleased to see that QPR were losing. Other teams losing can often bring as much joy as our own winning anyway. At the time, QPR, Brighton, Charlton and Millwall were all proving a far more reliable sauces of enjoyment than Palace.

The next day we were due to play Liverpool and our descent in the six months since that glorious 3-3 had been horrendous. We'd lost our manager and replaced him with Warnock, we'd lost match after match, we'd lost our enthusiasm and our direction and we'd certainly lost our solid defence. We were also possibly going to lose our owners and that scared me that we'd lose our identity and unity. I was almost at the point of not caring about the results. For the first time ever, and I don't say this lightly, but with me being thousands of miles away and Warnock in charge, I was starting to wonder if I was losing interest in Palace. However, the little smirk on my face at QPR's deficit probably suggests I was over-reacting. Still, the overall downward spiral made me sad, exaggerated by the man in charge.

In the cheesy, student-esque club, I danced and chatted to Michaela's friends and allowed myself a wry smile as Three Little Birds came on to the dance floor. The song, not pigeons or parrots or attractive young ladies. Afterwards, we retired to an Irish bar for G&Ts, but I just wanted to go home. Well, back to Michaela's, who'd kindly given me her room and bed for the weekend. I was exhausted.

The next day, my final one in KL, Michaela woke me early so that we could make the most of the day and sightsee the city. After a banana leaf breakfast (basically a curry presented on a giant banana leaf), we went to the markets, which were mainly filled with tourist tat of the towers and tacky Christmas accessories, as well as more emotive keepsakes in tribute to the casualties from MH370. Once again, I noticed the vast array of European football shirts available, including a red Cardiff City one. Maybe their Malaysian Bond Villain owner's plan to market them to the East was working after all?

Away from the local's Asian markets, KL is known as the shopping capital of South East Asia and it was in the main central mall that I saw the most impressive Christmas lights of my life, despite Christianity being the third most celebrated religion in Malaysia. To be honest, the mall was filled with brands and chains, which could have been anywhere in the western world. In fact, with the ever increasing economy of the city, a bit like Singapore, it felt like it could be in Europe in many ways.

The afternoon took us to Government Square and a couple of museums, before cooling down with some ice cream as we completed our tourist filled day. All we needed was an 'I heart KL' t-shirt to complete the look. After a brilliant weekend, I said my goodbyes and Michaela dropped me off at the coach station to get my bus to Melaka (or Malacca), where Tom was going to meet me. The coach journey is advertised to be between two and six hours long, so I was hopeful that the four hours I'd given myself was enough time to arrive and find a bar showing the Palace vs Liverpool game.

Chapter 21 - Come Rain or Shine – *Melaka, (Malaysia) 23rd-25th November 2014*

The journey south was fine, time wise, but it was marred by an almighty downpour and swirling winds that seemed to follow me down the entire way. I arrived at the deserted Melaka coach station at around 9pm. 45 minutes or so before we kicked off against Liverpool in South London.

Instantly, I spotted a difference to Kuala Lumper. No one spoke English and wifi was sparse. As it hadn't been a problem to either use my phone or communicate with locals in the capital, I'd naively assumed that I'd be alright to sort out the finer details of my arrival upon entering the town. How wrong was I?

The opening signs were good. A small café showed replays of Bolasie terrorising the Liverpool defence from the previous May as they built up to the match. I instantly gravitated towards the coach station cafe, bought a cup of Malaysian tea and began to watch the pre-match preview, but the angry little Asian lady behind the counter had other ideas. After a minute or so, she began to shout in her local language and ushered me out of the cafe. I think it was due to it closing as opposed to me doing anything wrong but I couldn't be sure. I tried to watch her small flickering screen through the window but she swiftly switched it off when she realised.

Unsure as to where my hotel was and immediately surrounded by non-English speaking taxi drivers as the rain hammered it down outside, I tried to direct them to 'an Irish bar', believing that a) everywhere in the world seemed to have an Irish Pub and b) they always seemed to show sport, so the odds of them showing Liverpool were strong. However, this was met with confused looks and more Malaysian shouting amongst the taxi drivers.

"Hotel?" they would shout at me, unable to understand my response that my friend had booked the hotel and I couldn't remember its name.

Eventually, aware that the game was now only about twenty minutes away, I spotted a familiar sign. A brand almost as big as the Premier League. McDonalds. I hastily made my way to the golden arches, despite the heavy rain continuing to fall, followed by six taxi drivers and confused instructions, as they argued over their bait (me). There, I looked up the hotel name. Finally, I was able to break the hearts of five taxi drivers and opt for one to take me to where I was staying. The hotel Tom had booked was mid-range but more than comfortable. We'd paid slightly more than I'd budgeted per night but hadn't gone overboard. The room was large and clean, the facilities were excellent, including the rooftop pool and the reception desk was helpful.

I dumped my bags in the room and scanned the TV for the football, which was kicking off as I flicked through. Unfortunately, the only sport channel was showing the Abu Dhabi Grand Prix as Lewis Hamilton picked up his second world title. But I didn't have time for that. I had a game to watch. I didn't even change out of my drenched clothes. For weeks, I'd been feeling discontent with Palace. I hadn't cared. I hadn't even thought about them. Especially after my huge effort and the anti-climax of the Sunderland game in Surfers Paradise. But now, there was a game on and I felt an unexplainable desperateness to watch it. Even alone. With naïve hopefulness, I asked at the front desk if they knew of any bars that showed the Premier League but I received a negative response, so I asked them to book me a cab. Through broken English, they told me to hail one outside the front of the hotel.

Smash! Smash! Smash! Smash! Smash! Smash! As I got to the entrance to the lobby, I could hear the rain beating down on the pavement with all that it had. Malaysia didn't want me to watch this game, but that only made me more determined to see it through. To try and be part of it from afar. My inbuilt addiction and instincts were far from cured.

It took a couple of minutes of cowering under a tree, barely protected from the rain and being viciously attacked by the wind, leaving me drenched through yet strangely warm and sticky in the way that a humid climate hits you, but I did manage to hail a cab. Thankfully, one who vaguely understood me. With his broken English, the friendly driver kept asking me which pub I wanted to go to and I'd reply *"One showing the EPL?"* or *"Premier League?"* or *"Liverpool?"*, which wasn't particularly helpful for either of us really. We both kind of understood what I wanted but I wasn't really sure how to achieve it – so I couldn't be too agitated that he wasn't either.

He took me to three or four bars, allowing me to run in to them through the monsoon and check if they were playing the game before I'd let him leave so we could move onto the next bar if needed. Unfortunately, none of them were showing the match. Each time, I returned to the car slightly wetter. In the end, we settled up and I began to explore without a chauffeur. After being given some vague hope by one non-football-showing bar owner, I jogged along the main, deserted street in the heavy rain, with the knowledge that there might be some reward at the end of it. Occasionally, the odd car would skid past, turning the puddles into tidal waves heading towards the dangerously pot holed pavement that I ran on alone. Suddenly, I heard something in the distance. The rain had slightly eased off by now, but the wind was still strong enough to carry the sound to my ears. A distant cry of the crowd. From the deepest, darkest corner of South-East Asia, I could hear Selhurst Park.

I began to move quickly, almost breaking out into a joyous run, desperately hoping that it wasn't a mirage in the football desert that I found myself in. As I got closer, I saw flashing blue light coming from around the corner. There was a bar with a giant screen outside the front of it. A giant screen showing 43 minutes on the clock. A giant screen that showed Joel Ward holding his head after having an effort saved. And in the corner, it displayed Crystal Palace 1 Liverpool 1.

I strolled in, wearing my soaked Palace shirt proudly and plonked myself on a comfy sofa in front of the screen. Immediately, I was approached by a waitress who informed me that the restaurant (not bar as I'd assumed) didn't serve beer but this didn't bother me in the slightest. Beer or no beer, I was more than at home. During the half time break, I ordered some fresh watermelon juice and a rice dish, while enjoying the replays of the first half action. Well, I didn't enjoy seeing Rickie Lambert put Liverpool ahead in the first minute but I did enjoy the scousers' nemesis and constant thorn, Dwight Gayle, equalising for us.

Quietly, I watched the second half, taking in the action of an edgy affair. The atmosphere sounded brilliant, but I was more than content watching from Asia. I'd gone through hail and thunder to see the game, alone, but for once, I didn't wish I was there. I was making the travelling dream work without missing Palace. Using the free wifi, I spent most of the half texting friends and family back home to allow me to discuss the match, despite the obvious difficulty of having no one beside me. There were a few Malaysians watching in their fake Liverpool shirts but I preferred my text company to joining them, especially as the ones that I heard weren't discussing the match in English.

Near the end, Bolasie, one of Liverpool's ghosts of Selhurst's Past, chipped the ball over two red shirts and charged towards the area. Once there, he teed the ball up perfectly for Joe Ledley to smash the ball past the keeper and give us a seventy-ninth minute lead. Selhurst erupted. I erupted as I jumped out of my seat, threw my arms into the air and let out a huge yelp of delight. The local Liverpool fans looked bemused, the family dining out on a table near me looked terrified. I simply punched the air again and grinned towards the red shirts.

I'd barely sat down and was still texting back home, using capitals to show that I was shouting as I'd realised that actually shouting for real in a Malaysian restaurant was slightly inappropriate, when we got a free kick three minutes later. Jedinak stood over it. What happened next was a thing of beauty. And I'm not talking about me nearly sending the table that I was sat at flying. Our inspirational captain curled the ball beautifully into the top corner of the net. The keeper stood no chance. For the second time in six months, we'd humiliated Liverpool in front of the world. We'd gone from the team that broke Liverpool to the team that tortured them. As they left, one of the Malaysians walked past me and shook my hand. He said *"I hate Crystal Palace!"*

This was great news. It is not hate that we should fear, but indifference. Liverpool will never be able to feel indifferent towards Crystal Palace again. Oh, how the mighty have fallen since that 9-0 defeat. Since that result, only the fifth Palace game after my birth, we've held a strange voodoo over Liverpool. Since that 9-0, we'd had ten victories. My personal record was now thus:

Live: W4, D1, L1
Radio: W1 D0 L0
TV: W1 D0 L0

After the game, I struggled to find a cab as it was around midnight and everything seemed closed. I certainly didn't see any bars and it began to dawn on me how well that I'd done to find the game. Back at the hotel, I met Tom, who'd arrived from Singapore, and immediately I burst out with enthusiasm about the match. It was a shame really but it felt like an anti-climax. I'd gone berserk for the goals and had been frantically WhatsApping post-match, but without friendship or beer, I felt a sad distance from the action. Although, not as much anguish as my Dad was feeling after he'd turned down a free ticket from Pavel. Soon after, I headed to sleep as we had a busy couple of days ahead of us.

I really liked Melaka. Exploring the small town, I spent the next couple of days wondering around museums, the Palace (not Crystal but Sultanate) and religious buildings. I loved learning about the rich history of the World Heritage Site that had been traded as freely as Premier League footballer between the Dutch, English and Portuguese in the past thanks to its excellent port and shipping potential. It's funny to think about what was worth money in the past. Everyday goods such as sugar and tea had sky high values that reflected the market and dominated economies. As ever, these things don't last and the value of assets decrease over time. Just look at Chris Armstrong, or indeed any other player that we've ever sold to Spurs.

The food was brilliant too as we had feast after feast of rice, chicken, duck, pork and seafood. All served with a different spicy sauce of one kind or another. And that's not even mentioning the variety of noodles and soups that we tried. In the evening, we found a few nice bars along the river and a couple in the old town, where we enjoyed a few cool beers in the hot evening. The settings were beautiful, the history was rich and the company was excellent. It was a fantastic short break. However, it says a lot about the size of the place that we felt we'd completed it before our two full days were up and spent our final couple of hours playing ten-pin bowling. The longer I was there, I felt more and more privileged that I'd been able to find somewhere showing the Palace game.

But even rarer than finding a Palace game in Melaka was something else. Something incredible. I even brought myself to mumble something that went against all I believed in. I said to Tom, "Warnock got his tactics spot on!" Having said that, I still didn't like the guy, but he did deserve some praise. See, football fans aren't always narrow minded and loud mouthed hypocrites. Just most of the time.

Crystal Palace...3 Liverpool...1
Selhurst Park, 23/11/14
Premier League

Palace: Julian Speroni, Martin Kelly, Scott Dann, Damian Delaney (Brede Hangeland 36), Joel Ward, Mile Jedinak, Joe Ledley, Jason Puncheon (James McArthur 76), Yannick Bolasie (Barry Bannan 86), Marouane Chamakh, Dwight Gayle.
Subs Not Used: Wayne Hennessey, Wilfried Zaha, Fraizer Campbell, Andy Johnson.

Liverpool: Mignolet, Johnson, Lovren, Skrtel, Manquillo, Allen (Can 74), Gerrard, Lallana (Borini 72), Coutinho, Sterling, Lambert.
Subs Not Used: Jones, Toure, Moreno, Leiva, Markovic.

"The 3-1 was a different game to the three all. It was more difficult because we were in a poor position at that time. Again, we went 1-0 down but had the strength to come back and thoroughly deserved to win when we kept at it, stuck in their faces, got our rewards and got two goals in the second half to eventually see them off, which got us back in the mix of things because we'd had a slow start that season. Obviously, I quite enjoyed my free kick too!"

Mile Jedinak

Chapter 22 - The Jungle, an Island and Thailand – *Taman Negara National Park & Perhentian Islands, (Malaysia) 25th-29th November 2014*

That evening, I paid 170 Ringgit (roughly £25 – or au$55 as I was working in) to travel 80km by taxi from Melaka to Gemas, a small Malaysian town with a large railway station. I guess that makes it the Crewe of Malaysia. From there, I was to get an overnight 'Jungle Train' 300km north to Jerantut, which is a gateway into the Malaysian National Park. The Jungle.

In the taxi, I admired the spectacular daily thunder storm and was glad that I was safely in a car (well, as safe as you ever can be in a car in Asia) rather than chasing through it to find a Palace game.

The train journey was long and not particularly comfortable, especially with the air con turned up to full blast and my warmer clothes packed away in my rucksack. My arrival in Jerantut wasn't ideal either. It was 4:30am. A taxi driver followed me as I tried to get my bearings and repeatedly shared his seemingly only English phrase, "Give me ten ringgit, I find you hotel!"

My brief investigations showed me that I had few other options, so I finally accepted his offer and got into his door-less cab. He took me to a hotel and banged on the caged entrance, waking up the middle aged owner who came down in nothing but his rather loose boxers. He charged me 30ringgit for the night (well, 2 hours) and told me that I needed to be awake early to catch a bus if I wanted to go to Taram Negara (the National Park) as it was off season and there was only one a day.

I had planned to take the intriguing option of a river boat to sail into the heart of the jungle but he informed me that because it was the 'off season', no boats were running. The 'Off Season' was really beginning to annoy me. It involved beautiful weather of 30 degrees each day, with one heavy storm in the afternoon or evening. It wasn't stopping me from doing anything that I wanted to but it seemed to dictate that tourists were advised not to visit and services were much more infrequent.

It was only after my early morning wakeup call that I discovered my next dilemma. My wallet was basically empty, as were all of the cash machines in the vicinity. If I ventured further out, I would miss the only coach of the day, leaving me stranded in an empty town, but if I didn't get cash, I wasn't sure how I'd be able to cope. There was unlikely to be any signs of the western world in the middle of the jungle, let alone cash machines.

In the end, I boarded the bus. The journey was stunning. I'd first noticed in Brazil, but had since felt the same in Asia and Australia. Things just feel so much better when there are palm trees about. Maybe Palace should plant some around the side of the pitch at Selhurst Park to raise spirits during cold, January 1-0 defeats. From watching some A-league games on tele, I'd noticed that the Australian team, Central Coast Mariners, had some planted behind the goal at their home ground, which was unadventurously named 'Central Coast

Stadium. Mind you, it didn't seem to be doing them much use, they weren't doing much better the Western Sydney Wanderers, who were still rock bottom of the league.

Anyway, through the jaw dropping surroundings, I arrived in a secluded little village situated across the river from Taram Negara. It was deserted and our coach load, which consisted of me and a French couple, hardly filled the area with activity either. The village had mixture of wooden built hotels, restaurants, shops and small huts. On the river, there were four barges moored up, all of which were picturesque functioning restaurants, surrounded by nature. I could hear the sounds of birds, listen to the splash of the water and dream of seeing a tiger on the night tour. Unfortunately, I quickly felt less cut off from the world by the almost instant sighting of a local child in a Manchester United shirt.

The branding of that club is incredible. The kid wearing it had no concept of what Manchester United was or where it came from but he still wore the shirt and liked it regardless. When I see a Palace shirt, even in South London, the little boy in me allows my heart to skip a beat and exchange an inane grin or thumbs up with the owner of the said shirt. I wonder if United fans feel the same? I doubt it. They're too common (the shirt's frequency rather than the personality of the fans – in most cases anyway). Even in the middle of the Malaysian Jungle.

Money was tight but it showed me how cheap South East-Asian living could be. My 61 ringgit (£11.55/au$21.28) got me:

- 10r on one night in the hostel – I had my own room that overlooked the river.
- 7r on brunch - sweet sour chicken, rice and fresh watermelon juice - on a floating river restaurant.
- 2r on three 1.5L bottles of water.
- 1r on a boat to Taman Negara.
- 1r entrance to the National Park.
- 5r for permission to take photos in the park.
- 5r to go on the world's highest tree-top canopy walk.
- 1r on the boat back.
- 3r on fresh lychee juice.
- 10r for a meal in nicest floating restaurant - black pepper beef and rice, and a watermelon juice.
- 2r on some more water.
- 5r on nasi lamek for breakfast (a Malaysian dish of rice, chicken, fish and chilli sauce)
- 2r on boats to and from the National Park.
- 7r on the bus back to Jarantut.

It was incredible value for money. I loved my two (incredibly humid) walks in the jungle too, where I met monkeys, 1.5m lizards, foot long giant centipedes, various bugs and birds, and the French couple. Although, it was after my meeting with the French couple that I made my scariest two findings of the journey. A real life, wild snake that stood to attention and hissed at me after the French guy nearly stepped on it. But even more terrifying than that, I discovered a group of two or three locals in the street, playing football while wearing FlyMalaysiaAirlines QPR shirts.

Maybe there really was some global pull of worldwide branding. If Josh Harris did buy Palace, would kids in States suddenly be donning a red and blue shirt with an eagle as these children were here? Would that be even cooler than having four South London born owners? Did we even need a foreign owner to make that happen? If my travels had taught me one thing, it was that wherever I was in the world, from Brazil, to Oz, to the Malaysian Jungle, if people liked football, they now knew who Crystal Palace were and could tell me a little about us. And that's after just one season in the top flight (well, possibly just one comeback vs Liverpool). Imagine how big we could become if we stayed in this elite league (and continued to embarrass the scousers).

Anyway, later that afternoon, I got the bus back to Jurantut, finally withdrew some more ringgit and booked an overnight coach to Khota Bahru. From there, I planned to head on to the Perhentian Islands, a small group of coral-fringed, white sanded, jungle filled islands. However, as with Taram Negara, I had been warned that it was the 'off season'. Not that this bothered me. It hadn't stopped me so far and I'm more than happy to do things by myself, hence my habit of attending lower league pre-season Palace matches.

Buoyed by my ability to sniff out football (and wifi) in the middle of the jungle during the off season, I set about my next challenge. To find a way of watching the Swansea vs Palace game , while I was on the 'limited electricity' Perhentian Islands. A quick google search suggested that finding food and water would be tricky. Let alone Premier League Football. Although I had a plan, I was still slightly concerned that electricity was inconsistent during the off-season. However, my research from a small wooden shack by the Jaruntut coach station led me to believe that there was a hotel which was open and had a 'computer room'.

The coach bookings operator, who'd allowed me to use the computer in his shack, noticed that as well as researching the Perhentian Islands, I was doing some writing about football. He informed me that he liked 'Hotspurs', but he also noticed that I'd typed the words 'Queens Park Rangers', at which he shouted "Fernandes!" after their Malaysian owner. The fact that a Premier League side was owned by a Malaysian certainly filled him with pride. I suppose it's similar to when GB win a gold medal in the Winter Olympics. The fact that we all know little or nothing about the sport that's being competed in doesn't stop our national pride in celebrating the win as our own. Simply having a Malaysian national being involved in the Premier League was enough for this guy. Which was just as well really – because QPR certainly weren't going to win anything.

Before catching my bus, I allowed myself to dip into the Western World and have a Pizza Hut, which cost me 50r – nearly equal to my entire outlay for two days in the jungle. Sat on my own in the corner, I began to observe the locals. At the price I was paying, I realised that it was likely to be wealthier Malaysians dining with me but I noticed a complete change in etiquette. By and large, when I'd seen Malaysians eat, they'd used their hands – even for curry dishes. However, in Pizza Hut, one of the few restaurants that it would be acceptable to use your hands to eat with back home, everyone seemed to be using a knife and fork.

As with my train from Melaka, despite large and comfortable seats, my overnight journey (223km north) was a nightmare for the same two reasons: blasted air-conditioning and early arrivals. Now, I might sound a bit of a 'Moaning Michael' for complaining about having aircon in a hot country and public transport arriving early but bear with me. Firstly, it was freezing. Despite preparing trousers and a coat this time, I was shivering most of the way. All of the locals had prepared themselves with thick blankets, scarfs, woolly jumpers and warm hats. It was ridiculous and surely a waste of money? Was there no controls on the bloody thing to tone it down?

As for the punctuality, arriving a couple of hours early to an away game on public transport might be a bonus, allowing extra drinking time or a chance to see a new city. But arriving at a coach station in the middle of nowhere (well Khota Bahru) at 4am, when it's advertised as arriving at 6am, is pretty useless.

For the umpteenth time, I was surrounded by local taxi drivers all demanding that I got into their cab and telling me that unless I went right now, I'd miss the only ferry to the Perhentians. This wasn't really a problem as I was keen to move on but they all shouted at me that it would cost 100ringgit (£20ish). The scrap of all of them pushing each other out of the way as they threw their arms forward, trying to grab my attention, reminded me of a bundle as fans scraping for a player's shirt as he chucks it into the crowd on his way out of a club.

Eventually, with no wifi or way of checking if the information that I was being given was correct, I had to agree to get into a cab to take me to the boat. The journey was about an hour and after a lack of sleep on the coach, I slept the entire way. Before the sun had risen, I was dropped off at the deserted port and my driver left me, saying that there should be a boat soon. I looked around. Other than a family of wild goats munching on some nearby grass, there were no other signs of life. Feeling more than a little conned, I fastened my rucksack to my arm, used my other bag as a pillow and lay down on a bench to sleep.

"Per-ren-yon? Per-ren-yon? Per-ren-yon?"
I was woken by a small, toothless Malaysian shaking me as he repeatedly stated a word in his thick accent that sounded nothing like how I'd previously

understood 'Perhentian' to be pronounced.

"Errrm, Perhentian Islands?" I replied, ignoring his presumably correct pronunciation.

Exaggerating all his movements to compromise for the lack of spoken understanding after waking me from my exhausted slumber, he pointed towards a small electric jet boat. This must have been the only ferry of the day that I'd been told about. In a futile attempt to be vaguely prepared, I'd read online that I shouldn't pay more than 30 ringgit for the ferry. Despite plenty of haggling, he charged me 50, after originally asking for 100. However, as I was his only customer, he wasn't going to drop any further.

The boat ride was magical. Gorgeously, the sun rose over the beautiful islands as the salty water gently sprayed on my face from the bobbing speed boat. It was a feeling of freedom and escape. It was what travelling was all about. I may have felt conned and alone but I was also on an adventure. I was doing what I wanted, on my terms.

Upon arriving, I wondered around the first island, which although beautiful, was ruined slightly by the litter dumped on the beaches. It was well and truly off season; everyone had upped and left the day the busy period had ended. Many locals move to Langkawi, an island on the other side of Malaysia, where the weather is more favourable for tourism and income. However, for me, the empty nature of the island added to its charm. There I was, on an island that has previously been voted the world's most beautiful, and I had it to myself. I couldn't help but feel that it would make the most perfect honeymoon.

As predicted, the accommodation options were limited. Out of the dozens of hotels on the island, only three were open. I picked a chalet on the beach, with (controllable) air-conditioning and an en suite. It cost a mere 40 ringgit (£8) for the night. As I was surrounded by amazing coral and sea life, I was gutted to discover that not only were all of the scuba diving centres shut, but I couldn't even find anywhere to rent a snorkel. Fortunately, I was able to scratch the surface (well not actually scratch it as I didn't want to damage anything!) of the underwater world as I had my goggles from swimming in Sydney.

However, I had a more pressing concern, as I lay on the empty, picturesque beach in the afternoon heat. It turns out that the internet doesn't always tell the truth. Only the restaurant of the big hotel was open. Not the computer room. In fact, there wasn't any internet on the island, which meant there'd be no way of watching Palace. The 'free wifi' signs that were all around the ghostly restaurants, bars, hotels and chalets were taunting me as a luxury from another time.

In the evening, I met a couple of fellow Englishmen – the only other tourists on the island. They'd arrived on a later boat at a much more reasonable mid day time, for a much more reasonable price of 30 ringgit. Not that I was bitter or anything. Anyway, they were having a short break from their challenge. The two cousins had taken a year out of work and flown to Indonesia. From there, they'd given themselves a year to cycle back home. While travelling, I often heard people say that they'd done the most amazing things or met the most amazing people, but with these two, I was genuinely in awe of them.

After a very secluded day of swimming, snorkelling and sun bathing, it was lovely to have some company in the evening at the only open restaurant on the island. Even if the limited menu was incredibly expensive. There were no drinks other than water available, and the prices charged were higher than those advertised on the menus left out from the high season. I guess it was an extreme version of the business model adopted by kiosks in football concourses. You don't need to have good customer service, high quality produce, wide variety of choice or a low price when there's no competition. Pay up or go hungry.

The reason that this beautiful day was considered the 'low season' and the island had about ten people on it, rather than the thousands that visit it for the majority of the year, was the ten minute heavy downpour in the afternoon. Apparently, sometimes that makes crossings difficult. However, I was convinced that the island was missing out on tens of thousands of pounds worth of tourism by shutting itself off in this way.

The next day, partly because one day of self reflection and alone time was enough and partly because I wanted to try and at least follow the Palace game that evening, I decided to leave the islands, after briefly visiting the second one to see the amazing coral just meters from the shore in Tuna Bay.

Back on mainland, once again I was confronted by taxi drivers at the coach station who tried to claim my custom over local busses with flattery.

"Where you from?"

"England" I replied.

"Who you support? Manchester? Tottenham? Arsenal?'"

"Crystal Palace!" I replied proudly, expecting that to throw him.

"Ah yes. Crystal Palace. Liverpool no like!"

Despite his acknowledgement of my club, I chose to pay 3 ringgit for a bus back to the coach station, rather than 100 for a taxi, and then set about my next challenge: Get to Thailand and find somewhere to watch Swansea City vs Crystal Palace. The first bit was easy enough. I was lead to a bus by the non-English speaking station operator and I began to talk to the driver. Our broken conversation went like this,

"Thailand?"

"Ah Thailand!" he replied, pointing to the floor of his bus.

"This... bus... goes... to... Thailand..?" I responded, arrogantly hoping that a slower and louder response would be clearer.

"Thailand!" he repeated.

"Thailand?" I quizzed again, pointing inside the bus.

"Thailand!" he replied, pointing at the 5 ringgit sign next to him.

Well that seemed about as definite an answer as I was likely to get so I paid the money. We travelled north for about an hour or so as the bus got hotter and fuller. There wasn't another backpacker in sight. I was certainly doing things my way. After a while, we stopped and people groaned. The driver was pushing himself towards the back of the bus. Amongst a mass of rolling eyes and sighing, which I was tempted to join in with, I realised something. He was heading for me! He pointed at me and then towards what looked like a motorway toll and shouted, loudly and slowly for the foreigner, *"Thailand!"*

Chapter 23 - Crossing the Border – *Krabi, (Thailand) 29th November – 1st December 2014*

I clambered off the bus with my giant rucksack on my back and smaller, but still rather hefty, backpack on my front. I was carrying more weight than Neil Ruddock. The bus turned left and as it did, a few of the passengers continued to point out of the window at the arches ahead.

Above them, I noticed a small Thai flag and guessed that I was at the border. Slowly, I dragged myself and my luggage to the edge of Malaysia, had my passport stamped and was allowed through. There was a small bridge, a lot of traffic and not much else. I'd made it to Thailand but this was very much the 'off season'. Pre season hadn't even begun yet!

I knew, from looking at vague maps, that I wanted to go to Krabi as it was the closest place that interested me. I'd seen it advertised in a travel agent's window on Oxford Street and it had pulled my attention for two reasons. Firstly, it had looked nice enough and secondly, it was obviously quite touristy. After plenty of alone time in the jungle and Perhentians, I was ready to mingle. Besides, if it was touristy, I was more likely to be able to find the football.

However, this lonesome bridge was far from touristy. In fact, the limited English from the few officials who were mulling about left me wondering if they'd ever had a Brit crossing this particular Malaysian/Thai border before. I had no idea what to do and neither did they.

"Krabi?" I asked desperately.

I was met with blank faces.

Eventually, it became clear that I wasn't actually in Thailand. I'd been stamped out of Malaysia but not yet stamped into Thailand. I had to cross the bridge that I was dillydallying on and go through customs on the other side. Once I'd argued my way through (they didn't like the fact that I couldn't give them an address that I would be staying at so after lots of shouting in Thai, they eventually settled for 'Bangkok') I finally stepped out into Thailand. Immediately, I was surrounded again by people offering me a lift. However, this time, they weren't taxi drivers. They were motor bike riders!

In Liverpool the previous year, I'd gone to our rare 3-1 defeat against the red side of the city and the night before the game, I'd come across some dodgy taxi drivers. One had taken me to the wrong hotel and one had started to drive with the meter on, before explaining that he had no idea where my hotel was and it was up to me to direct him. However, at least I spoke a dialect of the same language as scousers. Here I was, in a tiny Thai border town, being offered a lift on the back of a motorbike to a location I didn't know, in a language I didn't know, without any helmet or protective gear, while carrying a 15kg rucksack and a 5kg backpack. It brought being a dodgy cabbie to a whole new level.

Concerned for my safety, I turned back inside the terminal, found the border police and explained my situation. I needed to get to either a train or coach station so that I could get to Krabi. To do this, I also needed to get some local currency. The local plod was more than helpful. He took me outside, pointed at the motorbikes and then summoned a bloke over who was sitting at the side of the road.

"He want Thai baht!" he explained to the man, while pointing at me.

It seemed that the local currency exchange was a man sat on the pavement. Considering I had no idea how many baht went into the Australian dollar, English pound or Malaysian Ringgit, I decided to pass on the chance of a roadside exchange. However, I had little other option than to get on the back of a motorbike and travel the 5km to the coach station, stopping off at a cash machine on the way. It was there that I learned that $1 = 33baht or £1 = 50baht.

At first, I clung on for dear life to the back of this bike but soon, I realised that everyone actually was driving pretty calmly. Unlike Kuala Lumpur, this place wasn't overcrowded and people didn't drive like maniacs. However, there was some crazy stuff going on. I saw pre-teen children driving motorbikes, with even younger brothers on the back, we overtook one grey-haired granny, happily holding an umbrella to protect herself from sun as she rode along one handed, and plenty of parents rode with their toddlers who wore no protection on the front of their bike. To think my five year old niece is scared of getting in a car for fear of being sick.

At the coach station, I learned that the next trip to Krabi was an overnight one, meaning that I'd miss the Palace game after all. Although, I was told that some of the busses had wifi so I might be able to at least follow the game online, even if the internet was unlikely to be strong enough for a stream. Mind you, even a stream on a Thai coach would be better than the fuzzy picture I'd watched our game against Swansea on in the previous season.

I'd seen the game in Patricks Irish Bar in Crystal Palace and the picture was so jumpy and blurry that I had no idea what was happening. Unknown to us, it had also fallen ten minutes behind the live action. It was only the mad celebrations in the pub that informed us Glenn Murray had returned, and scored to equalise long before we saw it on the screen. Although, it did allow me to start one of my wittier chants,

"We're guna score in a minute! Score in a minute!"

Anyway, in a desperate attempt to find the game before booking the coach, I had a quick look around the town of Sungai Golok, but there really wasn't much there at all. I decided that I had no chance of watching the match whether I stayed or not, so I booked the coach.

The wait was about six hours or so and I used the time wisely – to read up on the latest Palace news. I read about a new link that the club had set up with Mumbai FC. Many people on the forums were sceptical of any benefit of such a connection, but I thought it was great. It was another small step into making

Crystal Palace Football Club known worldwide. Mumbai has a population of nearly twelve million people and it had to be a more likely destination of extending the fan base than the Malaysian jungle, which had clearly been successful for QPR. Especially with the new and heavily funded Indian Football Super League, I was hopefully it would mean a splurge of red and blue in another corner of the world. If nothing else, they might learn that we're good for stuffing Liverpool.

While I waited, I struggled to find places serving food that appealed to me. However, I was far more concerned that I was missing the football than worried about my stomach. Although I'd been feeling distanced from Palace, I still had a strong natural desire to be able to see, discuss and ultimately moan about every game. Especially after the win in our previous match. Before setting off, after discovering that there was to be no wifi on the coach, I asked my Palace WhatsApp group to keep me informed by text about the events from South Wales.

Fortunately, I'd finally learnt and prepared for the freezing conditions of the journey and I was able to sleep much better than on previous overnight trips. Unfortunately, as with the Manchester United game, my subconscious was playing tricks on me making it hard to differentiate between when I had actually received a text and when I'd dreamt it. This resulted in me regularly waking up and having to check my phone.

Eventually, soon after midnight, I received a text from Pavel, who wasn't at the match but had been following the game.

"1-1... Bony with the first goal... Apparently Swansea all over us in the first 15-20 mins.. Then Gayley got injured and we brought on McArthur and started playing much better.. Cham got fouled in the box... Jedi scored the pen... Jedi brought a cricket bat into the centre circle before the game as well..."

The cricket bat was a tribute from our captain to his fellow Australian, Phillip Hughes. The batsman had died aged just twenty five, while playing the game he loved when he was hit on the head by a ball. As always with tragedy in sport, it reminded us that it's just a game. I will never forget the feeling I had when I walked into a pub in Wimbledon one March evening in 2012 and was confused as to why the FA Cup game on the tele had been suspended.

Slowly, news filtered through that the Bolton defender, Fabrice Muamba, had collapsed during the game after suffering a cardiac arrest. His heart stopped for 78 minutes but amazingly, he survived. To hear of someone coming so close to death while playing the sport that we all love, was harrowing and ended our evening prematurely. While all death is tragic, especially in one so young, when it grabs someone in the heat of such a familiar moment like that, it somehow feels even closer to home. Thankfully, Muamba lived to tell the tale, even if he never played again. Still, as gutting as that must be for him, it must have put sport into perspective. Hughes was never allowed that chance.

After reflecting on those tragic events, it seems almost disrespectful to return to the match. An hour or so of broken sleep later, I received a second text from Pav.

"1-1 full time... I think it is a great away point for me"

I agreed but I couldn't reply as I had no credit on my Australian phone.

At around 3am, we were all woken for a toilet break. When I returned, there was confusion as the Thai conductor seemed to be insisting that I changed coach. No one else, just me. This hadn't been mentioned at the coach terminal. I didn't think I smelt that bad. Still, unable to communicate with anyone, I repeated the word 'Krabi' a lot and I held on tight to my bags. At 4am, my new coach pulled into a quiet, empty road and I was ushered off the bus unaccompanied.

"Krabi?" I asked, hopefully.

A slightly confused driver gave an unconvincing nod back and then the door shut, and once again, I was alone, not knowing where I was, without a hotel, in the middle of the night because a coach had arrived ahead of schedule.

Soon enough, I was met with Asia's answer to leeches football agents: a taxi driver. They really will lie, manipulate and double cross to scam as much money out of you as possible. So once again, I found myself and my two bulging bags loaded onto the back of a motorbike and off we rode into the night, looking for a hotel in Krabi Town, which was about 3km away from where I'd been dropped. Although, my driver told me that it was 9km to ensure that I didn't opt to go for a midnight stroll.

As soon as he realised that I was English, he wanted to speak EPL. He was a Chelsea fan but knew of Crystal Palace

"You lucky. You beat us!" he told me, referring to our John Terry inspired win in the previous season. I grinned, but not too much. After all, I was riding on the back of his motorbike in the middle of the night, without a crash helmet.

The first place he took me to was on the waterfront. It looked amazing. And I'm sure it was, but at 3500baht (£70) a night it should be! So we carried on looking. Ideally, I wanted a hostel so that I could meet other backpackers to explore with. He took me to a couple more hotels which were closed, before we moved onto another expensive one. Eventually, he took me back to where the coach drop off was and I settled for a small, dingy and cheap hotel. I paid for one night, well a few hours, and decided I'd look again in the morning when I wasn't dictated to wherever he wanted to take me. The lack of wifi meant that I couldn't read up on the game but to be honest, I wasn't that fussed. It was a decent result but hardly ground breaking stuff. Besides, I had a new town and country to explore.

The next morning I got a local bus, which was actually a van with benches in and no back, and found a hostel in the town centre. The brilliant thing about using hostels when travelling is that you immediately meet people. Defying any shyness from my younger years, I tended to burst into rooms, introduce myself and immediately find out what was going on. On that morning, a young Finnish girl was going for some breakfast so I joined her. To be honest, conversation was slow as we struggled to find common ground and simply shared our experiences of Asia thus far.

As we were splitting after our morning meal, an internal battle was won. There'd been a question that I'd wanted to ask her since meeting her. Every time conversation had hit an awkward silence, my mind had gone to one addiction fed thought. Part of me didn't want to ask. Part of me felt that it was a question from my younger years when I had a one track mind and couldn't hold a conversation about anything else. But part of me needed to know and it was that part that forced my hand. I asked.

"Do you know who Aki Riihilahti is?"

Her face lit up. *"Of course I know him. He is a legend. He is different to most footballers. He is a good man. You must support Crystal Palace. Aki is very popular in Finland so your team is too."*

After that, conversation was easier. We'd found our common ground. Despite her lack of interest in football, we shared a love of the former Palace and Finnish midfielder, Aki Riihilahti.

The rest of my time in Krabi was spent feeding monkeys, relaxing on the beach, exploring caves, visiting temples (including one stunning one at the top of an incredibly steep rock face), going to Palaces (none made of Crystal), eating and drinking at the night market and then heading out to some bars in the evening, where I noticed Southampton vs Manchester City was on in the background. However, despite this, I had a strange lack of interest in the EPL. I was out with non-football fans and although they were virtual strangers to me, I still had more intrigue in them than the game on the screens. While I still had the odd Palace-inspired blip into addiction, my obsession with football was definitely weaker than it once was.

Although, despite not focussing on football, I couldn't help but notice that it was all around me. There were Everton shirts everywhere on locals, donning the 'Chang' sponsor: Thailand's highest best beer. Most of the shirts were fake, but the Chang logo was proud and large; leading me to wonder if the beer company were producing them. However, what pleased me more, was that there were a few people in Krabi FC shirts – one of Thailand's professional sides. It was my first evidence of South-East Asian football and I was pleased. Around the town, there were billboards and badges. I mean sure, there was more evidence of Manchester United and Liverpool around, but this place was proud of its own team. I liked that. It recognised that football could exist locally as well as globally. To me, neither can thrive without the other.

Swansea City...1 Crystal Palace...1
The Liberty Stadium, 29/11/14
Premier League

Swansea City: Fabianski, Rangel, Bartley, Williams, Taylor, Ki, Shelvey, Sigurdsson, Routledge (Barrow 64), Montero, Bony (Gomis 74).
Subs not used: Tremmel, Amat, Richards, Britton, Carroll.

Crystal Palace: Julian Speroni, Joel Ward, Brede Hangeland, Scott Dann, Martin Kelly, Mile Jedinak, Joe Ledley, Jason Puncheon (Wilfried Zaha 81), Yannick Bolasie, Marouane Chamakh (Fraizer Campbell 66), Dwight Gayle (James McArthur 21).
Subs not used: Wayne Hennessey, Zeki Fryers, Barry Bannan, Jerome Thomas.

Chapter 24 - Oh Phuk-et – *Phuket, (Thailand) 1st-3rd December 2014*

From Krabi, I took a coach to Patong Beach in Phuket. Compared to Malaysia, I'd already noticed a difference in the culture and attitude towards tourists in Thailand. Being English meant two things. Firstly, I supported an EPL team and secondly, most importantly, I was seen as a walking cash machine. Phuket made it very easy to understand why.

The place was crawling with obnoxious Brits and Aussies: out for a shag and a cheap booze up. Any natural beauty of the area or enjoyment of the luxuriously warm sea was ruined by the underlying tense atmosphere of the area. The locals hated the tourists as they showed no respect to them or their country, but they relied on them for money. The tourists hated the locals as they felt consistently ripped off and lied to, but they relied on doing business with them for their holiday activities. Patong Beach is a party area for the western world to use for drugs, booze and ping pong shows. The Magaluf of Asia.

I realised what I'd arrived at straight away, as I wondered around the town, dripping with sweat, carrying my two bags while fruitlessly searching for a hostel to stay at. I hated it already: the bars, the tattoo parlors, the English writing everywhere, the string of northern football shirts, the sex shows, the fast food chains, the signs for 'Full English Breakfasts' and 'Steak Dinners', the absence of culture. However, at least there were dozens of places advertising that they showed the English Premier League – Palace were due to host Aston Villa on my second night. For that reason, I was glad to be there.

Anyway, after an hour of searching, which I was beginning to think would never end in the scorching temperature, I saw a sign for a 'Backpackers Hostel'. I'd finally found the Holy Grail. Although I had a tantalising few minutes, still dripping with sweat from the sheer heat, as the women on reception scoured the booking system for availability. Once I'd checked in, I met Nathanial, an eighteen year old from Bromley (although criminally he didn't support Palace), a Welsh girl called Jade, who'd been backpacking for nearly three years without returning home or seeing family, and Lucy, a nurse from Guildford, who was having a gap from work before joining the London Air Ambulance Service.

That evening, the four of us went to play pool and were constantly harassed by offers to watch ping pong shows and asked to buy tat from desperate locals. As we walked along, we practically had to pass picket lines of sellers. The whole area was money driven and corrupt as the western tourists ignored the poverty thrown in their faces. In that way, it was not too dissimilar to the way that the Premier League carries out its business as lower league sides fall into administration. But when you're part of it, you just don't care.

The next morning, I woke to the sight of a bare naked, snoring, white bottom on the bunk bed opposite mine, and the sound of a shrieking little Thai lady who was angry at my laddish roommates for the excessive amount of noise they'd created the night before. Most of the day was spent on the beach, but I also spent a considerable amount of time enquiring as to which bars would be showing Crystal Palace vs Aston Villa that evening. I needn't have bothered. On the main strip, there was an 'Aussie Bar' that showed 'Every EPL game'. That'll do!

In the evening, Lucy and I sat on the main strip of bars drinking beers as we observed the mobs of British tourists getting rowdy, and the ladyboys dancing up and down the street. Inevitably, the Magaluff comparisons were easy, like most of the girls in the area. The strip was lined with bars playing the same crap music, offering the same drinks deals and semi-naked dancers on the bars. I would love to take the moral high ground and question the motives of people travelling half way around the world to find what they could see in Blackpool, but what was my main motive for the evening? To watch Crystal Palace.

After a while, we went to a second bar, which although similar to the first, had the novelty of housing a shark in it. However, at 1:30am, disaster struck. Lucy decided that staying up any longer was not a priority and she wasn't going to watch the game with me. I couldn't believe the rudeness. I'd just met this girl and she deemed sleep more important than watching Crystal Palace play on TV at three in the morning. I still had an hour and half until kick off and I now had no company.

I must admit, I did consider not watching the game. However, after the disappointment of not seeing the Swansea match, I decided to stay out alone, despite the rain that had begun to fall. Besides that, Villa hadn't won in nine and were one of the few teams in the league who were even worse than us. In fact, they'd only scored three goals in that time too. Surely we were favourites? The first place I headed to was the Aussie Bar. You know, the one that claimed to show 'Every Premier League game live'. Well, they were only showing the Manchester United and Liverpool games, despite there being six Premier League matches that evening.

Inevitably, having had a few beers, and feeling a sense of injustice, I got into an argument with the bar manager as he refused to change one of the many screens to show the Palace match. Even though no one was actually watching the other games. Luckily, Palace's tradition of kicking off at 8pm UK time instead of 7:45 allowed me an extra fifteen minutes to find the game.

The second bar I went into agreed to change the channel if I purchased a drink, which was fair enough. Unfortunately, I realised that I was out of cash. With just a couple of minutes to go until kick off, I sprinted back through the rain to my hostel to get some more Baht from my locker. When I returned, true to our words, I bought a beer and the girl behind the bar switched the screen to show Crystal Palace against Aston Villa. There I was, in an empty bar, at 3am, in South Thailand, watching my beloved team alone. It goes against everything I enjoy about football: the social element, the togetherness, and the tribal traits. It was a show of pure commitment and addiction. I couldn't face missing it.

I watched the half surrounded by ladyboys, bemused bar girls, possibly prostitutes, and repetitive chart music booming around the otherwise empty bar. Such is the prevelance of working girls in South East Asia that it became hard not to be skeptical of any native female who spoke to me.

The half itself was frustrating. Palace were the better team, although mainly because Villa were so dreadful. We'd huffed and puffed against a weary and thoughtless opponent, but it was my beloved Palace who went into the break behind. Scott Dann, our usually reliable defender, who was reportedly being watched by the England manager, Roy Hodgson, made a horrendous error where he decided to keep the ball in play to avoid giving away a throw in on the half way line. Sadly, while he saved us from conceding a harmless throw in, he gifted possession to Villa's star-man, Christian Benteke, who duly ran through on goal and scored. Thankfully, in those grotty surroundings, I'm sure my early hours, drunken language wasn't anything new to the bemused bar girls who sat and watched me rage.

Unfortunately, the bar staff soon realised that keeping the bar open purely for me was unlikely to be hailed as a leading business model and at half time, I was asked to leave so that they could close.

Still, I didn't consider it a problem. Although many were shut as it was now nearly 4am, plenty of bars were still open. Avoiding the ladies who were physically grabbing me in the street, I simply nipped over to the bar next door, where I was directed to the DJ (and TV controller). As he spun his decks, he raised the TV remote control above his head and whizzed through every channel, stopping at various points for me to examine the teams on show. Regrettably, not one channel owned by the bar showed Selhurst Park and off I trudged to find the game elsewhere.

Undeterred, I passed a couple of bars with their shutters down as I did my best Yannick Bolasie impression: ducking, turning, shimmying and weaving my way past opponents – working girls blocking my route to find Palace in this case, rather than hapless full backs trying to stop our winger. Quickly enough, I found another open bar – complete with TV screens, chart music and half naked girls dancing on the bar. Once again, I was thwarted as the British owner refused to change the channel from the United or Liverpool games.

After my latest refusal, I rushed out into the street once more, conscious that back in South London the players would have nearly finished their half time oranges and to their relief, Warnock's northern drones would be all but over. With time running out, I began to get firmer and grumpier to the many generous offers I was receiving.

"No thank you," turned to *"No, I don't want to go for a f***ing 'good sexy time'!"*

Soon, I found yet another bar with TVs, showing the football. I pleaded with them to change it over. I couldn't bear the thought of leaving a Palace game half watched. Villa had been atrocious. I was sure we were going to get back into it. Not watching it wasn't an option.

"We change channel if you buy me drink!" came the answer from behind the bar, without even the smallest hint of a cheeky smile.

"Fine!" came my frantic reply.

"...and you buy all my friends a drink too..." she added, pointing at her fellow bar staff, sensing the desperation in my answer.

"Yes whatever! Just look for the game!"

She went to find the remote control, via a quick and excited giggle with her colleagues, before she began to flick through the channels.

"This one..." *"No!"*

"This one..." *"No!"*

"This one..." *"No!"*

"This one..." *"No!"*

"This one..." *"No!"*

Then I was interrupted. Someone tugged my arm and I instantly turned to see who. I was met with a smile and a familiar question.

"Hey, where you from handsome?" (Well, it was familiar in Phuket, if not in London or Sydney!)

"I JUST WANT TO WATCH THE BLOODY FOOTBALL!" I replied and turned back to the screen.

"This one..." *"No!"*

"This one..." *"No!"*

Each time, my repeated answer became a little slower and a little more depressed as the realisation came to me that not only had the second half kicked off, but it was unlikely that I'd find anywhere to watch it. I don't know who was more gutted. Myself or the bar staff. They'd lost their free drink.

The bar next door was showing football too but as the bar staff wore a Manchester United shirt and very little else, I decided that it was unlikely to be a successful destination. Finally, I began to accept my fate and that staying up until 4am had been fruitless; I'd have to follow the second half on twitter at the hostel – in the dark and alone.

As I returned back to my bed disappointed, I noticed a small, seedy looking bar, fronted by two nearly naked Asian ladies and decided make one last attempt. I asked the bouncer if they'd change the channel and he assured me that they would for any paying customer. Excellent! I'd finally made it. I went to the bar and was told to sit down. Once I was seen to, I bought an expensive half pint, much to the annoyance of the waitress who tried to insist on me having a full pint. However, I really wasn't in a drinking mood but was more than happy to buy a beer in exchange for the game.

Sure enough, I asked at the bar and a man was summoned to change the channel. My persistence was rewarded. In all their glory, five minutes into the second half, red and blue shirts flashed up on the screen. I had my Palace fix. Right, now for the points I thought. Then something hit me. I realised something. I'm not sure what I saw first or whether it was the combination of a few things: the posters, the bouncers, the girls, the side doors or the hidden rooms. Whatever it was, it quickly became apparent that I was watching Crystal Palace vs Aston Villa, at 5am, in Thailand, in a brothel.

"Hi, where are you from handsome?" enquired one girl while stroking my arm, less than a minute after my drink had been delivered.

I glanced over towards the bouncer and then back at the screen in front of me. My quick and rude dismissal from earlier wouldn't do here. Not if I wanted to carry on watching Palace.

"London," I replied, not taking my eyes of the screen. *"I'm cheering my team from London, Crystal Palace!"*

I sussed that as well as trying to hint that I wasn't interested in paying for sex, I might as well try and convert a Thai prostitute to my addiction.

"Ah we cheer them together!"

Maybe my plan was working.

On the pitch, Palace's attempts to break down a flimsy Villa defense were no more successful than girl's attempt to break down mine. After sitting next to me for a couple of minutes and trying to engage in football related conversation, while I largely ignored her in favour of tutting and sighing at the collapse of the Palace attacks, she upped and left. What was upsetting was that Villa were actually playing appallingly. They weren't organized at all, and they continued to give us the ball on the edge of their area, but we didn't create a single clear chance. We were clueless.

My lack of interest in the continuing stream of girls seemed to only increase their determination as I appeared to be some sort of challenge to them. Making sure that I was always polite to the working girls as the bouncers looked on, my frustrations and anger at the football began to boil over. Considering I was in a brothel, perhaps it was appropriate that my favourite word appeared to be 'f***ing'. With my new favourite adjective usually being followed by 'useless' or 'pathetic' or 'Palace' or 'Warnock'. Mainly Warnock.

The game dragged on, as did the propositions. Usually, when you're chasing a game desperately, time seems to vanish as the opponents eat up precious seconds and the match slips away from you. However, that night, such was my confidence that we could play for a month and not score, time seemed to pass ever so painfully slowly. We created nothing and Warnock's lack of subs was as baffling as his appointment had been. He just watched on hopelessly as we created nothing against a woeful Aston Villa side. Still, I'm sure he blamed the referee. It couldn't possibly be Neil Warnock's fault that we had one win in eight. There was to be no happy ending that night.

Around five am, I got back to the hostel after our 1-0 home defeat. The next morning, I left for Koh Tao to do some scuba diving.

Crystal Palace...0 Aston Villa...1
Selhurst Park, 2/12/14
Premier League

Palace: Julian Speroni, Martin Kelly (Jason Puncheon 89), Scott Dann, Brede Hangeland, Joel Ward, Mile Jedinak, James McArthur, Yannick Bolasie, Wilfried Zaha, Marouane Chamakh, Dwight Gayle (Fraizer Campbell 46).
Subs Not Used: Wayne Hennessey, Zeki Fryers, Barry Bannan. Jerome Boateng, Jerome Thomas.

Aston Villa: Guzan, Hutton, Clark, Okore, Cissokho, Cleverley (Richardson 89), Westwood, Cole (Sanchez 8), Weimann, Agbonlahor, Benteke.
Subs Not Used: Given, Herd, Lowton, N'Zogbia, Grealish.

Chapter 25 - Over Land and Sea – *Koh Tao, (Thailand) 4th-7th December 2014*

I've been fairly lucky with my away game travels. Many years ago, I went to Plymouth for a game that was frozen off, but as I was staying with a friend for the weekend, it didn't feel quite as frustrating. Twice I've had trains back from Cardiff delayed for over an hour – once because of kids playing up and once because of Crawley fans smoking in the train's toilet. I've had a pretty horrendous midweek return from Villa Park and a six hour journey to Leicester. But overall, I've not had too many horror stories. I even managed to avoid the sixteen hour return trip for a game cancelled at Goodison Park by dropping out at the last minute.

Yet there are many retold tales of cancelled coaches, mad motorway dashes, missed trains, frantic phone calls and financial blunders in the name of addiction to football. However, none of my journeys for Palace could compare with or prepare me for my 290km - but eighteen hour - journey from Phuket to the island of Koh Tao, where I intended to do an Open Water Scuba Diving course. Despite many travel agents, well men at the side of the road, offering me a similar deal, I'd opted to book the trip through my hostel for a hefty 1000baht (£20ish)

It started easily enough. After a rice-based breakfast with Lucy in one of the few places that was open (presumably most places didn't bother to open before mid day as everyone was too hung over to get up), I was collected from my hostel by a minibus at around 11am. The non-English speaking drivers sped around the back streets of Phuket collecting other backpackers with bags similarly oversized to my own. There was one main concern though. As pure courtesy dictated that I introduced myself to my fellow passengers, I noticed that no one else was heading to Koh Tao. In fact, most of them seemed to be heading to Krabi. While my geography of Thailand is sketchy, I immediately noted that this was in the opposite direction to where I wanted to go, which is never ideal.

All I could do was ask the driver *"Koh Tao?"*, while offering a slightly confused face with a small dose of panic creeping in and when that didn't work, I simply used the traditionally ignorant 'Brit Abroad' next step. I repeated it: louder and slower. He gave me a rather unconvincing thumbs up in reply – prompting the Scottish guy next to me to enquire *"Krabi?"*, with the same mystified and ignorant undertones as my own enquiries. Similarly, he too received a thumbs up, resulting in minimal reassurance or comfort for either of us.

Without an option to leave, or a willingness to give up on my 1000 baht and doing my best Ashley Young impression by diving out of the minibus, we were forced to grin and hope. I mean, we were in a minivan claiming to go in two completely opposite directions with a non-English speaking driver. What's the worst that could happen? I doubted anything could be as bad as Palace were the night before.

Once we got onto a road that was as close to a motorway as Thailand has to offer, we mysteriously pulled over. Time passed as the bemused passengers tried to detect a reason for our halt. Eventually, an unfamiliar female Asian head poked its way into the mini bus and quizzed *"Koh Tao?"* As instinctively as Clinton Morrison in the six yard box, I grabbed my bags and followed. I was led to an empty minivan, where my bags were loaded into the boot, while the original van pulled off and disappeared into the distance. Once I was in, I waited. And waited. And waited. For about an hour the driver and I sat in silence at the side of the road. As fruitless as it was, at least I'd known what I was waiting for the night before when I watched on hopelessly for a Palace goal. Here, I had no idea.

Finally, a group of Scottish lads piled onto the bus and, such was their size, they literally filled it. While they weren't actually going to Koh Tao, their destination was in the right general direction of north east. In a style that was so cramped that I longed for a Kings Ferry Coach back from Burnley or Preston or some other northern hell hole, I spent three hours jammed up against the side window of the van. The service station offered little respite either. Well, the Asian equivalent of a service station anyway. It was a dusty car park with two or three fly-covered noodle and rice-based dishes being piled into a bowl at an overpriced rate. After opting for a tube of Pringles, which I discovered to be only half full when I opened them, we continued for a further three uncomfortable hours before the bus stopped again.

Using no more than the word 'off' and some exaggerated hand gestures, we were once again made to change transport with little or no explanation. By now, it was starting to get dark and as there was no sign of any phone signal, I had no idea where I was. We were greeted by a Thai couple, who were handed a wad of notes by our driver before he continued his onward journey. As for us, the Scots and I were left at an old, crumbling house with a small army of dogs making use of the large empty spaces around it. Our hosts, the middle aged couple who'd seemingly been paid to receive us, could just about communicate that we would be picked up from there and taken on to our next destination. Although, they estimated a two hour wait for the others and five for me.

However, to my surprise, a mere hour of growling dogs later, I was collected by a rather large man with a truck. While he seemed to be only able to state the word 'ferry', I was convinced he snarled *"Get in my van!"* with a Ray Winstone accent at one point. Ignoring the clear hesitation on my face, the Thai couple happily urged me into the back of the truck, where I sat on a seatbelt-less bench. As I tried to get my bearings and make sense of the situation, the owners of the shack handed over a, slightly smaller, wad of baht and cheerfully waved me off. There was more exchanging of money than agents handle in Premier League transfers. And it all seemed to be over me.

The truck set off in the dark; through a string of backstreets and sharp corners, throwing me from one side to the other, as I clung onto the wooden sides of the truck with one hand and my bags with the other. After about five minutes or so, we picked up an Irish girl and finally, eight hours into my journey, I'd found someone else who was going to Koh Tao. She worked on the island as a 'Free Dive' instructor, and held the Irish record for holding her breath underwater. Of course I was impressed with the achievement but I couldn't help wondering how much Irish free-diving competition there was.

Anyway, not only was she tremendously reassuring as she appeared to confirm that I was actually being taken to Koh Tao and not being sold into the Thai sex trade, she also gave me advice on dive centers and hostels for the island. A short drive later, we were deposited at the ferry, where once again, my driver handed over some notes to the men at the docks and left us to it. There, myself and the Irish girl waited for a couple of hours before our boat set sail. It might have only been a short time, but such was my tiredness and frustration at repeatedly having to wait throughout the day, that it felt as long as a Bob Dowie transfer saga.

After an exhausting day, I slept for the entire journey and only woke when the crew shook me into a state of consciousness as we arrived at five in the morning, eighteen hours after I'd set off from Phuket.

Upon arrival, I found a dive centre and hotel that I was happy with, before immediately beginning my course. Happily, I spent three brilliant days learning how to scuba dive and discovering a beautiful underwater world. Such was the intensity of the course and the exhaustion it caused, I didn't really think about Palace once. Although, as we waited on our boat for the 'Advanced Group' to finish their dive, I enjoyed chatting to a Belgian Anderlecht supporter. I loved the passion that he spoke about his club with. Any football fan can identify with that.

It was interesting that as they'd won Belgium league title for the previous three seasons, he said that both he and the club were prioritizing the Champions League this season, which was really affecting their home form. Unfortunately, it had all been to no avail anyway as they slid out of the Champions League group stages, despite credible draws away at Arsenal and Borussia Dortmund. However, unlike most English clubs, they were delighted to be allowed into the Europa League and be given some more European adventures.

I also admired that he had no more than a passing interest in the Premier League. He couldn't understand what all the fuss was about, preferring to focus on both his club and national Belgium side. Despite his lack of close attention to the league, he did know of Crystal Palace though. He didn't know our players, or manager, or ground, or badge, or mascot, or anything else about the club. He simply remembered one thing.
"Didn't you ruin Liverpool's title?"

After three long but magical days of diving, I received my certification and set about my next challenge: to find a bar showing Tottenham Hotspur vs Crystal Palace. It was only when I reflected on the fact that I hadn't thought about Palace or been frustrated over the Villa game or angry about Warnock or worried about losing or looked at the BBS once in three days that I actually realised we were playing Spurs that evening. With Tottenham being a reasonably big club (although I'd never admit this to my Spurs supporting brother) and the kick off time being a quite reasonable 10pm, I was fairly optimistic about finding the game. After dinner in a beautiful restaurant with Ken, the Belgium, and Tjimon, a Dutch guy from the course, where we listened to the gentle sound of the sea as we tucked into our selection of curry and rice dishes, we set off to find the match.

Enthusiastically, I led the way. Running parallel to the shore was a vine covered pathway through the palm trees that felt like it belonged in a fairy tale (hopefully one where Palace managed to beat Spurs away from home) and it was littered with bars either side. One of them had to show the game. Surely? The first bar we reached had a giant projector, but also had a sign next to it stating 'This is not for football'. Disgusted, I marched out and onwards to the next bar, followed by a slower and less marchy couple of Europeans.

The three of us strolled/marched down the beautiful ocean road, as I ignored the palm trees and beaches, focusing mainly on listening for the voice of Andy Townsend or Ray Wilkins to drown out the sound of softly breaking waves and lead me to a bar with the Palace game. Five or so minutes later, I heard what I was waiting for. As if I was a bird responding to a mating call (Do eagles make mating calls or is that just blackbirds?), I darted forward and into the venue, grinning as I saw the sign by the entrance stating 'Football Bar'. Unfortunately, despite my best protests, I was repeatedly told *"We show Arsenal"*. Well I wanted to watch a North London side, surely that's basically the same thing?

Once again, I led my uninterested companions along the fairy-tale-esque path towards the end of the rainbow, which would hopefully have a Palace game showing under it. Through my time on the island, I hadn't cared about football. I hadn't shown this side of me. I'd had a brief Anderlecht-centered conversation with Ken, but that was it. Tjimon had no interest in the beautiful game so I'd simply talked about other things. Was this a sign that I was growing up? I could actually have other interests and hold other conversations. Or was it simply a sign of my discontent with our club's leader? My irrational hated of Warnock. I'd always believed irrationality was an important part of being a football supporter, but I didn't like this. I simply felt empty. I felt like we had an outsider in the camp and I didn't feel comfortable in my own home (well, Palace). This irrationality wasn't breeding anger but an emotion far worse. Indifference.

However, as a football fan, something changes inside you at a certain point. I'd shown indifference for weeks now when we weren't playing, but come match day, as with the Villa game, which had taught me absolutely nothing, I had another irrational thought. It was nothing to do with Warnock. It was a deep need to watch the game. To be as close to my Palace as possible. I don't think that will ever leave me. It was 2:45pm on a Saturday (9:45pm local time) and I was desperate to find it. Even if we were certain to lose. Again.

The next bar wasn't far away and hosted a giant screen next to an enormous swimming pool. I quite fancied watching the game while bathing. I've never seen a Palace game in my swim suit before. Although, I have stood at a match in front of a group of guys dressed in lifeguard outfits for some reason. Maybe they'd heard ahead of my football pool party plan and had simply got the wrong game?

Once I was in the bar but not yet in the pool, I changed tack and asked if they'd show the 'Tottenham game', which considering I was the only person in there, and was promising two (less interested but equally happy to buy beer) customers, who were following me at a much more holiday-like pace, seemed a reasonable request.

"Liverpool. Just Liverpool!" I was told.

My flippancy ensured that I enquired if they'd show Stoke City (who the scousers were playing against that night) but I was given the same short, sharp response.

"Liverpool. Just Liverpool!"

As there appeared to be an empty bar for Arsenal and an empty bar for Liverpool, I did wonder if there was a Crystal Palace bar. Maybe that's why the others were so sparsely populated?

Anyway, as soon as the other two arrived, I was already waving them on to the next bar. It had spectacular views and a gorgeous garden, where live music was creating a busy and fun atmosphere, but it contained not even the slightest hint of Palace so we walked on by.

A couple of minutes later, I saw another screen. Once again, Liverpool were being shown... and Arsenal this time, but then, in the far dingy corner, I saw a glimpse of red and blue - I ran in. One minute and two seconds had gone and the score was 0-0 but I'd found it. Sure, I'd ignored a range of lively and beautiful bars for a dingy, male dominated hang out that could have been anywhere in the world, but so what? I could watch Palace take on Spurs. I just had to hope that the island didn't experience one of its regular power cuts during the next ninety minutes.

Ken, who'd declared that he wanted Tottenham to win thanks to their Belgian contingent, went to the bar and ordered our customary terrible Asian lager, while I tried to explain the match to Tjimon. I realised that if I thought I'd taken my eye off the ball with Palace, it was nothing compared to my ignorance to the wider ramifications of the league. I genuinely had no idea how Spurs were doing.

Upon finding the game, I sent a message to my Palace WhatsApp group showing my discovery. Dan responded with a picture of his Battersea living room showing a stream of the match, and Pavel, rather too smugly, sent a picture from the ground. It wasn't quite the usual camaraderie of an away game, but we were all showing our commitment to the cause and a desire to be part of the match in our own little way. While they (unlike me) hadn't quite done it literally, it felt like we'd all gone over land and sea to follow Palace.

Then suddenly, I heard it. I familiar cry. I'd been wrong. The sound of a background crowd and familiar commentators weren't my mating call. Something else was. Something that makes me drop my shopping and turn in the street. Something that deep-rooted instincts insist I repeat upon hearing. Something that makes me search out the origins of and gives me an instant interest in the source of. Something that impresses me and makes me buzz with excitement. Something that announces my arrival in far away towns. *"EAGLESSSSSSSSSSSSS!"* was screamed out across the bar. And not by me! I repeated the call and we gracefully flew towards our fellow species. There and then, the pair of us declared the opening of the first meeting of the Koh Tao Crystal Palace Supporters' Club.

And Palace rose to such a momentous occasion. It was almost like news had reached North London and the players were determined to put on a show. We went for the throat and attacked Spurs from the off with Bolasie and Zaha showing exactly why we rate the pair of them so highly. Our hosts couldn't cope. One piece of skill from Yannick was so sublime that it earned him his own move on the next FIFA game. People all over the world can now train their fingers to select the correct button combination and recreate a moment of sheer brilliance that is now known as 'The Bolasie Flick' – which a little bit of research has informed me is a '5/5 star trick'. Even after watching it multiple times, I still have no idea how he did it. With his back to two defenders, he spun one hundred and eighty degrees and as he did, he flicked the ball up his shin and past the bemused defense. From there, he charged into the area and but for a bit a bit of composure from Joe Ledley, who fired over, would have got one of the greatest assists of all time.

During the brilliant but goalless first half, I did turn to a fairly bored looking Tjiman and say *"I bet you didn't expect your Asia trip to take you to a crap bar, with only men inside, to watch Crystal Palace?"*
I was right, he didn't.

Once the half came to a close and I began to allow myself to actually communicate with those around me, I had a genuine first. I had a thoroughly enjoyable and intellectual, if a little bit politely insulting, conversation with a Millwall fan. To be honest, such was my enjoyment, I even considered ignoring my instinct of calling the local zoo to inform them of the escapee.

I also chatted in depth to a Burnley fan. We had a lot in common to be honest. We both empathised with the near impossible task of survival thanks to the financial imbalance of the league, but we also both enjoyed being Premier League underdogs and didn't fear going down. Another shared passion was our mutual hated of Warnock. Genuinely, I felt sorry for him as the pub wouldn't show QPR play against his beloved Burnley, which left me even more relieved that we were playing one of the bigger sides in the league that day. Gosh, I can't believe I just wrote that about Tottenham. Rather unhelpfully, I suggested to the Burnley fan that should have gone to Malaysia where Tony Fernandes' involvement in QPR had made them disproportionately popular. The pair of us genuinely wished each other good luck for the season, despite being direct rivals for relegation at the time, with Burnley slightly ahead of Palace in the league. Although, he did say that he wouldn't have been able to bring himself to say that if I'd tried to stand up for the 'Vile Warnock'. His words, not mine.

As Palace played bloody well but couldn't score, news of both Brighton and Millwall getting trashed came through (5-1 and 3-0 at Derby and Middleborough respectively). Not even this turned discussions sour with the pleasant Millwall chap.

Back in our game, Jason Puncheon had a late goal correctly ruled out for offside and the game finished 0-0. However, it had been an entertaining match and we'd played well. It was also the start of a run that I hoped would last many years: Palace had never lost a game while I was a certified diver. Although, it did also continue my run that we'd never won while I was in Thailand!

But there was something that was more important to me than daft and meaningless personal statistics that I like to over exaggerate the importance of. I'd been in excellent company throughout, from both football devotees like myself and avoiders like Tjimon. I also noticed that a mixture of a cut down in the amount of alcohol that I was used to, and having thin blood from the diving, meant that I went to bed merry in more ways than one that evening, despite only having three beers. My last night on Koh Tao had been the perfect celebration of completing my course for a number of reasons: Palace's players had redeemed themselves for the previous Tuesday, I'd had a thoroughly enjoyable time with the friends I'd made on my course and I'd met some fellow football addicts. Not even a Millwall fan couldn't ruin that.

Tottenham...0 Crystal Palace...0
White Hart Lane, 6/12/14
Premier League

Tottenham: Lloris, Dier, Vertonghen, Fazio, Davies, Bentelab, Mason (Paulinho 65), Eriksen, Lamela (Chadli 46), Kane, Soldado (Lennon 82).
Subs Not Used Vorm, Rose, Kaboul, Stambouli.
Palace: Julian Speroni, Martin Kelly, Scott Dann, Brede Hangeland, Joel Ward, Yannick Bolasie, Mile Jedinak, Joe Ledley, James McArthur, Wilfried Zaha (Jason Puncheon 65), Marouane Chamakh.
Subs Not Used: Wayne Hennessey, Damian Delaney, Barry Bannan, Jerome Thomas, Dwight Gayle, Fraizer Campbell.

Chapter 26 – Bangkok – *8th-10th December 2014*

After a seafood brunch and a long final walk around the beautiful island of Koh Tao, I got a rather choppy boat back to mainland Thailand. Upon arrival, myself and the other passengers were herded into a port where we had to wait for two hours before continuing on with our journey. When our 'bus' (well, cage on the back of a lorry) arrived, twenty of us piled into the back and squeezed onto two long benches as tightly as cattle being taken to market. Once again, I had to weigh up the morality of being transported in this way. Animal rights protestors would be up in arms if Millwall supporters were carried in these conditions.

A short journey later, we were deposited at the side of a busy road and told to wait for our coaches. I felt like I'd been upgraded from the terrace at Luton to a private box at Wembley when I boarded my luxury 'VIP Bus'. I had a huge comfy chair, a soft foot rest and even a blanket to compensate for the ever chilling air conditioning. For the first time on any overnight trip, including my travel in Australia, I was able to sleep and sleep well.

However, I was rudely awoken when once again my coach arrived early. My journey had been advertised as arriving at 6:30am, which would have given me a decent amount of sleep, and a full day in my destination, but it actually arrived at 3:45am, meaning that I needed to find a hotel room in the middle of the night. Sleepily forcing my tired eyes to stay open and dragging my bags behind me, I made my way to my next destination: Khao San Road, Bangkok.

Khao San Road was dirty and full of tacky bars – just like a small Patong Beach. Along the pavement there were scrawny stray cats chasing rats the size of rugby balls. Tourists were having massages by the side of the road, which was still fairly busy with party-makers trying to pick up a late night partner, as others spewed out the alcohol that their bodies couldn't consume, adding to the filth and rat food on the floor. However, even spewing or being in a massage chair or any other late night occupation wasn't enough to put off the locals who were trying to sell their tat.

Eventually, I found a hostel. On the door there was a sign that read 'I'm toilet, back soom'. After waiting at the entrance for a few minutes with no return coming any time 'soom', I decided to look elsewhere. Feeling the inevitable tiredness that comes at 4am, I quickly found a cheap room for 200 baht (roughly £4) so I could get some sleep and reassess my accommodation options in the morning.

The next day, after discovering that Palace had been given a brilliant sounding FA Cup draw away at Dover, I checked out early and gave myself two objectives: find food and find a hostel where I could meet people to explore with. Food was the easy part, Khao San Road is full of cafes and bars serving various Asian dishes and eventually, I settled on a small café where I got a Thai Green Curry. I used my location as an excuse to indulge in such a breakfast. Just like I use a midday kick-back home as an excuse to start boozing at 11am.

However, I soon went off the place when I spotted a small part of the graffiti that covered the entire toilet walls. It read 'BHAFC'. I had to fix this if I was going to stay and eat in this establishment. I took a pen out of my backpack and wrote '...0 CPFC...2'. I suspect my editing added value to the property and it certainly improved the experience for anyone who needed to use the facilities in the future.

Content with my food and content with my vandalism, I moved on to find a hostel, which took a great deal more searching and sweat than I'd expected. When I did find one, I met an eighteen year old girl called Freya, who'd been teaching in Vietnam, and we immediately headed out to explore the city together.

The pair of us negotiated a price for a tuk-tuk to take us to the famous temples and giant bhuddas around the city. Provided we allowed for some 'extra' stops, we were told it would cost a mere 40 baht (80p).

"Are you English?" enquired our driver as we set off down the first bumpy road in his smoke chugging vehicle.

We politely nodded in response. By now, I'd been in Asia long enough to know what the next question would be.

"Who do you support?"

"Crystal Palace!" I replied.

"Me too!" he enthused back. Could it be? Had I found the beginnings of a Thai fan base? Was the local so mesmerised by Bolasie and co that he'd ignored the glamour clubs and plucked to love all things red and blue like myself? Had our former Thai youth player, Teeratep Winothai, not only been a football manager legend, but also condemned thousands of innocent Asians into loving our club? Or was the driver simply after a tip? The Liverpool badge on the back of his tuk-tuk suggested it was the later. As did his lack of knowledge on the club when I asked him who his favourite player was. I was crest-fallen. He may have been simply after a tip but that didn't give him the right to have built up my hopes, only to dash my dreams.

After getting the football club formalities out of the way, he began to tell us about the city and temples that we were visiting before he suddenly stopped at a tailor's shop and insisted that we went in to talk to the man. Freya and I did our best acting before politely declining all the offers we were made, which made the shop assistant rather sharply turn off the charm and tell us what he thought of English tourists in no uncertain terms. By the time that we reached the fourth tailor, the whole routine had become as boring as Peter Taylor's football and we finally understood why our temple tour had been so cheap. We weren't paying the drivers wages. The shops were buying our custom from him.

Once the T&T tour of tailors and temples was brought to a premature end as the driver said that he wanted food but the cynic in me says that he realised we weren't buying suits, the pair of us walked to a small temple before going to see the floating markets.

That evening Freya and I went to a rooftop bar in Khao San Road to have cocktails and the next morning she was gone. That's one of the downsides of travel. With everyone moving all over the place to try and squeeze as much in as possible, you don't necessarily get to know people properly before having to say goodbye.

The next day I went to see some more Wats (temples) and discovered a place of worship of my own – a pub in Asia selling decent beer. I'd found a Brewdog pub and vowed to return later in the day so that I could drink the Scottish beer in a fourth different continent (Sydney in Australasia, England in Europe, Sao Paulo in South America). I then made my way to the Vinanmek Palace and on my way I spotted the Thailand Education building, which had a giant picture of the king on the front. While I have no idea of the state of Thai education, I suspected the King couldn't be doing any worse than Michael Gove was back in England.

The building was highly impressive (as you'd expect from a Palace) and not even having to wear a sherong to cover my legs could put me off it. Inside, I marvelled at the thrones, crowns, artwork and jewellery of the royal family and I loved that the King owned 'Royal Elephants'. I imagined all the others bowing their trunks to the crown wearing creatures and wondered if elephants considered Wayne Rooney as a privileged or even royal elephant thanks to the money he owns for clumsily powering his way through opposition defences?

By the time that I'd finished wondering around the Palace, I was hot and ready for some refreshments so I decided to head back to the hostel and look for some companionship. The room was full but as can be the problem with a hostel, there was no one who I wanted to spend my evening with, so I decided to nip out to get some food. While enjoying some duck and rice, I began to chat to a guy called Michael, who'd been living in Kuala Lumpur.

One of my favourite things about football away days is that striking up a conversation is incredibly easy. The odds are that the Palace fan next to you in Preston or Barnsley is going to have enough of a common ground that you can fairly easily chat away. Backpacking offers the same principle. Although I probably wouldn't be best friends with Michael back home (nor him me), I could easily chat to him about my experiences in Asia as they compared with his. We started talking about KL and the rest of the conversation followed easily. Fairly quickly, we'd learned enough about each other to want to formulate a shared plan for the night.

First we went for a couple of Brewdog beers before jumping on the back of motorbikes to be taken to The Banyan Tree Hotel for a drink on the top of the 650feet high hotel. As we enjoyed a cool beer in the warm evening heat, we took in the stunning sunset across the city. From there, we went to get some street food and started to talk to a Swiss girl, who joined us as we went to Pat Tong – the red light area of Bangkok that does Ping-pong shows. Not wanting to fund the industry that sells many Thai, Cambodian and Vietnamese girls into a life of slavery, I waited with a drink in the downstairs-prostitute filled bar while the other two went to the show. The whole area, which was as packed as the Arthur Wait toilets at half time, made me sad. Thailand is a naturally beautiful country that shouldn't need that industry to entice English tourists.

However, sadly, that is the way of life in South East Asia. Girls from the countryside, or Cambodia and Vietnam, go to Bangkok for three to four years so they can send some mich needed money back home.

I spent the next day discovering the city in more detail. Unfortunately, thanks to a visit from the King, the Grand Palace, which looked absolutely stunning, was closed. In fact, dare I say it, from my view outside of the Palace's borders, it looked even more spectacular than my Palace: The Holmesdale Road stand at Selhurst Park. As I strolled around the walls of the Palace and watched on as the heavily armed security ensured a safe arrival for the country's leader, I began to think about Thaksin Shinawatra, the former owner of Manchester City and ousted Thai Prime Minister.

Despite originally being popular in the role and being re-elected as Prime Minister in 2005 by an overwhelming majority with the slogan 'Building Opportunities', his decision to not pay any taxes when he sold nearly two billion dollars worth of shares in his telecommunications corporation angered many important people within the country.

To be fair to him, I guess he went against the grain of most politicians and actually managed to deliver on his election promise. He did build an opportunity – for himself. However, even Harry Redkapp and his dog Rosie would have done well to avoid the guilty verdict of 'Abusing his Power' and the two year prison sentence that went with it.

Before the trial, Shinawatra had bought Manchester City for £81.6m in a move that could be cynically suggested as a publicity stunt for protection. Amazingly, he'd managed to pass the Premier League's 'fit and proper person' test for potential owners, despite effectively being on the run at the time. Still, clearly crime does pay because he has never served a day in prison as he lives in exile and he was allowed to sell the club for £200m, to go with the millions that he stole from the country he was elected to lead.

During my walk around the walls of the Palace, surrounded by poverty and desperation, I wondered if the current rulers of Thailand were just as corrupt, or if the embarrassing incident had ensured that laws on corruption and personal gain from those voted into power had been tightened.

Despite having mixed feelings about giving money to the Thai government in the form of an entrance fee, I couldn't help but be disappointed to miss out on seeing the Palace. From a young age I've struggled to cope with missing out on things. That's one of the reasons that I can't bear to miss a Palace game. Even when on the holiday of a lifetime on the other side of the world.

However, regardless of the Palace closure, I found so much more to see in Bangkok: the ministry of defence, which was surrounded by giant cannons appealing to my inner child, a locals' market, complete with stalls selling live turtles, snakes and fish, various small temples and I even managed to wonder into the middle of an extravagant private school while happily snapping away on my smart phone, before I realised what it was. I can only imagine the reaction of our hyperbole press and politically correct, scare mongering culture in England if a tourist was seen doing that. The school I'd taught at made national news as there was a rumour of an unidentified visitor.

On the way to the train station to leave, I stopped off at The Golden Mount Temple for another view of the sun setting over Bangkok for the final time as I was heading north to Chiang Mai. However, at the station, I was once again amazed at the passion of locals to their football. In Brazil, I'd found the stereotype of children playing the beautiful game wherever they could (with whatever they could find) to be fairly accurate. However, I'd started to notice more and more children playing football in the street in Thailand and Malaysia with the same youthful enthusiasm as anywhere else in the world. While they didn't have local heroes to look up to and emulate, the widespread access of the Premier League gave them the role models (in football terms if not morally) to aspire to. I'd begun to wonder if that one day, not too far off, these countries would start to produce players from poverty like they do in the football-mad South America.

At the station, I spotted another comparison. I'd been in Sao Paolo for the Chile vs Brazil World Cup match. With the official fan park already full, we searched cafes and bars to find somewhere that we could sit and watch the game. No matter where we went, the streets were crammed as hundreds of Brazilians huddled around windows to peer through and catch the game so they could cheer their country on. In Hua Lamphong Station, Bangkok, dozens of locals crowded around a giant screen to watch Thailand beat the Philippines 3-0 in the AFF Championship – a biannual competition between countries in South-East Asia.

While the numbers watching might have been smaller and the match held far less worldwide interest, the passion of the crowd and the desperation to watch of those huddled around was just the same. I loved it. The football was little above the Scottish lower leagues in terms of ability but as a Palace fan, who am I to judge others for watching crap football? I was delighted for the forty or so locals, who had that familiar glint in their eye that comes from watching your own beloved team win, to find out that Thailand went on to lift the trophy two weeks later.

Happy with the result, I boarded my train for the fourteen hour overnight journey north, which at least gave me some time to reflect. Before arriving in Bangkok I'd been very sceptical. I was worried it would be just like Patong with prostitution and binge drinking being offered, and very little else. At least the fixture list dictated that I wouldn't see another Palace defeat here! However, despite my first impressions, Bangkok had been a lot cleaner than I'd imagined, even if it was faster-paced and busier than my liking, with crossing the road becoming a game of Russian Roulette as motorbikes, tuk-tuks and cars whizz by with little regard for traffic lights or sign posts. Even green pedestrian lights.

I was beginning to think of travelling like going to an away game. As I'd grown up in Berkshire, I didn't have any Palace mates when I first joined the Palace away game trail, and would travel to matches alone. Over the last eight years, I've built up and army of acquaintances and friends who I now attend matches with. Around Asia, the travelling was the same. Although I started alone, I wasn't scared because I knew the main event would be good – the match on an away day or the sight-seeing while backpacking – but it's not that you go for. It's the people you meet, the stories you make, the journeys you have and the places you visit. This was turning into the greatest away trip ever.

Chapter 27 - The North Thailand Burnley Supporters Club – *Chiang Mai, (Thailand) 11th-14th December 2014*

I slept for ten of the fourteen hours on my overnight train to Chiang Mai, with the personal fan and small curtain by my cramped bed giving sufficient comfort to allow for a good night sleep. In the morning, I was able to fold up the bed and adapt it into a pair of chairs for myself and the Spanish girl who'd resided in the bunk below me.

Back in England, I'm more than used to trains – mainly from Palace away days – and have become familiar with all the main routes around the country. My favourite stretches of track are actually at different ends of England: along the Devon coastline between Exeter and Plymouth, and through the Lake District on the way to Carlisle. This trip reminded me of the latter. Of course, everything was a bit more extreme: the landscape, the distance, the vegetation and the wildlife. But there were similarities too, and not just that I was travelling from the capital to a town in the North West.

On the train, I reflected on the fact that I'd been surprised at how prominent the teams in Krabi and Phuket had been, especially as I later discovered that neither of them were top division sides. I'd also been impressed that Bangkok United merchandise had been readily available in the capital city. I love the idea of people supporting their local team. It's bad enough when people in the Home Counties ignore their local sides for the big clubs, without folk on the other side of the world doing it too.

I understand why Thai people support Manchester United or Liverpool or Real Madrid. I get that living in poverty, they must be in awe of the glamour and stardom of those teams and players, but surely they should support their roots too? Surely they should pop along to their local team to see if that one day, the exploding popularity of the sport will produce a superstar of their own. From their own modest streets in the way that happens time and time again in Brazil and Argentina.

As well as that, it would provide them with the ever burning hope that football fans from England allow to flicker and use to drive us to return week after week. The Premier League's research suggests that the popularity of the league in Asia is down to the crowd's vocal backing. Surely Asian supporters could take a leaf out of Western Sydney Wanderers' book and try to create an atmosphere to be proud of for themselves, despite the dreadful football. The Wanderers fans had set out with a dream two years previously and were now competing in the World Club Championship; one game away from facing Real Madrid. The few lucky fans that were able to travel to Morocco for it might get to see the global superstars in a uniquely special way – against their local no-hopers.

Anyway, the fact that Thai football was prominent enough to sell merchandise in the streets left me intrigued by football in the country I was visiting. I was disappointed to discover that it was the off season and no matches were taking place that weekend, or I'd have loved to have taken in a game in a new continent. I had hoped that the World Club Cup was in Asia again and I would have considering going to see the Wanderers if it had been feasible. But it wasn't. However, it did make me think about Thailand football fans. I wondered if there were any who followed their side around the country.

Bangkok to Chiang Mai is 690km each way and took 14 hours by train. That's quite a commitment – at least they can be thankful that Sky Sports won't move the games to a bloody Monday night. And besides, despite the length of journey, it would be a lot cheaper than following football in England (although perhaps not if you consider the comparative wages). The catering was better too. My train had a reasonably pleasant restaurant on board, rather than the usual under stocked and overpriced buffet carriage that resides on the English cross country routes. I've often wondered if there's a market for a 'Wetherspoons Carriage' back home?

While travelling north, I also thought about the results. I've had some particularly lively and boozy train journeys home from wins 'oop north – complete with me leading various songs about Palace, Brighton, Mullery, Cantona and Alan Lee – but I'm not sure even I could celebrate a win for the entirety of a fourteen hour journey home. Also, being a Palace fan, I had to consider the likelihood of having a fourteen hour slog after a terrible 1-0 loss. Drinking to forget the pain wouldn't be a problem, but still having a liver at the end of it might be.

Eventually, with my mind in a strange parallel universe of Thai football, we arrived at the final stop on the line: Chiang Mai. I loved the ancient city, surrounded by a wall built nearly 700 years ago to try and defend against Burma and armies of the Mongol Empire, which had conquered most of Yunnan in China. Having come from the craziness of Bangkok, I loved how calm and peaceful it was – thankfully the wall hadn't been required to defend enemy assaults for hundreds of years. Roughly the same time as the last Peter Taylor led team made a meaningful attack. But now, rather than worrying about war, the city now lived for yoga and finding an 'inner peace'.

The time I spent in Chiang Mai was relaxing if lonely. I found a cheap but comfy hostel to stay in and didn't really click with anyone there, so I mainly rested and explored alone. I wondered around the Buddhist temples of the city, taking in their splendour and in the evening, I went to the Night Bazaar, where local tradesmen came down from the mountains to sell their goods. Many stalls sold scarves and shirts for Chiang Mai FC as I once again let my mind wonder to the practicalities and popularity of football in the region. I also particularly enjoyed the array of rice and noodle dishes, as well as fresh fruit and juices available in the city's food market.

Local life was calm and simple, and I was happy to fit into that for a few days. However, with my mind rested, it allowed itself to wonder back to my first addiction far more frequently than it had done previously as I dashed around the country. I decided to have an extra day in Chiang Mai. As well as allowing me a period of rest, my research suggested that I was more likely to find the Palace vs Stoke City game in this quiet town than my next destination: Luang Prabang in Laos.

On my second day I went on an elephant tour, where I was horrified by the treatment of the animals, despite a clear improvement on the past. It was definitely something that would have been worth spending extra on as some of the more expensive places have taken on a role of being a sanctuary to boost their appeal to tourists. After the elephant trek, and various other activities such as sliding down waterfalls and white water rafting thrown into the day trip by the side of the road travel agent, I relaxed with a Thai massage, where an elderly little lady threw my body about and beat me up.

My battered body was dealt another blow when I returned to my hostel to discover that Western Sydney had lost the Quarter Final of the World Club Championship 3-1 to the Mexican side Cruz Azul. This was despite being 1-0 up in the 89th minute. Unfortunately, after holding out for most of the match, once they'd conceded one, the heavens opened in extra time. The Real Madrid dream was over.

Soon enough, it was Saturday night again, which for me didn't mean dancing like Whigfield, but it meant trying to find an obscure football match in an obscure location. My posts on the BBS had borne no fruit, and I was still none the wiser as to how to find the game. Enthusiastically, I went to the newer and livelier part of the city as I suspected the pretty but quiet and traditional old town wasn't a breeding ground for Premier League football.

My first port of call was a pub called The Red Lion. My internet research had informed me that this was the home of 'Clarets in Thailand' – the North Thailand Burnley Supporters group. I suspected that in order to be able to keep their website's promise of showing 'every Burnley FC match live' then they needed to have a range of TVs – as well as a subscription to a suitable sports channel. Apart from anything else, I quite liked the idea of a North Thailand Burnley Supporters Group.

When I arrived, I discovered a pub that was clearly British owned. Everything about it from the name, to the pub sign hanging outside, to the London Pride being served behind the bar reminded me of a traditional English old man's pub. There was a notice on the door listing the matches for that evening:

Burnley vs Southampton
Leicester vs Manchester City

It was a shame we were playing Stoke City really. We were due to face Manchester City a week later, which would have been far easier to locate. Despite the disappointment, I went in anyway and the Clarets in Thailand were easy enough to locate. Well, The Claret was anyway.

The group consisted of a single dedicated fan. It was a bloke in his 50s, whose years of excess beer showed on his enormous gut, but he came across as a knowledgeable and kind guy. He was with a Scottish friend, whose years of excess beer showed on his brain. He was older and skinny, speaking with a stutter and slur. Although he supported Glasgow Rangers, he had been to many games all over the UK but seemed to sit quietly in the main, listening to his opinionated Lancashire friend. However, he would suddenly burst out into random stories - some great, some dull. He reminisced about his love of watching West Ham in the 60s, and Scotland beating England (The World Champions) at Wembley in 1967. He talked about seeing Spurs draw 4-4 with West Ham, and watching Ipswich Town in Europe. I loved it. There was a genuine passion in his eye when he spoke, whatever the game was.

The three of us chatted all things football in the hour or so before the games. Outside of our beloved game and one-eyed passion for our own respective clubs, I had nothing in common with these two alcoholic expats, but I had great fun regardless. I like Burnley and their fans' attitude. The Claret of North Thailand said that he looked to Palace from the year before as an inspiration to stay up. He wanted his side to achieve, but saw the importance of not going for broke to stay in the league. He'd seen it all before with his club, and he couldn't believe his luck of living in a world where he could watch every Burnley game, live from the North of Thailand.

Before kickoff, he recommended a pub to me where I might find the Palace game so I bid the pair of them farewell and I went for my Saturday evening hunt. He'd directed me to an empty Irish pub with multiple screens and they agreed to show it, as long as I put 1000baht (£20) behind the bar as a 'spending insurance'. As well as guaranteeing me a screen for the game, it basically meant I could drink what I wanted at no extra cost. Twenty years of following Palace has taught me that the team (especially when managed by Warnock) were unlikely to display £20 worth of value so I was tempted to simply push the beer limit of my deposit and get lashed up (something that would be nearly impossible back in London for £20). However, sitting on my own in a pub in North Thailand, watching a screen with no sound, not even Palace could drive me to drink heavily.

The first thing I noticed about the match was the low sun over the main stand, which created a real glare on the cameras for the first ten minutes or so. In fact, I received three picture messages complaining about a similar issue from London: one from Dad, one fromfriend Dan at the game and also one from my mate Chris, who was having the same issue at Griffin Park. Quite why he felt the need to inform me, I don't know. Anyway, it was due to looking down at my phone to respond to those messages that meant I wasn't looking when James McArthur headed us 1-0 up just 11 minutes in. With no sound to grab my attention, it was only during a replay that I realised we'd scored and I let out my customary yelp of delight.

Unfortunately, thanks to the fact that I was watching a game that no one else within a 500 mile radius was likely to care about, I didn't have anyone to share my yelping and happiness with. Therefore, my grin and natural energy was being pushed into the buttons of my mobile phone to try and share the feeling with some of my friends back in South London. And it was for that reason that I missed the second goal of the match too. Stoke's equaliser.

Despite the exciting start, the rest of the game was drab, with neither team looking like scoring. After the dour 1-1 draw, I went back to see the Burnley supporter to find out their score, wish him well and thank him - I'd not have seen the game without his help. Mind you, maybe that would have been a blessing?

Burnley had won 1-0, putting them ahead of us in the league and prompting mixed emotions on my behalf. On one hand, I was genuinely chuffed for my new found friend. He'd been welcoming and helpful without need, allowing us to bond over a shared passion and international language. Football. In many ways, I wished I'd stayed in his pub and watched his game. At least I wouldn't have needed to spend most of the match on my mobile phone in order to share and discuss it. However, on the other hand, Burnley's good form, despite being favourites for relegation, had put even more pressure on us.

What was more important to me? Being able to talk about football and use it as a vehicle to meet people and share our love, or Palace actually winning on the pitch. That evening, with me in a faraway city where I had limited companionship, it was certainly the former. The isolated experience made me resolve to try and watch the Manchester City game the following week with some good company, even though the thought did occur to me that the match would be better for Palace without Kompany, the City defender. Although, the whole evening did make me wonder that if there was a Chiang Mai Burnley Supporters Club, why hadn't anyone set up a Crystal Palace one?

That way I could have enjoyed the terrible game with my second family: My football club. I realised it wasn't Palace who'd ruined the night; it was loneliness. A horrible emotion, but an emotion that has been cured by Palace many times before. Being a football supporter, particularly of a less popular team, is a binding thing. A bind that's created dozens of friendships for me, introduced me to hundreds of people and initiated thousands of conversations.

Us Brits have a reputation for being miserable and avoiding communication with strangers (Just look at the tube – or don't look as that could create an awkward eye contact that we all aspire to avoid) but no one can tell me that football fans avoid that bizarre form of socialising with strangers. No, as football fans, we thrive on it.

Crystal Palace...1 Stoke City...1
Selhurst Park, 13/12/14
Premier League

Palace: Julian Speroni, Martin Kelly, Brede Hangeland, Scott Dann, Joel Ward, Mile Jedinak, James McArthur (Barry Bannan 85), Joe Ledley, Yannick Bolasie, Wilfried Zaha (Jason Puncheon 60), Marouane Chamakh (Dwight Gayle 77).
Subs not used: Wayne Hennessey, Damian Delaney, Jerome Thomas, Fraizer Campbell.

Stoke: Begovic, Bardsley, Shawcross, Cameron, Pieters, N'Zonzi, Wilson, Diouf, Bojan (Arnautovic 54), Walters, Crouch.
Subs not used: Butland, Huth, Whelan, Adam, Assaidi, Ireland.

Chapter 28 - The Power of Football – *Luang Prabang, (Laos) 14th-17th December 2014*

The next morning I was on the move again. I'd researched getting a boat from Chaing Mai to Luang Prabang in Laos, but as much as I liked the idea of sailing to a new country, the reality was that it would have meant spending nearly three days in horrendously uncomfortable conditions with too many people crammed into a tiny boat, atrocious toilet facilities and limited eating opportunities. As I didn't want to recreate an Asian version of the Arthur Wait concourse during half time, as well as live there for 48 hours, I opted to take the short one hour flight. As well as saving me time and comfort, it also allowed me to discover a Leicester City club shop at the airport as their Thai owners looked to boost their brand.

Flying into Laos over the stunning mountains was a beautiful experience. I wanted to compare the bumpy up and down landscape to Palace's fortunes but the truth was that they were closer to Chelsea's or Liverpool's: lots of peaks in a staggeringly close proximity to each other. We'd be happy with a lonely mountain of success. Although, it did feel a bit more like a Palace rollercoaster as the bumpy plane got lower and lower without any sign of civilization, let alone an airport. We appeared to be descending fast towards untouched marshland. I've never been so relieved to spot a runway when it floated into view at the last minute to save us as if it were Tony Pulis appearing to avoid a disastrous drop. Nothing spectacular, but enough to save us.

In Laos, I was keen to tick off the main attractions of the area as soon as possible. Wanting to move on from my lonely experience in Chaing Mai, I'd decided to research a livelier hostel to ensure plenty of opportunities to share my experience with fellow backpackers. After checking in, I headed straight to the Kuang Si Falls with some people from the hostel: a Swiss guy and an American girl. The falls were as spectacular as some of Ashley Young's. Dramatic drops were interspersed with bright blue pools of fresh, sparkling water for swimming. Although the freezing temperature of the pools made the reality slightly less appealing than the appearance had originally suggested.

Later on, I had another first experience. I went on the back of a motorbike. Adam, an Englishman from the hostel offered to take me out to explore the area. On the whole, I felt safe and excited but a trip down a bumpy dirt track to see a second set of waterfalls reminded me of watching Palace play. My destiny was in someone else's hands. Just like the players control and determine my health and emotion on a Saturday afternoon - or evening when I'm on the other side of the world. Both experiences are terrifying, bumpy and horrible to watch, as you race across rocky ground. You know that anything could happen at any moment to seriously hurt you, but you can do little more than clench your fist, grit your teeth, watch on and hope – while your stomach does somersaults

That evening, after climbing to the top of the hill in the town centre to visit Wat Chom Si for the sun set, I headed to the town's market for some street food with a group from the hostel. We then moved on to bizarre but trendy outdoor bar that would have fitted in nicely in the 'hipster' parts of East London. Only the warm weather reminded me that I was in fact on the other side of the world. Eutopia, the bar by night and meditation centre by day, was little more than a wooden shelter with mats on the floor to sit on. However, it had motorcycles stuck to the ceiling and poles around the edge of the cover, boasted a stunning view of the Mekong River and had an enormous garden filled with palm trees. Maybe you wouldn't get that in East London?

The night was a happy one. Our group had come together with no history or previous friendship and included as many nationalities as an Arsenal team sheet (English, Austrian, Swedish, Canadian, French, American, German, Dutch, Polish, and Australian). However, just as sharing similar experiences with football fans leads me to think of strangers as friends, sharing travelling tales built a bond for the night. The 95p beers probably played a part too.

Unfortunately, it drew to a close all too quickly as Laos enforces strict drinking laws insisting that bars are closed at 11pm. Outside the bar, we were approached by multiple taxi (well, tuk tuk) drivers, who offered to take us to the bowling alley. As the out-of-town lanes are an 'entertainment venue' and not a bar, it's allowed to stay open late, while still serving beer. Myself, Adam, my motorbike acquaintance, and two Canadian girls decided to use this excuse to a have a competitive drunken bowling match and continue our boozing.

At the bowling alley, a group of tourists in the lane next to us took great delight in giving me a congratulatory high five after one of my less-beer affected throws got me a strike.

"English?" they enquired, as they pointed at me. The lack of surrounding words to the question suggested that they had about as much command of our language as I had of theirs. I nodded.

"Chinese?" I returned the 'question'. They nodded.

"Manchester?" was their next enthusiastic enquiry. Based on my previous Asian experiences, the second question was usually about which football team I support, rather than my geographical location within my homeland.

I shook my head vigorously. *"No! No! No!"* They may have been asking an innocent question but I couldn't let them believe that I supported Manchester United. This was bigger than them simply finding out who I supported. This was about giving them an education. An education into English football culture.

In Asia, they'd probably never met anyone who didn't support 'Manchester' or 'Real Madrid', but in England it's different. We have thousands of supporters turning up to watch games at every level, every week. Supporting a football team for us isn't about winning or glory; it's about passion and pride. It's about our dedication and addiction. It's more than a hobby. It's a way of life. And for many of us, that means supporting a loser. Something most countries can't understand.

With that in mind, I proudly professed *"CRYSTAL PALACE!"*
Then something strange happened. They didn't look confused. Despite the fact that it was now established that we shared about seven mutual words, they said two that transported me to a happy place. To Selhurst Park. To memories of getting a name printed on the back of my shirt as a kid. To memories of singing with Bolton Wanderers fans while watching Palace at West Brom. To memories of a red card at Loftus road, late night TV coverage, missed penalties vs Nottingham Forest and the 2002 World Cup.

It might not have played such a huge role as it had in mine, but Crystal Palace Football Club had made a small impact on the childhood of these Chinese guys in front of me.

"Ah Crystal Palace... Zhiyi Fan!"
The former Chinese Captain and Palace defender/striker might not have turned us into the immediate super power that Mark Goldberg had intended, but it had clearly increased awareness of our club in the Far East.

Fan Zhiyi and his eighty-eight appearances for Palace allowed us to understand each other, communicate and bond. We laughed, smiled, enjoyed and respected one and other. All in the name of one Chinese footballer. They burst into a song. Obviously, I knew none of the words (what with it being in Chinese and all) but I shouted the two I knew. Zhiyi Fan. This footballer, who was relatively unknown to most of the western world, had been a hero of my childhood and a hero to these guys too. Nearly eight thousand kilometers away. Soon, three adults, or as close as men can get to being adults, were linked in arms, jumping and singing about a fairly average Chinese footballer, who'd once played for my team. And that, is the power of football.

Russell Parker, Palace fan in Namibia

Since promotion to the Premier league in 2013, I have seen just about every Palace game here on TV and 90% of those were live. We have a South African satellite company called DSTV which shows up to five/six live premier league games every Saturday and Sunday.

Pre-promotion was a different story, the odd Championship game was shown live and there was a highlights programme once a week, which was the best you could hope for.

When I lived in Namibia in the mid 90s, my next door neighbour, who worked with me on a contract, was and still is a Palace fan. On two occasions, such was our feeling of being cut off from the club, we were drinking in our local bar on a Thursday night and decided to go back and watch Palace for the weekend. We flew from Namibia on the Friday night, landed at Heathrow on Saturday morning, hit the pub and then the game. At full time, we headed straight back to Heathrow, and were back in our local in Namibia on Sunday evening. We did that twice and in true Palace style, lost both games.

My other story from those days was the play off Final against Sheffield United, when the game was shown on TV here, but five hours late so we had to do the 'Likely Lads' approach and keep away from the result.

Our usual pre-match routine (I say 'our' because the whole family of four are all Palace fans) is fairly straightforward. I coach football here in Namibia as well as my day job, so we usually have league games on Saturday mornings. After that, it's back home for a pre-match beer and on with the shirts to watch the game.

However, there is one more tradition in the Parker household and that is called 'Clarence time'

We have a labrador called Clarence, and if Palace are holding on for a draw or win with ten minutes to go, I walk the dog. I even get text messages from friends at the game in the UK telling me it's now 'Clarence time!' It all started in the play-off semi final away to Brighton when we went one nil up and I couldn't stand the pressure so eventually I took the dog for a walk, only for my son to call me when Wilf scored the second. The poor dog had the shortest walk in history and I turned round and went straight home.

In terms of other Palace fans in Namibia, I am sorry to say that the Parker family is it, now that my neighbour has long been back in the UK. Local interest in Palace has obviously improved after promotion and I regularly get comments about my CPFC car registration plate. Interestingly, when I first came to Namibia in 1988, I was still young enough to be able to play football so I joined a local team and once they knew I was a Palace fan, everyone asked about Wright, Bright and Salako.

For the 3-3 Liverpool game, we were on a family break in Cape Town and watched the game on TV. South Africa has a large Liverpool fan base and my son and I had many comments when wearing our Palace shirts the next day.

As far as a special memory is concerned, it is really about a game we couldn't watch rather than one we did. The relegation last game of the season against Sheffield Wednesday. It wasn't shown on TV here and I couldn't stomach following online. I made the decision to go to the gym instead and time a run to finish at the final whistle.

Once I finished, I went to the changing room and turned my phone on. Immediately, I received two calls telling me the result. Luckily the gym was empty because anyone coming in to the changing rooms would have seen a middle aged man covered in sweat with tears running down his face.

I have always felt that being abroad it is even harder and more emotional than being at the games. It may have something to do with my 11 year old son, who despite all the boys he knows in Namibia following the big teams, has stayed loyal to the Palace family tradition.

We go back every season to see a couple of games and my son did not see them win live for seven games. However, his first live win was the play-off win against Watford, and his first Premier league game was the away win at Villa when Gayle scored. That is still one my best Palace moments.

Chapter 29 - My Time in 'Nam – *Hanoi, Halong Bay, Ho Chi Minh, (Vietnam) 18th-23rd December 2014*

I'd loved my time in Laos and was gutted that I'd only spent four days in the country so I hadn't had the chance explore it any further than Luang Prabang. If I'd had my time again, I'd have definitely scheduled more time there and less in South Thailand. I loved how relaxed and laid back the lifestyle was. The French influence from years of colonisation was still strong, with some of the best traditions still being prominent: Namely, fresh baguettes and pastries.

On my final morning, I visited some the area's temples and found myself comparing the experience to the home crowd at the Emirates or Old Trafford. The people who were there didn't really belong. The place of worship was full of tourists talking photos, rather than believers who it had been built for and really meant something to. They'd been priced out in favour of money paying visitors. However, as with large stadiums, I couldn't help but be impressed by the incredible architecture.

Ok, I don't really want to call Old Trafford 'incredible' thanks to my hatred of the Manchester club, but I couldn't downplay the brilliance of the Buddhist temples. Although, I do have a strange attraction to sports stadiums, big and small. I'd even asked Adam to pull over on his motorbike when we passed the Luang Prabang stadium so I could have a little nose around. I was disappointed to find that the small 10,500 stadium wasn't the national one. That's in Vientiane.

However, that was the only sign of football civilisation that I saw. During the four days that I'd spent in Laos, there were no Palace games and it was just as well. I'd have certainly struggled to find anywhere to watch them. From Laos, I took another short flight. This time to Hanoi in Vietnam.

Hanoi was about as different to Luang Prabang as physically possible. It was busy, dirty, congested, pressured, rushed and hectic. I soon forgot the relaxed and laid back nature of Laos. However, for completely the opposite reasons, I loved the place. It was a brilliant kind of crazy.

Within minutes of arriving in the Old Quarter of Downtown Hanoi, I'd spotted a sign stating 'Manchester City vs Crystal Palace shown here next Saturday.' Finally, I was being rewarded with an easy match to watch. To make matters even better, the fact that it was a lunch time kickoff in England for Sky TV meant that it would kick off at 7pm Vietnamese time. Suddenly, I was pro-modern football and rescheduling matches for the international market. Something that had been the bane of my life back home.

I had been slightly worried about finding the game. Despite spotting several United, Arsenal, Chelsea and Liverpool shirts during my wait to have my visa authorised at the airport, I hadn't seen any 'Citeh' shirts. I guess money can't buy you love in Vietnam. Well, I suppose it can but that's another debate for another, seedier, book. However, the major teams were everywhere in the 7.5million populated city: billboards, adverts, posters, fake shirts.

Yet alongside the pictures and dreams of millionaire footballers, there was poverty and a cost of living so low that even Simon Jordan couldn't build up a debt. At the airport, I'd casually strolled up to the ATM and withdrawn 3,000,000 dong. Roughly £90. I assumed our former orange owner had thought he was using dong when he handed over three million pounds to Leicester for Ade Akinbiyi. Once I arrived, I drank beers ranging in price from fourteen to eighty pence, happy hours were simply free beer, a night in a hostel cost £1.50 and meals were less than a pound.

On my first evening, I spent 90p on a bowl of pho (pronounced fur), which is a noodle soup, flavoured with ginger and coriander, spring onions and slivers of chicken, pork or beef. It was delicious and I couldn't get enough of it over the next few days. Especially as I could season it with fresh chilli, chilli sauce, lime and garlic. Four of my favourite flavours. I'm sure my healthy portions of each did wonders for my breath.

After that, I went to a bar with a few people from the hostel. The streets were packed with tourists and locals alike. Non drinkers were desperately trying to make a living and sell their goods as they hassled and bartered their tat, badgering each member of each group individually. As the police arrived, everyone had to frantically clear the roads and strictly stay on the pavements for a fear of a fine. An act the 'old bill' observed, before they were paid off by the local establishments and the roads were filled again.

That evening, I went to bed with the ringing sound of beeping in my ears. Hanoi allegedly hosts roughly four thousand motorbikes but from my experience, that seemed like a huge under estimate. Streams and streams of bikes went past me, from the whizzing to the crawling, the sublime to the ridiculous. Some with one person on, some with three or four. The town was motorcycle crazy. All the bikes did have one thing in common though. They were all beeping.

Bikes beeped because they'd been cut up or pedestrians had run out into the road. But that's normal, right? They were the core base of the noise, keeping the beat. They core beeping was interspersed with additional beeps because people were driving the wrong way, or a dog had changed into the road, or a lady has stopped to pick up the fruit she'd dropped off the back of her bike, or because a pet cat had jumped off the back of a bike, or because there were terrified and trapped pedestrians in the middle of the street, or because pedestrians were in the way as a motorcyclist drove on the pavement to avoid the main traffic. However, on the whole, there didn't seem to be a particular reason. Most were just joining in with the high-pitched, continuous screech.

It wasn't just at night either. They were still going with just as much venom when I woke the following morning, and with just as many ridiculous reasons. Back home, we save the art of beeping our horn for when we're really riled up by the stupidity of fellow drivers... or even occasionally as a friendly gesture to grab the attention of a friend.

The only time I'd experienced a constant buzzing of horns like this was coming away from the Hawthorns after the final game of the 2001/02 season. The Baggies beat us 2-0 to secure promotion ahead of their arch rivals, Wolves. Outside the ground, I think the jubilant drivers were trying to collectively build up enough noise to be heard at Molineux, eleven miles away. Perhaps, a dramatic success for Hà Nội T&T Football Club (or in Vietnamese: Câu lạc bô Bóng đá Hà Nội T&T – try making a chant for that!) might have explained the constant racket. However, it would have had to have been a very dramatic victory as the beeping lasted on every road throughout my entire time in Hanoi.

Such was the congestion and a lack of any form of the Green Cross Code, crossing the road was quite a traumatic and daring event. In Bangkok, crossing the road had seemed like a game of Russian Roulette, whereas here, in the absence of traffic lights or pedestrian crossings holding any sort of meaning to the drivers, it held a closer resemblance to a suicide attempt. Each time I made the mad dash through the traffic, my heart-rate was taken back to the final few minutes of the Play-off Final at Wembley.

Throughout my second day in the Vietnamese capital, I did the tourist things in the city: visited the war museum, Hanoi prison (or The Hilton as it was ironically named by American soldiers) and the Hanoi museum, shaped as an upside down pyramid. The history of Vietnam is both fascinating and tragic in equal measures. Scars from the conflicts of the past are very evident to this day. In fact, they refuse to acknowledge the American attacks as a 'war', instead referring to them as the 'American's illegal aggression in Vietnam'. Little known to me, before the thirty year clash with our neighbours from across the Atlantic, they'd had a long battle for independence with the French, which I was fascinated to learn about.

Laos had embraced the French influence on their culture, but the Vietnamese War Museum took great pride in announcing that '...*after the French army was annihilated by the brave Vietnamese heroes, some tried to flee to Laos but they were ALL captured*'. They'd even ensured that the English translation was read out by a disgruntled French lady; possibly one of the captured escapees. Presumably they were ALL taken to the Hanoi Prison, where I was informed that any tales of bad treatment were further lies from the Americans/French.

While there are many proven cases of illegal and immoral behaviour by American soldiers in their country, I couldn't help but find that reading about the war in Vietnam was a bit like reading a supporters' message board after a match. The write ups were incredibly one-eyed and biased. The general view on the American War/Illegal Aggression/Vindictive Torture was that the yanks loved bombing schools, hospitals and innocent puppies, while the rest of the world begged them to stop.

After an evening which combined excessively cheap drinking and a water-puppet show, complete with live music, smoke and dangerously explosive indoor fireworks, I set off the next morning for a tour to the World Heritage Site of Halong Bay.

I'd found booking the trip difficult. The internet was full of tales of woe where people had been on dangerous and rotting boats, unsafe for travel. However, a lot of the recommended trips were expensive and my funds were running low. I also knew that I didn't want to simply go on a booze cruise. Unfortunately, this meant that I ruled out the tours that most of the people in the hostels were sailing on.

For my trip, the 6am start time had left me in a miserable starting mood, which wasn't helped by the cramped bus for the four hour journey. I was amused by our stop off at a Vietnamese equivalent of a motorway service station. Local sellers were offering their life-size stone statues. In England, we occasionally have signs stating 'Strawberries Sold Here' as traders try to pick up some passing money, but I couldn't imagine many scenarios where these things would be bought on the off chance by passing tourists.

"Oh go on honey, we'll just pick up this 500kg, six foot, stone statue and bring it back as hand luggage!"

Once we arrived at the bay, I began to suss out who was on my ship. The was a half Indian, half Australian couple with two primary school aged girls, an English couple from Norwich in their 40s, a single mum from Canada with French born kids aged 15 and 11, a Korean guy with his Mum, neither of whom spoke English, an older German guy, a 40 year old Russian women with a large supply of vodka, a Chinese couple who spoke no English and an Estonian girl about my age. I must admit, my first thoughts weren't full of optimism for my new crew mates.

I didn't instantly fall in love with Halong Bay either. Don't get me wrong, the rainforest-topped limestone islands, surrounded by emerald water and rising mist were beautiful, but I'd been so spoilt over a short period that it now took a lot to stun me. Although, I was soon under the mysterious bay's magical spell as we took kayaks out to get a closer look at the islands and explore some of the caves. On one of the islands, we made the short but steep trek to the top for a stunning view of the sunset. As I walked with the Canadian mother and her eleven year old son to the summit, the boy turned to me and asked *"Do you like football?"*

Suddenly, I was no longer the outsider. His previously unimpressed face lit up. Instantly, I was transported back to another world. I was back at school; in a world of trading football stickers, fanaticising over dream team line ups, arguing – possibly even bullying – over classmate's preferred players and clubs. The secondary school playground is a harsh place to be, but it's a lot easier if you're clued up on the latest results, fashionable opinions and latest football console game. Its only made simpler if you're actually a decent player.

Throughout the early evening, I kept my new, young friend occupied by listing and comparing our favourite players, just like I'd done in many lessons (just to clarify - when I was the student not the teacher) with friends at school. The pair of us showed each other our football manager games and offered advice. I also explained to him who Yannick Bolasie was as he designed a Ligue 1 XI to face my Premier League XI. Soon, I realised that football fans are still kids. It wasn't just his face that'd been lit up. Mine had too.

Unfortunately, I have grown up enough to understand that social acceptability meant that I shouldn't only talk to the children on the boat and conversation would have to veer from football at some point. However, the initial burst of child-like communication was enough to turn his teenage sulky mood into one that embraced the trip, and enough to open conversations for me with the rest of the group. The connection with her son had got me chatting to the mother, who it turned out was a moderately successful and famous filmmaker in Paris, with most of her work coming from India or South-East Asia.

As we enjoyed our slightly strange 'East meets West' cuisine, I started to chat to the rest of the group. By the time the sun set behind the picture-esque islands, we were fishing for squid without bait while drinking beers that were priced at an extortionate 30,000 dong (£1) and conversation was flowing between the randomly assembled group of holiday makers. All of us enjoyed the gentle sound of the waves and moonlit surroundings on deck, while the vodka-fuelled Russian danced about happily on her own, as the crew drank and smoked in the corner over a game of poker. There was a bizarre happiness on board. The bay was as stunning and relaxing as you could wish for and everyone was soaking it all up.

The next morning, we sailed back to shore, taking in a Vietnamese cooking lesson on the way (i.e. we watched someone make a spring roll), before getting the cramped bus back to Hanoi. Back in the crazy city, I skyped my Mum and brothers, who were celebrating their pretend Christmas on the Saturday before as they wouldn't be together on the actual date, and I wished them all season's greetings. To be honest, since seeing the decorations in Kuala Lumpur, nearly a whole month previously, I hadn't really clocked that we were now just days away from xmas. And to me, that means only one thing. Loads and loads of football!

I'd agreed to take Debra's son to watch the Manchester City vs Palace game that evening and was delighted that this one would take very little commitment on my behalf. It kicked off at 7:45pm local time, which was very social for drinking beers, and there were adverts everywhere for the match. It was almost too easy.

I found a local cafe down the road from the hostel that was showing the game and we sat down as the only Europeans in the venue. I bought myself a

42p beer and Oreal, the kid, a 20p bottle of coke. I think he enjoyed his introduction to my beloved club, as did the Manchester United supporting, Vietnamese owner, and the three of us cheered on Palace together. We played well in the first half, perhaps edging a 0-0 half against the World's Richest Club.

At half time, I tried to move to a different bar as the cafe didn't have wifi. Not only did I feel that Debra should be able to contact me as I was looking after her son, but I was supposed to be sending updates to Dan and Pavel, who were at a wedding back in England and unable to follow the score otherwise. The wonders of the modern world whereby I was watching a game being played in Manchester from Vietnam and relaying the action to friends in Surrey. Unfortunately, on my search for somewhere more suitable, I only found a Cameron Jerome loving, Norwich fan, who was watching a stream of their game against Derby in the hostel lobby.

Once again it reminded me how lucky I was that Palace were in the Premier League during my time away. As much as I'd had to settle for bizarre locations and some lonesome viewing, I had managed to watch nearly every Palace game live. This dedicated Norwich fan had built up this match to vital importance. Thanks to the lack of opportunities to see his Championship club, his relationship with them had become more distant and therefore more personal and selfish. Despite the fact that they were top of the league, this one match mattered more to him than any other as he could actually see it. Disappointingly for him, Norwich were losing, even though Cameron Jerome had scored his eleventh goal of the season. Our former hit-man managed just two in twenty-nine games for us in the previous year.

Anyway, after sending some messages back to England, I returned to the original café. Unfortunately, before I'd even arrived, 'Citeh' had scored, and minutes later, they finished the game off with a second. To be honest, considering the difference in finances of the clubs and the impressive first half performance, I wasn't too fussed. I'd almost expected defeat before the match.

I spent most of the second half taking in my surroundings. A young boy, no older than six or seven, loitered around the cafe, desperate to get a glimpse of the football. Using thumbs up and down, alongside exaggerated child faces of emotion, we established that he liked Manchester United, but not Manchester City or Chelsea. As City repeatedly strolled through our defence, he sat as glumly as I did. The obsession with football and allowance of it to take over his state of mind and mood reminded me of myself, even if he was roaming the streets of Hanoi alone at an age when I wasn't allowed to play without supervision on the green in the middle of the quiet, Berkshire cul-de-sac that I grew up in.

The commentary made me laugh too. It was in Vietnamese and I'd learnt from a friend who lives in China that the well-known players are given a 'local' name to make it fit in with the rest of the commentary. However, other than Bolasie, the Palace players weren't given this luxury. The constant background blur of fast-paced Vietnamese coming from the TV was interspersed with the odd recognisable word of 'Jedinak' or 'Speroni'.

City scored a third late on as Yaya Toure cruised through our defence like a Rolls Royce and classily placed the ball powerfully into the net. At full time, I sat and stared - not miserable, not cross, not even anti Warnock. I just had a feeling of not caring. We played well, their squad was 'desolated', and had resorted to having James Milner up front. They hadn't even played well, yet they still sailed to a 3-0 win. It wasn't even an old and rusty boat like I'd toured around Halong Bay on. Their second eleven had been a lavish cruise liner. For the first time in a long time, I felt anti-Premiership or Premier League or whatever this greedy, spoilt brat of a division wanted to call itself these days.

We'd been unlucky in a way. Of course we had. We always are against the big boys, especially away from home. There'd been a huge deflection on first goal, McArthur had a goal wrongly disallowed, and we'd actually gone toe-to-toe with them, but it was a predictable result.

Manchester United...2 CPFC...0
Liverpool...3 CPFC...1
Chelsea...2 CPFC...1
Manchester City...1 CPFC...0
Arsenal...2 CPFC...0
Arsenal...2 CPFC...1
Manchester United...1 CPFC...0
Manchester City...3 CPFC...0

Since promotion, we'd played eight games against the top five away from home, scoring just three goals. None of them had thrashed us, all of them had been decent games, but we'd lost all of them. We'd come up with Cardiff, who'd lost all five of their matches away at the top clubs with a credible four goals, and Hull, who'd lost eight of their nine, scoring three. The tigers 0-0 draw at Anfield being one result to celebrate out of twenty two games for the three of us. And the Premier League is supposed to be the most exciting league in the world?

I stayed to watch United draw with Villa after our game, much to the frustration of the cafe's owner. I think the Manchester club's inability to break down their opponent's ten men was the reason behind his frustration, but the language barrier meant that I couldn't be sure. Maybe my depressed mood was scaring his customers away and that was prompting his sighs and regular throwing of his arms? I hadn't seen any sign of local football but this guy and the little kid outside were clearly fanatical and passionate about their Manchester club. They were every bit as enthusiastic and excitable as fans back home.

Manchester City...3 Crystal Palace...0
The Etihad Stadium, 20/12/14
Premier League

Manchester City: Hart, Zabaleta, Demichelis, Mangala, Kolarov, Fernandinho, Navas, Milner (Fernando 82), Silva (Lampard 69), Nasri (Sinclair 89), Toure.
Subs Not Used: Caballero, Sagna, Boyata, Reges, Ambrose.

Crystal Palace: Julian Speroni, Martin Kelly, Scott Dann, Brede Hangeland, Joel Ward, Yannick Bolasie, Mile Jedinak, Joe Ledley (Barry Bannan 89), James McArthur, Jason Puncheon (Jerome Thomas 84), Fraizer Campbell (Wilfried Zaha 67).
Subs Not Used: Wayne Hennessey, Adrian Mariappa, Damian Delaney, Dwight Gayle.

Chapter 30 - Christmas in Sydney – *23rd December 2014- 4th January 2015*

From Hanoi, I flew down to spend my final night in Asia in Ho Chi Minh City in the south of the country, from where I was set to fly back to Sydney for Christmas. There was one must-see attraction, The Vietnamese War Museum, and after a five hour delay on my flight, I grabbed a taxi straight from the airport to the museum. The history is as interesting as it is staggering. Learning about the affects of Agent Orange, which was used by the American soldiers was simply stomach churning.

Eventually, after three weeks travelling up Australia's East Coast, ten days in Malaysia, two weeks in Thailand, five days in Laos and six in Vietnam, I was returning to Sydney. I'd spoken to the managers at Scruffy Murphys and annoyingly, they went back on their word from before I left. Despite the promise, I was told that I wasn't needed. Thankfully, as I was now almost entirely out of dollars, I had already arranged and paid for accommodation back in Sydney for the xmas period.

I was going to live in Vaucluse, a very wealthy area of Sydney, with Sarah, who I'd previously worked with, and two of her friends. When I arrived back in Australia's largest city, it felt incredibly quiet and calm, almost tranquil, after being in Vietnam. I lugged my bags on trains and busses to our temporary home, which was a huge family house with a beautiful sea-view. The English expat owners had decided to go home for the festive period and we were renting their place while they were away.

However, if the house was above my expectations, Western Sydney's performance was below it. They'd played ten, drawn three, lost seven and were yet to record a single victory. Now us football fans are superstitious. Especially me – I partly blamed myself for City's opener against Palace on the previous Saturday as I was late back from my WIFI hunt and missed the goal. However, I didn't realise that me starting to support a team could affect them quite this much. Having joined them as the champions of a continent, they'd somehow transformed into the worst team in the country.

Sarah's friends proved pleasant enough – another Irishman called Alan, whose complete lack of interest in football made conversation difficult. To be honest, I am occasionally able to speak to non-football fans, as proved by my other new housemate, a Norwegian girl called Camilla. She was brilliant and we got on instantly, but I was disappointed by her ignorance towards Johnny Parr and Steffen Iverson. Not that I have a one track mind or anything. However, with Alan, while I don't think either of us would have a bad word to say about the other, dialogue was often mutually painful. In such circumstances, football is often a translator that eases communication but was it was always awkwardly absent with Alan.

Christmas Day was a surreal experience. It started well as American Rich joined us with some friends; Hayley, Rachel and Jackie. We started the day with an ocean swim and, without wanting to sound too much like a spoilt brat as equally I didn't buy any, a noticeable lack of presents to open was upsetting. As it was Sarah's second Christmas down under, she was desperate for a touch of home and a traditional roast turkey. However, Rich and I were after a more Australian experience. In the end, we had both: A Barbeque at around 11am and we finally sat down to an amazing Christmas lunch around four pm. Both Sarah and Alan had previously worked as chefs and didn't disappoint.

The problem with spending Christmas away from home is that everyone's different traditions don't always mix. Some people spend the day watching TV; others are used to it being banned. Some want to spend the day cooking; others are desperate to relax. Some want to play board games, whereas for others, the mere word 'monopoly' has traumatic ramifications. To be honest, my main Christmas tradition is to be able to escape it all on Boxing Day to go and watch Palace.

So the next day, after an afternoon at the races and an evening drinking, I left the group early to head home and watch Palace host Southampton, using Sarah's laptop to stream it. Mind you, when I say I left early, I meant that I took the final bus home and was set on the sofa not long before the 2am kick off. The Vietnamese time of 7:45pm was a distant memory. The stream that I eventually found was jumpy and blurry, and in the end, it disappeared completely. After five minutes of following the game on the BBS, it returned. I flicked over to the necessary tab just in time to see a Southampton striker round Speroni and score.

At half time, I found a decent stream, but I shouldn't have bothered. Southampton scored twice more in the first eight minutes of the second period. The game was over. I watched the pointless half at three am, tired and bored, and sat almost as quietly as the Selhurst crowd. Even the Holmesdale Fanatics had stopped singing.

Most of my anti-Warnock agenda had been loosely based on principle, but now, he was proving to be a disastrous appointment results-wise too. As time edged towards four in the morning, I slammed the laptop lid down and sulked off to bed with ten minutes remaining. It was only the next day that I discovered Scott Dann's consolation. Much is said, accused and debated about fans that choose to leave the game before the end, but on that depressing Boxing Day, things were so bad that I left my armchair early.

The next day Warnock was sacked. I didn't feel smug, or happy, or any other emotion than relief. They club were second bottom in the league and frankly, only going in one direction. Of course, sacking Warnock wasn't going to be enough on its own. The list of potential managers in the summer had been pretty depressing.

I spent the next few days wondering around the city and exploring, as well as swimming in the sea and generally enjoying the sun. I also set about looking for a job and trying to continue to pursue permission to teach in Oz. It felt very natural to be back, made even easier by the fact that wherever I went, I seemed to see Palace shirts: the beach, George Street, Central Station, everywhere.

The day after Warnock's sacking, Palace were back in action as the Christmas games come thick and fast. We were away at QPR, effectively the source of my Warnock hate, so in many ways they were a fitting opponent. Our London rivals were sat just above us in the table, two points clear of relegation.

Around midnight, I used Sarah's laptop to find a stream to watch Tottenham play United. It made me miss the relaxed nature of watching football at home. I was simply enjoying a game between two teams that mattered very little to me. In Oz, everything was a huge effort: going to the pub, staying up late, going out socialising. This was the first time in the four months that I'd been away that I could just lie down on a comfy chair and switch off in front of the football. The score or game mattered little. The escape was there.

Unfortunately, once your own team becomes involved, enjoyment goes out of the window. I watch football to enjoy it. I watch Palace because I have to. I watch Palace because it's a routine, because I'm devoted, because I want them to win, because I have history with our club, because my Dad's from the area. But not to enjoy the match. That might come afterwards.

When people arrive at the cinema, or a gig, or a play, they're smiling. They're paying for entertainment to entertain them. But not at football. Look around at the turnstiles before a game, or in the seats at 0-0. No one is smiling, no one is happy, no one is enjoying it. At football, we pay an extortionate price for entertainment to make us miserable. The entertainment is the pain and the strain and the underlying desire that once it's over, we might be happy. And if we can't be truly happy, we'll be happy moaning.

Having Keith Millen in charge rather than Warnock might have made me happier pre-match, but I was just as jumpy and nervous and unnecessarily aggressive through my gritted teeth as ever during the game. The match was poor but we were a lot more organised than we had been against Southampton two days earlier. As well as that, and this may well be my anti-Warnock agenda, but the players looked a lot more interested and fired up than they had in the previous few defeats. Either way, we battled to a tense 0-0 draw.

Despite the match ending at four am, I couldn't sleep after that. The emotion of football makes it impossible to immediately switch off, even after a 0-0 draw at Queens Park Rangers. I spent an hour calming my body down after the game by reading the BBS and catching up on other scores. However, it wasn't until the next morning that I heard the big news of the day. After Newcastle's 3-2 win over Everton, which lifted them to eighth, Alan Pardew had left the stadium immediately, amongst rumours that he was set to become our new boss. He was certainly a step above the depressing list of potential managers that had been bandied about in the summer.

New Years Eve arrived and I still hadn't got a job so I was delighted to be able to head out for the night. I'm never a fan of the occasion back home but this was my only chance to experience it in Sydney and I was keen to make the most of it. Rich and I met some of his friends and headed to Manly. There, we barbequed and drank craft beer, looking out towards Sydney and the legendary firework display at the harbour bridge.

On the ferry home (a brilliant way to get back from a night out!) I was messaging my Dad about the rumours over Pardew, as well as Peter Crouch, who was linked to us at the time. While we agreed that we both wanted 'Super Al' to return, our opinions differed over Crouch. Dad still hated him from the days when both Palace and Andy Johnson were in direct competition with him in 2005. I pointed out that now I was in 2015, I was far more forgiving and progressive thinking than him, who was stuck in 2014 thanks to the time difference, but he'd soon catch up.

The next day brought about more football, and all but confirmation of Pardew's appointment. It always amazes me that managers receive smaller salaries than the playing employees. While we build a powerful 'relationship' with the troops on the pitch, in my experience, it's the sergeant in the dugout who provides the strongest bond. I've been enraged by managers into having a foul mood and demeanour for months on end in a way that a single player has never managed.

My entire outlook on Palace changed with Pardew's appointment. Suddenly, I had an optimism and belief that we could survive, and a renewed will for them to win. Previously, I'd been so focussed on wanting Warnock out that I couldn't even really enjoy the rare victories that we did have. Super Al was not only an improved manager, but a Palace man too.

Once again, I stayed up until the early hours to try and get a glimpse of my beloved club. Unfortunately, the streaming website, wiziwig, had been shut down and I was lost. How could I see them now? The BBS bore no fruit and suddenly, I was cut off from Palace. If I'd known earlier, I'd have made the trek to central Sydney to watch us in the Royal Exhibition Hotel, where Russ was the single member of the supporters club, watching alone. In fact, he was the only member of clientele in the entire pub. Apparently, post midnight on New Year's Day isn't the most popular time for people to frequent pubs, even with the pull of Palace.

Unable to watch, I listened to the first half of the game on Bet365's website, where Pardew's presence in the crowd told us all that we needed to know. On the pitch, the commentator went through the usual radio routine of over-excitement, energised squeals and confused ramblings to seemingly go out of his way to give me as little detail as possible on the actual events. I did decipher from his screaming that Bolasie had gone through on goal and hit the bar, when he should have scored in the commentator's opinion.

During the half time break, with all the other results going against us, I fell asleep. I didn't intend to or realise that I had, but suddenly, it was morning and

I was forced to look up the result. Once again, we'd drawn 0-0. Millen had been reliable as ever and steadied our sinking ship for Pardew to take us on. However, we certainly did need to push on. The two 0-0 draws had left us without a win in eight and languishing in the relegation zone.

Once again, I continued job hunting the next day and this time, I received a trial shift at the backpackers' bar, Sidebar. Under the stress of being followed around and corrected at every turn by an overzealous supervisor, I blew it. As soon as I left, I knew the job wasn't to be, even though they said they'd be in touch. I hated having such close observation as I did my job. Each time I used a slice of lemon instead of lime, she'd sigh and throw the drink away and on the occasions where I forgot to give the customer a straw, there were groans louder than those heard at Selhurst Park when Calvin Andrew was sent to warm up.

Suddenly, I began to feel some empathy for professional footballers. If my ability behind the bar and confidence could be destroyed by a five-foot-two, nineteen year-old, power hungry, supervisor, then how on earth must they feel, when twenty thousand people tell them to "f*** off" in unison as they lose the ball? However, while they are given thousands of pounds a week to compensate this, the forty-odd bucks that I received for my shift wasn't going to keep me fed for long.

However, with me set to run out of money any day, I did get a job in a bar at the Opera House. I worked in Opera Kitchen, a bar and restaurant under the world famous building. Even during the trial shift I felt an irrational hatred towards the job. It involved limited interaction with customers: it seemed dull and there was no time for communication with colleagues. However, like Alan Pardew, I had a new job at one of the most impressive locations around.

The next day, I went to celebrate with my housemates at an Irish Bar in Bondi. The live entertainment sang an array of anti-English, pro-IRA songs that would only be matched for hatred and one-eyed-ness in a football stadium. After the jolly Irish night, I began to research how to watch our FA Cup game against Dover that evening.

Out of all the games I'd missed while being away, this was the first one that I was truly gutted about. I'd seen us play all of the Premier League teams in the past and am likely to see us play them again. However, we hadn't played against a non-league side since 1982 and it might be another thirty-odd years before we play another one, especially away from home. Let alone the chance to play again at Dover. This is something I'd missed and am highly unlikely to recreate.

I love the FA Cup, even though Palace's record since I started supporting them in 1996 is pretty horrific. Prior to this match, we'd played thirty-seven FA Cup ties, winning ten, drawing nine and losing eighteen, having never gone past the fifth round. However, there's something magical about the draw and the optimism, anyone can beat anyone. Even if that was a slight worry against

Dover. I've seen us lose to Bury and Cambridge and other such teams, but to lose to a team from the SIXTH tier of English football would be a new low. Being unable to watch the Villa game had shown me that I now expected the right to watch Palace on TV from anywhere in the world. I didn't appreciate it anymore as the novelty had worn off. However, I can only begin to imagine the excitement of an exiled Dover Athletic fan at being able to see their game live. Unfortunately for them, their team was completely overwhelmed by the occasion.

I suspect Pardew was dreading this as an opening match. It was a potential banana skin of epic proportions. Luton had become the first non-league side for 24 years to beat a top-flight one during the previous season by getting the better of Norwich, and for Pardew to start an already difficult looking job in that manner would be a huge blow. He must have been even more relieved than most as Scott Dann powered home two first half strikes. Late on, Dwight Gayle scored a third in what was a completely flat match. As happy as I was to avoid the embarrassment, I did feel sorry for Dover. It was their biggest ever game and they simply offered nothing.

Over Christmas, my friend Pavel had proposed to his girlfriend using a pun involving a picture of Scott Dann, so it not only was it fitting for our centre back to turn into a goal machine, but it also prompted our Palace whatsapp group to try and persuade our friend Cliff to propose to his girlfriend. His reluctance was summed up by his response, *"I'll propose when Kevin Doyle scores!"* Unforeseen by him, within minutes, Doyle had not only been subbed on, but he also scored our fourth goal. Just when he'd thought the Irish striker's spell at the club couldn't get any worse; the disastrous signing had made him go ring shopping.

To be honest, unlike the QPR game, sleep wasn't a problem after the match. I'd been as relaxed watching as the players had been on the pitch. Even in a 4-0 win, I couldn't enjoy it.

A few days later, still prior to receiving my first pay packet from the Opera Kitchen, our three week contract at the Vaucluse house ended. Unable to afford or face another hostel stay just yet, I took up Richard's offer to sleep on his sofa until I had some funds behind me. The plan was to spend a month building up some money and then move to Melbourne to discover and work in a new city, where, like Palace under Pardew, I could start afresh.

Crystal Palace...1 Southampton...3
Selhurst Park, 26/12/14
Premier League

Crystal Palace : Speroni, Mariappa, Dann, Delaney, Ward, Jedinak, McArthur, Ledley (Zaha, 66), Punchewon, Campbell (Gayle, 48), Bolasie (Kelly, 71).
Subs Not Used: Wayne Hennessey, Jerome Thomas, Barry Bannan, Brede Hangeland

Southampton: Forster, Yoshida, Alderweireld, Gardos, Clyne (McCarthy, 86), Schneiderlin, Ward-Prowse, Davis (Wanyama, 55), Bertrand, Mane, Pelle (Long 71).
Subs Not Used: Davis, Tadic, Reed, Targett

Queens Park Rangers...0 Crystal Palace...0
Loftus Road, 28/12/14
Premier League

QPR: Green, Isla, Dunne, Caulker, Hill, Hoilett, Barton, Henry, Fer (Vargas 65), Austin, Zamora (Phillips 75).
Subs not used: McCarthy, Ferdinand, Onuoha, Mutch, Wright-Phillips.

Palace: Julian Speroni, Adrian Mariappa, Scott Dann, Damian Delaney, Joel Ward, James McArthur, Joe Ledley, Mile Jedinak, Yannick Bolasie, Jason Puncheon, Wilfried Zaha (Fraizer Campbell 67).
Subs not used: Wayne Hennessey, Martin Kelly, Brede Hangeland, Barry Bannan, Jerome Thomas, Kevin Doyle.

Aston Villa...0 Crystal Palace...0
Villa Park, 01/01/15
Premier League

Aston Villa: Guzan, Cissokho, Vlaar (Clark 15), Okore, Hutton, Bacuna, Cleverley (Grealish 64), Sanchez, Weimann (Cole 82), Agbonlahor, Benteke.
Subs not used: Given, Clark, Lowton, N'Zogbia, Robinson.

Palace: Julian Speroni, Martin Kelly, Damian Delaney, Scott Dann, Adrian Mariappa, Yannick Bolasie, James McArthur (Barry Bannan 89), Joel Ward, Joe Ledley, Jason Puncheon, Wilfried Zaha (Dwight Gayle 61).
Subs not used: Wayne Hennessey, Brede Hangeland, Jerome Thomas, Fraizer Campbell, Kevin Doyle.

Dover Athletic...0 Crystal Palace...4
Crabble Stadium, 04/01/15
FA Cup R3

Dover Athletic: Rafferty, Essam, Raggett (Nanetti 56), Orlu, Sterling, Bellamy (Wynter 69), Cogan, Deverdics, Payne, Murphy (Modeste 81).
Subs not used: Hook, Francis, Reid, Hook, Lock.

Palace: Wayne Hennessey, Joel Ward, Scott Dann, Damian Delaney, Martin Kelly, Barry Bannan, Joe Ledley (Adrian Mariappa 75), Stuart O'Keefe, Wilfried Zaha, Dwight Gayle (Jerome Thomas 72), Glenn Murray (Kevin Doyle 46).
Subs not used: Chris Kettings, Brede Hangeland, Adeline Guedioura, Jason Puncheon.

Chapter 31 - Focussing on Palace – *Sydney, 4th-24th January 2015*

It was a strange time after moving into Richard's place. When I'd left Sydney to go travelling, I'd felt that I had roots in the city: friends, commitments and a job. However, the time in Vaucluse felt like a seaside holiday and when it ended, I felt a little bit lost. I was desperate to move and I hated the new job. Palace's run of results wasn't helping either. We'd won just one league game in thirteen.

While I'd been travelling, Palace's form hadn't got to me, but now I was back in Sydney with an unfulfilling job, my anger towards the club had rocketed. The irrational resentment of my employment started on my very first shift, when I was forced to miss the first Asia Cup game that I'd pencilled in - Uzbekistan VS North Korea.

I loved the idea of watching two nations that had no footballing history (minus one famous game vs Portugal), playing in a 90,000 stadium in Sydney. Admittedly, part of my interest was the fact that it might be my only ever chance to actually see a North Korean. Incredibly, over 12,000 others showed up to watch the match, demonstrating the increase in interest in football down under and acceptance of really crap football. Would we manage a crowd that high in London for the same fixture?

By all accounts, Uzbekistan's 1-0 win was a terrible match, although made slightly more amusing by the North Korean fans/army 'ultras' constantly bouncing to the tune of 'Kim Jong Un! Ole! Ole! Ole!' However, the feeling of missing out on a unique event irked me and added to my frustration in the job. The one thing that I did like about my first shift was chatting to an Italian Lazio fan as we wheeled the bins to the garbage dispensers under the Opera House at 2am. He was excited for the following day when he could watch the Rome derby but he bemoaned the general lack of coverage of Serie A compared to the Premier League. Which is bizarre really, because growing up in England in the 90s without Sky TV meant that I saw more of the Italian league than our own.

However, I was less interested in his comparisons of the Rome derby to the Merseyside one thanks to the traditional 'family' nature of it and far more interested in chatting about my favourite Italian and Lazio subject – Just One Lombardo! Although the great Italian winger helped Lazio achieve five major trophies (the Cup Winners Cup, Serie A, the Supercoppa Italiana, the Coppa Italia and the European Super Cup) and he helped Palace achieve relegation, administration and near oblivion, it was clear that I held him in much higher regard than my Italian colleague. Lombardo's professionalism, skills, flair and precision were so far ahead of his team mates in SE25 that it makes it unlikely that we'll ever have a greater player.

Of course, it was a different era, when Italian internationals didn't routinely come to England and Blackburn Rovers could win a title with a midfield of Sherwood, Batty, Wilcox and Warhurst. Nowadays, I don't think he'd stand out as high, but at the time, it was simply magical watching him. If football is an escape from the stresses of life, watching Attilio in red and blue was an escape from the stresses of Palace.

After the shift, I had a four mile walk home, where I collapsed on Richard's sofa and set an alarm for 4:30am – Palace were due to host Spurs that night in Alan Pardew's first league game in charge. However, when I woke, at around quarter to six in the morning, we were already behind. I couldn't be bothered to find a stream on Richard's laptop so I went to the loo and returned to sleep. But unfortunately, I couldn't. My Dad was at the game with my brother, who is a Spurs fan, and there was no way that I couldn't follow, despite my tired and defeatist state.

"I'll watch til we go two down," I thought to myself.

The clock showed 33 minutes left for me to endure as I sleepily closed the pop-ups around the stream. Minutes later, Joe Ledley was taken down in the box, although replays suggested that the defender clipped the ball first, and Dwight Gayle smashed home the resulting penalty. Selhurst (except my brother) went wild and I smiled. It was all I felt. It was an 'oh good' moment, like when you're given a packet of sweets in the street as a promotion or receive a nice text from an old colleague. It wasn't the usual pandemonium that erupts inside me when Palace score, especially to equalise against one of the big teams. Being so far away, and on my own, and so tired, meant that I simply didn't have any energy for Palace.

The positive side was that I wasn't even nervous as the game went on, even after Jason Puncheon had brilliantly fired us ahead with a strike from the edge of the area. Although, despite my sleepy and repressed mood, I did manage to wake up most of the house with an almighty cheer for the goal. However, at full time, I simply rolled over, and slipped back to sleep.

Over the next few days, I worked long shifts, getting angrier and angrier towards the seagulls that swooped around the harbour. Horrible creatures – thieving from plates, aggressive to children, but ultimately cowardly when challenged. Imagine being symbolised by them – flying vermin. I remember at the time, despite Palace's upturn in form, feeling constantly angry and the seagulls seemed to be my outlet for that. Cruelly, I had a burning desire to kick them, and hard, but thankfully, I never acted on this brutal craving. Instead, I frowned around the restaurant, doing the bare minimum and no more as I actively tried to disengage with the job. I didn't want to like it.

I'd trusted the previous job at Scruffy Murphys. Despite initial reservations, I'd grown to love it; the people, the clientele, the management, but upon my return, they'd gone back on their word and not appointed me. I wasn't going to make the same mistake again and learn to like this job. It was a short term solution and I'd be gone within the month. In the meantime, I'd resent the job and daydream about kicking seagulls, mainly because of their Brighton connection.

As well as the job at the Opera House, I took an early morning role in the cellar of the Backpackers bar, Scary Canary. The job was four morning shifts, each 2-3 hours long and meant that I got free accommodation. Unfortunately, it did mean ending one job at 2am and starting the next at 6am, but neither required much brain use and I could always sleep in the day.

The following Saturday, after spending the day with Richard and some girls in Manly, I needed to get a boat back across Sydney to work for the evening. Once again, I escaped in to my own mind of regret as the others enjoyed an evening drinking in the sun, while I collected plates and cutlery for tourists at the Opera House for a mere $17 an hour – far less than I'd been earning at Scruffys.

My frustration was increased by a German colleague, usually so efficient, who was adamant that he wanted us to go slow in the early hours to gain an extra half hours pay. I, on the other hand, was adamant that we should work our nuts off to ensure we finished in time to get to the Royal Exhibition for 2am, when Palace kicked off in Burnley.

The 'compromise' meant that I finished around 1:30 and, as the busses had stopped running for the night, I had to run across the city to make the game. Thankfully, the Palace supporters' pub was outside of the 1:30 lock-out area in the centre and I arrived at 2:13am, with Palace already 1-0 down. I said hello to the small, dejected group of Palace fans in the corner. Not only were we losing, but a large group of Chelsea fans had taken over the main screen, which had left us shunted to the back of our regular pub. There really is no loyalty in the game these days, even in Sydney pubs.

By the time that I'd nipped to the loo to get changed from my work gear, Palace were 2-0 down, and the six of us sat there, listening to Chelsea fans sing, as Burnley thrashed us. Maybe Pardew wasn't the savour after all. Thankfully, just as I was considering leaving, Dwight Gayle scored to get us back in the match and just after half time, Puncheon scored again to level it up. The six of us jumped up. Suddenly, my companions went from five guys who I'd met in a pub to five mates. We were back in the game. In fact, such was our absorption in our match, combined with Chelsea's arrogance in victory, we didn't even hear their cheer for their fifth goal at Swansea.

Late on, we pushed for the win. Glenn Murray, who'd recently returned from his absurd loan spell at Reading, hit the bar and we thought the chance was gone. However, Dwight Gayle, the striker that Warnock had refused to play, had other ideas. His last gasp winner sent the six of us loopy. At full time, we sang and jumped, hugged and screamed, and most importantly, ordered a tray of drinks to celebrate. It was only a good five minutes or so after full time, when the six of us finally returned to any sort of normal state, we realised that despite having nearly as many goals as we had fans, the Chelsea lot had left.

I wondered, do we care more as fans of a crap club? And I guessed not. After all, the Chelsea lot had stayed out until 4am to watch their side. However, the routine-ness of their victories robbed them of something. If we'd won 5-0, we'd be dancing on tables with joy for weeks, but we'd also expect to lose 1-0 to Barnsley on the following Tuesday. The fact that Chelsea had probably won 5-0 already that season and almost certainly would again, definitely took the edge off the occasion for as them. Whereas for us, a win, any win (except maybe vs Dover) was vital. After the pub shut at five in the morning, Jordo, a guy that I barely knew, gave me a lift home. Why? Because I'm Palace, and so is he.

And that, in two matches sums up what watching football is all about. It's a collective sport. Beating Burnley, a side who were destined for relegation, meant far more to me than beating a Spurs side, supported by my brother and flying high in the league. Why? Because I (not Palace) did it with friends. Either way, post Warnock, Palace were on the up again!

The next day, I moved into my new accommodation. If I thought back about my previous Sydney accommodation, then Bounce (my first hostel) was like Manchester City. It was expensive and they'd spared no expense and filled the place with luxury. Nomads was Leeds United – a huge organisation that's dirty and rough, and ultimately, not very good. 790 on George was cheap, but reasonably kept and had good company, possibly the Fulham of hostels. However, Base, behind Scary Canary where I started to work in the cellar, was like QPR – it was expensive but actually pretty s***. Thankfully, I received free accommodation.

I spent the little spare time that I had trying to chase up an accreditation to teach in Melbourne, as I didn't want to be stuck in another dead end job when I arrived in Australia's second biggest city. At Scary Canary, as I also lived there, I started to make more of an effort with my colleagues and got on well with everyone without especially clicking. However, with work taking over, the weeks became fairly dull and I lived for Saturdays, after midnight. The Burnley game had relit my passion for Palace and the will to see the supporters group. Other than Rich, they were the closest that I had to friends out there.

I had a bond of memories and loyalty. Two ingredients that come naturally amongst football fans. We may not have even met in May 2004, for an event that had cemented the our group leader's love of Palace, but we'd all shared our play-off victory together in one way or another. Just as we'd experienced relegation the following year, and stayed loyal with it. We've all fought in the same battles and wear the same scars. We might not all know each other personally, but we know how our minds work on a Saturday afternoon (well, Sunday Morning in Oz).

Therefore, it was gutting that the following week, our FA Cup match at Southampton was not due to be televised anywhere in the world. I guess this is the equivalent of an away game. Home or away didn't matter in Oz as the commitment was the same. However, Sunday's televised matches, Midweek games and FA Cup ones are immeasurably more difficult to follow. This was only the second match of the season that wouldn't be shown down under.

In the day, I had a very different experience to following football. Debra, from my Halong Bay cruise, had messaged me to say that she had a friend performing at the Sydney Opera House and asked if I wanted a free ticket. Of course, I jumped at the chance. Now, when she said that she had a friend performing, I'd assumed that she meant someone with a violin at the back of the stage somewhere. The show was the French-silent film, The Artist, with a live orchestra.

Before the show, I met her friend in one of the private bars for a glass of champagne. It turned out that he was the conductor of the music for both the film and live show, Ludovic Bource. Bizarrely, before a shift waiting on tables, I was having a drink in the VIP area of the Sydney Opera House, with a Golden Globe and Oscar award winning musician. I didn't think he'd appreciate my musical awareness of 'Oh South London...'

The show itself was brilliant. Even as someone who isn't especially enthusiastic about that kind of thing, I was hooked from start to finish, possibly slightly biased from meeting my new star-studded friend beforehand. I hadn't been that star-struck since August 2005 when I bumped into Iain and Bob Dowie after a 1-1, Andy Johnson inspired draw away at Norwich in a service station when I was 16.

After my shift, which wasn't as good as the performance, I met Richard and two friends, Haylie and Emma, in Scary Canary to get us some cheap drinks. I'll be honest enough to admit that with Palace out of sight, they were close to being out of mind too. I didn't get many chances to relax thanks to my hectic two-job schedule and I was enjoying a rare evening off. I only remembered the game when I received a message from Dan in London saying "What the hell is going on with Palace?"

This really was an irritating message to receive. What did it mean? It told me nothing! We were just as likely to be 5-0 up as we were to be 5-0 down. Quickly, while still on the sticky dance floor of the bar, I directed myself to the BBC website on my phone for an update. After 21 minutes, it was two all. Twice we'd been behind, but goals from Chamakh and our new signing, Yaya Sanogo, had clawed us back into it. Maybe Palace could be as exciting as an Oscar winning performance after all. The problem now was that I'd started to invest in the match.

I wanted to leave it. I wanted not to care. But I'm me, and Palace are Palace. The night out became less significant. Regularly, I'd check my phone and drinks were drunk quicker as the nerves for the night grew. Soon, I received another message. This time from Pavel. 'YESSSSSS' was the simpler, clearer and more direct approach this time.

"Who got it?" I relied.

"Cham again! We're the famous Crystal Palace and we're going to Wem-ber-ley!"

After that, I let the match go a little bit. I stopped checking for scores and waited for friends to inform me. Receiving good news would be hard now.

From a winning position, we were only likely to muck it up – not extend our lead. Long after the bar had closed, I was still drinking with colleagues in the hostel behind the pub, and news filtered through that Palace had held on for the 3-2 win.

The following morning, we were woken with news that they'd been noise complaints against us by other guests. Typically, my main contribution had been a loud scream of delight at full time, followed by a solo rendition of 'Allll, Super Al!' However, bizarrely, Palace's result wasn't even the best thing about that evening. Neither was the chance to socialise and get to know my new colleagues, and even the cheap drinks had been topped. The other results from the world's oldest cup competition that day were quite brilliant.

Chelsea...2 Bradford...4
Manchester City...0 Middlesbrough...2
Cambridge...0 Manchester United...0
Liverpool...0 Bolton...0
Tottenham...1 Leicester...2

Amazingly, with Arsenal not due to play until the next day, we were the highest placed team definitely in the 5th round.
However, life, like Palace, has a nasty habit of bringing you right back down as quickly as it builds you up. The next day, at the end of a long and busy shift for 'Australia Day', I suffered my first experience of genuine racism. Four bald and burly guys, who'd been kicked out of the bar next door, came into our restaurant just before closing. While I was cleaning up, one of them asked me where their burgers were. As I didn't know anything about them, I asked to look at their receipt so that I could check for him.

Well that was it, my request unleashed a barrage of foul-mouthed abuse about me, the restaurant, being English, my attitude and anything else that popped into their heads. In my mind, I stayed calm throughout, offered solutions to the complaints and politely asked them why they were questioning my attitude. However, as their language became more colourful and the insults more personal, I walked away, before explaining the situation to my boss.

It was the first shift that I'd worked with the top boss as he'd been away when I was appointed and he went to speak to the angry customers. When he returned, he accepted that they'd been offensive, aggressive and unreasonable. However, rather than kick them out, or even support me, he gave me a lecture. He told me that by speaking to them, politely, as acknowledged by our own security, I put myself in a situation where my safety was put at risk. He then continued to say that if I had been attacked, the incident would have reflected badly on the restaurant and he'd have been forced to sack me.

Often in life, I link my own successes and downfalls to Palaces. Of course, it's unlikely that me getting a job had much to do with Palace surviving the drop in 2010, or a Palace promotion helped me with a work promotion, or my girlfriend dumping me was because of a semi-final defeat in Cardiff, but inside, I can't help but link the two. In my mind, events in my life are defined and remembered by Palace's fortunes at the time. It becomes harder and harder to remember what led to what. Was I thrilled about the job and Palace matched the mood? Or did I take the emotion from the football with me to boost my confidence in life? Or is it that the football simply takes too much of my thought-time and when I should be concentrating on work, or relationships, or exams, or any other acceptable form of improving oneself, instead I'm thinking about football?

However, in January 2016, I was miserable, on a come down from the end of my travels and a realisation that, despite meeting and socialising with hundreds of new and interesting people, I only really had one friend, Richard, within 17,000km. On top of that, I was working two jobs for people who I had no respect for. But strangely, my misery didn't infest itself onto Palace as I'd come to sub-consciously believe that it would. Palace really were an escape into having a social life and giving me some rare, joyful and resentment free, winning moments.

Crystal Palace...2 Tottenham Hotspur...1
Selhurst Park, 10/01/15
Premier League

Palace: Julian Speroni, Martin Kelly, Scott Dann, Damian Delaney, Joel Ward, James McArthur, Joe Ledley, Barry Bannan (Adeline Guedioura 46), Jason Puncheon, Dwight Gayle (Fraizer Campbell 87), Glenn Murray (Wilfried Zaha 74).
Subs not used: Wayne Hennessey, Adrian Mariappa, Brede Hangeland, Jerome Thomas.

Tottenham: Lloris, Rose, Vertonghen Fazio, Walker, Eriksen, Stambouli (Soldado 75), Dembele, Townsend (Capoue 69), Chadli, Kane.
Subs not used: Vorm, Kaboul, Davies, Paulinho, Lennon.

Burnley...2 Crystal Palace...3
Turf Moor, 17/01/15
Premier League

Burnley: Heaton, Trippier, Keane, Shackell, Mee, Boyd (Sordell 90), Marney, Jones (Wallace 90), Arfield, Ings, Barnes (Vokes 73).
Subs not used: Gilks, Duff, Reid, Kightly.

Palace: Julian Speroni, Joel Ward, Scott Dann, Damian Delaney, Martin Kelly (Adrian Mariappa 83), Jason Puncheon, James McArthur, Joe Ledley, Wilfried Zaha (Adeline Guedioura 70), Yaya Sanogo (Glenn Murray 78), Dwight Gayle.
Subs not used: Wayne Hennessey, Brede Hangeland, Jerome Thomas, Fraizer Campbell.

Southampton...2 Crystal Palace...3
Saint Mary's Stadium, 24/01/15
FA Cup R4

Southampton: Forster, Clyne, Gardos (Targett 46), Fonte, Bertrand, Elia, Cork (Long 59, Seager 73), S Davis, Ward-Prowse, Tadic, Pelle.
Subs Not Used: K Davis, Isgrove, Reed, McCarthy.

Palace: Wayne Hennessey, Martin Kelly, Damian Delaney, Scott Dann, Joel Ward, Wilfried Zaha, James McArthur, Joe Ledley, Fraizer Campbell (Glenn Murray 81), Marouane Chamakh (Jason Puncheon 65), Yaya Sanogo (Adrian Mariappa 78).
Subs Not Used: Julian Speroni, Brede Hangeland, Barry Bannan, Dwight Gayle.

Chapter 32 - The Asia Cup – *Sydney, 9ᵗʰ-31ˢᵗ January 2015*

It comes as a huge surprise to people that I'm not really a fan of International football, especially the England team. A fact that becomes even harder to fathom when people realise that I went to Brazil for the World Cup, far further than I've ever travelled for Palace. However, those flabbergasted individuals all have something in common, they're not football addicts. Not in the way that I am anyway. They may have a love of the game, but they have a different relationship with it. They're not obsessed by one club.

I may not have ever kicked a ball in anger for Palace (I usually kick the chair in front to express that particular ugly but regular football emotion), but I feel part of something - a niche group. An outrageous crowd of rebels who fight tooth and nail to defend our club against the evil empire of famous Premier League clubs. Part of the fun of supporting a crap team is the fact that we're different; we're not all about winning trophies and success. Just as well, I hear you chuckle. We're South London and proud. We're a club that represent our area, and (despite being born in Berkshire), that's the 'we' that I characterise.

Now, I'm sure you could argue that having been born in England, but not South London, I should feel more representative of my country. However, I don't have the familiarity with my country. I haven't been through the pain, and built connections and routines. I don't go every Saturday. No one does. It lacks the regularity. How many people can afford the time or money to not only follow England, but sustain the same level of dedication for years on end? Entering adulthood (in the vaguest possible use of the word) has even impacted on my Palace attendance; imagine if that commitment was to prance across the continent on jolly-ups to Macedonia and Lithuania every few months? For the vast majority, restricted by careers and family, it couldn't be done. Giving up Saturdays for Palace is much more realistic and routinely achieved.

I haven't made friends through being an England fan as everybody jumps on the bandwagon. John Smith, Joe Bloggs and a middle class housewife from Surbiton are England fans, not 'cos they like football, or will feel the heartache, or have spent years agonising over the game, but because it's fashionable in the moment. They'll put their passion back into a box at the end of a World Cup and leave it there for another two years. Imagine being able to switch off after a Palace game or even for the summer? We couldn't do it. We're an intimate society at club level. A cult; not a fashion.

We like to think that you can't choose your football team and that forms the bond but the opposite is true. I couldn't pick my country but I did pick Palace. My Palace friends all had different journeys to supporting our club – some were born locally, some inherited it, some loved a player, and one liked the colours as they matched CSKA Moscow's. However, we all chose Palace, all of us fell in love with our red and blue way of life and we all bonded at the games.

Together, at the hundreds of matches we've attended, we've argued, despaired and cheered. We've hugged and drank, screamed and sang, booed and swore, debated and become bemused. Emotion is indescribably high at live football, yet the roller coaster goes on forever. Often appearing to be more of a never-ending Haunted House at Palace as the predictable ghosts pop-up, such as last minute goals galore, managers repeatedly walking out and financial woes a plenty. However, over the last twenty years, there's barely a story or result about the club that I couldn't recall – in such great detail that it not only astonishes friends, but it also terrifies me.

Alternatively, with England, I attended my first ever match aged 24, in Brazil, at the World Cup. The team had played twelve or so games just to get there. I'd only watched one on tele and couldn't even tell you who they'd played. I was a cheat. I didn't deserve to be there. I couldn't feel the pain when Suarez scored to knock them out, because they were out, not me. I hadn't earned the right to feel angry or upset. My main motivation was to enjoy the party in the home of sexy football and frankly, seeing England was more of a coincidence than the action of a fan. And I suspect I was far from the only one out there with that attitude.

A few die hard England fans criticized me for wearing a Palace shirt, but I didn't care. I was far more interested in finding the Palace flags and shirts out there than finding an England win. Incidentally, as I was with Brentford and QPR fans, I'll point out that not only did I see a much greater number of Palace shirts than either of their clubs, but we were also far more famous worldwide too. QPR might have had the Brazilian goalkeeper but we'd just 'f***ed up Liverpool'.

Still, the best thing about the World Cup was socialising with fans from all around the world. Each city we visited was awash with colours and cultures. The Chileans took over Rio and taught us local swear words, Salvador belonged to Portugal and educated me in taunting Liverpool in Portuguese, the Uruguayans, who were keener to talk about Suarez than Gonzalo Sorondo, our former centre half, filled Sao Paolo with parties and songs. And the Columbians were everywhere – and buying drinks for everyone! It's almost enjoyable in the usual sense of the word. You know, like going to the theatre or cinema, where you pay to be entertained, and it's sociably acceptable. Shoppers and passersby don't look on in fear at the unruly crowd. Instead, they join in with the party.

Imagine having a tournament with 32 club teams. They'd be mayhem. The police wouldn't know where to build their walls. I've heard of the Football League Centenary Tournament held at Wembley in 1988, which was contested by sixteen professional teams over two days. However, the fact that it had disappointing crowds suggests that it didn't particularly capture supporters' imaginations in the way that it could have done. Of course, the 80s were a different era of hooliganism and policing too. I suspect a similar event now would easily sell out, if the police allowed it to happen.

Anyway, the Old Bill wouldn't know what to do. How could they separate

Arsenal and Spurs, while also splitting the Manchester clubs, and keeping Millwall away from everyone? The atmosphere would be terrifying and aggressive. People would lock up their houses and the police would lock up the pubs. Yet at the World Cup and in international football, everyone – men, women, children, families – all sit together in the ground and drink together outside, even after a defeat as the tribalism is diluted. With the noticeable exception of England travelling to Marseille anyway.

In some ways I even miss that. I love the conflict of football. Not violence but a battle of wits and trash talking that exists between rival fans. Maybe it comes from having three competitive, stronger and older brothers? Maybe it's a result of the school playground, where I had to stand up for my own s*** club as no one else supported them. But when I meet up with my friends who support a different team, such as Jak who supports Brentford, I enjoy spending the time putting his team down as he abuses mine. At international level, other than Russia with my friend Pavel, I don't know enough passionate supporters of other nations to fight against. However, even with my Russian friends, I have watched an international match between our nations sat side by side, without any form of resentment.

However, by comparison, I wouldn't want to sit next to my Tottenham supporting brother and watch us play Spurs. I'd hate him if we were losing (note how the football fan can only focus on his own side's fate, ignoring that my brother's team was actually winning – other environments might allow me to be pleased for him) At football, I'd argue ferociously if he defended the ref, scorn at his attitude if he supported his team, and almost certainly irritate him immensely whie abusing him horribly if we actually took the lead. However, I'd have happily sat at the game, drinking beer and discussing it with a Costa Rican in Belo Horizonte as England drew 0-0. In fact, I'd have probably preferred it. But not watching Palace. No, watching my addiction brings me no joy, but turns me into a sub-human species of aggression and nerves for ninety minutes. That's the power they hold over us. That's the bond I've built with our club.

Of course, part of the reason for my lack of attachment to international football might be nothing to do with the above reasons. It might be that international football celebrates the game in the way that club football never can. We're all too filled with inbuilt-Neanderthal-anger to celebrate it. I hate Manchester United and their players, which means I hate Wayne Rooney and Rio Ferdinand and Ashley Young. I hate most of the England players and I especially hate John Terry for his thuggish, obnoxious and racist traits, before I even begin to think about him being the symbol of another thing I hate, Chelsea Football Club. I hate that I'm supposed to cheer these arse wholes as I come from the same country, when I'm allowed to boo them (and far worse) most other weeks.

But the hate goes far deeper than detesting a few key players. I think it goes back to 2005 and Andy Johnson's England debut. In my younger days of football obsession, I'd been proud to support our nation. I fondly remember going berserk while celebrating wins in Euro 1996 and the famous 5-1 in Germany. However, the excitement I felt before England's friendly with Holland on 9th February 2005 was immense. Unfortunately, he was humiliated. He was played out of position and although he was given four further caps, he never really got a fair chance. On behalf of AJ, I was fuming.

He was the embodiment of a hard working player. In many ways, he was limited by international standards, but he'd put everything into making himself the very best he could be. He'd scored 21 Premier League goals in one season for a relegated team with limited goalscoring chances, but he was pushed out by lazy, over-rated, under-achieving regulars. Take Steven Gerrard, some of his performances for Liverpool were inspiring, even to neutrals, in a way that Nick Hornby captured non-Arsenal fans with Fever Pitch. However, for England, he was half the player. I hate what I perceive as a lack of effort and commitment from the so-called world class players. I'm far more used to Palace's ability-lacking grafters like Peter Ramage and Clint Hill.

But that's what football does to us otherwise reasonably rational humans. I'm not a hate filled person and I don't 'hate' the England team. But watching Palace and putting so much energy into supporting my club has left me having a reason to 'hate' just about every single other team and so many other players in the country for one obscure reason or another. With England, I don't have that resentment to their enemies (other than Germany for breaking my heart in 1996). I simply don't care one way or the other for them.

I think part of the problem with England players (and fans for that matter) is the sense of entitlement. They've put very little in. They're not there every week. Yet, they think England are a big footballing nation and should be the best. Very comparable to West Ham in many ways. They've achieved buggar all since 66, yet the fans have unrealistic demands that not only should they win, but they must also play great football. When the reality is, which everyone seems to forget, they're actually pretty crap and have a rubbish atmosphere. West Ham are regularly out of the top division and England should perhaps remember that qualifying for major tournaments has been by no means a given in that past as it is now.

At Palace, we expect to be crap and we usually are, bar the odd hiccup of unnerving success. It's best that way. We're used to it. We don't fall down and hurt, so we return with the same acceptance of familiar uselessness in the following season. Whereas the expectation is built up for so long as England win qualifiers, everyone forgets that in reality, they're hopeless on the pitch and haven't beaten a decent nation in a competitive match since 2002. The nation expects, the team disappoints, and the fans become disillusioned and uninterested in a way that couldn't happen at club level. The automatic renewals of direct debit on our season ticket and regularity of fresh hope ensures that.

Rightly or wrongly, the hours that I've spent on the club – not just at matches, but defending them rigorously in the school playground, agonising over them in the pub, searching train websites for cheap travel, reading books, programmes and forums, telling uninterested girlfriends and workmates about my Saturdays, reliving great moments in my head, day dreaming while in a shop or on the morning commute, and generally being a one-minded, one-eyed, Palace fanatic has given me a sense of ownership of the club. An amount of time that the pure irregularity of matches wouldn't allow an England fan to waste. In my head, Crystal Palace are my club as much as they're the chairman's. Although I've done a deal where I don't get to make any major decisions and they don't ask me to stump up millions of pounds – just thousands on tickets, travel and accessories. An ownership I just don't feel over Rooney, Beckham or Wembley.

However, I might not love international football but I do love live football. So the Asia Cup, hosted by Australia thanks to their dubious relocation to their nearest federation, was as good as any excuse to take in some extra matches during my Palace exile. Made even better by the fact that the home nation's captain was none other than Palace skipper and legend, Mile Jedinak.

In fact, such is my loyalty to club over country, if I'd been given the choice between watching England or Australia in the World Cup, I'd have picked our skipper every single time. Had England been in the Asia Cup (well, let's face it, Australia sulked and got in to the competition (In a similar style to the way that they gate crashed the Eurovision Song Contest!) so why can't we? There's not that much difference in distance), then I may have even cheered our criminal cousins over us.

Unfortunately, my eagerness wasn't rewarded. Just like me, Jedinak was no more than a spectator in the stands for Australia's 4-0 group stage victory against Oman. Our leader had managed to injure himself before the game. The match itself was slow and turgid, and although the crowd was an impressive 50,000, the majority were fairy uninterested.

Richard and I met up with two German guys who we played five-a-side with and spent the second half with them. Such was our lack of interest in the match, and familiarity of the English laws about drinking in view of the pitch, we missed the start of the half as we finished our beers in the concourse, forgetting that you can be trusted to drink and watch football simultaneously in Oz. Having already seen off Kuwait 4-1 in the opening match, where Mile scored a penalty, Australia's victory meant they'd qualified for the quarter finals after just two matches. Which was just as well really, as they lost their final group game 1-0 to South Korea, with Jedinak still injured.

To be honest, the tournament was happening very much in the background. While there was a decent level of interest in the games, it was hardly football-mania in the way that it would be if the European Championships came to England.

Group C, which consisted of Iran, UAE, Bahrain and Qatar, was never likely to be a classic. Although, the six games averaged crowds of nearly 12,000. I guess the size of the country made it harder for people to travel to different stadiums, as matches were played in Sydney, Brisbane, Canberra, Newcastle and Melbourne.

Also, the lack of away following detracked from the games as most nations only had a handful of followers. At least they showed some consideration to the fans and ignored the temptation to place a game in Perth. It was hard enough in the World Cup for the England fans to travel 4,000km from Manaus to Sao Paolo, but to ask the thirty or so ultra-keen fans from Uzbekistan to do the same distance in the Asia Cup seemed a bit much.

Work life for me was so busy that I didn't get any opportunities to watch matches on the tele. I saw the odd bits of games during my breaks in the Opera House staff room, but not enough to get a real feeling for the competition. So the longer it went on, the more one-eyed I became about it. Being in Oz, had made my relationship with football very Palace-focussed. There was no Match of the Day or following other games as finding time and locations to see my beloved first team was hard enough. However, my interest in the Asia Cup was even more narrowed than focussing on one team. I was obsessed by a single player – who'd missed most of it so far anyway!

Jedinak returned to captain the country for their 2-0 quarter final win over China as they marched on to a semi-final vs United Arab Emirates, who'd shocked the competition's favourites, Japan, in the previous round. A match that Richard had gone to, leaving me bizarrely jealous that he was watching crap football as I kicked out at the violent, vulgar seagulls at work. Football was my only escape from work: Palace matches on a Saturday/Sunday morning, and live games in the Asia Cup. The fact that the game was Japan vs UAE didn't bother me. I wanted to go and watch a game, drink some beers and escape from my sixty-hour working weeks. However, the fact that I needed to frantically save to move to Melbourne meant that I couldn't afford to give up any shifts.

I set a deadline that I would go to the final of the Asia Cup at the end of the month, which my Dad had bought me tickets for as a Christmas present, and then move to Melbourne for the start of February. Once there, I could forget all about my bitterness, and the Opera house, and 2am finishes, and seagulls, and Scruffy Murphy's rejection, and six am alarm calls for my cellar job at Scary Canary. And that was because once I was in Melbourne, I had a plan.

Way back in November, at Rainbow Beach, before I went to Fraser Island, I'd met a girl who worked for a teaching agency in Melbourne. Although I was having just as much problem with receiving certification to teach in Victoria (the state that Melbourne is in) as I was in New South Wales (Sydney's state), she'd told me that I'd be able to get work as a Teaching Assistant, working with autistic children. The idea charmed me. I didn't want the stress of being in charge of a class, but the thought of being able to work with children, earn money, and still have a life around it, appealed to me a lot. However, until then, I had to slum it in under-paid and unfulfilling bar work.

The semi-final fell on a Wednesday, which was good because that was my day off from my early morning cellar job. I made the most of it and slept for thirteen hours, showing quite how sleep-deprived my body was. My schedule was crazy and I was forced into taking Del Boy's mantra of 'sleep being for wimps'. However, my body knew little about this and I often needed to snooze in the day, between my two jobs.

That night, the opera house had no shows and the weather was horrendous. Like us, Sydney's summer seemed to consist of 'three hot days and a thunder storm'. Yet, there were two major differences. Firstly, after the thunder storm, they had three more hot days and secondly, the hot days were all about 40 degrees and beautiful. Our restaurant, positioned under the world famous venue, was entirely outside and relied on shows and weather for its business. Therefore, we had little else to do but stand under the covers and watch the spectacular lightening crash down around Sydney.

No matter how magnificent this might have been, it didn't impress my boss, who sent me on an early break. In the staff room, I slumped into the chairs with my dry staff burger and watched the first half an hour of Australia's big game. It was over within fifteen minutes as Australia scored twice early on, neither of which were from Jedinak. But that didn't bother me as the result meant that I was going to be in the stadium to see a Palace captain try to win an international competition.

Make no mistake, I was genuinely excited for the final against South Korea. For me, it was as close to seeing Palace as I was going to manage all year.

Before I'd even left the hostel in the morning of the big match, I'd bumped into a Palace fan. Mark, an Aussie from Brisbane who'd caught the Palace bug during his own working holiday in England. The excitement for the day was built further by the fact that I'd planned my entire life around it.

My planned move to Melbourne had been delayed by getting tickets for the match, and I'd juggled days off from both my jobs to enjoy an entire day of drinking for football. This game excited me as much as most Palace games. Pre-match, Rich, Mark and I went for lunch and drank at the Opera Bar in over thirty degrees heat, surrounded by some of the world's most famous landmarks. The picturesque tourist location was as different to my Palace routine of a dingy South London boozer as possible. Back in London, Palace were hosting Everton that day so after the Aussie game, I intended to head to The Exhibition for a double celebration.

By five o'clock, our spirits were high, with jagermeister being the main culprit. The train journey was packed with yellow shirts but was once again, showed the difference between football cultures. In Brazil, the England fans had partied on the train to the out-of-town stadium in Sao Paolo with constant song in a manner that I'd become accustomed to while following Palace. My Brentford supporting friend had never seen anything like it and absolutely loved it. For me, it was fun, but no different to trains taking me to Watford, or

QPR, or Chelsea from Clapham Junction. However, in Australia, the hordes of fans who were packed onto the train taking us to the ANZ stadium, showed no interest in joining in with our songs.

Chants of "When Mile, Goes Up, To lift the Asia Cup, I'll be there, I'll be there!" and "He's big, He's hard, He'll kick Korea's arse! Jed-in-ak! Jed-in-ak!" were met with smiles, laughs and thumbs up, rather than any appetite to join us. In fact, the only engagement that we received was not from Australians, but some Brazilians wearing red and blue Bahia shirts – the team I'd fallen in love with while in Salvador the previous June.

As always, I focussed on the Palace in the occasion. Predictably, the match was of a low quality and I was disappointed in the average-ness of Jedi's performance. The atmosphere was poor too, but I did bump into a dozen or so other Palace fans. Some were proud Aussies, who idolised their captain. Some were Western Sydney fans, with Popovic's influence. Some were expats. However, all of them had felt a need to wear a Palace shirt to a match between South Korea and Australia, 17,000km from Selhurst Park.

While finding 12 Palace fans in a crowd of nearly 80,000 might not sound like a lot. Other than golden home shirts or red away ones, I didn't see another badge more represented. Unlike Manchester United or Liverpool shirts, I don't expect to see Palace ones. Even passing a fellow Eagle in Battersea forces a smile onto my face, so the idea of finding multiple ones in Sydney at an event that didn't really have anything to do with Palace uplifted my spirits far more than the game or beer.

However, Jedinak nearly sent the entire crowd, especially me, wild when he found the roof of the net with a free kick midway through the first half. Just before the interval, Australia did take the lead, although they showed a real lack of consideration for my dreams by not involving Jedinak at all. And for the majority of the second half, they looked comfortable with their lead as Korea lacked the quality to break them down.

Unfortunately, football isn't kind. Football is cruel and the closer you get to achieving something, the further away it feels. Nerves kicked in, mistakes were made and with seconds remaining, Korea scored to rob the host nation of their first ever trophy and take the game to extra time. Extra time was as tentative and flat as you'd expect in a final with neither team wanting to make a mistake and the crowd still hurting from conceding in the last minute.

However, while Rich and I were debating if we wanted to get a final beer for the second period of extra time, Australia regained their lead with a scrappy goal, which seemed a fitting winner for both the match and the tournament. The second period passed without much concern for the hosts and the final whistle was greeted with jubilation by the vast majority of the stadium, including me. And just as I had done at Wembley, I beamed with pride as Mile Jedinak, the Palace captain, lifted the trophy.

After the ceremony, we took the party to the Royal Exhibition so we could not only celebrate the result, but hopefully cheer Palace onto yet another victory. The pub was packed with gold shirts and the atmosphere was buzzing. Loudly and drunkenly, I burst into the pub and immediately lead the crowd in an array of Jedinak songs. I may have only been cheering him for his Palace connections but it certainly made me more than popular in the bar.

Rich and I were joined by Mark, from earlier in the day, Russ and Tom, two of The Exhibition regulars, a group of four Palace fans who'd come to the game from Melbourne, and another Palace fan from Brisbane. Despite a fairly disappointing 1-0 loss to a poor Everton side, the evening was thoroughly enjoyable. There was a happiness about the place after Australia's triumph. Of course, it was easier to feel less anger and aggression as Palace had risen from the relegation zone to thirteenth thanks to our wins against Tottenham and Burnley, as well as gaining a morale boosting cup win.

However, once more, the day had been about two things. Surprisingly, neither of which were winning. One was the usual Palace bond. Despite being from different countries, and of different ages, and values, and incomes, and stages in our Palace love affair, I'd absolutely loved meeting so many Eagles throughout the day. The other was my friendship with Rich. I'd been so lucky that this guy who I'd met in a hostel had somehow turned into an incredibly close friend. Honestly, I don't know what I'd have done if he hadn't allowed me to stay with him before I'd got the two jobs. It was a reminder that at least I did have some roots in Sydney, alongside discovering a lack of potential for Teaching Assistant work, that persuaded me to put my move to Melbourne on hold.

However, what was strange about our friendship was that while my obsession with Palace seems to bring out the more competitive and irritating sides of my personality and often makes friends detest my beloved team, Richard seemed to adopt them as his own. Even to the extent of cheering Jedi with me.

At the end of a long but brilliant day, on my way back to the hostel, an old man approached me and tried to chat. Having experienced many of the old drunks wondering around Sydney city centre on plenty of occasions, I kept my head down and tried to walk on.

"Oi!" he slurred after me.

Wearily, I glanced back and noticed something. He was waving a red and blue scarf at me. He was another Palace fan who'd come up for the Australia game from Melbourne. As he didn't know about our Exhibition meet ups, he'd found a different pub showing the game. Immediately, the two of us burst out into song. And to be honest, that summed up the day quite well. There I was, in the streets of Sydney at 5am, singing Palace songs with a drunken Australian pensioner, after a Palace defeat and our captain had lifted a major international trophy.

Crystal Palace...0 Everton...1
Selhurst Park, 31/01/15
Premier League

Palace: Julian Speroni, Joel Ward, Scott Dann, Damian Delaney, Martin Kelly (Wilfried Zaha 66), Jason Puncheon, James McArthur, Joe Ledley, Dwight Gayle, Marouane Chamakh (Jordan Mutch 25), Yaya Sanogo (Glenn Murray 71).
Subs not used: Wayne Hennessey, Adrian Mariappa, Brede Hangeland, Fraizer Campbell.

Everton: Robles, Baines, Jagielka, Stones, Coleman, Besic, Barry, McGeady, Mirallas (Oviedo 68), Naismith, Lukaku (Kone 90).
Subs not used: Griffiths, Distin, Alcaraz, Gibson, Barkley.

"It was a big tournament for myself and the fact that it was back home in Australia was pretty significant. It meant and awful lot that we won it in front of our own fans and was a huge achievement for us as a nation and as a team. We still use our victory now for motivation going forward and it gives us a belief that things can happen if you get everyone pulling in the right direction."

Mile Jedinak

Chapter 33 – Miserable – *Sydney, 1st-7th February 2015*

The two jobs continued to keep me occupied as I cleaned pipes, mopped floors, carried barrels and took stock takes in the morning, slept in the middle of the day and then waited on tables, emptied bins and took orders by night. Often, I would work all seven days of a week with six evening shifts and four morning ones. Occasionally, I booked time off to play five-a-side or watch Palace but generally, I worked every hour I could. As trying to find some work in schools was providing more blanks than Palace under Trevor Francis, I was determined to earn as much money as possible, as quickly as possible, and then go travelling again. This time to New Zealand.

One benefit of working between six and ten am at Scary Canarywas that it allowed me to message people back home and follow the football news more. Although the hostel manager seemed to have a strong dislike towards me and be critical of my personality when he couldn't fault my work, I liked the fact that I was given a list of jobs for the week and it was my decision to decide when I did them. Thankfully, the bar manager and I had a much better relationship and he just about kept me sane, despite the lack of sleep.

Another benefit was that I also managed to follow the climax of the January Transfer Window. On Deadline Day, Palace signed Lee Chung-Yong from Bolton and re-signed Wilfried Zaha permanently. Although Wilf hadn't looked like his old self since returning on loan from Manchester United, it was definitely a coup to get our former youth product back for a fraction of the price that we'd received for him two years previously. It had been a busy month for us as we'd already signed Jordan Mutch from QPR, Yaya Sonogo from Arsenal on loan, and Shola Ameobi on a free transfer. None of them were especially exciting but at least they seemed more planned and an upgrade on Kevin Doyle and a basically retired Andy Johnson (like we'd signed in the summer).

The next day, I felt a duty to indulge in a first. I watched the Super Bowl. Rich had engaged in Palace so much that I felt I should follow his first sport. In a way, I was intrigued. With all the games at Wembley and a potential London franchise, I hadn't really been swept along by all the excitement. Anyway, thanks to the time difference, the game kicked off in midmorning, rather than middle of the night slot in England. I did my morning job and then headed to Rich's for beers, chilli, hot dogs and "football".

A few of us had taken the Monday off work for the match and beers were already flowing when I arrived. As much as I tried, I just couldn't be captured by the sport. Even more than rugby, it was far too stop-start for my liking. However, Rich was adamant that it was the regular breaks that helped to make it popular in the States, especially to the TV companies, and it was a lack of intervals and advert opportunities that made the broadcasters reluctant to go with the tidal wave of enthusiasm towards 'soccer'.

In-between my early morning and late night shifts, I found it hard to use my time productively. As we were in February, it was still very much summer time down under and my tan from Asia seemed to actually be fading, such was my sleep pattern. During the sunny days, I generally lay in bed, watching films or reading the BBS, as I drifted in and out of consciousness.

When I was at work, I seemed to be developing a never-before-seen habit of arguing with managers. The problem was, I had no respect for the bosses, who showed no respect to me in the way that they spoke, and I also had no respect for the jobs. While it may be arrogant, working in bars felt like a waste. Mentally, I had no sort of challenge and the manner of the jobs (being in the cellar for one and simply delivering food/drinks in the other with little or no customer interaction) meant that I got no social satisfaction out of them either. I worked alone in the cellar, except for the manager who I couldn't stand, and the Opera House forbid and monitored discussion with colleagues during shifts.

The more I resented the cellar job and felt devalued, the more I took liberties. As with the Asia Cup, the Palace connection had given me an interest in the African Cup of Nations. Both Yannick Bolasie and Kwasi Appiah were representing their countries: D.R. Congo and Ghana respectively. In a perverse way, I'd kind of hoped they'd both do terribly and get knocked out in the group stages so they'd return to help Palace in their battle for Premier League survival.

However, as they'd both reached the semi-finals, and would be still out there for the third/fourth place playoff anyway, I now wanted them both to win. Instead of working, I followed the games on twitter as Bolasie's D.R. Congo lost to a star-studded Ivory Coast, but Appiah, a player who'd barely had a kick for us, helped Ghana into the final. Unfortunately, Kwesi and his team mates' achievement was over shadowed as the game was delayed by thirty minutes for crowd trouble, while fans and players alike feared for their safety.

That evening, I had another run in with the top boss at the Opera House. However, this time, I received an Official Warning. One of the duty managers had told me to do something one way, and the top boss told me to do it another way. I explained to him that I didn't mind which way it was done, but the managers needed to be consistent in their approach. To be honest, he seemed to accept that but didn't like me questioning him. He was the employer and I was the employee. While I knew that I had a valid point, and politely explained to him why, I also knew that I needed to change my attitude there or I would be sacked. Arrogant or not, I knew that I was easily replaceable. I hated the pettiness.

Things continued to frustrate me at every turn. It just seemed like everything was against me. Due to the lack of sleep, even little things seemed like a huge effort. I spent days chasing my Superannuation payment from Scruffy Murphys as I wanted to merge it with my Opera Kitchen one, but when it eventually came, I found that I'd been charged $300. 15% was tax, and I'd also been paying $15 a week in various charges, including one because I didn't set it up myself (Scruffy Murphy did as they insisted it was their policy), and another which apparently I'd agreed to when I set it up. They missed the irony in that...

And that's just the way the luck seemed to be going. In our promotion season, Palace had gone on a terrible run, where we tried to bottle promotion. In it, we seemed to come across every form of misfortune possible and that's how my life felt. While bleaching plastic 'glasses' one morning for the backpacker bar, I managed to destroy my phone, which had my photos from Asia on it. Anything that could go wrong, was going wrong. Except one thing. The one thing that I usually can rely on to go wrong! Palace.

Eventually, the weekend came and I'd negotiated to finish my shift at midnight so I could get to the Exhibition for Palace's 2am kick off against Leicester City, who were rock bottom of the league. Their early season thrashing of Manchester United had long left the memory after just two wins in eighteen subsequent matches. Despite our upturn in form, and Leicester's horrendous run, I, if not Russ and Jordo and the other 6 regulars in the pub, was still nervous. We are Palace and things tend to go wrong when they shouldn't.

Football was my escape from life and unhappiness, but that didn't mean that it wasn't still within me. Starting to 'relax', I was only a couple of beers in when I had my latest outburst of anger and frustration. I'd like to think that other than with my Spurs-supporting brother, I'm not the most argumentative person. Until it comes to Palace that is. It doesn't matter what it is: a disagreement about a player, an incorrect recalled memory or even the mere name of Neil Warnock. However, usually there's a shared understanding with Palace fans but not that night. A fellow fan dared to have a differing opinion to me. He wanted Jedinak, my hero, dropped.

Immediately, my response was verbal aggression rather than dialogue. It was only when the argument got embarrassingly heated (although purely fuelled by passion and entirely verbal) that I decided to take myself away. Soon enough, we'd bought each other pints and apologized but it showed me how much self-loathing and bitterness I was carrying around with me. Looking back, it was ridiculous. I was living in Oz, surrounded by friendly company, earning enough money, having amazing opportunities and Palace were winning. But none of that cheered me up. As a substitute, I preferred to focus on the fact that I was single, that I was missing the Palace games, that I was working too much, that I couldn't teach, that I had terrible sleep patterns, that I'd decided to hate my job, etc. So instead of enjoying the sun, noticing how many great people I was working with, revelling in the fact that I could watch Palace with fans and enjoying a stress-free job, I cursed seagulls and argued with a fellow eagle. I even considered coming home.

Once again, my insecurities made me question what was the purpose of me staying was. Even the bits I liked, felt like a London Lite. Sure, I had a group of Palace mates, but I had a closer group back home. Being able to watch the games was great, but I was actually at the games in England. Richard was a true and close friend, but I had dozens of them back home, rather than one to rely on. It just seemed that I was living for football, exactly as I had been in 2013 when I'd been fed up in London, and it seemed ridiculous to be designing my life around watching something on tele at 2am on a Sunday Morning. In truth, I was on a come down to reality after an amazing two months of travelling. Well, that and my inability to deal with change.

Once the game kicked off, Palace shoved my negativity to the back of my mind. I led the songs and forgot my gloom. If football is an relief from life, singing at football is reprieve from the stresses of watching the games. Leicester peppered our goal with shots and crosses. Thankfully, Speroni, our long standing hero, was equal to the task. He rolled back the years and produced a master class to keep the Foxes at bay, meaning we were still holding them at 0-0 after the first forty-five minutes.

One of my biggest complaints about Warnock had been his inability to change matches with his substitutions. In fact, he rarely made them until the final few minutes. On the other hand, Pardew's early tactical switches had turned the games against Tottenham and Burnley around. And in Leicester, he did it again. He dragged the ineffectual Jordan Mutch off the pitch at half time and added a second striker in Yaya Sonogo. Although he didn't score, his strength and powerful running caused problems throughout the half.

Ten minutes into the half, Joe Ledley nodded home from a corner to put us 1-0 up and the seven assembled devotees in Sydney jumped, screamed and hugged in jubilation. Particularly for me, the release of anger was therapeutic. The fact that I wasn't in Leicester didn't bother me.

We held on through a nervous finale and Nigal Pearson, their manager, showed the stress of a relegation battle by attacking James McArthur, who'd turned down a move to Leicester in the summer. As the tension built, closeness within our group grew and fingernails disappeared. Eventually, full time arrived and was greeted with cheers and hugs, and even a sweaty embrace with my pre-match antagonist.

We stayed and celebrated in the pub until it closed, posting victorious pictures with Russ' giant red and blue scarf that were retweeted by eagles around the world. News filtered through of losses for Brighton, who still weren't safe from going down to League 1, and Charlton, and Millwall. The Bermondsey Neanderthals demise was particularly sweet was it was sealed by three former Eagles: Sean Scannell, James Vaughen and Jacob Butterfield. In a strange way, I didn't know what to make of the evening. In little over a month, we'd gone from being almost certain to go down in my mind, to a position where relegation would be a disaster. Should I be grateful as it justified me living for Palace? Or should I be sad, as I knew that this would be as good as it got for the week. In fact, it was all I really had to show for the week. A trip to the pub for a 1-0 win against a side that were rock bottom of the league.

Leicester City…0 Crystal Palace…1
The King Power Stadium, 07/02/15
Premier League

Leicester City: Schwarzer, Konchesky, Morgan, Wasilewski, Simpson (Vardy 79), Mahrez, Cambiasso, James, Schlupp (Albrighton 66), Ulloa, Nugent (Kramaric 71).
Subs not used: Hamer, De Laet, Drinkwater, King.

Palace: Julian Speroni, Joel Ward, Damian Delaney, Scott Dann (Brede Hangeland 46), Martin Kelly, Jason Puncheon, James McArthur, Joe Ledley, Wilfried Zaha, Jordan Mutch (Yaya Sanogo 46), Dwight Gayle (Adeline Guedioura 78).
Subs not used: Wayne Hennessey, Adrian Mariappa, Fraizer Campbell, Glenn Murray.

Chapter 34 - Newcastle, Twice. – *Newcastle, (Australia) 8th-15th February 2015*

Sunday – worked 6pm-1am at the Opera House
Monday – worked 7am-10am at Scary Canary & worked 5pm-2am at the Opera House
Tuesday – worked 7am-10am at Scary Canary & worked 6pm-2am at the Opera House
Wednesday – worked 7am-10am at Scary Canary & worked 6pm-2am at the Opera House

I shouldn't have been moaning really. Taking on two jobs had turned around my finances as quickly as Palace's form. Like the team, I'd been dead and buried at Christmas but working so hard meant that I was once again saving hard. After one of the shifts, I began to speak to Camilla, who I'd lived with at Christmas, and we formulated a plan. I knew that I needed something to focus on now that I'd decided against moving to Melbourne. Between us, we decided to go to New Zealand for the entire month of April.

In light of our form and my determination to watch as many games as possible, I'd switched my Thursday morning cellar shift to Wednesday so I could see Palace host Pardew's former club, Newcastle. The night before, I'd spent time match making my Dad with my friend Pavel so he could borrow his season ticket for the game. Any normal person who has to wake at 6:30am most mornings after four or five hours sleep might choose to use their day off for a lie in. But no, not me. I wanted to watch a fairly mundane fixture. I was so focused on Palace being my life that I couldn't contemplate not watching.

Weary eyed, I headed to the 24hour Cheers Bar for 6:45am, where I met Ben, who was a new manager at the Opera House. We'd got on from the start and although he was an Arsenal fan from Bristol, he was keen to take in any football. He was new to Sydney and liked the idea of breakfast beers for Premier League football. Admittedly, my choice of beverage was a cup of tea. Well, for the first half anyway. Being a Palace fan, forty-five minutes of live action sent me further towards alcohol, especially when Papiss Cisse nodded the Geordies ahead just before half time.

I couldn't believe how busy the bar was. It was the early hours and it was packed out with people in suits before they headed to work. There were Southampton fans, frustrated by their 0-0 home draw with West Ham as they agonized over whether they could get Champions League football; Chelsea fans leapt with glee as Willian scored a last minute winner against Everton, and fans from both Manchester clubs as they secured comfortable victories. All of us, football fans of all ages and clubs, lived in harmony. Admittedly, Cheers had felt rough and edgy on a Saturday night, but everyone who frequented it on a cold

Thursday morning in February was simply there as they were hopelessly desperate to see their heroes.

Mind you, it wasn't all fraternising with the enemy. There were four of us fixed on our screen – Ben and I, and two others. One of them wore a Newcastle shirt, so I'd assumed they were both part of the Toon Army until I struck up a conversation with them midway through the first half. The other was an Eagle, who'd made a special effort to turn up to see us play against his mate's side. Social media also prompted me into dialogue with another eagle in Sydney. One holiday maker from South-London was up early watching the game, but unfortunately he was in Kings Cross, another English-inspired part of town.

Pardew rung the changes early again by throwing on Fraizer Campbell and Yannick Bolasie. The two of them combined when our recently returned star from the Dominican Republic of Congo crossed for Campbell to slide home the equalizer. Ben cheered nearly as loudly as me, as I infected him with my passion for the club. After this, Palace had their tails up and could have won it when Bolasie set up Zaha but he missed the decent chance. Still, once again, quality management had earned us rewards and we were a point closer to guaranteeing safety. After the game, I said bye to Ben and went back to bed, setting an alarm for my evening shift.

The following night was to be the final of eleven straight days of evening shifts since the Super Bowl. A shift that ended at 3am as I filled up pots of tomato ketchup for my money. As always, my social life had revolved around football. I'd booked the weekend off so that I could travel to Newcastle (New South Wales, not England) with Richard to see Emilie Heskey's former club, Newcastle Jets, take on Western Sydney Wanderers.

Newcastle might have been 300 miles away from Sydney and New South Wales might have banned drinking alcohol on trains, but it was the second closest away game of the season, after Sydney FC. We'd jumped on a train for 8am and were in our Central Coast destination by midday. Before matches, I've done a whole range of bizarre and strange activities, usually revolving around alcohol, but not always. In York, I visited the train museum. In Blackpool, I rode on a rollercoaster. In Cardiff, I took in a rugby game, and once against QPR, my pre-match was spent at Craven Cottage, watching Fulham play Everton (and AJ). However, in Newcastle, I had a first for a pre-match routine when I swam in potentially shark-infested water. The sea was rough and the knowledge of the recent fatal shark attack was chilling.

Although, I felt more at home when, after a few pints in a lovely craft beer bar in the centre, we got a cab to the ground. In the absence of a suitable pub by the stadium, we nipped into a liquor store to buy Jägermeister and red bull. A ritual that had started in London and Rich and I had carried on in Oz, starting with the Asia Cup matches and now taken to Newcastle.

Three-thousand fans had marched north from Sydney for the chance of seeing a 'local' away game. In a strange way, I felt a bit of a traitor. Until Western Sydney had started up and appointed Poppa two and a half years previously, Newcastle had been my Australian team thanks to their red and blue striped kit. However, due to my previous matches, and Popovic's appointment, I was very much in the Western Sydney camp.

Since I'd last seen the Champions of Asia, they'd played fourteen games, drawing four and losing ten. They'd somehow transformed themselves from the kings of a continent to the worst team in their country. Newcastle weren't much better mind. They had a mere eight points from a pathetic season and sat just above the Wanderers, with both teams cut adrift from the rest of the league. However, the dramatic fall from grace didn't stop the Sydney fans.

They were constant in their wall of noise throughout an abysmal goalless first half. As I'd found previously, the continuous singing was accompanied by a regular supply of flares and military trained choreography – we were told to crouch or wave our arms or salute at various points. Yet this time, I did begin to question it. I've been to plenty of Palace games where I get boozed up and lose some focus on the match, often getting carried away with the vocals passionately barking from one stand to the other, but here, the fans didn't seem to even notice the game.

Dubious refereeing decisions weren't met by a barrage of abuse and anger, there was scarcely a sigh as the majority simply sang their way through the match. They certainly didn't stop to moan at the players, which was just as well really as passes rarely hit their target and 'we' failed to even register a hint of a chance in a miserable first half performance. No matter what happened, they sang and sang and sang. In fact, the only thing deemed worthy of stopping for was telling other fans to raise their voices.

The second half was slightly better as Western Sydney began to carve out some chances and twice managed to put the ball in the back of the net. Unfortunately, both times the referee ruled them out, which I assumed was to the frustration of the away crowd but I wasn't sure as they happily carried on singing anyway. Regardless, it frustrated me. With seven minutes left, a minute after the second of these strikes had been disallowed, the Wanderers' fans finally stopped for breath. The referee went from villain to hero as he pointed to the spot.

In the fifteenth match of the season, the previous years' top club had a chance to win for the first time. After a brief cheer, the Wanderers returned to song – not for the player charged with taking the spot kick, but for the club. It's always about the badge. Like the fans, the striker showed no nerves in the situation. He dinked it down the middle, before charging over to the away faithful to lap up the praise. The Wanderers fans even stopped singing and let mayhem prevail as they went crazy for the goal. Over halfway through the season, finally, this was their moment.

Or it should have been anyway. Newcastle offered nothing in response for the final seven minutes. Their performance had been feeble. It was only in stoppage time when they began to lump balls forward to salvage a point. With just a minute of the three "added on" remaining, a fairly innocuous strike from the edge of the area hit a red and black arm, and the referee pointed to the spot. The Jets had a penalty of their own, which they smashed into the top corner to equalize. For the second time in the week, I was disappointed with a 1-1 draw against Newcastle.

After the match, Rich and I found a pub packed with fans. The atmosphere was much more English in there. Considering that the Wanderers fans who I spoke to seemed to idolise our Premier League crowds, they'd actually made more of a European atmosphere with long, continuous and bouncy tunes. In England, we prefer short bursts of abuse directed at the ref, the opposition, our rivals or a mouthy fan in a Matalan t-shirt at the front of the opposition's section, rather than focusing solely on cheering our team. However, in the pub, Sydney FC were on the tele and the robotic party was replaced by humorous and demeaning chants.

Tired from the early start and midday drinking, the pair of us needed a power nap before heading out in the evening. We nipped back to the hostel and I had my first ever post-match snooze. Around eight o'clock, we wearily got up and headed into town, heading for the Honeysuckle area of bars by the river. To be honest, the evening was a disappointment. Newcastle is a small and quiet town. Despite being the seventh biggest settlement in Australia, it hosts just 400,000 people. Cardiff, with a similar population, is the 17th biggest city in the UK. Yet it felt like even fewer than that. The entire 'vibe' of the place was that it was a quaint, little seaside town, comparable perhaps to Littlehampton.

However, unsatisfactory as it was, the lack of a long night out (most places closed well before the 1am lock out rule), wasn't what bothered me. Palace had, in my opinion, their biggest game of the season so far. If not the biggest, then definitely the most exciting. The FA Cup 5th Round. Home to Liverpool.

Unfortunately, it had been picked to be on tele at 5:30 in England, which meant a 4:30am kick off in Oz. Ideally, I'd dreamed of there being a pub or club showing the match, but even a small amount of research showed that was highly unlikely. Plan B had been to stay out until kick off and then watch it on the hostel computers, but that proved impossible too. So when I collapsed in my slumber at about 1am, I set my alarm for 4:20 in the morning, having already purchased some tokens to use the reception room computers.

With Palace now close to being safe in the league, I was fully focused on the FA Cup. Mind you, even if we weren't safe (which we weren't quite yet), I'd have still favoured taking on this huge opportunity. If we could beat Liverpool (and we knew we could) then only Arsenal and Manchester United remained for us to be scared of. West Brom and Villa of the Premier League, Reading and Blackburn of the Championship and League 1's Bradford City were the rest of the draw. We weren't ever going to get another opportunity like this. Indeed, I was so excited, that I didn't actually get to sleep until about 3:30am, by which time it was barely worth sleeping at all.

The FA Cup is what got me into club football. Other than Euro 96, my earliest football memories are of the cup and the end of the 90s, when I first followed the game, just about still had the magic of the BBC giving up a whole day of TV for cup final coverage. It probably further fuelled my cup passion that I started visiting Selhurst in the doomed 1997/98 season. You know, the one where we didn't win a home league game until April. Anyway, our dismal home form meant that my first, seemingly mythical, Palace win at Selhurst, was against Leicester City... in the FA Cup with a Bruce Dyer hat trick. Proof, if ever it was needed, that anything really can happen in the magical competition.

I remember the 1997 Cup Final when Chelsea beat Middleborough. All of my Berkshire-born primary-school friends supported Chelsea and carried their jubilant celebrations on for months, much to my annoyance. A bitterness that deepened and was fed every Saturday as BBC's Football Focus showed a clip of Dennis Wise lifting the trophy. Each week, I vowed that one day, that would be Palace. That it would be Ray Houghton, or Andy Roberts, or Andy Linighan, or Dean Austin, or Haydon Mullins, or Neil Shipperley, or Tony Popovic, or Mark Hudson, or Shaun Derry, or Paddy McCarthy or Mile Jedinak, who featured on Football Focus (or any other football show) lifting the famous, old cup.

The fact that there is such a long list of low-key (to the outside world) names helps you to understand how long that I've wanted this. It was nineteen years ago that I first set eyes on the biggest realistic trophy that Palace could win. Who else, other than football fans, even remembers what they wanted when they were seven? Let alone still wants the same thing. Each year, the chance and dream arrives, only to disappear just as quickly.

At least the league usually gives you a glimmer of hope towards achieving your aims, and as Palace fans, they're usually pretty low threshholds. Finish 6th in the second tier or 17th in the first. However, in the FA Cup, blink and it's gone. As I regretted before the Dover game, our record is horrendous in my time following the club, and this, the 5th round, was as far as we'd got over those nineteen years of desire and yearning.

And Liverpool, with Pardew, it just seemed like fate. I'd already declared that I would come home for the final. I didn't care how much a ticket would cost on the black market. Of course, being abroad, meant that I was highly unlikely to qualify for a ticket in my own right thanks to the disgustingly low allocations given out by the FA. Mind you, coming home for a final wasn't even a dilemma, whatever the needs or cost. It was a potential semi-final that I wasn't sure about.

Anyway, we had to get past Liverpool first (and someone else after that) before I should have even begun to think about a semi-final, but that's just not how football fans work. We dream, we plot, we hope, and we get hurt. I found the match on a stream, but the sound options on the computer were locked so I sat in silence, watching the game without commentary. As much as certain commentators can be irritating, sitting in silence was eerie. Also, bearing in mind it was nearly five in the morning and I'd barely slept, it required a lot of concentration.

In fact, the lack of excited squeals from the muted commentator meant that I didn't look up from my phone (I was sharing a link for the stream with my Dad) when someone put us ahead in the first half. I didn't know whether to laugh or cry as I waited for the replay to find out how we'd taken the lead and who'd done it. As it turned out when they eventually showed a replay, it was Fraizer Campbell with a tap in.

Unfortunately, the prematch arrogance grew and I felt a lack of surprise at our lead. Rather than thinking, *"Bloody hell, we might actually beat Liverpool here!"*, I was thinking *"Here we go again!"* and wondering how many more bemused South Americans and Asians and Yanks would be watching on as the scouse giants came up against their worst nightmare once more. Throughout the first half, we looked strong at the back and dangerous on the break, despite the second goal eluding us.

But some things never change. We should never believe as Palace fans, or expect. We should know what's round the corner as we've seen it so many times before that it might as well stop bloody lurking around the corner and just smugly stand in front of us waving. When we think we're onto something good, we inevitably cock it up. Martin Kelly lost his man and Liverpool equalised. Ten minutes later, Speroni spilled a freekick and we were behind. From then on, we never looked like coming back into the match.

When the computer crashed with five minutes left, I didn't even bother to try and load it again, so much was my certainty that the game was gone. Instead, I retired to my bed and followed the final moments on the BBC text updates. There was to be no final twist and as we had been for the previous nineteen years, we'd been dumped out of the cup before entering March. Although I was gutted, after building my excitement up so much, I couldn't believe the fact that the BBS, our supporters' online forum, was already full of anger and moaning. Yes, we'd been a bit flat after falling behind, but considering where we'd been a couple of months ago, we couldn't really complain. Finally, with the sun coming up, I crashed back to sleep.

On the way home the following day, as I regretted that this was likely to be the closest that I would get to an away day while abroad (and it felt more like a weekend away to visit a new town with a match thrown in rather than a football-based trip – as much as I liked Western Sydney, they just weren't Palace) I remembered the challenge that I'd set myself in Brisbane of finding a place named after all 92 football league clubs. The station named Cardiff, just outside Newcastle, was my first prompt, which reminded me that I had just been to Newcastle and I'd gone through Torquay on the way there.

Once I was back home in Sydney, I crashed. Not only was I exhausted by Palace depriving me of sleep, but I also knew that I had a 65 hour working week ahead of me.

Crystal Palace...1 Newcastle United...1
Selhurst Park, 11/02/15
Premier League

Palace: Julian Speroni, Joel Ward, Brede Hangeland, Damian Delaney, Martin Kelly (Yannick Bolasie 67), Jason Puncheon, James McArthur, Joe Ledley, Wilfried Zaha, Marouane Chamakh (Dwight Gayle 65), Yaya Sanogo (Fraizer Campbell 25).
Subs Not Used: Wayne Hennessey, Adrian Mariappa, Jordan Mutch, Glenn Murray.

Newcastle: Krul, Janmaat, Coloccini, Williamson, Haidara, Gouffran, Colback, Sissoko, Cabella (Dummett 85), Cisse (Abeid 78), Perez (Riviere 89).
Subs Not Used: Woodman, R Taylor, Anita, Obertan.

Crystal Palace...1 Liverpool...2
Selhurst Park, 14/02/15
FA Cup Round 5

Palace: Julian Speroni, Martin Kelly (Adeline Guedioura 63), Scott Dann, Brede Hangeland, Pape Soaure, Yannick Bolasie (Wilfried Zaha 71), Joel Ward, Joe Ledley, Dwight Gayle, Marouane Chamakh (Jason Puncheon 46), Fraizer Campbell.
Subs Not Used: Wayne Hennessey, Adrian Mariappa, Damian Delaney, Glenn Murray.

Liverpool: Mignolet, Sakho, Skrtel, Can, Moreno, Lallana, Allen, Henderson, Coutinho (Lovren 77), Sturridge (Lambert 77), Markovic (Balotelli 46).
Subs Not Used: Ward, Johnson, Manquillo, Borini.

Chapter 35 – Opposites at The Exhibition – *Sydney, 16th-28th February 2015*

Another reason why Palace are so special to me is summed up by when I started to communicate with them about selling my first book in the club shop. I found Steve Browett, the club's co-chairman, and Mike Pink, the club's Head of Consumer Sales, to both be brilliantly enthusiastic and caring about their jobs as well as the club. Having owners and employees who went out of their way for a supporter and a supporter's product, even as we enter a stage in the club's history where they try to widen the global brand, really is what makes my club special. Note the use of the use of the word 'my' there. It is deliberate. Unlike Ron Noades or Simon Jordan, the previous chairmen during my time following the club, the current owners really make the fans feel valued and listened to.

As well as Browett and Pink, I also contacted our former defender, Matt Lawrence, on Twitter. He too was delightfully positive and helpful to my project, offering to read the book and write a foreword for me. Having such a positive response from Matt provoked me to email the current clubs of five or six other players to discuss the 2009/10 season with. Almost immediately, I received excellent and excited responses from Danny Butterfield, Johnny Ertl, Paul Hart and Julian Speroni.

The passion that those former players had for our club was infectious and the spirit was clear, even a few years on. They'd been the rock that the club had been built on. With the club doing so well, it was easy to forget how far we'd come in just four years, when going out of the FA Cup was the least of our worries. However, what made me even prouder was that the team spirit and atmosphere that we'd created in 2010 when we faced oblivion, seemed to be living on in 2014, as we pulled towards the top half of the Premier League.

Since coming back from Newcastle, I'd done five closing shifts and three early morning ones. At least the absence of a midweek Palace match meant that I'd had one lie in during week to recover. In fact, I even managed to build up some sort of personal life with trips to the beach and Hyde Park during the daytime with colleagues from both of my jobs. It was tiring but it had to be better than wallowing in my own self pity and only socialising for Palace, right?

However, Palace was still the main event. So as soon as I finished my shift at around 1:30am on the Saturday night/Sunday morning, I set about sprinting through Sydney to make it to The Royal Exhibition in time for kickoff of our game against Arsenal. There, I'd arranged to meet Ben again, my boss from the Opera House, which was just as well really. No other Palace fans showed up. In fact, with West Ham away (well not playing, meaning their fans were away) and Chelsea fans retreating to their original pub since their invasion for the Burnley game, we were more or less the only people in the boozer, other than an argumentative drunk Irish man and a group of inebriated teenagers. Without football, our pub that was open until 5am, simply wouldn't be able to survive.

As with previous sprints across town, I was given little instant reward. Our new left back, Pape Souare, just eight minutes into his Premier League debut, managed to miss-control the ball, lose it, and then foul an Arsenal striker in our own box to give away a calamitous penalty and gift the Gunners the lead. He'd nearly done the same a week previously against Liverpool.

It got worse for us just before half time. Arsenal scored again. One of the disadvantages of watching on TV is that before I could get over the disappointment of conceding, the replays were already rubbing salt into the wound by showing me that it had been marginally offside and should have been disallowed.

To be fair, in the second half, Palace created plenty of chances but we didn't register a shot on target until the 84th minute and by then, it was surely far too late. Although, four minutes into stoppage time, I did manage a small cheer as Glenn Murray bundled home his first goal of the season in red and blue. The ex-Brighton legend had looked to be heading out of the exit door on Deadline Day but he surprised and delighted us all by signing a new contract. Bafflingly, but not as bafflingly as sending him on loan to Reading; he had barely played since signing his new deal. However, it was great to see him grab a morale boosting consolation in the 94th minute when he'd been thrown on as a substitute.

The goal had scarcely provoked a reaction for me as it had seemed so hopelessly little so late on. I'd smiled, and been pleased for Glenn, but I couldn't see how it would help us – and in the end, it didn't really. But we did come oh so close to creating something oh so special. One minute later, in the final minute of five added on, Bolasie got the ball out wide and beat his man. Murray rose to meet the cross at the far post and nodded it down against the inside of the woodwork, before it bounced harmlessly away.

It'd looked a certain goal. I'd sent myself flying off my stool in delight. Never mind an eruption of delight at Selhurst, I could have matched it on my own in the empty Sydney pub at 4am. The agony wasn't lost on the landlord either (nor the importance of football fans in his pub I suspect) as he came over and gave me a free schooner of ale. Still, kind as it was, it meant very little to me at that point.

The following week was long and busy. I worked another fifty hours, as I seemed to become more and more popular at the Opera House with the management, even being given special responsibilities occasionally. Nothing spectacular, but being given a microphone to communicate and solve problems with those in charge, or being asked to run the pass, as the final line of defence for food, before being sent out.

I must admit, it showed me how child-like I am. In the classroom, I'm always amazed about how much it means to kids to be asked to take the register to the office or send a message to another teacher, and the errands that I'd been given in the restaurant weren't much more challenging than that. Yet for some inexplicable reason, being chosen for a job made me take a lot more pride in what I was doing and how I presented myself. I even shaped my long, scruffy travelling beard, produced the occasional smile and spent less time daydreaming about kicking seagulls.

Mind you, it wasn't any better at the other job. Ralph, the top boss, seemed to hate me for anything and everything. One morning, I arrived to discover that the industrial fridge door was broken and there was a leak in the roof of the cellar. When I told him, he set off on a foul-mouthed rant at me for destroying his business. Another day, he raged at me for not stocking the bar, with a delivery that hadn't arrived. Still, I kept my mouth shut, avoided him at all costs and did the bare minimum. The irony was, if he actually looked at the jobs that I was doing, I'm sure he could have criticised me fairly. Unfortunately, his erratic rants were not so much about my job, but dependant on his own mood and situation.

As time went by, and I again started to do more and more around town, such as work on my book, go for dates, play volleyball, cook meals and partake in pub quizzes, basically anything with people who were fast heading towards that brilliant relationship of friendship, the cloud that I'd previously been under seemed to slowly raise itself from over me. Not completely, but partially. The problem with feeling sorry for yourself is that you often don't have a real reason for it, which makes the misery and outlook hard to explain.

In many ways, I wish it was like football. When you win, you're happy. When you lose, you're sad. But in life, it's far more complicated. Previously, I'd believed that Palace could be completely directive of that cloud but in recent weeks, I'd finally accepted that life, and being happy in it, and particularly friendship, was more important to me than Palace. The wins alone hadn't been enough to clear me of my misery (although they'd been a great distraction) but the recent defeats (admittedly to Arsenal and Liverpool) hadn't been enough to derail my recovery.

The following Saturday, after a week of late nights and early starts, I was so exhausted that as soon as I woke, it was time to eat my evening meal and head to work for my five o'clock shift. Palace were kicking off early against West Ham (12:45pm London/11:45pm Sydney) so I'd booked myself as 'unavailable' for after 11pm, meaning I had a short shift with an exciting event to look forward to at the end of it. And what an excitement it was! This was the match that I'd been waiting for. The Royal Exhibition Derby Mark II.

Thanks to the earlier kick off, the trains were still running when I finished so I had a slightly easier dash through town. Upon arrival, the pub was packed. There were about 25 or so Palace fans and a similar amount of Hammers. Everyone had been saving themselves the week before, when I'd sat alone in the same pub, for this. We'd been humiliated earlier in the season but this was our moment, and we wanted to show that this was our pub! As soon as I entered, I marked my arrival with a song. At the beginning of the season, I'd very much been an enthusiastic visitor, like I was for the Western Sydney games. But now, I was the chief cheer leader! Although not as pretty as the Crystals, I was just as keen...

The mood in the pub was worrying. People had seen our team sheet and couldn't believe that Jordan Mutch was starting ahead of Jason Puncheon. Still, it didn't really bother me. The West Ham games were as close as I was likely to get to being in a Palace crowd for a match all season and I intended to sing my heart out and make the most of it! I'd brought some support too: Dave, my friend, who was a chef at Scary Canary, as well as Ben and Rich, who had all vowed to join me and unite in song to drown out the enemy. Within minutes, my voice was going horse and Jordo brought me a jug of Pale Ale on the understanding that I'd carry on singing at the front!

However, as loud as we were, the Hammers seemed to have the upper hand on the singing... until we scored. Glenn Murray's weak header bounced and spun like a Shane Warne delivery and the red and blue of the pub erupted. There was pandemonium... in half of the pub.

The night was brilliant. All of the Palace regulars were there, and the occasional guys, and even a few new members, including a guy called Mark, who was travelling the world. He and I got talking as he'd just booked a trip to New Zealand, as I had. Unfortunately, Camilla had dropped out and I'd decided to do a tour bus trip alone, but it turned out that Mark and I would be in the land of Kiwis together. Hopefully finding obscure ways to watch Palace.

There was another fan from Thailand, who'd met an exiled eagle in his home land and had adopted us as his club. Since moving to Australia, it had been far easier for him to see Palace as Premier League football wasn't as prominent when he lived back home as it is now. Additionally, there was another fan who was new to Sydney called Dave. He was around my age and had just moved over to start a new life with his girlfriend. All in all, there was about thirty eagles in the pub that night. Old and new, everyone fitted in perfectly to the Palace family. Although, despite our lead and the Hammers dreadful league form, the noisy bunch from East London wouldn't let us forget they were there, especially as we'd moved in to steal the best seats before kick-off.

Half time came and went as the beers flowed. During which, Jordo and the leader of the Hammers group did a joint speech to announce a friendly between the fans so that money could be raised for the Dylan Tombides fund. He was a former Australia and West Ham youth player who'd died a year previously. As often is the case, when faced with a heart-breaking tragedy, humans come out fighting and are determined to bring some good into the world to balance out the pain. And contrary to some police forces' beliefs, football fans aren't too dis-similar to humans really. The "Dylan Tombides DT38" charitable foundation was launched with the aims of "fundraising, raising awareness of testicular cancer and of the education of young people on the subject."

Still, that cause was for another day. The early hours of the morning in Sydney were for Exhibition Pride and celebrating three points. Early in the second half, Scott Dann put us two 2-0 up. Alongside the masses, I leapt up in the air. Unfortunately, when I landed, it happened to be on the foot of a rather large and rather irritated West Ham fan. Thankfully, he was able to spot that it was a pure accident and could easily have been the other way around if his team weren't quite so rubbish. Although I didn't point that out to him at the time, I apologised, quickly and desperately, because as I said, he was very large.

Minutes later, Murray scored his second and our third. I even managed to jump, hug and scream without putting the ankles of any Hammers in danger. We were in dreamland and the enemy was stunned. After each beautiful goal, once we'd calmed down from the initial celebration, I'd turned to our fan base and led the raised hands and suspense raising 'woooahs', before crashing my arms down onto the table to begin our chant of "We Love You...".
Exactly as the fans in the ground were greeting each glorious goal.

The party was on and revenge for the defeat in my first Palace match at the Exhibition was sweet. Even if, Palace being Palace, we made a bit of a meal of it in the end as my three favourite players made some howlers. First, Murray was sent off for a needless second yellow as Pardew was desperately trying to sub the ticking time bomb off. Then, Speroni gifted them a goal as he only got a weak hand to an average shot and minutes later, Mile Jedinak elbowed a Hammer in our area, which thankfully all of the officials missed or it would have surely resulted in a red card and penalty. Not that I noticed at the time – I was far too busy leading the singing and dancing.

As our nerves grew, while our opponents both sensed the advantage and realised that they had nothing to lose, the echoing loud sound of Forever Blowing Bubbles rose through the pub, drowning us out. Suddenly, it wasn't our pub and it wasn't our night. Our opponents may have been losing on the tele but they were winning at the bar. With five minutes to go, finally beginning to believe that we might hold on to a precious three points and surely Premier League safety, I stood on my stool, turned to face our loyal Sydney fan base and screamed "SUPER AL'S RED AND BLUE ARMY! C-P-F-C!"

It had the desired effect. The chant continued for the final five minutes as well as the five added on. Try as they might, West Ham couldn't raise their voices to match us. We'd won. On the pitch in East London and in the Pub in Sydney.

After the game, I knew I had a responsibility. When they'd smashed us in August, the Hammers had been dignified and gracious in victory. This was going to be difficult for me. I am a child at football. Not only had we thrashed them, we were now eight points clear of relegation and sitting comfortably in twelfth place. I wanted to sing and gloat and be smug into the night. They're some of the football emotions that I enjoy the most, because we all turn into a bit of an arse when it comes to watching our team win. However, it really wasn't appropriate. The majority of the Hammers' fans had shown throughout the season that they were great guys.

As it was, both sets of fans stuck around for hours after the match, mixing and drinking together. Palace and West Ham. Fraternising with the enemy and as far as I know, I didn't manage to upset even one of them. Maybe I really have grown up a little. Still, when I did eventually make it to my bed at around 5:30am, having watched the three o'clock kick offs, and the start of the evening match, I fell asleep as content as I'd been for months.

Crystal Palace…1 Arsenal…2
Selhurst Park, 21/02/14
Premier League

Palace: Julian Speroni, Joel Ward, Scott Dann, Damian Delaney, Pape Souare, Wilfried Zaha, Jordan Mutch, Joe Ledley (Shola Ameobi 79), Jason Puncheon, Dwight Gayle (Glenn Murray 79), Fraizer Campbell (Yannick Bolasie 56).
Subs not used: Wayne Hennessey, Brede Hangeland, Martin Kelly, Mile Jedinak.

Arsenal: Ospina, Monreal, Mertesacker, Koscielny, Chambers, Coquelin, Cazorla, Ozil, Sanchez (Gabriel 89), Welbeck (Gibbs 76), Giroud.
Subs not used: Szczesny, Bellerin, Rosicky, Wilshere, Walcott.

West Ham United…1 Crystal Palace…3
Upton Park, 28/02/15
Premier League

West Ham United: Adrian, Jenkinson, Reid, Tomkins, Cresswell, Song (Nene 61), Kouyate, Noble, Downing, Valencia, Sakho.
Subs not used: Jaaskelainen, O'Brien, Collins, Demel, Jarvis, Nolan.

Palace: Julian Speroni, Martin Kelly, Damian Delaney, Scott Dann, Joel Ward, Mile Jedinak, Jordan Mutch (James McArthur 33), Yannick Bolasie (Joe Ledley 82), Jason Puncheon, Wilfried Zaha (Shola Ameobi 71), Glenn Murray.
Subs not used: Hennessey, Pape Souare, Brede Hangeland, Dwight Gayle.

"Did the rise of the club surprise me? Not really. The on-field stuff we took care of on a daily basis and we always had a belief - that was a key thing. If we were set out in the right way and organised, we always gave ourselves a fighting opportunity. We had the players that could go out and win us games, but we also had guys who could do the other side of games as well, like keep clean sheets. Over the years, I don't think anyone at the club could have predicted where we'd be now but sometimes when it came to Crystal Palace, there were no boundaries. You just thought like that and you never allowed yourself to think 'Oh we're Crystal Palace, we should be restricted to this and that'. You just never thought about that. We just went and did what we did on the field and with the support that we had behind us, the fans, we really did feel that we could do anything and achieve anything. I think everyone outside of the club started to notice us too and it was great what the football club had become, and it's still progressing now."

Mile Jedinak

Chapter 36 - The Losing Week – *Sydney, 1st-6th March 2015*

Day	Morning	Afternoon	Evening
Sunday	Slept and recovered from the West Ham game	Went bowling with Scary Canary friends	Worked 5pm until 1am and then went to a packed Cheers Bar for Liverpool vs Man City with Opera House friends
Monday	Worked 7am – 10pm	Slept	Worked 5pm until 2am
Tuesday	Worked 7am – 10pm	Slept	Worked 5pm until 2am
Wed	Watched Palace vs Southampton at 6:45am	Slept	Went to Western Sydney vs Guangzhou Evergrande
Thursday	Worked 7am – 10pm	Slept	Worked 5pm until 2am
Friday	Worked 7am – 10pm	Slept	Worked 5pm until 2am

As I've grown older, I've learnt that I really shouldn't let football dictate my mood, but as you can see from the table above, during that week in early March of 2015, I had very little else to allow my frame of mind to go on. My shifts were deliberately planned around the two events that I wanted to do: watch Palace and Western Sydney. I won't bother you with any details around the rest of the week and will merely fill you in on the Wednesday, where I once again found myself looking inwardly towards what being a football fan is all about.

Beep-beep! Beep-beep! Beep-beep! The sound that fills us with dread as we wince our eyes and send a tired, wriggling arm to search for the snooze button on our phone lying by our pillow. I'd love to report that when it's for football, or as close as Palace can muster to football, I'm more excited than if it were for work. I'd love to report that I jumped out of bed with glee and began singing Glad All Over, building myself for the match. But I didn't.

I might have done. If this were a cup final, or a big match, or even a chance for revenge over some minor incident that had happened earlier in the season. But it wasn't. It was just one of thousands of games that we wake up for, we attend, we muddle on through and then we return home, neither full of hatred, or regret, or bitterness, or sadness, or joy, or any other particular emotion. It's just what we do as football fans. We turn up because we have to and see what happens. In many ways, as football matches go, this was very much your every day work routine.

Unlike the Newcastle game, Cheers Bar seemed to be empty for this one. Just like ours, the other games had very little pull towards them (Hull vs Sunderland & Villa vs West Brom). Mark, the Palace fan who I'd met othe previous Saturday and would be in New Zealand when I was, joined me and we ordered cups of tea just before kickoff. Anyone who has read my first book will appreciate that this had the same effect on our bladders as beer.

The game was turgid and the company was tired. Don't get me wrong, Mark is a great guy and is now one of my good friends. However, the pair of us were exhausted in the early hours and the football gave us very little to cheer. Saints offered nothing, we offered nothing. Mind you, we couldn't complain as we drifted aimlessly towards an eighth consecutive unbeaten away game. The previous seven being against QPR, Villa, Dover, Burnley, Southampton, Leicester and West Ham.

Unfortunately, with just a few minutes left, one of my long-standing heroes let us down, and not for the first time recently. Speroni is a legend at Palace. I've worshiped him for as long as I can remember, longer than many of my friendships in fact. However, against Liverpool, Arsenal, Everton, Burnley, West Ham and now Southampton, he'd conceded softly. We lost 1-0 thanks to his late error, but it wasn't that which upset me. I was convinced that when I turned up to see us play the on following Saturday, and longer term when I returned from OZ, my Number 1 wouldn't be Palace's Number 1.

After the game, Mark and I parted. We agreed to meet around four at Central Station, and he went to the beach while I went to bed.

Beep-beep! Beep-beep! Beep-beep! Hearing it twice in a day was simply cruel...

I hadn't been to Paramatta for a Wanderers home game since that electric semi-final when I'd first fallen for the club. Since that jubilant night, when I'd gate crashed the joy, I'd brought my own favourite football guests – despair and misery. Since the Newcastle game, they'd lost three more on the bounce, including a 4-3 home defeat to Sydney FC.

However, they now had a chance to forget their A-League form of no wins in eighteen and play in the Asian Champions League. The competition they were the holders of. Unfortunately, it wasn't going to be easy as the opponents for the evening, Guangzhou Evergrande FC, had genuine pedigree too, winning the competition themselves in 2013 and having a World Cup winning captain, Fabio Cannavaro, as their manager.

Despite the smaller crowd, the singing was still non-stop. Although disappointingly, we were unable to buy tickets in the RBB (Red Black Block) where the bulk of the atmosphere was, because we weren't members. Mind you, a mixture of highly enthusiastic travelling fans and the large Chinese population in Sydney meant that there was a sizeable and vocal away crowd too.

Thankfully, The Wanderers rose their game to the occasion and played far better than they had done a few weeks previously in Newcastle. Unfortunately, their opponents were far better too and took the lead midway through the first half. After the break, during which we were disappointed to only meet World Cup Winning Captain, Favio Canavaro, as we tried to make contact with Tony Popovic*, Mark and I continued to work our way through beers and the game came to life. Although they might have helped, I don't think the beers were the sole reason for our enjoyment either.

My adopted team deservedly equalised ten minutes into the second half with a goal from a corner. Finally, the rest of the ground joined in with the songs from the RBB enclosure – the crowd situated behind the goal who are dedicated to singing and go out of their way to protect their non-stop atmosphere. On their website, they announce this:

"Anyone in the RBB bays is expected to get involved. The RBB bays are for making the noise, not just to listen to it.
You are required to chant. To stand. To participate in tifos. Your view may be obscured.
We welcome people who want to learn and get involved. For those who don't want to get involved at all, move to another bay so more people who do want to be involved can do so.
We want to create the best home end in Australian sport.
We must work together to achieve this"

It was clear that they keep to this too. Regrettably, I'd only been able to sit in the family stand at the far end for my previous visit, but for this match, I'd got us tickets as close to them as possible. Even before the equaliser, to a man, they'd been bouncing, singing and 'tifo-ing' as one. In fact, despite the team undoing all their good work two minutes later by falling behind again, the RBB remained just as supportive and constant. Even conceding a third ten minutes later didn't stop two-thousand strong crowd of dedicates.

Although, the goals did take the sting out of the rest of the crowd, until the fourth official rose his board to announce that there would be seventeen minutes of time added on thanks to a horrific clash of heads between the

---

the more you read that as a non-Palace fan, the less it will make any kind of vague sense.

Chinese goalkeeper and one of his defenders. This destroyed my previous record of 11 additional minutes in a game at Crewe Alexandra, when Julian Speroni made his only sub appearance for Palace, after a long injury to Gabor Kiraly. Palace being Palace, we conceded in the 99th minute to draw 2-2 after Clinton Morrison had scooped the ball over the bar from five yards with it seeming easier to score at 2-1 after 95 minutes.

Inevitably, its being able to quote factual but irrelevant nonsense such as this that had earned me the nickname of 'Statto' in Oz – well, specifically, in The Royal Exhibition Hotel. Pitifully, I didn't actually have to look up any of that. It's just there, in my brain, uselessly swirling around with hundreds of other results, thousands of other scorers and hundreds of thousands of useless and painful memories that my club has given me. I found it hard not to think of Palace when watching the Wanderers at the best of times, but with a Palace fan next to me, it was impossible.

Back in Sydney, the atmosphere was ramped up again as it was my side this time who scored in the excessive stoppage time. We had 14 more minutes of time added on to grab an equaliser. Sadly, try as they might, the players couldn't quite give the crowd the result they deserved, which I suspect had been the case for the entirety of the season. However, they did get their revenge in China, winning 2-0. Although that wasn't enough to put the Wanderers through the group, winning away at the eventual winners of the competition was a rare highlight in a pathetic season for the incredible RBB.

Southampton...1 Crystal Palace...0
St. Mary's Stadium, 03/03/15
Premier League

Southampton: Forster, Bertrand, Yoshida, Fonte, Clyne, Wanyama, Schneiderlin, Elia (Tadic 59), Djuricic (Ward-Prowse 78), Mane, Pelle (Long 70).
Subs not used: K Davis, Gardos, Alderweireld, S. Davis.

Palace: Julian Speroni, Martin Kelly, Damian Delaney, Scott Dann, Joel Ward, James McArthur (Shola Ameobi 83), Joe Ledley, Wilfried Zaha, Jason Puncheon, Yannick Bolasie, Dwight Gayle.
Subs not used: Wayne Hennessey, Adrian Mariappa, Brede Hangeland, Pape Souare, Jerome Boateng, Jake Gray.

Chapter 37 - The Cricket World Cup – *Sydney, 13th March 2015*

I'm still not really sure how it happened. At first, it was just the occasional after-work drink, but as I became closer to my colleagues: Fabian, a Swedish man who I would deliriously make bad puns with while we emptied the bins at 2am, and Joey, an English lad around my age who was out in Oz to play cricket, as well as various others who'd found themselves in Down Under for plenty of differing reasons, I began to go out after work regularly. It almost became the norm. Without meaning to, I'd carved out quite a hectic social life around my sixty-hour working weeks. Sleep became more and more of an abstract concept and I embraced Sydney life, rather than treating it as a working boot camp where I could save to go travelling.

Although, with all the money my long hours had brought, I had got a bit excited in booking things. As well as the five week tour of New Zealand, I booked a camper van to drive along the Great Ocean Road, trips to Melbourne and Canberra, a few weeks in the Philippines, some time in Hong Kong and a one night stop off in Munich, before heading to a stag do in Cologne. If the time between January and March had been solid work, I was set to reap the rewards.

However, now that I'd built up a solid network of friends, such as Tony, Jordo, Mark and Russ at The Exhibition, Fabian, Joey, Alice, Michael, Gabriella and Ben at the Opera House, Dave and Alex at Scary Canary, and of course Rich, as well as dozens of others who I knew and was keen to see more of, I was now having to balance my spending and saving. In some ways, it had been simpler when Palace was my only outgoing.

Having seen England vs Costa Rica in Brazil, a damp squid after England's two previous defeats, I was keen to try and outdo my football World Cup experience with the cricket equivalent. My first disappointment was that England's only game in Sydney was their final one in the group stages, against the mighty cricket nation of Afghanistan.

To be honest, I wasn't that bothered by England's opening match loss to Australia, although I received a fair amount of stick from my host nation. I wasn't even that fussed when they proceeded to lose to New Zealand and Sri Lanka too. Despite the disappointment, it meant that the final match, the one that I was going to, should be the decider as to whether they'd qualify or not.

However, when they managed to lose to Bangladesh and eliminate themselves from the competition before they'd even reached Sydney, I was slightly irked. Suddenly, England vs Afghanistan seemed like even less of a worthwhile reason to take time off work. I'm sure the England fans who'd travelled to Adelaide for the Bangladesh defeat were thrilled at the prospect on their 1375km journey to Sydney.

Although, to be honest, I didn't feel particularly sorry for them. Just as I don't for Palace fans when they go to a midweek defeat at Sunderland. As a sports fan, you know the risks when you book it. You know that the team inevitably lets you down and pay dozens, or hundreds, or in this case, thousands of pounds regardless. The only way to enjoy travelling long distances for live sport is to accept that the actual event is an excuse for the socialising and the journey, so you need to focus on that, rather than one unreliable factor! The result.

When you think about it, often the games that we remember most fondly, aren't the trips to Wembley or semi finals because we know, deep down, that we can't control them. We can't make the most out of a defeat and have a good day regardless. We know we have to win. Whereas losing 3-0 at Nottingham Forest, after losing 5-0 at Derby the week before, with a 1-0 home defeat to Crewe Alexandra sandwiched in-between can have a certain charm about it. A humiliating joy, where anger passes into humour and the self deprecation of a sports fan grows strong. You wearily accept those weeks and months of totally abject performances from overpaid professionals with an understated smugness of knowing that when you do win at Wembley, it's those matches that you'll reflect on, and make it all so special.

My three weeks in Brazil were some of the best in my life as I enjoyed the coming together of the world to unite for football, the food and culture of a different continent, the stories and friendships I made, the parties I danced at and the world-famous landmarks I visited. Honestly, I hope that anyone who made the commitment to come to Australia with the Barmy Army, specifically for the cricket, can reflect on their holiday as affectionately as I can, despite the equally pitiful England showing and early exit.

Still, Rich, Ben, Dave and I headed to the SCG (Sydney Cricket Ground) with hopes of a good day out and we weren't disappointed. Within the hour, England had bowled through four of their opponents top four batsmen, before rain stop the play. A familiar tale throughout the day.

As a child, all I wore was Palace shirts. It was a uniform and a statement. Admittedly, it was partly down to a horrendous lack of understanding of fashion, something that still eludes me to this day. Although, I have gleaned that other than at Palace matches where I have no intention of going out afterwards, and for playing five-a-side, wearing a Palace shirt is not an acceptable dress code. However, I'd learned at the football World Cup that it was a very good conversation starter so, along with many other England fans who were mulling around the barely-quarter-full stadium, I decided to support the England Cricket Team by wearing an English Club Team's football shirt.

Before rain had started to ruin the day, Dave, a Palace fan who'd recently moved to Sydney with his girlfriend and had been at The Exhibition for the West Ham game, spotted my shirt and gravitated towards me like a moth to light. Soon, it wasn't just Palace fans that I was attracting. A Glenn Murray loving, Carlisle fan approached us to talk about Cumbria's finest striker. I love chatting to lower league football fans. The ones who are used to real s***. Despite the fact that Palace were heading towards a third straight year in the Premier League and a second consecutive mid table finish, I still think of Palace in that bracket and identify far more with supporters of Carlisle than I do with a moaning Spurs fan.

Next, I chatted to a rather dejected Bolton Wanderers fan. He'd only come to watch England play cricket so he could avoid having to see his team that in his words "Dougie Freedman destroyed!"

It's funny, for most of my life, Bolton have been above Palace in the football pyramid, but the turnaround had been dramatic. Since relegation, their debts have spiralled and their team deteriorated. The only other Bolton fans that I've met in my life (I try to block out the racist ones on a train back to Manchester after we won 1-0 there in our promotion season) were some lovely guys I met in Birmingham before we played West Brom away in 2009. On that day, they talked about drawing 2-2 away at Bayern Munich. A reminder to all fans of fluctuating clubs like ours that you must enjoy the highs because less than ten years after that historic result, the Lancashire side were losing to Yeovil Town in a league game.

Although it wasn't all bad. Just like me after our defeat at City earlier in the season, he'd grown bored of going to the big clubs and losing. In eleven straight Premier League years, they'd had one draw and ten defeats at Anfield. He was fed up with it and even now, with Bolton doing so badly, he didn't miss it. At least the defeats are less predictable in the Championship.

As always with fans of differing clubs, we looked for common ground. As well as Freedman, we were able to compare our club's views on Paddy McCarthy, Barry Bannan, Neil Danns and our new signing, Lee Chung-Yong. While he was less than complimentary about our former contingent who'd ended up at the Reebok, he raved about "our new Koren", who was still to make his debut thanks to an injury before the transfer.

After a rain break of about forty-five minutes or so, the players came back out and the Afghan batsmen, cheered on by a tiny but very vocal crowd, showed a bit more resistance than their higher order teammates. However, the fact that I was at a, admittedly meaningless, cricket World Cup match didn't let my mind wonder too far away from football. I chatted to Wolves and Villa fans, Charlton and West Ham, as everyone drank together, applauding the odd wicket that England got between the many rain breaks.

At one point, as I nipped to the loo, another football fan approached me. "Palace scum!" he snarled.

I was a bit taken aback, but in the spirit of the day, it wasn't particularly past the normal lines of juvenile banter.

"Who do you support?" I replied, with a smirk.

"Brighton! Palace scum!" he replied.

As always, I find it hard to leave comments like this. People attacking Palace feel like people are attacking my family. However, I have learned from one ill-advised comment to a Brighton fan that caused mayhem and moderate violence, that responding with abuse, even attempted wit, is ill-advised.

"We are scum, but at least we're Premier League scum!" I replied, with a grin, ignoring the conversation that I'd just had with the Bolton fan about joys of the lower leagues. The idea was that while I stood up for Palace, I didn't respond with an insult and we could both be happy with our little attacks so we could continue to enjoy our day, supporting the same side!

Well that was a mistake. He charged towards me and blocked my way to the toilet.

"F***ing Palace scum, c***, I f***ing hate you, I wouldn't piss on you if you were on fire!"

Now, I know that watching Brighton must make you angry, but this seemed a slight over reaction, especially when you're on holiday in another hemisphere, watching a different sport.

Realising that anything I did could further escalate the ridiculous situation, I simply asked him to not stand so close.

"I'm just standing here, what the f*** are you doing?" came his slightly unhinged reply.

"Trying to go to the loo!" was my honest response and with that, I walked away.

Unfortunately, that wasn't the end of it. I'd heard him shouting obscenities my way as the door shut and when I returned, there he was, waiting for me. What followed was one of the most surreal threats of my life. He didn't want to 'f*** me up' in the ground as he'd get kicked out, so he wanted to exchange numbers so he could smash me outside the stadium. I politely declined the invitation and tried to walk away, but this moron, who must have been in his thirties, continued to block my path. Thankfully, at this point, the stewards finally intervened and let me go as he shouted obscenities towards me.

I suppose wearing a Palace shirt could be perceived as provocative, and I shouldn't have given an initial response, but the actions of one idiot really ruined the day as I was always looking over my shoulder after that. It provoked an angry reaction from my friends too, who wished they'd been there to stand up for me, although I fear that would have simply built up the aggression more if he'd had something to respond to. After all, he hadn't actually laid hands on me.

But there's a huge pity in the whole sorry situation. We like to think that we've evolved since the moronic days of the 70s and 80s and we have. It wouldn't have been purely verbal intimidation back then, but we still live in a world where someone 17,000 miles from home, watching a different sport, cheering the same nation, can get that irate about a football shirt. The same clothing had initiated five or six great conversations throughout the day but I wouldn't wear it again to a similar event. It's simply not worth the hassle.

Neither was the match really. England had been set a small target after Afghanistan's innings was rained off after 36 overs. When the players trudged off for a fifth time, with heavy rain falling, England already out and pitch blackness surrounding the floodlit stadium, we decided to call it a day and head for drinks elsewhere. If they were able to come back on, England would surely win, but by this stage, who cared?

My final thought for the day was that after seeing England's final group game of the football and cricket World Cups, should I try and make it a hat-trick? As a protest against rugby, I was tempted to book a ticket for the final game of England's group match when they hosted the Rugby World Cup once I was back in the country in October 2015. As it turned out, they didn't need me as their Jonah. Even without my ill-fated presence, the rugby team had managed an equally pathetic showing as English sport reached its lowest ebb. Three World Cups. Three group stage disasters.

Chapter 38 - The Match Day Routine – *Sydney, 14th March 2015*

The following day, I was given one of the strangest compliments – a twelve hour shift. They were usually reserved for the favourite staff, and it was even more pleasing that it was all on my terms. Mainly, that I would finish at 11:30pm so that I could get to The Exhibition to watch us play QPR in the 'early' kick off... at midnight.

To my surprise, despite a reasonable turn out from the Palace crowd of Tony, Dave (from the day before), Russ and two or three others, as well as Ben coming with me, we were actually outnumbered by a large QPR contingent, who'd turned up to attack our ground, well pub. But thankfully, metaphorically with song, rather than tossing petrol bombs in through the window or anything like that.

While they were loud at first, three easy first half goals from Zaha, McArthur and Joel Ward (his first for the club in nearly 100 games) soon shut them up. In fact, I felt sorry for them. QPR were pitiful. A 'team' full of disinterested individuals with a part time manager after Harry Redknapp walked out as he wasn't able to waste any more money on the shambles he'd created. Don't get me wrong, Palace played well for our 3-0 half time lead but I think our Sydney Supporters' team could have given Rangers a match that day, such was their lack of bottle and commitment.

The following day, I received an email from Clint Hill, who was subbed on at half time and restored some pride in the team, with some memories from our 2009/10 season for my first book. As he talked about the commitment and effort of our administration-struck side, who battled on through adversity, it was clear what he thought of the current mess that he was lumbered with.

As the fairly dull second half was played out, with nothing happening on the pitch, we began to keep ourselves entertained by singing.
"Oh... South London! (echo) ...Is Wonderful... (echo) Oh South London is wonderful! It's full of tits, fanny and Palace! Oh South London is wonderful..."
Which, of course, was responded to by the QPR fans in the pub, who retorted with a rendition claiming that it was in fact West London which was wonderful and coated in tits and fanny. However, this prompted the West Ham and Arsenal fans, who were waiting for their match to kick off, to join in with North and East London renditions. Soon, the four corners of the pub were merrily singing off against each other, announcing their part of London, while in a Syndey pub. It was brilliant and certainly served as light relief for the Rangers' fans, rather than wattching their demise.

Before the game, I'd taken the decision that I needed to avoid spending so I wasn't going to drink. It was now just a few weeks until I was set to start travelling again and every cent mattered. Unfortunately, when you start crossing over from being people who you watch football with to friendship, it makes decisions like that quite hard. Football is an incredible ice breaker, especially when people support the same side and share the same history.

When I was younger, I used to say that all Palace fans are friends of mine, but as I've got older, I've realised that just like the Brighton-supporting moron from the day before, there are Palace supporting morons too. The previous day could have easily been a Palace cretin abusing a Brighton fan. If someone is racist, or abusive, or nasty, or in any way an unlikeable, distasteful character, wearing a red and blue shirt doesn't change that. However, what tends to happen is that when you start talking about football with the vast majority of human beings who are able to avoid vile traits such as those, you move on to talking about other things and then you start to meet up and do activities in a world outside of the pub at 2am, which takes you away from simply being part of a cult, and moves you into friendships based on, but not reliant on, your club.

And if you're in the pub at 2am with a group of friends, who you are starting to want to see as much as the football, then when you say that you're not drinking as you're saving to go travelling, they tend to offer you drinks. Yet when you turn down drinks from friends, on the basis of not having enough money, they tend to not take no for an answer. Despite my protests, which you may or may not choose to believe were fairly strong, schooner after schooner of ale was sent in my direction and by the time that the game petered out to a 3-1 Palace win as QPR scored a wonder goal for a consolation, I was fairly drunk. Surrounded by friends. That night, the feeling I had was just the same as being at Selhurst Park for a home game. Watching Palace wasn't an event, it was a weekly routine to see friends.

Crystal Palace...3 QPR...1
Selhurst Park, 14/03/15
Premier League

Palace: Julian Speroni, Martin Kelly, Damian Delaney, Scott Dann, Joel Ward, Yannick Bolasie, Joe Ledley, James McArthur, Wilfried Zaha (Adrian Mariappa 57), Jason Puncheon (Dwight Gayle 55), Glenn Murray (Yaya Sanogo 80).
Subs not used: Wayne Hennessey, Brede Hangeland, Pape Souare, Shola Ameobi.

Queens Park Rangers: Green, Yun, Caulker, Onuoha, Furlong (Hill 46), Phillips, Sandro (Kranjcar 85), Henry, Wright-Phillips (Grego-Cox 85), Taarabt, Austin.
Subs not used: McCarthy, Vargas, Hoilett, Zamora.

Chapter 39 - Becoming a Film Star – *Sydney, 21st March 2015*

I'd hated the job at the Opera House. In fact, I'd actively tried to be rubbish at it and I'd relentlessly argued with the top boss, so it was more than a surprise when he summoned me into the office to offer me a promotion! However, as I had just a couple of weeks remaining until I left Sydney again, I had to not only reject the offer, but resign as well! Becoming a Head Waiter in a restaurant was hardly a dream job, such as becoming a superstar actor or footballer, but it was nice to be recognised regardless.

Well, I might not have been offered the chance to be paid as an actor but on the morning of my final Sydney game before travelling, I did discover that I was going to star in a short film. Palace had contacted one of our members, Tony, about sending some footage of our Sydney group to the club for a montage about the Stoke away game, which had been designated as 'Palace on Tour Day'. Our group, the New York Eagles, Steve Browett, Mark Bright and Five Year Plan (a fanzine) would all be filmed going about their match day routines. In order to show off our location, Jordo and Tony wanted to film them picking up me from the Opera House after work for the match. My 1am collection from in front of the world famous building, and naturally a huge 'eagles' cry, was included in the final cut.

To be honest, we had a lot of fun making mini clips of us arriving at our pub, The Exhibition, and little tit-bits, most of which were never to be seen again. We'd been asked to send clips from before the game, during the match, at half time, and some post match analysis. The realisation of a childhood dream in becoming an actor enticed a slightly larger than usual crowd out, although nowhere near as many as we'd had for the Hammers matches.

On the whole, the first half on the tele failed to match our excitement of being on camera. In fact, I even suggested to Tony that he filmed some of our songs at 0-0 as we might not feel like singing later in the game. It was just as well too as after 14 minutes, Stoke took a deserved lead. Tony decided that we needed to film a reaction so he flicked on his camera, and giving a 'selfie' shot of the two of us, introduced what had happened. I wanted to swear, and rant, and slam my fist down on the table in frustration, but I didn't. Somehow, having a camera show me what I look like when Palace concede made it all seem pathetic and embarrassing.

Of course, everyone in the pub and thousands of Palace fans at matches and many close friends have seen my overreactions to moments of what can only be described as pure devastation, such as going 1-0 behind to Stoke in a meaningless match, but I didn't want to see it myself. I bit my lip and shook my head, unable to communicate any dialect without swearing.

The half continued with Stoke on top. It was hard to be too angry, such was the incredible run that we'd been on since Christmas, but it was also difficult to continue to muster up much interest in the filming either. Suddenly, with Palace losing, it all seemed a bit pointless. Then, just before half time, we were awarded a soft penalty. A ball was played over the top to Bolasie, who jumped into the goalkeeper with his foot up high. The keeper and him collided in midair, and the referee pointed to the spot. When you're playing well, and you're on a run, you just seem to get the luck. There's no way that we'd have been awarded that spot kick earlier in the season.

Of course, for filming a crowd, a penalty is the perfect moment to capture. We all winced as Glenn Murray placed the ball on the spot, amid huge protests from the Stoke players, and Tony headed to the back of the pub where he could film both the projected screen at the front, and the back of our heads. As Murray slammed home the spot kick, the Palace contingent in Sydney leapt as one, as did the fans in the ground, and the Hong Kong Eagles, and the New York lads, and Palace fans everywhere. It was even admitted by one member of our group at half time that the goal had been celebrated with extra venom thanks to the potential stardom in our reaction to the goal.

If we'd over reacted to the penalty, then no exaggeration was needed a couple of minutes later when Zaha met Murray's flick on and slotted the ball past the goalkeeper to give us a half time lead. While the nature of our first goal had allowed planned and perfectly filmed celebrations for back home, the second prompted sheer and delirious mayhem. Beer went flying, someone's stool landed on my foot and each of us boisterously hugged each other. Palace were winning. Although that moment wasn't caught on camera, our half time analysis was certainly more upbeat, if a little less tactical than it would have been five minutes earlier.

The second half was nervous on the pitch as I led the singing in the pub. We were loud and proud, and trying to include a repertoire that didn't involve swearing, which is actually quite hard with football chants. For some reason, I didn't think songs about Ron Noades' mother being a lady of the night, or homophobic chants about Brighton, or songs about South London's filling of tits and fanny would be appropriate for a video on the club's official website. However, at full time, we were more than able to sing that we were Glad All Over.

So, with Palace having completed their job on the pitch, with a 2-1 win over Stoke, it was down to Sydney's latest film stars, Tony and I, to give our post match analysis. Now, as not all of the beer that we'd purchased had been launched in the air after Zaha's winner, we were a bit blurry eyed by full time so coupled with the fact that we'd won, we decided not to go into the finer details of the match. The two of us headed outside to the front of the pub and belted out,

"IT'S FOUR IN THE MORNING AND WE'RE STAYING UP!
FOUR IN THE MORNING AND WE'RE STAYING UP!"

Amazingly, our drunken, witty song didn't make it onto the final video. Although, the night didn't end there. We continued to celebrate being an incredible 11th in the Premier League until around six in the morning.

The club's video can be watched on Palace's Facebook page here:

https://www.facebook.com/officialcpfc/videos/10153138955515762/

After the Stoke game, I continued to take every shift that I could in my final week before travels, but I also decided to try and socialise as much as possible. The thing with backpacking is that you never know who you're going to see again and who you've lost. Happily, I spent a lot of time in Darling Harbour, and at the beach, and playing five-a-side. I couldn't believe the generosity of my five-a-side team mates on my last game when they bought me drink after drink to wish me well.

At the Opera House, I was also given a brilliant send off and they offered me a job for when I returned. Although I didn't see eye to eye with the bosses at Scary Canary, I still had a fun night saying goodbye to my colleagues, where again, the generosity of everyone astounded me. I'd miss having them as work mates as there was no way that I'd return to the job when I came back. Jedinak even celebrated my farewell with a goal for Australia against the World Champions, Germany. Mile was a true Australian hero and he plays for Palace. My ears pricked as I heard his, and our, name everywhere after his goal.

Soon, it was time to go. Ben and I jumped on a train to Canberra, where we'd spend two nights before heading to Melbourne for a few of days. After that, Rich was joining us and we'd rented a camper van to drive along the Great Ocean Road. From there, I'd fly to New Zealand, where I'd spend five weeks on a tour, and I'd finally return to Sydney for the end of the season.

Stoke City...1 Crystal Palace...2
The Britania Stadium, 21/03/15
Premier League

Stoke City: Begovic, Pieters, Shawcross, Wilson, Cameron, N'Zonzi, Adam, Arnautovic, Ireland, Diouf, Crouch (Walters 78).
Subs Not Used: Butland, Bardsley, Wollscheid, Whelan, Sidwell, Teixeira.

Palace: Julian Speroni, Pape Souare (Martin Kelly 70), Scott Dann, Damian Delaney, Joel Ward, Joe Ledley, James McArthur, Wilfried Zaha (Dwight Gayle 80), Jason Puncheon, Yannick Bolasie, Glenn Murray (Shola Ameobi 86).
Subs Not Used: Wayne Hennessey, Adrian Mariappa, Brede Hangeland, Yaya Sanogo.

Dave Jones, founder member of the New York Eagles.

Thankfully, watching Palace on TV in the US is much more accessible than in the UK. Palace reached the Promised Land in 2013, which was the same year NBC's new $250 million 3 year rights deal kicked in. This enabled the US powerhouse network to show every single Premier League game live. As much as television rights back home with Sky cause unbearable frustrations with fixture changes, the international rights for expats is a God send. As one of the less 'fashionable' teams stateside, we find the majority of our games on one of the 'spillover channels', NBC Premier League Extra Time. However, on occasion - particularly when we play live on Sky in the UK - Palace are broadcasted to over 300 million Americans on national TV for their viewing pleasure (or in the case of the Holloway era - torture). NBC network - home of Friends, Saturday Night Live and the Tonight Show - for 2 hours every few weeks goes from Central Perk to Selhurst Park. The American Dream is alive and well.

The rights to the Football League in the US are owned by beIN Sports - a subsidiary of Al Jazeera of all networks. During the two seasons we played our trade in the Championship while I was living in New York, catching Palace on TV was a rare treat...if you can call a 4-0 home defeat to Birmingham a 'treat'. For the majority of games I had to make do with streaming Palace radio - just like I did in London for away games that I couldn't make - so it was actually quite nice to hear familiar voices when you've just moved 3,500 miles from home. The times Palace were on beIN Sports usually coincided with when Palace were on Sky. The 5 hour time difference between London and the East Coast certainly makes the midweek games tricky with work schedules, but for the playoffs I would swim the Hudson River to watch the games. Using precious holiday days to go to a bar on a Friday and Monday afternoon baffled most of my colleagues at the time. They didn't get it, but I simple had to. Not least as otherwise I'd be at risk of being fired for abusive language or dancing on my desk singing "E I E I E I O".

It was while watching the second leg of the playoff semi-final at a midtown Manhattan bar called Legends - a bar soon to become the adopted home of Palace fans in New York - that I first met fellow Palace expats Owen and Steve. As the only Palace fans in an empty bar on a Monday afternoon, we toasted Wilf and agreed to meet up at the same venue for the final. The New York Eagles fan club was born. Falling on a bank holiday Monday and thanks to the BBS, the Palace faithful drew a crowd of 20 or so for the final. After racking up a tab the size of the Empire State Building, the owner of Legends, Jack, agreed to let us have it on the house if Owen formally set up the NY Eagles on social media and made Legends its home. Email chains, Facebook posts and tweets later, the NY Eagles have a fairly well drilled match day routine. Typically kick-off is at 10am on Saturdays, so we'd all congregate downstairs at Legends around the TV showing the boys in red and blue. As we've grown in Jack's affections over the years, we get upgraded to the main TV on occasion - much to the amusing annoyance of fans of 'bigger' clubs. You can usually spot those nursing a hangover from the night before as they may kick off with a coffee or water. For the rest it's morning beers from the get go. It certainly puts an edge on your Saturday when you stumble out onto Fifth Avenue at noon after 4 pints of Guinness, but when you've beaten Chelsea away, it's a beautiful thing.

The NY Eagles has grown impressively since inception. At the start, there would typically be 4 or 5 of us each week and now, we consistently get around 15-20. The great thing about having the bar in Manhattan is there is a constant stream of Palace fans on holiday who want to catch the game before their trip to the Statue of Liberty or The Brooklyn Bridge. In fact, on two occasions Steve Browett popped in with his family while they were in transit from their holidays. The first time they came Bolasie got a hat trick in a thumping 4-1 win away to Sunderland, and the second time we earned a hard fought draw against West Ham. Even Josh Harris and David

Blitzer, shortly after buying a stake in the club, popped by for a midweek game while in NYC for meetings. I was at work and missed this occasion, but from what I hear they proved to be very engrossed and impressively knowledgeable about the club. This season our guest of honour was Steve Parish. Pre-match Steve was happy to discuss any matters with the club, and fielded probing questions on transfer rumours expertly. For both Parish and Browett, the thing that hits home when watching Palace games with them that we sometimes forget, is they are fans like us. They join in the songs, swear at the referee, and roar every counter just like us. Steve Parish's face during the final few minutes of the Bournemouth game when Dann got the last minute equaliser was particularly memorable.

The interest from locals has grown notably season by season. Tim, Bryan, Sunita, Mike, and Brian are a few that all take the American patriotic adoration of the Eagle to the next level, each with their own unique story. Special mention goes to Bryan, who at the tender age of 15 watched his first 'soccer' game on TV in 2004: Crystal Palace v Arsenal. We all had a lot of love spreading after Aki's equaliser, but across the Atlantic, Bryan was hooked for life. What's even more remarkable is Bryan lives in New London, a small town in Connecticut that's a six hour round trip from Legends. Some of us expats travel over an hour from Long Island or Coney Island in Brooklyn, but this is simply remarkable for someone who despite the sport saturation enjoyed here with the NFL, NBA, MLB and NHL, kept following the club through the Championship years.

One game that I'll always remember but didn't manage to watch was 'Crystalbull'. The game happened to be one of those dreaded weekday games played during the working day on the East Coast, so unfortunately, I was in the office for the occasion. At 3-0 down, I was for once joyous to be at work. Tracking the game from my desk, spreadsheets and presentations served as welcome distractions.

When Delaney's goal went in, my eternal (and mostly painful) Palace optimism was in gear. At 3-2 I knew I lost focus on everything around me for the next 10 minutes and at 3-3 it was pure euphoria. It's after games like that where I feel the most homesick. One of my fondest memories in recent years is when we beat Liverpool 2-1 in the League Cup semi-final in 2001. Rubins scored a belter and Selhurst was rocking. After the joy of the 3-3 result, I began to feel a sense of regret at not being at yet another famous night at Selhurst.

My fondest memory of watching Palace from across the Atlantic was a forgettable game: a dire 0-0 draw. This game was against the 'mighty' Philadelphia Union, when Palace travelled to the US for their pre-season tour this past summer. Palace came to Philadelphia as part of a tour in 2014, but unfortunately I was back in London for a wedding at the time. I certainly wasn't going to miss this one. A good couple hundred or so Palace fans showed up for the game, all within a designated 'away' section which is something you don't normally see in US Sports. The previous game for Palace was the FA Cup final, so the stadium, atmosphere, and importance were at polar opposites, but it was nice to get back to business after all the 'what-ifs' since May. Outside of the game, it was amazing to see Philadelphia turn red and blue. We all met up at a bar in downtown Philadelphia a few hours before the game, then hopped on one of those long yellow school buses to the stadium. James McArthur was injured for the game, but chatted to fans and posed for photographs. Steve Parish also met fans in the stands at halftime. After the game, the team then travelled across the continent to play in Cincinnati and Vancouver. The game in Cincinnati drew a crowd of 35,000 - 10% the population of the city of Cincinnati. That match also had the highest attendance of any 'soccer' game in North America that weekend. Yes that's right, more people came to see Jordan Mutch play than Gerrard, Pirlo, Kaka or Drogba.

Chapter 40 - Canberra, Melbourne and the Great Ocean Road. – *Australia, 30th March-7th April 2015*

Canberra, a capital city built to avoid offending either Sydney or Melbourne, seemed to do exactly that. The 'city' was built in 1913 and has developed little non-political history since, with a population even smaller than New South Wales' Newcastle. However, I absolutely loved my couple of days there with Ben. It's relaxed. Despite being the political capital, there isn't the hectic rat race that we'd usually associate with capitals as it was planned and built to be small, spacious and calm. The city's main landmarks are the impressive Parliament House, which stands behind the equally grand 'Old Parliament House', and the highly impressive war memorial and museum. It was fascinating to learn about the war from a different prospective. It was almost like reading a different team's message board after a game.

The other notable building was the Canberra Stadium, home to rugby league and union teams, but notably, not a soccer side. Of course, London isn't a fair comparison as our fourteen professional teams are more than the ten that they have in the whole of Australia, but I was sad that the capital city didn't have its own side, despite failed bids for an A-League franchise in 2009 and 2012. However, with the likely expansion of the ever more popular A-league in 2017, Canberra is expected to try again. Until then, the 25,000 stadium that can be seen from most places in the fairly low-built city, will continue to torment the socceroos in the capital. Although, as frustrating as it must be, it's not quite the white elephant of the National Stadium in Brasilia, Brazil's purpose built capital and 75,000 stadium that I'd visited in the previous June.

Melbourne too greeted me with a giant stadium, the Etihad, home of five different AFL teams and occasionally Kevin Muscat's Melbourne Victory soccer side. Immediately, it became clear that this was a city obsessed with sport. Being tourists, Ben and I headed straight to the Eureka Tower, Melbourne's tallest skyscraper, and took in a view of the city. From high up near the clouds, we could see the MCG, home of Australian cricket, the Melbourne Grand Prix race track, Victoria Racing Club, home of the Melbourne Cup, Melbourne Park, home of the Australian Open and AAMI Park, home of both Melbourne Victory and Melbourne City FC. All of which were walking distance from the city centre.

After that, and I'd coincidentally bumped into Alan who I'd lived with at Christmas, Ben and I met up with Lauren, a friend of mine from University, who was living out there. Lauren had really embraced Melbourne life (the sport, the artistic side, the craft beer scene, the rooftop bars, the beaches, the weather) and was desperately trying to get sponsored to stay out there. She loved it. If Sydney is like being in Central London, then Melbourne has a feel of Shoreditch or Camden about it. Kindly, Lauren became our tour guide, taking us to a mixture of touristy areas, trendy backstreets and quirky bars.

Straight away, I regretted my decision not to move to Melbourne. Whether it was purely because Lauren sold the city so well and we got on so comfortably, I don't know, but my initial reaction was that I got the city more and liked its vibe. Who knows whether I'd have felt the same if I'd have spent longer there and had to work? A point pairly worth thinking about. Although, just like Sydney, I managed to find some more places named after English locations (well, more of interest to me, football teams) as there are areas of Melbourne called Mansfield, Doncaster, Newport, Cheltenham, Blackburn and Tottenham. As well as two roads called Southampton Drive and Bolton Drive.

After a few excellent days, Rich joined Ben and I as we collected our ridiculously decorated camper van before setting off on the Great Ocean Road for our next adventure. Palace fans back home, becoming irritated by my annoying wave photos, asked if I'd changed alliance and started supporting Charlton or Gillingham now that I lived in a moving house. I certainly hadn't. However, a mixture of clear blue skies, stunning scenery, brilliant company, wonderful wildlife, luxury eating, barbeque breakfasts (and dinners), high quality beers, vineyards, dreamy driving (maybe I should make it clear that it was dreamy thanks to the location rather than because it was after the vineyards on this list), cheese sampling, sea swimming, beautiful beaches, relaxed evenings of card games and childish hooting and tooting at fellow campers did mean that I didn't really get a chance to think about Palace much, even if they were due to play Rich's Manchester City on the final Monday of our trip.

The most famous attraction of the road was The Twelve Apostles. Although only eight of the spectacular erosion created offshore limestone stacks are remaining, they still make an amazing sight. I even took a photo of me posing with a Palace shirt to promote my first book, which was now just days away from being published. However, I was even more wowed by the Loch Ard Gorge, with its crashing waves creating a spectacular bay in the cliffs.

I also loved the 'London Bridge' natural arch formation, which collapsed twenty five years ago, leaving two Australian tourists stranded. Unfortunately for them, when the national news filmed them being saved by helicopter, it turned out that not only were they both skiving from work that day, they were also both separately married and having an affair.

Along the road, I continued to collect places in my challenge to see locations named after all 92 football league sides. I found Bristol, which I could count twice for City and Rovers, Torquay, Chesterfield and Peterborough, which was far more beautiful than its shared name back home, even though the English version did host my favourite ever Palace away game when two very late goals from Andre Moritz and Kagisho Dikgacoi gave us a 2-1 win, sent us to the top of the table and created mayhem in an over-filled terrace,

On our final night, as we sat with a beer in our hand, watching the kangaroos run free in the field next to us, I felt a sense of sadness to be leaving this behind. The three of us had become incredibly close over a short five day break. Yet the odds were that we'd never be together again. I was jetting off for my tour of New Zealand, Ben was moving to Queenstown to live with his girlfriend and Rich was flying off to work early the next morning. Although I would see them both individually again, it seemed like the end of an all-too-short passage of time.

Still, there wasn't too much of an emotional parting because for me, the excitement was only just beginning. At 8am the next morning, I was due to fly to Auckland, where I would meet up with Camilla, before I started my tour of the country. However, while I waited at the airport, Rich and I would go head to head as Palace hosted Manchester City. To my disappointment, Rich's internal flight was from a different terminal so we'd have to follow it alone. Although, I did have some dialogue on Twitter with Melbourne Airport as the two of us tried to find a way for me to watch it in the Terminal.

Despite the airport declaring that unlikely, Rich and I set off at a slightly earlier than the necessary 4am to try and watch the game. As warned, no bars were open and to make matters worse, the Wifi in Terminal 3 was rubbish, thus meaning I could see it at all, unlike Richard. Terminal 1 seemed to be the place to be as he watched a stream on his laptop while I had to settle with following the match on the BBS. Typically, thanks to a delay in opening security at the airport, the match kicked off while I was being scanned through the 'no phones allowed' immigration room so my imagination had to run wild about the events in South London for the opening stages.

As soon as I could, I used my phone to log onto the BBS and clicked on the Live Updates thread.

Comment	Location
The colours don't clash at all	Gold Coast, Australia
Murray went down very easily..	Kildare, Ireland
Flagged offside?	St. Albans
Don't think it was	The Midlands
COYP	-
Need to get closer to them in midfield	-
Definitely, need to do like we did vs arsenal and really get at them	Coulsdon
Murray rightfully upset that neither winger gambling on his headers.	-
Phew..Speroni a bit at sea there..	Kristiansand, Norway
Good save Jules. Great kick from hart!	Croydon
That's the 3rd time Murray has headed on the ball to no one - Zaha and Bolasie should be getting into positions to take those	Connecticut, USA
ooooooh!	Worcestershire
Good save by julian after giving me a heart attack	Gold Coast, Australia

Hennessey would have got sent off	Spain
palace fans in full voice	Worcestershire
Brilliant by Kelly and McArthur covering the goal line	-
Definitely giving Toure too much space.	Connecticut
Gonna miss Jedi for this me thinks	-

All of those posts were written between 5:05am and 5:11am and made as much sense to me then as they do now. Instead, I just enjoyed the fact that it was clear that all around the world, at ridiculous times, people were following our game and sharing the experience online. However, clearly, following the game on the BBS wasn't going to be a particularly informative method of keeping up to date as most people obviously had streams to discuss, rather than posting facts about what was happening.

With the stress of relegation all but gone, rather than hang on to Twitter's ramblings, I decided to do some proofing of my first book. I was so absorbed by that task that I almost forgot that the game was happening until I received a text from Rich saying 'Offside :('. Now, I had a sneaking suspicion that my friend's sad face was likely to be good news for me, but I needed confirmation. Back to the BBS I went.

Goood goall..no offside..no way..hmm.	Norway
what did i tell ya about GM!!! YERSSSSSSSSSSSSSSSSSS	Melbourne, Australia (I wasn't alone)
Amazing just amazing we really are an amazing team	Middlesbrough

While Rich and his multi-million pound friends would continue to moan about the fact that it might have been marginally offside, our former defender and foreword writer for my book, Matt Lawrence, possibly the only person who supports Palace and Millwall, summed it up best by tweeting:
"It wasn't offside. If it was offside, Manchester City would have taken a free kick. They didn't. They took a centre. Stop moaning. 1-0"
Surprisingly, Rich didn't agree with him. Regardless, offside or not, we'd scored our first goal against City since being promoted back to the big time.

Still, my response on Twitter was just as childish. Naturally, I used it as a chance to make a dig at Warnock, who would still be whining about our 'bad luck'. To me, it seemed simple. Play well, play Murray and you make your own luck. A message that was retweeted multiple times. The more I tweeted, about the success of Pardew, Palace and Murray, the happier I became and my excitement grew. For the third time in little under a year, after seeing off Liverpool and Chelsea in 2014, were we going to finish a team's title chase?

Unbelievably cruelly, just as the second half was about to kick off, I lost all internet connection. Not knowing what was happening was torture. Pavel, who was watching at home thanks a knee-shattering incident in a champagne bar, sent me a message asking what the score was. This confused me as I thought he was watching live and the request should have been sent the other way. *'1-0'* I quickly replied as I realised that the Whatsapp message signalled the return of my internet!

'Nope, 2-0, Puncheon!"

Sitting alone in the waiting area by my plane, I leapt for joy. We were 2-0 up against the reigning Champions of England.

Within minutes, I'd seen the goal on Twitter, which was a spectacular free kick and the South American commentary that accompanied it only added to the excitement. As my internet connection came and went through the second half, my nerves grew. There was no way that I could focus on a different task now. I was refreshing twitter every few seconds as it was far more informative than the screams of desperation and randomness on the BBS.

City fans moaned about a Glenn Murray clearance off the line, seemingly with his hand, but once again, the luck went our way as the referee waved play on.

"Glenn Murray, Glenn Murray, Glenn Murray, Glenn Murray, Saving Goals for Palace, Glenn Murray, Glenn Murray," was my much loved and retweeted message. Rich simply sent me some rude words and accusations.

I must have been one of the first people ever to cheer when my flight was delayed as it meant that I'd be able to follow the ending before take-off. Imagine if I'd had to turn my phone off with our goal still under siege. Mistakenly, someone posted a tweet saying *'Still 2-1, come on Palace!'*, which gave half his followers a heart attack. When had City pulled one back? They hadn't; it turned out to be a typo. Unfortunately, within seconds it seemed to be more of a prophecy than a typo. By the time that he'd explained his mistake, Yaya Toure had scored for City. We had 12 minutes to hang on.

This was no longer needing Palace like I had earlier in the season. This was now pure enjoyment, which in turn meant pure stress and worry and pain and tension. A form of enjoyment that's unique to football and makes no sense.

As we entered stoppage time, I handed my boarding pass and passport over to security, surely arising suspicion as I shook with excitement and nerves. Constantly, I refreshed my twitter feed, begging for time to disappear and Palace to hold on for a famous victory. Then it happened, just as I walked through First Class on the plane. Every head turned my way as I let out a giant and unplanned *'YESSSSSSSSSSSSSSSS'*.

The result was confirmed. We'd won and, slightly red faced with embarrassment, I was ushered away from the highly paying customers, who didn't particularly appreciate my relief.

Once in my seat, still grinning from ear to ear, I needed to do something. I needed to react. However, I'd already had one involuntary explosion of delight on the plane and I couldn't do another, could I? Quickly, before takeoff, I nipped to the lavatory, not to release my bladder, but to release my elation and relief. Once in the privacy of the Emirates 406 Airbus' toilet, I jumped for joy and punched the air as if I was at Selhurst Park, celebrating our win with friends and family.

After that, I did some proofing about a 1-1 draw with Barnsley just five years previously. Look how far we'd come! And like me, heading even further from home to New Zealand, could Palace continue to travel further away from what I knew? Could we actually stop being an also-ran Championship side, and establish ourselves in the big time? Since Pardew had come in, winning hadn't been the gold dust that it was under Pulis, or Warnock, or Holloway. Premier League wins, whoever the opponent, seemed to be fast becoming the norm!

Crystal Palace...2 Manchester City...1
Selhurst Park, 06/04/15
Premier League

Crystal Palace: Julian Speroni, Joel Ward, Scott Dann, Damian Delaney, Martin Kelly, Wilfried Zaha (Dwight Gayle 88), James McArthur, Joe Ledley, Jason Puncheon, Yannick Bolasie (Pape Soaure 84), Glenn Murray (Yaya Sanogo 83).
Subs not used: Wayne Hennessey, Brede Hangeland, Jerome Boateng, Shola Ameobi.

Manchester City: Hart, Sagna, Demichelis, Kompany, Clichy, Silva, Fernandinho (Milner 88), Toure, Navas (Nasri 77), Dzeko (Lampard 65), Aguero.
Subs not used: Caballero, Zabaleta, Mangala, Fernando.

Chapter 41 - Shaun Derry and the Bay of Islands – *Auckland, Bay of Islands, Hot Water Beach, (New Zealand) 7th-12th April 2015*

I arrived in Auckland around midday and immediately met up with Camilla, who now lived there. The pair of us caught up as we wondered around the harbour, trekked up a mountain overlooking the city and found an array of craft beer bars. I liked Auckland. Often, it is seen as the biggest and ugliest city of New Zealand but as I hadn't yet seen the rest of the country, it still felt small and relaxed compared to what I knew. Also, the beer was brilliant.

From Auckland, I'd booked on the Kiwi Experience coach tour. I'd have loved to have made my own way around the country but in the absence of any pre-arranged company, I needed to settle for an organised excursion. First, we headed north to the Bay of Islands and immediately, the beauty of the country was evident. Our first 'toilet break' was at a stunning waterfall.

The company was pleasant if not immediately amazing. But it didn't have to be. Part of the fun of travelling was being thrown in with a group of people who you don't necessarily have a lot in common with except your immediate ambition. In this case, to see as much of New Zealand as possible, and the fact that there was a group of people, who I'd experience it with and share meals and evening drinks with, was good enough.

In many ways, it reminded me of my teenage days of travelling to Palace away games alone. I'd never do that now as the frequency of my travels meant that inevitably I did pick up friends along the way. However, in some ways, I miss the freedom of jumping on a train to Doncaster or Sheffield by myself and striking up conversations for hours on end with people who I have nothing in common with bar the colour of my shirt.

When we arrived at our location, we discovered that the enormous bay has one hundred and forty-four islands and hosts some spectacular wildlife. In some ways, I wished I'd taken the option to do some further scuba diving there but, despite the better than expected April weather, I decided to wait for warmer climates. I did however, go on a sailing boat tour, where we not only saw dolphins but we also encountered a killer whale. There's something quite magical about watching giant animals roam free in the wild.

In the evenings, the freedom of being close to no one allowed me to talk to everyone as we barbequed on the beach and drank into the night. I was devastated to learn that although there was a guy from Bromley present, he wasn't a Palace fan. Yet I was just as pleased to bump into a Welsh girl who I'd met in Phuket five months previously. Just like Palace away days, the travelling scene is smaller than you'd think and repeatedly bumping into the same familiar faces is inevitable.

During my second day, we went on a tour to the very north of the island, visiting Cape Reinga, the beautiful most northern tip of the country, bodyboarded down the giant sand dunes and drove along '90 Mile Beach', which is actually only 55 miles but some terrible estimates based on how long it took cows (or was it Shefki Kuqi?) to walk it meant that the beach developed a rather strange name.

That evening, I received a short but exciting message.

Hi James,

*If you'd like to give me a call on 07********* we can have a chat about the book.*

Kind regards

Shaun Derry.

Receiving an email from Shaun Derry, while I was slightly tipsy, was both exciting and bizarre in equal measures. However, trying to explain my thrill to people who had no interest in football, let alone Palace, was quite difficult. It was just three days until I published my first book so with little time to lose, while slightly drunk in New Zealand, I phoned Shaun Derry on Whatsapp, who'd only recently been sacked by Notts County, and conducted a phone interview about his memories of the 2009/10 season.

I woke up the next morning with a slightly sore head and a need to check my phone to confirm that it hadn't been a strange alcohol-induced dream about our former captain. Before leaving to return to Auckland, I visited the Waitangi Treaty Grounds, where the Māori and British signed an agreement about the future of the country in 1840. A date considered to be the founding of their country. Interestingly, the contracts were written in two different languages and had slightly different wording, which means that they're still being contested to this day. The British one said that they would govern the country, whereas the Māori one suggested that they would govern it together. Either way, a desire to stop the French was the successful motivation behind the alliance.

After my mini-retreat in the north, I spent another night in Auckland, where I received my foreword from Matt Lawrence, who was juggling his visiting in-laws with finishing my book, and official confirmation from our Chief Executive, Phil Alexander, that I could use a club-owned photo on the back cover.

From there, I headed to Hot Water Beach. On the way, we stopped at the stunning Cathedral Cove, where I swam in the 'refreshing' sea and began to make closer friendships within the tour. I'd spend the next few days with Tom, an eighteen year old on a gap year, Max, a twenty-five year old German scientist, who came across as a bit of a traditional James Bond villain (Maybe he'd get on with Vincent Tan?), Natalie and Lily, two lovely best friends on a gap year, and a couple of girls from Essex, who it would be easy to judge upon meeting (they spoke like they were on the famous show and knew half the West Ham team) but proved to be incredibly lovely people.

Hot Water Beach is a natural phenomenon. Within two hours either side of low tide, it is possible to dig into the sand allowing hot water to escape to the surface forming a hot water pool. The water, with a temperature as hot as 64 °C, filters up from two underground fissures located close to each other. Tourists can dig large holes to create a pool akin to a jacuzzi so they can relax and soak in the thermal water. Unfortunately for us, the tide decided to not go out far enough and the best we could do was stand in the sea and as our feet sunk down into the sand, we'd occasionally get a scolding blast of undiluted, boiling hot water to burn our toes.

That night, after some early evening card games, I set an alarm and headed to bed early. In the middle of the night, I had two exciting things happen. First, I was finally going to click publish and release my book. Secondly, I was hoping to use the computers on the campsite that we were staying on to watch Palace away at Sunderland. Despite the extortionate price of $1/ten minutes, I'd organised enough change in the day so that I could keep the game alive.

At 3am, with New Zealand's time difference really not favouring Premier League football, which is probably why I'd already noticed that it wasn't in your face in the way that it was in Sydney, my alarm woke me up and I headed to the cold computer room. Everything was ready, my manuscript had been through its final read-through and proofing in Auckland and I'd added in Derry and Lawrence's contributions. I clicked publish. Unfortunately, I'd have to wait for 'up to 12 hours' until it became live. As well as that, I ordered fifty copies for the club shop.

The next part proved more difficult as the old computers weren't fast enough or updated enough to maintain a stream. With the score 0-0 at half time, I resigned myself to returning to bed at around four in the morning.

Keen to check if the book was live and find out the score, I set an early alarm for the next day. I wasn't over the excitement of seeing my book available for the general public to buy when I loaded the BBC website. The headline sent my joyous mood over the edge.

"Bolasie hits Hat-trick as Palace thrash Sunderland!"

We'd won 4-1 with our winger, who couldn't shoot, scoring three! We really were flying.

Delighted with life, I spent most of the day humming the heartbeat tune as I walked around caves and incredible scenery with my German friend, Max. Despite living in the centre of the football mad Munich, he barely knew who Arjan Robben, Frank Ribbery and Pep Guardiola were, such was his lack of interest in football. However, thanks to me, he now has no doubts as to who Yannick Bolasie is, or the fact that he *"Runs down the wing for me!"*

Sunderland...1 Crystal Palace...4
Stadium of Light, 11/04/15
Premier League

Sunderland: Pantilimon, Jones, O'Shea, Vergini, van Aanholt, Gomez (Johnson 59), Cattermole (Bridcutt 65), Rodwell, Wickham, Fletcher, Defoe.
Subs Not Used: Mannone, Coates, Reveillere, Buckley, Graham.

Palace: Julian Speroni, Joel Ward, Scott Dann, Damian Delaney, Pape Souare (Martin Kelly 35), Mile Jedinak, James McArthur (Joe Ledley 69), Wilfried Zaha, Jason Puncheon, Yannick Bolasie (Yaya Sanogo 71), Glenn Murray.

Subs Not Used: Wayne Hennessey, Brede Hangeland, Dwight Gayle, Shola Ameobi.

Chapter 42 - Wellington Phoenix – *Rotorua, Taupo, Wellington, (New Zealand) 13th-19th April 2015*

The tour continued and friendships grew. Although I had only known him for a week or so, Max and I became closer and closer. We also became friends with some Scottish and Irish girls, who just about forgave me for being English. As for the travelling, we crawled and swam through the caves in Waitomo, we drank in microbreweries, we pretended to be hobbits at the Hobbiton film set, and visited geysers in Rotorua. The only disappointment was that the weather dictated that we couldn't do the Tongariro Crossing, a twenty kilometre trek over volcanic peaks, also passing over Mount Ngauruhoe, which was used as Mount Doom in The Lord of the Rings films. Instead, we had to spend the day bathing in the natural thermal pools in Taupo and visiting the spectacular Hakka Falls. It's not a bad old life.

I'm not sure if it was due to how busy I was, or whether Palace were doing so well that I had nothing to worry about, or even if it was the fact that actually watching the games in New Zealand was proving difficult, but I would say that it was the furthest my mind has ever been from Palace. Not just geographically either.

New Zealand has a population of just under four and a half million and they are absolutely rugby mad. In the UK, despite having a population that is over fourteen times bigger, other sports behind our beloved football barely get a look in. However, in New Zealand, by the time that you've taken away all the rugby devotees, and a handful of cricket ones, that doesn't leave many people who want to commit to obsessing over football. Especially as the Premier League kicks off at 4am for most of the season. The powerful league's branding may be spreading like wild fire in Oz, but it will take an unbelievable effort to crack the kiwi's sporting culture.

With such antisocial kick off times, genuine pedigree in other sports, a lack of natural interest, no particular national football idols and very few competitive international matches against anyone but small islands, it's no surprise that none of the broadcasting channels forked out on the TV rights. Instead, a website allows you to buy a 'Premier League Pass' to watch the games on any device you wish. So, as I was staying with my friend Joe in Wellington, I was delighted that I'd be able to use his pass to watch our game against West Bromwich Albion.

I didn't actually know Joe that well. He was an old school friend of my Palace mates: Pavel, Dan and Cliff. I'd met him as, despite becoming a Charlton season ticket holder when they were in the Premier League – one of the masses bussed in by the club to cash in on Zola and Bergkamp playing at the Valley, he's a passionate Middleborough fan and had been to Palace vs Boro matches before. I'd also played football with him in England as he used to organize a Thursday night five-a-side kick about, which I'd taken over when he left for New Zealand some eighteen months previously. However, I didn't know him that well and was pleasantly delighted when he offered to put me up for my weekend in Wellington.

I met Joe in the centre of the small and beautiful capital city on the Friday night and after dropping my bags at his, we headed straight out to see the local game, Wellington Phoenix vs Central Coast Mariners. Despite not being in Australia, Phoenix, whose all time top goal scorer is former Palace winger Paul Ifill, compete in the A-league and unlike my Wanderers side (who'd now actually won two matches as well as drawing six and losing sixteen), were actually having a really good season.

They were in a straight fight with Adelaide, Sydney FC and Melbourne Victory for the title. Now, this is where it gets confusing. Even if they won the league, they wouldn't be able to qualify for the Asian Champions League as they are part of the New Zealand FA, who are part of Oceania confederation, rather than the Australian one, who are part of the Asian confederation. Things were getting even worse for Phoenix as despite their high league position, the A-League were threatening to take away their franchise thanks to their low attendances. An average gate of 8,500 was the second lowest in the league, even though the Westpac Stadium has a capacity of 34,500.

Despite a pitiful attendance for a title chasing side of around six thousand, I quite enjoyed the atmosphere. It wasn't as loud or consistent or ferocious as the brilliant scenes in Sydney but it was more... English and humorous. They sing about Wellington being full of 'Wind, Rain and Phoenix' and made puns on their player's names. The small faithful also stuck to chants such as repeatedly singing 'Ernie Merrick's Yellow Army' as we would for 'Alan Pardew's Red and Blue Army'. I also liked their 'simple' song that they sung about their opposition.

"I've got a song,
It won't take long,
Central Coast are rubbish!
Second verse,
Same as the first,
Central Coast are rubbish!"

Joe told me of a story when the Sydney FC goalkeeper had got into trouble for getting drunk on the flight over for an away game, the crowd had relentlessly sung at him *"Our goalkeeper drinks responsibly!"*
Perhaps the more English than European atmosphere reflected the demographic of the crowd and the fact that they seemed to be mainly followed by British expats. I spotted numerous English football shirts in the small crowd, including three Palace ones.

Unfortunately, their football, especially their goalkeeper, seemed similar to their singing – humorous. They slumped to a 2-0 half time deficit. As these teams were both higher in the league than the dross that I'd seen in Newcastle,

I tried to pin point exactly what it was that was better about them. I commented to Joe that they seemed to move the ball between themselves a bit quicker than the other sides I'd seen, but as he pointed out "That's not necessarily deliberate!"

The second half was little better but in the style of potential champions, Phoenix scored three goals in the final twenty minutes to steal a victory from the jaws of defeat. The six thousand present had been given a treat and as it was the Friday evening game, the home side temporarily went back to the top with just one game remaining. Sadly, with other results going against them, they finished fourth and lost their Final Series match (a playoff between the top six at the end of the season to win the Grand Prize) 2-0 at home to Melbourne City.

After the game, Joe and I went to various bars and celebrated the result as our own. Although, with the exception of one bar, where the players visited to pose for pictures and then drink with the fans, (imagine the scandals that would happen if Premier League fans were trusted to do this back home!) the city didn't seem to take much notice of the result. Personally, I was just disappointed that Paul Ifill (who no one will be surprised to know was injured at the time) didn't show up at the bar. He might not have been my favourite ever player. In fact, he was fat, lazy and useless for most of his time in SE25 – and I'd generally shouted that at him from the terraces, but I'd have been happy to have had any connection with Palace at the time.

The next morning, I woke with a very sore head to news that Middlesbrough had beaten Norwich 4-3 to go to the top of the Championship. Joe had set a 6am alarm to watch the crunch match and hadn't felt it fair to wake me. To be honest, I wouldn't have minded. Such is my addiction that any game will do. We also learnt that Bromley had won the Conference South and were promoted to the top level of non-league football for the first time in their history. This was something that both of us could celebrate. Joe, as he was from the area, and me, as it's my connection to South London and Palace because my Dad grew up there, while falling in love with his local side, the Glaziers.

Much of the next couple of days are a blur as the pair of us drank heavily, wondered to various view points, visited the museum to see the giant squid and ate fresh food from the markets. Wellington is the ultimate hipster town. It's full of craft beer, avocado and Joe Ledley beards. While I was more than happy to drink copious amounts of high quality beer and eat the odd avocado, my beard and dress sense didn't stand up to the locals inventive standards.

However, whether it was because Joe was so settled and happy there, or whether it was that, like in Melbourne, I'd had such fun with my host, I don't know – but I spent much of the weekend mulling over a potential move to Wellignton. Joe was keen and adamant that I'd be able to find teaching work and live properly out there. And besides, what did I have to return to London for? Other than Palace of course!

I'd have no job, no flat, no potential flatmates and no girlfriend. All of the things that I'd missed in the past, were no longer waiting for me. It's funny how things change. Just three months previously, I'd been thinking about going home early but now, I was considering how I could avoid going back at all. I wasn't even finding it that difficult to completely miss out on Palace. Maybe the naturally enforced cold turkey was helping me get over my addiction?

Thanks to a combined drunken effort by Joe and myself, I didn't even get to see the Palace vs West Brom game in Wellington. We'd returned from a full days drinking in time for the match but as he fell asleep and I couldn't log into his computer after accidently logging out, I couldn't load the match. Sleepily, I followed the first half an hour or so on Twitter with Palace 1-0 down and by the time that I'd woken in the morning, with a second splitting head ache in as many days, we'd lost 2-0. To be honest, I didn't have the motivation or interest to find out any more than that.

Crystal Palace...0 West Bromwich Albion...2
Selhurst Park, 18/04/15
Premier League

Palace: Julian Speroni, Joel Ward, Damian Delaney, Scott Dann, Joe Ledley (Pape Souare 46), Mile Jedinak (Dwight Gayle 46), James McArthur (Yaya Sanogo 79), Jason Puncheon, Yannick Bolasie, Wilfried Zaha, Glenn Murray.
Subs Not Used: Wayne Hennessey, Brede Hangeland, Martin Kelly, Shola Ameobi.

West Brom: Myhill, Dawson (Wisdom 71), McAuley, Lescott, Baird, Gardner (Olsson 80), Fletcher, Yacob, Morrison, Berahino (Baird 88), Anichebe.
Subs Not Used: Rose, McManaman, Sessegnon, Ideye.

Chapter 43 - South Island West Coast – *Kaiteriteri, Westport, Lake Mahinapua, Franz Josef, (New Zealand) 20th-26th April 2015*

The Sunday was just as drunken, although we did stay sober enough for a game of five a side in the evening, and by the time that my ferry departed for the South Island on the Monday morning, I felt like a student before mid day. The ferry was long and painful, as my hangover stopped me appreciating the full beauty of the scenery. In fact, that could be said for the entire day. Upon arrival, after being reunited with my Kiwi experience tour, we were herded onto a coach and set off on a five hour journey to see the beautiful beaches of Kaiteriteri.

Sadly, Max, my German friend, was only touring the North Island and had returned home. However, plenty of familiar and friendly faces were still on the coach. In particular, Adam, a twenty year old Chelsea season ticket holder. Maybe it was the fact that I was so far from Selhurst Park, and so logistically cut off from the football that I didn't hold this against him. Amazingly, I even considered him a friend. The pair of us and a couple of girls, Jess, a geography post graduate, and Amy, a gap year student, formed a close group as we once again experienced the immediate bond of sharing our travels.

From Kaiteriteri, we headed to Westport for some surfing. After that, we were taken to a money spinning con that football clubs would be proud of. Kiwi Experience own a rundown lodge in the middle of nowhere. They take you there with no other accommodation options and charge you $50 to stay the night. At least they host a party... where they own the bar!

It mirrored a scheme that Palace announced at the time. The club claimed that it had frozen prices in all areas of the ground, which to be fair, was mainly true. I'd happily bought a season ticket for the following year and my return, even if I was a bit apprehensive about coming back to England.

However, in one area, they'd increased the price by £100 and given each purchase a £100 voucher to spend in the bar. Of course, for people who usually bought stuff in the ground, that wouldn't really matter. Indeed, some people wouldn't mind as they could simply change their routine to buy beers or snacks in the ground rather than outside. Yet, there was a slight problem. Even with only a small percentage of the supporters in that area visiting the bar, it was often full and people couldn't get in. So if everyone needed to buy a drink there every game to use their voucher, the supply of space certainly wouldn't fit the demand. It was basically a con.

Ironically, if the club had simply increased the price they'd have probably got away with it with minimal complaint. Unfortunately, they wanted the best of both worlds. They wanted to claim they were freezing prices and increase prices at the same time. Fans saw through it and complained at length. As they always do, the owners listened and found a compromise. Like the Palace fans in the Stephenson's lounge, I felt trapped by Kiwi Experience. However, in true football fan fashion, I moaned about the price, paid up and got on with it. We spent one night there before heading onto the highlight of the tour, Franz Josef Fox Glacier.

The experience was magical from start to finish. I'd have felt satisfied that I'd have got my $300 (£160) worth from the helicopter ride to the top so the three hour hike over the spectacular river of ice was a bonus. The views were stunning as we trekked, crawled and slid our way through the glacier. Upon our return by helicopter to the town, the group of us relaxed in the natural spas at the bottom to thaw out. In the evening, sitting with a quality beer by a warm fire in the pub, while reminiscing over the incredible experience, completed a perfect day.

Therefore, with me having such fun, it was almost scripted that while I was fast asleep at the end of a long but brilliant day, as content as I could be with life, my Dad and brother were sending me updates from Selhurst Park of our 2-0 defeat to Hull. Neither missing the game nor Palace losing bothered me. I was having to get used to this now. Well, the missing games – losing was still a small surprise under Pardew. However, maybe I'd found a cure to my addiction? This was the least that I'd been able to follow our results and it was the least that defeats had ever hurt me.

Was it the fact that we were now definitely safe? No, I'd still passionately be attending matches if I was in London. Was it the fact that I was on holiday? No, I'd been just as determined as ever to see our games from Asia, despite us being rubbish and Warnock being in charge. Was it the fact that the games were at antisocial times and I was so far from home? No, it wasn't that different to Australia on either of those counts, where Palace had not only stayed an addiction, but they'd helped me through the hard times. The only thing that I could think of was that for the first time since I fell in love with the club while listening to the radio as Dougie Freedman and Neil Shipperley scored the goals to take us up to the Premier League before my first ever match (the 1997 Play Off Final), Palace were out of my sight.

Had this started to take them out of my mind? Was simply not watching the cure? Because despite the absence of Palace matches and even the start of apathy towards my club's fortunes, I was actually seriously considering moving to New Zealand.

Crystal Palace...0 Hull City...2
Selhurst Park, 25/04/15
Premier League

Palace: Julian Speroni, Martin Kelly, Scott Dann, Damian Delaney, Pape Souare, Mile Jedinak (Chung-Yong Lee 65), James McArthur, Wilfried Zaha (Dwight Gayle 72), Jason Puncheon, Yannick Bolasie, Glenn Murray (Yaya Sanogo 58).
Subs not used: Wayne Hennessey, Brede Hangeland, Jordan Mutch, Joe Ledley.

Hull: Harper, Brady (Rosenior 84), McShane, Dawson, Chester, Elmohamady, Huddlestone, Livermore, Quinn (Ramirez 74), Aluko (Bruce 85), N'Doye.
Subs not used: McGregor, Figueroa, Hernandez, Sagbo.

Colin Moody, A Palace Fan in South Africa – *the days before Worldwide TV Coverage*

I arrived in Johannesburg in early January 2003, used to not being able to see Palace as much as I would have liked (as I'd been living in the Channel Islands for a number of years) but expecting it to be that much harder; Palace weren't exactly tearing up any trees in Division 1 (soon to be renamed The Championship in a year's time), and I wasn't expecting there to be a great deal of interest in the English second tier from abroad.

Of that I was right, but as luck would have it, my arrival coincided with a combination of some positive results and interesting draws in the FA Cup; as a result I got to see three live games within the first two months of living there; two v Liverpool and then the infuriating match v Leeds, where Dermot Gallagher managed to miss a handball, nominally on the goal line, as a goal was not given, but actually a yard or two behind it. Unfortunately, FA Cup coverage was not great and there was barely any analysis of that incident and no build up shown, meaning that I only got a cursory mention of the hostile reception given to Venables during the commentary.

For the rest of that season, keeping in touch was quite difficult; South African TV didn't show games from the second tier and the coverage of Premier League games consisted of the match, a bit of analysis and a run-down of the other Premier League scores. Results were obtained by text message from home, or a quick look online but by and large new and information was hard to come by. Fortunately, it didn't appear that I was missing a great deal and the most interesting news of the remaining months of the season was Francis getting sacked.

The 2003/4 season started with some kindly sole in the offices of Supersport (the local equivalent of Sky) deciding that it was worth broadcasting the feed from Gillette Soccer Saturday in the UK and so for the first couple of matches, there was up to date information and scores; unfortunately this was short-lived as room was made across the various channels for, first, Tri-Nations Rugby and then the Rugby World Cup. However, the shining light was that Supersport were now showing Division 1 matches that were being shown live by Sky, provided that there was no clash with something deemed more interesting!

Managing to find a pub to show the games was fruitless, the pecking order seemed to be South Africa International Rugby; International Club Rugby featuring a South African side; local Rugby; International Club Rugby matches, featuring a number of South African players in the teams; Premier League football; nothing; and so at about 2:30pm South African time, I settled down with a few beers to watch the mighty Palace take on Wigan Athletic. Unfortunately, I hadn't banked on the debacle to follow and severely under-estimated the number of beers needed that 5-0 defeat. Fortunately, it appeared that I was the only one who gave a s*** and so barring a few comments from friends that knew I'd stayed in to watch the game, I got away with barely a word said.

After that, it was back to trying to get hold of scores by text during matches, although somewhat bizarrely, a feed of Gillette Soccer Saturday was broadcast on the day that England won the Rugby World Cup, not that I was in the greatest state to pay much attention to it! Palace's fortunes steadied and shortly before Xmas 2003 an evening game away at Reading encouraged me to delay the start of an evening out; this was despite various encouraging words such as "last time you stayed in to watch them they got thrashed!". However, despite the scorns from friends, we marched to a 3-0 win and we were off and running!

Bizarrely, after that, despite Palace surging up the table, we didn't seem to be broadcast again. However someone on the BBS match threads had posted up a link that seemed to default through to Radio London commentary, which was useful on a few occasions; a glorious 3-0 home win against Sunderland was one such time. Come the Play-Offs and I'd managed to find a pub, which went on to become a regular haunt for a while, that would show the semis. I watched the Friday night first leg against Sunderland with a Huddersfield fan, who had a day layover on his way somewhere; my

yelling and shouting at the TV seemed to keep him entertained if nothing else. The following Monday in much about the same spot, I attracted the attention of a Newcastle born, West Ham fan; unfortunately for him we'd just gone 2-0 down and while I wasn't rude, I wasn't in a particularly talkative mood. At about 10:30, with me pretty much the only person showing any interest, I picked up my tab and was about to settle up, when a corner came in and... *"Bloody hell! We've scored! Get in!"*
"What does that mean?" says the barmaid.
"Extra time, I'll have another Castle!"
She did her best to appear pleased!

By the time extra time had finished, the pub had officially closed. However, the manager and a couple of his friends, drinking at the end of the bar, seemed ok for me to stay, *"Just so long as you only drink bottles, yah bru?"*
This was fine with me – as long as I could see Palace. The highs & lows of a penalty shoot-out when you actually really care about the outcome are excruciating, and seemingly bemusing to the guys at the end of the bar. That said, after Hughes scored the winner and I did a 'lap of honour' of the pub, the only bottles rule went out of the window as they started to indulge in a few shots
"Just to help you celebrate, yah"

Obviously, I wasn't in South Africa for the final!

2004/5 became much easier to follow – it's so much easier when you're in a league that people seem to want to watch. Premier League coverage consisted of the lunchtime Saturday TV live game; at least two 3 o'clock Saturday games; the evening Saturday TV live game; both Sunday live TV games; Monday night game. Any games that weren't shown live, were shown delayed, in full later; that in itself led to some odd occasions. I particularly remember leaving friends partying outside in their garden while I went inside and watched a re-run of a tedious 0-0 draw at home to Blackburn.

Games were generally watched at a few different pubs around town, or at home, depending on whether they clashed with any Rugby matches that were being shown. If the worst came to the worst, then listening via the aforementioned link to Radio London commentary had to suffice (a 2-1 win at Charlton in the League Cup was followed this way). The preference was to watch in a pub, where there were at least some other interested football fanatics. Despite looking, I didn't come across any other Palace fans in Johannesburg during the time I was there and despite trying, I wasn't able to convert any. Pretty much everyone I knew had already nailed their colours to the mast for Man U, Liverpool or Arsenal; although one lad was Leeds and sticking with it, no matter how far their fall from grace was going. The best that I got was people converting for the day, based on who we were playing; hence me getting jumped on by a couple of Man U followers, when Aki equalised against Arsenal one Saturday evening. Having said all that, Palace were better known in some quarters as a result of the tour in 1992; unfortunately, it seems we never built on any interest generated.

As the season started towards its' end, getting games on in the pubs became harder; the Super Rugby season had started and that took priority; unfortunately the games that I remember that we did get shown in live ended in resounding defeats; Arsenal and Everton away to name two. Football simply wasn't a priority at that time in that part of the world. Suddenly, towards the season's end we were on at home to Liverpool and 1-0 win gave hope of survival.

Our last home game wasn't shown live, the link to Radio commentary that had been posted previously on the BBS no longer seemed to work and broadband connections weren't fast enough to support streams, even if there had been one. I was left with a last resort of following by text commentary on the BBC website – tortuous, but in its' own weird way, a bit exciting

The moment of joy seeing that Crouch had been sent off, to be followed cruelly moments later with the words "SENT OFF! – Sorondo". Going into the dying seconds of a game, holding on to a 2-1 lead, constantly pressing refresh to suddenly see "GOAL! Crystal Palace 2-2 Southampton". Never have four words and a couple of numbers generated such a torrent of foul mouthed abuse to be shouted at...well no-one actually, I was the only one in the room. I appreciate that it probably wasn't half as gutting as being there, but still. The next day, watching the goal on a highlights package, with Higginbottom running the length of the pitch to the Southampton fans and screaming "We're still f***ing in it!" just about topped of a crap weekend.

And so the last game v Charlton. Surely that would be screened live? Well, no actually! Ah! but in a way, yes. The second half would be screened live on a "reserve channel" while the two main channels would show Fulham v Norwich and Southampton v Man U. After forty-five minutes of trying to follow by text commentary, while flicking the TV between the other two games was to be followed by an excruciating 45 minutes watching Palace try to, first overhaul a deficit and then hand on to the lead; as soon as Leigetwood gave away the free kick, I immediately though that could be costly, and then, bang! F***'s sake!

Dowie entered into the spirit of stupidity by bringing on a central defender to play up front, rather than a centre forward and then it was done. Fortunately, the cameras cut away to West Brom, so I was at least spared watching the clowns celebrating like they'd won the league, although having heard them already on the commentary, I had been given a flavour of what it would be like.

The one benefit of living abroad was that I was also spared the wall to wall coverage of the relegation in the media for the next couple of days and was able to wallow in disappointment without being force-fed re-runs of goals, celebrations etc etc. The flip side to that of course was that I was back to very little TV coverage and having to scratch around for news, results etc.

In the latter part of 2016, there were two live TV games, a 2-1 victory in the League Cup over Liverpool and 3-1 victory over QPR, which was memorable for two Marco Reich goals and quite possibly the funniest post-match analysis comment I've ever heard from Terry Paine; after a discussion about how well Palace had played and how well they could do that season the presenter asked Paine *"And*

as for QPR, what about them, are there any positives that can be taken from tonight?"
Paine, after a quick pause for thought, he gave a straight faced *"No".*

As my contract come towards its' end and I prepared to leave South Africa at the end of 2005, the ability to watch Palace started to drift away. Tthere was however an Oasis in the desert, a 3-2 win at Brighton, with Freedman scoring twice and a last minute winner from McAnuff, to cheer the soul.

And that was basically it, my time in South Africa was over. I actually got to see far more games than I had expected when I'd left, obviously helped by a storming run that ended in promotion to the Premier League. English football was well followed but, probably inevitably, it was the 'bigger', more well-known clubs that were supported; the bars that I found that were frequented by English nationals, generally seemed to predominately Man U or Chelsea fans and they were just as repugnant as they are at home. I preferred to watch with local South Africans but that tended to mean that I was restricted to only being able to watch Palace when they played one of the 'big' teams, or when our game didn't clash with another match.

Chapter 44 - Queenstown and the Deep South – *Wanaka, Queenstown, Dunedin, Invercargill, Lake Takapo, Christchurch, (New Zealand) 27th April-4th May 2015*

The further south we travelled, the more beautiful the country seemed to get. Even the heavy rain we experienced on the way to Wanaka couldn't ruin it as it simply added to the aggressive beauty of the dozens of waterfalls that we passed. Wanaka was a majestic small town surrounded by mountains and a large, gorgeous lake. With scenery like this outside, why would anyone want to stay up all night to watch the EPL? Unlike Oz, there was absolutely no appetite for it. Even when we headed on to the party town of Queenstown.

In the centre of town, there 50 bars in one square kilometre and despite this vast range of drinking outlets, none seemed to think there was much money to be made from 4am showings of the Premier League! And even if there was anywhere, I made the early assumption that nowhere was likely to show Palace games. However, with such a large choice of bars, I set about trying as many as possible, as well as the famed Furg Burger.

As April was now drawing to a close, so was the football season. Within days of each other, Bournemouth and Watford joined us in the Premier League, as Middleborough bottled promotion, having looked so strong when I'd been with Joe. Talking of Joe, he was strongly encouraging me to look into teaching opportunities in New Zealand. Although, despite my intrigue at the possibility, I was still treating this trip very much as a holiday. A holiday where I was planning to take my love of extreme experiences to a new level.

Often, I've talked about watching Palace being a form of punishment rather than entertainment and it was again that self-torturous peculiarity of mine that took me over when I signed up to do a bungee jump. Throwing myself off a ledge resting 340m up in the air may have been what I'd felt like doing in August when Warnock had been appointed, but by the time I was standing on the edge of the suspended high wire platform, I was physically shaking.

The jump itself was the scariest thing I've ever done. Tension at football is built up not just over ninety minutes as a collective group cheer, sigh and growl as one, but in the days and weeks before big matches as we talk, dream and pray about the match. The situation during the game is constantly changing as you face different types of pressure; holding onto a result, needing a goal, listening to results elsewhere. All of which you have no control over. Here, stood over an enormous drop, I technically did have the control, but the fear and suspense had grown over three days. I couldn't drop out (rather than off) now could I?

Like with football, I'd tried to plan for my emotions. Before important matches, I like to think about what it would mean to win, or how I'll deal with defeat. Of course, the reality is very different and rawness of the emotion stops you thinking about what you're doing. This was the case as I felt myself flop forward and freefall towards the earth. I'd intended to scream "EAGLESSSSSS!" as I jumped but the fear as I dived was too much. Despite the actual ten seconds of freefall being a bit of a blur, the adrenaline rush lasted for the rest of the day until I eventually collapsed in my bed for the evening.

The next morning, I was awakened by a German scream as a Dortmund fan let out a sound of relief at the full time whistle of their cup semi-final victory over Bayern Munich. Sensing my passion for football, or perhaps simply appreciating my vague interest, he emphatically told me about the match that he'd watched on his phone. From Queenstown, I visited Dunedin and Invercargill, the two southern-most towns of New Zealand.

The landscape and wildlife were amazing, despite the appalling cold and wet weather. However, the quieter nature of the trips gave me some time to reflect. Over the previous few weeks, I'd realised one thing. There was very little for me to return to in England. I'd have no job and by the time that I was back, most teaching posts would be gone. I'd have no girlfriend and my ex had recently found someone new. Besides that, I'd also sent some enquiring messages out to friends and no one was looking for a new flatmate so I'd be living with my Mum again in sleepy Berkshire, not only separated from the excitement of London, but also away from most of my friends, who'd long since left the area that we grew up in. Only Palace seemed worth returning for. Even then, I was coping just fine without them.

As I hadn't done any farm work or held any employment that was worthy of an Australian company sponsoring, staying Down Under wasn't a possible option. I'd vaguely looked at teaching posts in South-East Asia but it was the wrong time of year to apply for jobs there. However, Joe had really sewn the seed in my mind about moving to New Zealand, especially if I could find a teaching role in Wellington, rather than spend another year working in bars.

My 'Deep South' tour ended with a trip to Milford Sound. The journey was a thing of beauty as we weaved through the cliff faces and over crystal clear streams. Near the Sound, we stopped at the 'Mirror Pools', where the reflection doubled the magnificence of the view. Eventually, at the end of a long, long journey, we were taken on a marvellous boat tour, spying dolphins and seals, and being driven into the glorious waterfalls that filled the melted glacier.

Back in Queenstown, I said a few goodbyes to people from my tour and met up with Ben, who I'd explored the Great Ocean Road with as he was now living in New Zealand. At the end of a fun and drunken day with him, I followed the final day of the Championship season on my phone as no bars were showing it and many had closed.

I was delighted for Brentford, the only team that I'd seen Palace play against live in the season, as they clinched a playoff place during their first season back in the second tier. An achievement that had seemed inconceivable in August, despite their 3-2 friendly victory over us. For me, the idea of Bournemouth and Brentford, and terracing, being in the Premier League was brilliant. The more small clubs the better and it might make Palace and Selhurst look slightly less out of place amongst England's elite.

The surprise result of the day was Leicester, who had looked all but down after their defeat to us, beating Newcastle 3-0. When Pardew had left the North East club, they'd been 10 points ahead of us in 10ᵗʰ place. Now, just five months later, they were seven behind us and only three clear of relegation. To make matters worse, Pardew's replacement, John Carver, accused the players of stopping trying as two were sent off in their dismal defeat. Cruelly, as the bitter and smug fan that I am, I grinned throughout their implosion. Especially in light of their dislike and treatment of our 'Super Al'.

The following day, we headed to Lake Takapo, where I spent time relaxing and walking around the water. In the evening, I began to argue with a Norwich fan, who was still bitter and angry about Andy Johnson 'diving' in 2004 to deny them three vital points at Selhurst Park in a 3-3 draw. Now, I will accept I have a somewhat biased view. But, Andy Johnson was not a diver. I'll accept that Zaha throws himself to the floor, and Bolasie, and I've seen Johnny Williams, Tommy Black and Sasa Curcic do it in red and blue too. However, AJ was not a diver, and the ridiculous and wrong reputation he got for cheating not only denied us numerous clear penalties, but also led to him getting a serious injury at Reading after the referee gave him no protection all night. Not that I struggle to move on from Palace injustices at all...

Anyway, it wasn't AJ being accused of diving when I woke up the next morning. It was Eden Hazard. The Chelsea winger had gone down under minimal contact from Adrian Marriappa as Chelsea beat us 1-0 to secure the title. Further fuelling South London's anger, there were reports that John Terry had handled the ball in the Chelsea area. Not that the referee noticed of course.

After hearing the news, I caught the bus to the tragic city of Christchurch. Surrounded by collapsed buildings, we walked around the eerie city. Deserted shops still showed signs from four years ago before the first devastating earthquake. The only signs of life were at a temporary shopping centre, built in storage containers.

With little else to do, as all the bars and restaurants in the centre of town were closed, most people headed back to the hostel for the early evening. Although it seemed like a waste, it did allow me to catch my first glimpse of the 'EPL' in New Zealand as the evening sports news ran a short piece on Chelsea winning the league, allowing me to see brief Palace highlights. For what it's worth, I wasn't convinced it was a dive but at least I got to enjoy Speroni's penalty save, despite Chelsea scoring the rebound.

Chelsea...1 Crystal Palace...0
Stamford Bridge, 03/05/15
Premier League

Chelsea: Courtois, Azpilecueta, Terry, Cahill, Ivanovic, Matic, Fabregas, Cuadrado (Mikel 46), Willian (Zouma 86), Drogba, Hazard (Luis 90).
Subs not used: Cech, Ake, Loftus-Cheek, Remy.

Palace: Julian Speroni, Adrian Mariappa (Martin Kelly 60), Scott Dann, Damian Delaney, Joel Ward, Joe Ledley, James McArthur, Jason Puncheon (Yaya Sanogo 70), Jordan Mutch (Glenn Murray 60), Wilfried Zaha, Yannick Bolasie.
Subs not used: Wayne Hennessey, Brede Hangeland, Mile Jedinak, Chung-Yong Lee.

Chapter 45 - Palace up a Volcano – *Kaikora, Wellington, Taupo, Auckland, (New Zealand)*
5th-11th May 2015

Still deep in reflection at the devastation in Christchurch, we headed further up the east coast to Kaikora, where I swam with dolphins as the magical moments I was experiencing, coupled with Palace's mid table position, totally eclipsed the feeling of Palace losing three consecutive matches. After getting the boat back to the North Island, we stopped to pick up three extra passengers. Immediately, I recognised one of them. It was Mark – the Palace fan who I'd experienced my Palace and Western Sydney 'losing day' with.

He was travelling with his American girlfriend, Ashleigh. Encouraged by Mark, she'd adopted Palace after meeting him at the top of Machu Picchu in Peru, even if she had said that Crystal Palace sounded like a 'crack den'. Despite being on the opportunity of a lifetime, she was almost as keen to stay up and learn about our beloved club as she was to see New Zealand. Any football addict needs an understanding partner!

Eventually, I arrived back in Wellington, where I met up with a rather shaken up Joe. In between my two visits, he'd managed to fracture his spine while cycling. Thankfully, although he could barely move, he wasn't to experience any long term damage. Despite his injuries, he generously put me up for a couple of nights and we discovered a drunken bet that we'd made in my first visit. Our only recollection of it was the shaky film footage from the end of a night.

He was adamant that Palace were at the top of their potential and the only way was down, while his Middlesbrough team were coming back to 'greatness'. I'm not sure when 'Boro had previously been 'great' but I guess that's beside the point. Anyway, on the 18th April 2015, Joe had declared that Middlesbrough would be back above Palace within three years. Me being me (and drunk), I couldn't and wouldn't accept his depreciating trash talk about my club so I called him up on it. It was decided that whoever's team held a higher league position on 18th April 2018 would be entitled to an entire night of drinks purchased for them. An expensive price to pay for their football teams shiteness.

After managing to get a highly disabled Joe to the pub, along with Mark, and Emma, an Irish girl from the Kiwi bus, we proceeded to once again get heavily drunk. However, this time, my wallet and liver were delighted to discover that I'd made no further bets before we headed back to Taupo to try and do the Tongariro Crossing, which bad weather had denied us the opportunity to do on the way down south.

The next day, starting with a 5am wake up so we could arrive at the crossing for the crack of dawn (first daylight, not a young lady's bottom), was to have two enormous tests. Firstly, the steep and challenging 20km hike and secondly, Palace were set to face Manchester United. The early parts of the walk were pretty and easy, as the odd waterfall gave us a quick chance for a photo. Happily, I chatted about Palace with Mark as we comfortably moved along. Without realising it, I'd really missed having a fellow Eagle to share memories, opinions and statistics with.

In some ways, the early part of the walk mirrored our own season. Like the numerous signposts at the start of the trek, we'd be warned as to how difficult it would be to simply stay up after Pulis walking out. Furthermore, appointing Warnock had shown how hopelessly unprepared we were for the task. A bit like my footwear for the day. However, early wins against Leicester and Everton had masked the size of the challenge and fans began to dream again of a comfortable survival.

However, pretty soon, the terrain and steepness of the 'Devil's Staircase' wiped the smiles off our faces and began to show the challenge of the task ahead. It didn't take long before we were surrounded by a low cloud and the optional extension of Mount Ngauruhoe (better known as Mt Doom in Lord of the Rings) became impossible. It was all about simply completing the track ahead.

Just like the path, Warnock's results knocked the optimism out of the club as we couldn't look at improving on the previous season or enjoying the bonuses of the extra, exciting games that are brought about by a cup run. We simply had to find a way of staying up.

As we neared the top of Mount Tongariro, the cloud meant that our visibility was little more than two or three metres. Under our feet, the crumbly ground gave way as we trudged up the increasingly steep incline, while battling the strong wind. It wasn't fun and I was relieved for the suitable walking boots and warm hat that I'd rented before setting off.

Despite the Liverpool victory bringing a relief of tension in November and a supporting hand to our point's total, the Premier League ground was collapsing beneath us as we suffered defeat after defeat. Watching Palace was an uphill challenge and the reward was little. I couldn't see a way out of it.

Briefly, very briefly, the cloud cleared as we arrived at the summit. Suddenly, it was all worthwhile. My hand was shaking from the cold as well as the jaw dropping view. As quick as my frozen body would allow, I tried to reach into my pocket for my phone to capture the moment but before I could, the stunning sight looking into the volcano was taken away by the elements. Still, Mark and I posed for a photo in the mist with a 2013/14 home shirt to lay claim to the ground as conquered by Palace. We felt like we were at the top of the world and we wanted Palace there with us.

Finally, Warnock was relieved of his duties over Christmas as we fell to a pitiful home defeat to Southampton. Keith Millen, as he always does for his boyhood club, stepped in and restored some pride with a couple of uninspiring but vital 0-0 draws before moving aside for Alan Pardew to lead us into a new era.

As we skidded down the other side at pace, we took in the mystical, emerald blue lakes. Under Super Al, Palace beautifully charged from one Premier League victory to the next. This was perfection. After the main event and the excitement of the volcano, there were a few ups and downs before we cruised to the end of the path with a fairly boring and easy forest walk. However, like Palace's late season defeats, a tame end to the walk couldn't ruin its greatness.

No sooner had I returned back to the hostel, I collapsed in my bed. The day had been exhausting and my alarm was set for 4am. I'd conquered the crossing, now Palace had to take on Manchester United. Awaking at that time ensured a freezing and dark start to the day, which hardly ensured optimism for the challenge ahead. I set off on the short ten minute walk across the small town of Taupo with plenty of time to find Mark and Ashleigh's hostel. There, we intended to watch the game on Mark's laptop.

It was great to have some Palace company for a match. Since watching us beat Stoke at the Exhibition in mid-March, I had gone seven weeks without watching a Palace game. The six games in a row that I'd missed was my longest run in seventeen years and back then, it was because I was totally reliant on my father taking me to games. I couldn't and wouldn't understand why he didn't take me everywhere, home and away. What do you mean it's expensive? And you have other things in your life? And you'd have to pay for my brothers too? And you're tired? And we always lose? C'mon, this is Palace.

However, I couldn't blame anyone for this. I could only blame myself. Sure, it would have taken some serious commitment and meant missing out on some once in a life time opportunities, but in the past, I'd have done it. Maybe going 'cold turkey' in New Zealand really was curing my addiction? Especially as I was actually considering the possibility of moving to this football-less country. There again, the fact that I was shivering down the road in a small, Kiwi town at 4am to watch a game on a stream in a hostel suggested that perhaps I had a long way to go yet.

The living room at Mark's place was small, cold and surrounded by dormitories. Cheering too loud would be seen as rather disrespectful to the sleeping backpackers in the neighboring rooms. Although, the odds were, there was at least one Manchester United 'supporter' in the building from one country or another who'd be sleeping through the match, oblivious. Having said that, I'd done the same (bar some early hours tossing, turning, sweating and BBC following) for the return game earlier in the season.

Strangely, despite our previous three defeats, I was cautiously optimistic. Worries of relegation were long gone and Palace were looking for one, final big result to round off an excellent second season in the Premier League. Manchester United, while clearly stronger than under David Moyes' disaster, were still recovering from their post-Ferguson hangover and were nowhere near the threat that they'd posed in the past.

As usual, when I dare to show any signs of positivity towards my club, things didn't go to plan as my early morning effort was given no kind of reward. For the third time in four matches against the North-West giants, the referee awarded them a penalty, which Juan Mata dispatched. Not that I knew much about it. Mark, Ashleigh and I squinted at the freezing, spluttering and blurred picture throughout a terrible forty-five minutes.

By half time I was considering going home but luckily, the break allowed us to find a far better stream. Additionally, Pardew's half time introduction of Jason Puncheon allowed Palace to find a far better performance. One of my biggest criticisms of Warnock's second spell was his refusal to change games with the men sitting on the bench behind him. All too regularly, he'd leave the subs until too late into the match and the game was lost. Since replacing him, Pardew had won us numerous points with his early substitutions.

Puncheon should have had a penalty when he was tripped in the box after showing feet too quick for the lumbering white-shirted defender. However, the referee outrageously waved play on. Still, undeterred, Palace pushed on and got their reward from a Jason Puncheon freekick, which was deflected past de Gea in the United goal. Mark, Ashleigh and I erupted as if we were in Selhurst Park. The jubilant, erratic scenes of us doing a mixture of shouting, hugging and jumping were witnessed by exhausted and confused backpackers, who were sleepwalking out of their dorms to head off for the Tongariro crossing. They looked on unimpressed as they tried to come to terms with their early morning alarm.

After that, we went for the throat. (I mean Palace going for the win, I didn't attack any by standing backpackers in a random act of fatal violence to add a strange twist to the book) Zaha, McCarthy and particularly Glenn Murray had great chances to win it but all of them found de Gea in top form. Inevitably, after wasting chances, United punished us. Fellani nodded in a soft winner. He seemed to push our usually solid centre back, Delaney, into Speroni, which allowed him an open goal but it was hard to tell from the replays.

Minutes later, Murray nearly scored an exquisite equaliser as he controlled the ball in the air and spun towards goal, volleying it towards the top corner but predictably, United's Spanish keeper made a superb save to deny us for the umpteenth time. Yet in truth, it was United who looked more likely to score again. Speroni, not wanting to be outdone by his opposite number, pulled off a couple of brilliant saves to keep us battling right up to the final whistle but for the fourth consecutive time since being promoted, we'd battled hard against the red devils and lost.

Disappointed but not devastated, I headed back to my hostel and bed before later catching my final bus of the trip back to Auckland. There, I briefly met up with Camila again and said some goodbyes to people from the tour, before catching my flight back to Sydney for the final time.

Crystal Palace...1 Manchester United...2
Selhurst Park, 09/05/15
Premier League

Palace: Julian Speroni, Joel Ward, Scott Dann, Damian Delaney, Pape Souare, Mile Jedinak (Chung-Yong Lee 84), Joe Ledley (Jason Puncheon 46), Wilfried Zaha (Marouane Chamakh 85), James McArthur, Yannick Bolasie, Glenn Murray.
Subs not used: Wayne Hennessey, Martin Kelly, Jordan Mutch, Fraizer Campbell.

Manchester United: De Gea, Valencia, Jones, Smalling, Shaw (Evans 39), Blind, Herrera, Young, Fellaini, Mata, Rooney (Falcao 46).
Subs not used: Valdes, McNair, Periera, Januzaj, Wilson.

Chapter 46 - A Functioning Alcoholic – *Sydney, 11th-16th May 2015*

Within ten hours of being back in Australia, which felt far more like home this time than my return from Asia, I was back at the Opera House Bar. Unlike Scruffy Murphys before them, they'd kept their word and given me a job upon my return. I felt bad. Aware that they might not take me on otherwise, I hadn't told them that I'd only be back in Sydney for a few weeks before beginning my journey home. Not only did they take me back on but they offered me a promotion that I knew I couldn't take. As well as having a job to return to, for the first time, I had a permanent place to live. Rich's housemate had moved out and I'd been allowed to sleep in his room for my remaining time in Oz.

On the plane back from Auckland, I'd made an extensive 'to do' list of places to go, opportunities to take, bars to frequent and most importantly, people to see. Back at the Opera House, it was great to see some familiar faces, but such was the high turnover of staff, there were plenty of new ones too. At the end of my first returning shift, I jumped on the train home with Thomas, a new colleague from Bordeaux. As it usually does, conversation soon turned to football and I was quick to tell him that I supported Palace
"Oh, Marouane Chamakh!" he said with a huge grin, remembering his home town club's former hero.

The next morning, I woke to news that eclipsed Palace having a following in Bordeaux with its bizarreness. Kevin Muscat, the former Palace thug of a right back, was named A-league Manager of the Season. His Melbourne Victory side had won the Grand Final as Tony Popovic's Western Sydney finished the season in second bottom place. If ever I needed proof that I was a jinx to the clubs that I support, this was it. One season of me following the Wanderers had nearly destroyed them.

Another thing that I noticed was how normal it felt to be back in Sydney. When Mark – the Palace fan from Brisbane who I'd watched the Asia Cup final with – came down, I was able to show him around and take him to a range of my favourite places as we drank beers and chatted about Palace.

I also noticed a change in my ability to deal with the Australian climate. However, that did mean that if it was only twenty degrees, it felt too cold to go swimming. A concept that had amused me during my early days Down Under. However, the best thing was that around town, I was bumping into people I knew all the time. Through Scruffys, and the Opera House, and Scary Canary, and the two different hostels, and the Palace crowd, people from the Kiwi Bus, and the Wednesday night five a side, I finally felt like I had a large amount of friends in Sydney. Each day, I was going to different craft beer bars before and after work with different mates.

Back in the previous August, my arrival in Sydney had sparked a heavy feeling of loneliness. Only Palace and the fans at the Exhibition had been able to spark any life into me. Yet now, I was dreading returning home. All the things that I'd lost by moving, I'd now replaced. A flat, a close flatmate, an area I loved, a job I liked, five a side, and most importantly, friends. I'd even replaced Selhurst with The Royal Exhibition Hotel. Now, I was set to return to a jobless, flatness, girlfriendless England to live with my Mum in Surrey.

Therefore, I was making the most of my time out there. The money I earned from the Opera House was going straight on beer. While it wasn't healthy for the body, it was healthy for my mind to be so active. How no one at work noticed that I was turning up half cut, I don't know. I was regularly having three or four schooners before work and would sober up enough by the end of the shift to head to a bar with some colleagues. On top of that, I discovered an amazing bottle shop with over one thousand beers from around the world, including all my favourite Kiwi, Australian and English brews. It probably wasn't big or clever that I was paying Richard rent in beers either...

On Saturday 16th May, I headed into Newtown with Rich to tick some more bars off my hit-list before work. Thankfully, the Palace game against Liverpool kicked off at 5:30 in England, which now the clocks had jumped forward and back respectively meant it was a 2:30am kick off in Oz, rather than 4:30am as it would have been in the middle of the season. Seventeen thousand kilometres away from Anfield, the repercussions of this were that seven dedicated eagles could head to The Royal Exhibition Hotel for the final time in the season.

As soon as I arrived and began to lead the singing with Jordo, Sean, Dave, Paul, Tony and Russ, I realised that I was with genuine friends, who I'd dearly miss when I was gone. These weren't just Palace fans who I'd been able to share this chapter of our history with. These were the people who'd make my year abroad a success. Originally, they'd accepted me for who I am, a Palace Addict. However, now, I saw them as friends whose bond reached far further than simply sharing a beer and a singsong because we liked the same team.

All of them had purchased copies of my first book and I felt like a celebrity as we had a book signing session in the betting corner of the pub. For once, the game matched the occasion. Palace battered Liverpool at Anfield. Even the scousers taking the lead couldn't stop us. For the third time in recent weeks, Jason Puncheon scored directly from a free kick and we headed into the break on level terms.

The second half was simply magical as Palace stormed to victory with goals by the substitutes Wilfried Zaha and Glenn Murray. Loudly and proudly, the seven of us cheered the team on, constantly expecting us to fall apart at any moment. But we didn't. This wasn't the Palace we knew. This was a new team. A new club. As I'd been told repeatedly around the world in the previous year, we were the team that f***ed Liverpool.

The full time whistle was met with a huge group hug as we danced in disbelief at what we'd just witnessed. Jordo and I shared a meaningful embrace as he left the pub and I thanked him for the memories of the previous year. Iain Dowie, Andy Johnson and Neil Shipperley had captured his love of the club when he'd lived in England in 2004 but since then, he hadn't let go. Even in the days of Championship football and minimal coverage down under, he'd endeavoured to start up and maintain the supporters group. But it was more than that. Chelsea and Manchester United and Arsenal and Liverpool and Tottenham had supporters groups in Sydney. They were all organised by their clubs and had membership fees. We were simply a group of friends who loved the same club.

After the match, with the Exhibition closed, five of us, each carrying a copy of my book, wondered around Sydney looking for a pub to serve us so we could celebrate our win. Various places turned us down thanks to the Responsible Service of Alcohol laws, despite our claims that we were simply a midnight book club looking for a weekly venue. Eventually, we were allowed into the Gaming Room at Scruffy Murphys before I finally got home for 8am with the sun already out.

Liverpool...1 Crystal Palace...3
Anfield, 16/05/15
Premier League

Liverpool: Mignolet, Can, Skrtel, Lovren, Moreno (Sinclair 87), Gerrard, Henderson, Lallana (Lucas 65), Sterling, Coutinho, Ibe (Lambert 65).
Subs not used: Ward, Johnson, Toure, Allen.

Palace: Wayne Hennessey, Joel Ward, Scott Dann, Martin Kelly, Pape Souare, James McArthur, Joe Ledley, Jason Puncheon, Yannick Bolasie (Glenn Murray 82), Chung-Yong Lee (Wilfried Zaha 59), Marouane Chamakh (Jordan Mutch 76).
Subs not used: Julian Speroni, Damian Delaney, Mile Jedinak, Fraizer Campbell.

Chapter 47 - Preparing to Leave – *Sydney, 16th-24th May 2015*

The final few days in Sydney were manic. As well as some emotional goodbyes and ill-advised quantities of alcohol, I had all the nitty-gritty things to sort , such as closing bank accounts, closing and collecting my superannuation (pension), claiming my tax back and resigning from a job that I'd only re-started three weeks earlier.

I also managed to coinside my return with the free-bar (delayed) Christmas Party at the Opera House, where International Fifa Tournaments were rife. Team selection wasn't allowed. Instead, your nationality dictated which team you had to play as. While England wasn't too bad a choice, as I beat my French colleague 3-0 and lost by the same score to my Mexican co-worker (who disappointingly wasn't wearing a silly hat), I felt sorry for Alex, an enthusiastic Vietnamese lad. What I took out of the whole experience was pride that Palace's former youth product, Nathaniel Clyne, was now established enough to be seen as England's number one right back on the world stage.

There was also a strange discovery in that I found my favourite pub in Sydney during my final couple of weeks. I'd always walked straight past the Keg and Brew in Surry Hills, as it had looked like a standard, non-descript Aussie Bar. However, based on a recommendation from a friend, I checked it out. As well as an excellent range of well-priced beer, there was also a series of animal heads on the wall, which reminded me of Fawlty Towers. Additionally, it had the bonus of an attractive young bar girl, who one day, wore a Jurassic Park t-shirt. Every 90s kid's dream.

On my final Wednesday night, I played five-a-side by the rocks, another of my favourite Sydney areas. While the group weren't the close friends who I'd previously organised a game for back home, I couldn't have asked for a better setting. The outdoor pitch overlooked Sydney harbour and was next to two of my favourite bars. It certainly beat a sweaty sports hall in Victoria back in England. Usually, Richard and I would be the only ones to retire to the pub and undo any fitness improvement from the match. However, I was touched by everyone joining us after the game as it was my last week.

During the football based conversations afterwards, as we all compared our skills to Zidane, Ronaldo and Amir Karic (I'll let you decide who my game was based on), I realised something. We had eight different nationalities and at least one representative from each continent. All of our backgrounds couldn't have been more different, yet here we were, happily drinking in the pub after a game of football, sharing our common love. More than winning at Anfield, or me chasing around Asia in monsoons looking for a screen showing Palace, or waking up at 3am, or seeing homeless kids in the streets of Thailand kicking anything vaguely round, or seeing a QPR shirt in the middle of the Malaysian jungle, I think it was that moment that convinced me to write this book.

It was a unity for football that previously, I'd never experienced. There was no tribalism or trash talk that I usually love. Our teams were all so varied and different that we all wanted to learn about each others. Back home, football fans create in-fighting as I'll need to stand up for Palace and my friends will put them down, as I do to their (crap) teams. However, out in Australia, with us all exiled from home and our teams, we all simply shared a love of the beautiful game, rather than one club in particular. Football was our identity, rather than Palace.

My final week in Sydney coincided with Vivid, a yearly light festival that sees various buildings lit up over the two weeks to spectacular effect. I've always been amazed at the detail in which they could get on the Opera House. In particular, when one week they projected live images of the orchestra performance from inside. This got me thinking (always dangerous and usually about football), why don't they show live sport on the side of the Opera House? They had the technology to do it but seemed to have resisted the urge – or simply lacked my creative mind. I'd have thought that Australia's appearance in the Cricket World Cup Final that they hosted would have been the perfect opportunity to launch such an idea. Still, I had to be content with the Opera House and harbour-front skyline being lit up in red and blue for Vivid. Finally, the rest of the human race was seeing the world as I did.

Before the festival, I was asked to work with the company's handyman, Bill, to collect a temporary bar. After waiting three hours for him to turn up, as I lay in the sun being paid, eating and drinking for free, he collected me and we began to talk. You can probably guess what about. Bill was Lebanese born, but had lived in Australia for the previous forty years so when he started talking about Liverpool as his club, I rolled my eyes. However, I shouldn't have been so quick to judge.

He had an absolutely encyclopaedic knowledge of football. Passionately, he discussed the A-league, especially Sydney FC, as he was desperate for football to thrive in his adopted country. He could discuss Palace in detail as he tried to watch four or five Premier League games throughout the week to understand each team. Embarrassingly, he probably had a far better understanding of Palace's tactical on-field strengths and weaknesses than I did.

I love the club and support them intensely and obsessively. However, I rely on passion over any kind of football understanding to get my enjoyment out of the club. Past what I've learnt by playing football manager, tactics remain a mystery to me. Not that this stops me from hurling abuse at managers (especially Warnock) if they make a decision that I disagree with.

Bill had played State-league football as a central midfielder, who idolised both Patrick Vieira and Roy Keane. However, his love of the position and no-nonsense play, coupled with his desire for Australia to grow within the world's football standings, meant that he absolutely loved Mile Jedinak. However, Vieira was his main love, which he'd passed on to his son, who was now fanatical about Arsenal for that sole reason. In the former Arsenal captain's days, football in Australia was hard to find but it had still managed to inspire someone to love a club and fly over to England for games a couple of times a year. Could Palace do this now?

Yannick Bolasie was the most likely to grab the attention of international fans. He's everything that's sexy and marketable about football. He's quick, skilful and strong. He's unpredictable and willing to try new things in matches. Just ask the Spurs defenders who crowded around him as his bamboozled them with a piece of trickery that earned him his own 'skill' on a worldwide computer game. Maybe, just maybe, there'll be a depressed and obsessed twenty-five year old in Australia in 2030 looking back at his life after our latest 4am defeat to Barnsley, wishing he hadn't fallen in love with our Yannick as a wide eyed kid.

However, just as I was getting ahead of myself and began to think of the exciting possibilities of Palace being a world-wide brand, and revelling in my ability to watch Palace across the globe, I was given a heart-warming reminder of what the club is really about through a topic that is close to my heart. When CPFC 2010 took the club out of administration, one of the first things they did was to rip out Simon Jordan's 'Winning is Everything' slogan from the training ground and replace it with their own understanding of the club – 'South London and Proud'.

The shift was significant as it showed a real understanding of the club. If winning was everything, we'd have all given up years ago and probably climbed up the Crystal Palace TV mast to hurl ourselves off of it. However, winning isn't everything for us. Seeing youth academy players make their debut is. Admiring the home made displays of the Holmesdale Fanatics is. Passionately partying after a 0-0 draw at Doncaster is. Creating loud and proud atmospheres at home and away is what we do. Embracing in the glory of a dirty jerk chicken shop and a run-down pub is what we love. It defines us. Not winning. We don't do that well.

And it was that mentality that meant I felt more pride in one letter than I got from our wins against Liverpool and Manchester City combined. In many ways, a man's love of his football team is selfish. It incomprehensible for many around him but it regularly puts them out. It's allowing the actions of eleven other men to dictate your mood and easiness to be around. I often wonder if it was that feeling of being out of control that prompted so much violence in the 70s and 80s. By making the day about your own punch up, as much as the action on the pitch, then you can take back some control on the situation. You can handle that.

I suppose in a less animalistic way, that's what I do these days. I can't control whether Cameron Jerome fires over the bar from three yards or not, but I can contribute to the excellent atmosphere within Selhurst Park. We're used to losing. If we valued the art of winning matches too highly, we'd be back up the Croydon mast. We're never going to be the best football team in the country so we have to look elsewhere for our pride and bragging rights. However, the beauty of this letter was that it wasn't about bragging rights. It wasn't about taking control. It wasn't anything I'd done, or even anyone at Palace really, other than keeping the value of the club being for the community. It was about all of us. It was simply about how football has improved and it included the most touching relationship between a boy, his mother and a football club.

To all the team at Crystal Palace Football Club,

I wanted to write to tell you all about my son and the wonderful things being at the club has done for him this season.

As some background information, he suffers with Autistic Spectrum Disorder (ASD), he also has a severe speech and language delay with mild learning difficulties and dyslexia. Life can be tough for him as he tends not to speak or look at people he does not know well. New situations and places are also difficult for him to deal with. The one absolute passion he has in his life is football. However, getting him out of the house can be challenging.

We visited the club at the end of last season with a family member for a game and he told me he had enjoyed the game and wanted to return. As a family we tend to buy passes for places so if we should have to leave because of an "autistic meltdown" as we call them we can return at no extra cost, with this in mind I thought a season ticket might not be best for us as I had a view it would take until quite far into the season for him to feel truly settled. How wrong I was!

From the first moment I rang up, the staff in the box office were amazing and put me straight onto Pam.
Pam was wonderful, I felt she listened to my concerns and quite frankly my moaning, I did not feel rushed and she made me and my son feel valued as a customer. After the phone call I felt so positive about bringing [redacted name] to the games and knew if I had any problems Pam would be at the end of the phone for us. I cannot thank you enough it is not often I look forward to going somewhere.

The beginning of the season came and he was very withdrawn which I had expected, but we did not have to leave one game. The first breakthrough came around November time when a fan who was celebrating asked [redacted name] for a "High-Five" which he did with a smile, from then on I can truly say it has been amazing! He has started talking to other fans who have spoken to him. He has even started to move independently around the area of our seats. He asked if he could wait for the players to have his programme signed which I thought I would have to manage for him, again I was wrong he talked to the players, who were also incredible being patient with him and I felt they listened to him which I know he feels he does not get very often.

So we now have a young man, who regularly asks to leave the house to go and practice his Puncheon corners or his Zaha runs. I have just had a meeting with his school who have said this year he has started to speak out in class and has recently given a class presentation which is incredible. Which I think is without doubt the result of coming to Selhurst Park.

Therefore, I would like to say the biggest thank you to all of you and the work you do to help young people like my son. You have all helped him in every aspect of his daily life.

As someone who has aspirations to work with autistic children and also be a SENCO (Special Educational Needs Co-ordinator) in a mainstream school, the story really touched my heart. I think part of the beauty of this was that actually, it wasn't that the club went out of their way.

Kudos must go to Sunderland by the way, who have recently adapted a corporate, money spinning box into a sensory room to allow autistic children to enjoy matches without the stress of strangers, loud noises and unfamiliar smells. While things like that are incredible and absolutely deserve praise, I was so proud that a group of football fans, so often linked with violence, aggression and foul mouths (and smells too after the amount of beer consumed) were able to create an environment for a child with so many difficulties to thrive in. Yet better still, it wasn't done out of pity or politeness, it was done without them knowing. Just by being decent human beings.

Someone should alert the press. Football fans aren't animals. But sadly, no. John Terry having an affair, being racist and shop lifting, Steven Gerrard beating up a DJ in a nightclub, Ashley Cole's general scum-ishness, Joey Barton being Joey Barton, or other such horrible stories steal the headlines. The days of fans dragging our game's name through the mud are thankfully leaving us but sadly, the multi-millionaire 'heroes' on the pitch seem to be taking over the mantle for us.

Chapter 48 – The Last Game – *Syndey, 25th-30th May 2016*

Fox Sports had claimed that they show every single Premier League game live and until now, I'd found this to be entirely true. Even the early season Leicester City game, that it had taken two pubs, a variety of bar staff, a control room and a red button to find had kept in line with the company's claim. However, with all ten games kicking off at the same time on the final Sunday of the season, they lacked the channel power to show every game live. Unbelievably, presumably because Fox Sports have some kind of a totally irrational and unjustified hatred of our beloved club, they weren't showing the best game of the day: Mid-table Crystal Palace vs Mid-table Swansea City. To this day, I can't imagine why not. They were, however, showing a full match re-run at six am – two hours after the game was due to finish.

Before going to bed on the Sunday night, I turned my phone onto aeroplane mode. Such is the incredible coverage of social media these days, I knew it would be impossible to stop all of the Twitter, Whatsapp, Facebook and text messages firing through to my phone. Naturally, I live and breathe Palace so I usually try to grab every bit of coverage that I possibly can. However, one peek at any of those things, or one message from a friend who didn't realise my plan, and the result would be ruined.

I woke up at 5:30am on the Monday morning and set off to watch the match. However, this was different to all the others. I wasn't going to the Exhibition – mainly because it wasn't open. Interestingly, I could have created some symmetry by mirroring my opening day experience and watching the game at Cheers Bar. Yet that had been so impersonal and lonely so I think it would have been a horrible ending. Now, often with football, the matches write their own script. The way Hillsborough and Lloyds Bank played out in 2010 created the perfect ending to the story of my first book, but it wasn't that which motivated me to write it in the first place. It had started out as a challenge for me to go to every game in a season. I wanted to tell my story.

And I think my story in Australia could be summed up by the first and final matches of the season. Back in August, I'd been alone, watching a manager-less Palace lose to Arsenal in a rough Sports Bar with sticky floors and safety flaws, before heading back to my hostel to be shouted at by strangers after locking myself out of my dorm. Now, for the final game, I was heading over to Tony's flat for breakfast and the match, making the short trip from my flat, where I was living with one of my closest friends.

The game itself wasn't anything special but in the way friends do, we chatted happily about the match, and hundreds of previous ones that we lived through and experienced in different ways. Tony told me about being caught watching our 2003 win at Anfield through the window of a Thai family's house. When they saw him, they invited him in and were utterly bemused that he wasn't supporting Liverpool.

As we munched on our second half avocado and bacon, the pair of us erupted up off his sofa when Chamakh gave Palace a deserved lead. The rest of the match played out pretty quickly. We weren't nervous. Ok, partly because the game meant so little to us as a club but mainly, because the pair of us simply babbled gleefully about Australia, about the future, and about Palace.

At full time, a quick gesture from Pardew to the crowd showed us that other results had gone our way and we'd somehow sneaked into the top half of the table for the first time that season. Palace were a top ten side. In 2010, I'd gone to every single Palace game and we'd achieved our lowest league position in my lifetime: 21st in the second tier. Now, in the first year since I discovered the club that I hadn't been to a single match, we achieved our best season in that same time. That evening, I had to take a long, hard look at myself and my effect on the clubs I support. My presence in Sydney had seemed to have a similar devastating effect on Western Sydney Wanderers as I've had on Palace over the many years of my support. It can't all be my fault, surely?

However, I also had a think about the effect that the club has on me. In my first book, with the club on the brink of relegation and liquidation, I'd needed to be there for them. And it's just as well I was when I look back at my year abroad. During my lowest moments, in both of my first two job-less arrivals in Sydney, it had been Palace who'd been there for me. Palace that had made me friends. Palace that had given me purpose and focus. Sure, once I was settled or travelling, I hadn't needed the club as much and had put them to the back of my mind. But when I was unsettled, the club carried me. Suddenly, it dawned on me. All the money that I'd spent over the years on merchandise, tickets, travel and booze had been paid back. Like a true friend, Palace had been there when I'd needed them most, despite geographically never being further away from them before.

After the game, Tony headed off to work and I nipped into town to get some paperwork completed for my impending departure from the country. Of course, soon enough, I'd completed that and nipped to the pub to meet Fabian, my Swedish friend from the Opera House. Naturally, I persuaded him to frequent The Keg and Brew with me, my new favourite watering hole. By now, with England asleep, I'd switched off about Palace's top half finish and had totally forgotten about the red and blue shirt I was wearing.

As soon as I walked into the bar, the manager came over and made an announcement. He was a Palace fan. Immediately, I knew why I'd felt so at home there from the start. Although he'd moved over to Oz when he was seven, his Dad had demanded that he carried on the family tradition of supporting the club. Despite his love mainly coming from afar, and not even knowing about our Royal Exhibition meet ups, he'd spent 2013 in England and owned a half year season ticket, culminating with that glorious day at Wembley in the play offs.

Throughout the sunny and warm, winters Sydney day, various other friends came and joined me for a drink as I was soon to leave Australia for the

Philippines and begin my slow yet exciting journey home. Inevitably, I'll always associate 'years' with football seasons rather than January to December, but none more so than 2014/15. I'd arrived in Oz for Pulis' departure, two days before the first game, and departed just a couple of weeks after it ended with Super Al in charge.

On my final morning, I left Richard a goodbye present of a copy of The Palace Addiction in his flat with a special message for a special friend. I departed, safe in the knowledge that from now on, this part-English, part-American, part Australian, Manchester City fan wouldn't be able to check the football scores each week without looking to see how Palace had got on and be thinking of me. My work there was done.

Crystal Palace...1 Swansea City...0
Selhurst Park, 24/05/15
Premier League

Palace: Wayne Hennessey, Joel Ward, Scott Dann, Brede Hangeland, Pape Souare, Mile Jedinak, James McArthur (Glenn Murray 35), Wilfried Zaha, Jason Puncheon, Yannick Bolasie (Fraizer Campbell 80), Marouane Chamakh (Jordan Mutch 65).
Subs Not Used: Julian Speroni, Damian Delaney, Martin Kelly, Chung-Yong Lee.

Swansea: Fabianski, Naughton, Bartley, Fernandez, Richards, Dyer (Barrow 63), Cork, Britton (Grimes 69), Montero (Gorre 83), Emnes, Gomis.
Subs Not Used: Tremmel, Rangel, Fulton, Hanley.

"The biggest moment of the 2014/15 season for me was remaining in the Premier League. Of course, we tried to push on and climb up the table, and we finished with 48 points, which was a huge achievement for the football club. Back to back seasons staying up with not too many significant changes, some in personnel and management, but the large majority were the same guys who'd got us there in the first place. That was great to see. That's what made it special.

The overwhelming feeling was an immense positivity, primarily thanks to us being able to remain in the Premier League. Securing safety for the football club again and knowing that in the following season, the club would continue to try and grow again. That positivity was in the back of your mind as an employee of the club and member of the playing group. We knew the positivity would remain strong within the group."

Mile Jedinak

Chapter 49 – Football in the Philippines – *Manila,* Cavite, Cebu City, Oslob, Booljoon, Moalboal, (Philippines) *31st May-21st June 2015*

In my early days of secondary school, I'd become friends with a boy called Ash. Rarely for me, Ash didn't like football. Although, that hadn't stopped me once dragging him along to a rain-soaked 1-0 win away at Plymouth Argyle. Of course, he'd hated it. (But maybe I should have insisted on dragging him along again as a lucky charm?) However, what he didn't hate was visiting his mother's country. The Philippines. Regularly, he'd wax lyrical about the country he visited every year with the same passion and love that I'd speak about Palace with.

As a tribute to my old friend, I'd made a mask with his face on and wasted no time at all in finding someone to wear it at Sydney Airport. Originally, Ash had hoped to join me out there but as he couldn't, I decided to pretend he was in all of the photos that I sent home. It seemed right as he was the primary force behind me wanting to visit the country.

Talking of home, when I arrived in Manila, the Philippine capital, it might not exactly have reminded me of London, Sydney or Ascot but my cab journey did take me back to a time and place in England. Not knowing where I was, or the way to my hostel, I naturally jumped in a cab and as I wasn't a local, the driver took great delight in driving me around in circles. Not to mention feeding me a load of lies in his dodgy accent. I peered out of the window at the dark, dirty streets and strange smells, while I watched the meter rise and rise. Sure enough, it felt just like my arrival in Liverpool the night before we lost 3-1 at Anfield in 2013.

In fact, Manila reminded me of hotter and stickier Liverpool in more way than one: choking pollution, shady characters on every corner, muggings and unemployment-a-plenty, dodgy karaoke bars everywhere and brothels routinely on the corner of streets. Still, at least Liverpool hosts Stanley Park. I don't think I saw a single hint of green throughout my entire time in Manila.

In many ways, Manila is a tragic city. Signs of corruption and underfunding are everywhere. From the half-finished tram lines that run to a sudden stop, to the poverty evident on the side of the unfinished roads and the beginnings of pavements. Unlike the other manic and polluted Asian cities that I'd visited, such as Hanoi, Kuala Lumpar and Bangkok, tourism didn't seem to have reached this one. There was no one to show off to and people were stuck in a rat race to survive.

The Palace in me couldn't help but noticing the occasional 'Pulis' signs dotted around the city. Of course, I thought of the strict disciplinarian who'd been in charge of Palace the season before and deemed the Philippine Police Force an appropriate comparison. I suspected they could be brought to court over certain payments too, as it was soon to be announced that Tony would be.

Contrasted to the villainised Pulis, Selhurst Park was playing tribute to a Palace legend in Julian Speroni. His former club, Dundee, brought two thousand fans down to London for his testimonial in what seemed to be a magical night. In many ways, it was a frustrating one. The emotion of competitive games was easy to capture and experience from the other side of the globe, but despite watching the extensive highlights of the match on my phone, the pictures failed to give me the feeling for the occasion. Anyway, even if I was gutted to miss out, I was delighted for Speroni to be rewarded for all of the commitment, loyalty and breath-taking saves that he'd shown for Crystal Palace Football Club.

After a day and a night in Manila, I moved on to stay with Ash's uncle and cousins in Cavite, which is a small town just outside of the city. The hospitality and generosity of effective strangers was incredible. As well as taking me out for dinner and drinks, they also took me to visit the stunning town of Tagatay, where we could look out over Taal Volcano Island, an active volcano surrounded by the Taal Lake.

New Zealand had been the first country that I'd visited where football wasn't the way of life. Rugby had captured the small population enough to barely leave any scraps for other sports. However, after arriving the Philippines, I was relieved that the season had ended as even more so than for the Kiwis, football didn't seem to exist to the population here. I hadn't seen so much as a Barcelona or Manchester United shirt in a shop window. I highly suspected that watching Crystal Palace would be nigh on impossible.

In the evening, as we sat out on their balcony enjoying a couple of beers (curiously, thanks to the lack of decent fridges, Filipinos cool down their drinks with ice cubes which also helps to tame the inevitable hangover with the local 7% Red Horse beer), I had to raise the question with Kevin, Ash's cousin. Why was football so low profile? He talked passionately about the popularity of basketball, which was something I'd noticed as kids played the American sport on the street in the same way that children kicked a ball in Asia and Brazil. USA's occupation of the country had lasted for nearly fifty years and was still evident now.

Of course, unlike Vietnam, Indonesia or Thailand, where football was rife, the Philippines has its own world class, national sporting hero - Manny Pacquiao. Keven spoke of him as an inspiration. Children were imitating him in the playgrounds rather than Wayne Rooney or Yannick Bolasie as kids do back home. To think that our teachers in England complain that they have problems when the sport in the playground at lunch time gets too heated.

Talking of Wayne Rooney, he'd never heard of him, nor Manchester, let alone Manchester United. The only footballer he knew was David Beckham. Determined not to give up, I asked my host if he knew who Robert Gier was. I'd always taken particular interest in the barely known centre back as he'd gone to primary school and played football with my oldest brother. Furthermore, my Dad always claims to be his first ever manager.

After Gier left the scouts team that my father managed for a day, he went on to play Championship football for Wimbledon. In one game at Selhurst Park, he even slipped to allow Andy Johnson through on goal to lob the keeper and seal a 3-1 victory for Palace against the Dons. I assumed that was the impact of my Dad's coaching in his early career? Anyway, my reason for asking Kevin about this little known player is that he played 66 times for the Philippines, captaining them on most of those occasions but alas, he was still in the dark.

After that, even I didn't feel the need to check if he'd heard of Crystal Palace. It would be pointless. He came from another world. He'd never left his home country but his dream was to move to England. However, he knew so little of the reality of our culture and way of life, summed up by his ignorance towards football. An obliviousness that provoked me to think about the FIFA scandal that had recently broken.

For all FIFA members, which includes everyone from England, to the Philippines, to tiny West Indian islands, funding is almost as evenly spread among FIFA members as voting power is. More than 90 percent of associations received between $1.8 million and $2.1 million from FIFA Associate Projects between 2010 and 2014.Where had all the money gone? There was no evidence of pitches being created for children or a local league being supported to promote the game. Or even coverage of the national team to inspire future players and create opportunities. Literally, in my entire time in the country, I didn't see even one suggestion of evidence that this funding was being put to any sort of good use, beyond lining the pockets of a select few.

With a disheartened attitude towards football, I moved on to explore more of this beautiful country. My next stop was the island called Cebu and the chance to experience yet more of the country's brilliant hospitality as I stayed with Ash's girlfriend, Joy, and her family. Over the next few days, as well as treating me to copious amounts of Philippino food, Joy and her friends took me to various beautiful beaches, waterfalls and natural springs for some stunning swimming locations and tanning opportunities. The absolute highlight was the chance to swim with whale sharks in Oslob, a small town at the south of the island.

The night before I left Joy, we spent an evening with her friends and cousins in Cebu City. There, we frequented various bars, eating and drinking far too much. As the outsider, I tried to strike up some conversation with her cousin, Christian.

"Are you a big basketball fan?"

"No, I like soccer!" was his surprising response. Unfortunately for him, since the TV channels had stopped showing the Premier League games nine years previously, he'd barely been able to watch a match on the box. As far as he was concerned, football was stuck in 2006 and Henry might as well still be playing for his beloved Arsenal. Mind you, I'm sure there are Palace fans who wish they could freeze the Palace time continuum and leave us in 1979 or 1991?

Still, such was the lack of coverage and the ability to watch games, especially as the internet was nowhere near fast enough to stream matches, Christian had no idea that both Arsenal and his Spanish team, Barcelona, were playing in cup finals that night. Until 2006, he'd been able to watch games as avidly on TV as I had over the previous twelve months. Now, he only recognised one name off the Arsenal team sheet when I looked it up.

Mind you, there were quite a few I didn't know. Other than Palace, watching football had been hard for over a year now. Still, at the end of the night, I was able to cheer Christian up with the knowledge that Arsenal and Barcelona had won 4-0 and 3-1 respectively.

The next morning, it was time to say goodbye and thanks for the incredible generosity and welcoming nature of everyone I'd encountered. I was merely a stranger but thanks to knowing Ash, I'd been treated like royalty. Still, I wanted to continue my journey and explore more of this incredible country, so I headed to the small town of Booljoon. There, I stayed in a picturesque hotel by the sea, with a beach hut reaching out over the crystal clear water. Below the surface, an incredible coral sparkled in the boiling sun.

In the evening, one of the hotel workers swam out to sea and caught some fish by hand to barbeque for all of the staying guests. At first, I chatted to a group of guys from Scotland, who wore Celtic shirts. Like me, although for different reasons, they were delighted that Rangers had lost in the play offs against Motherwell to get promoted back to the SPL the previous day. I'd been gutted to miss out on seeing my Scottish side, Dumbarton, play host to the giants of the game from north of the border. Thanks to this Rangers failure, I'd get the chance in the following season. Maybe moving back to England was worthwhile after all...?

Additionally, as well as our joint pleasure over Ranger's failure, they shared my love of Joe Ledley and his incredible beard. One of them even claimed that Palace were his English side as his hero played for us. Unfortunately, that was about as far as our similarities went as they declined into a group of Glaswegian mess, playing various drinking games involving throwing vodka down their eye sockets throughout the night, and I decided to chat to some calmer visitors.

Next up, I moved on to Moalboal on the west coast of the island. There, I took my Advanced Scuba Diving course as I continued to try and escape from the impending reality of returning back to England. The days were hard work and tiring but the rewards were incredible. As the only student on the course, I had one to one tuition with my Latvian instructor, who knew of Palace because of our former internationals from his home land, Andrejs Rubins and Alek Kolinko, but his interest in football stretched little further than that. During my four dives, I saw a whole range of unbelievable wildlife on different dive sites.

On the boat back from one dive, I began chatting to another instructor, who was a Geordie living in the Philippines. Unusually for anyone from the North-East donning a black and white shirt, he didn't hate Pardew. In fact, he even rated him. Ah, but he didn't have to watch it every week I'm sure they'd argue. I mean, how could he while living in this football haven? As he put it, *"During the World Cup, you would flick through the channels and find eight of them showing chickens fighting but you couldn't see the biggest sporting event on earth!"*

However, I chose to see his more positive opinions on Pardew in a different light. If he was intelligent enough to choose to live on a beautiful Pacific Island rather than living in Newcastle, his views were probably worth listening to more than any of the fat, topless anti-Pardew fans in St. James' Park.

After a few days in the sun to recover from my tiredness of the diving (it's a tough old life isn't it?) and a couple more nights in Cebu City, I set off for my final Eastern Stop, Hong Kong. At the airport, as well as messaging the Hong Kong Eagles to try and organise meeting up for a drink, I began to apply for jobs back home. I was due back in England for early July so there was a serious lack of teaching roles available as staff have to announce any plans to leave by the May half term. Still, the idea of doing a mundane and unfulfilling job back home didn't bear thinking about.

However, the thought of living back at my Mum's house in sleepy Berkshire after eight years away in London and Syndey was horrific. Yet without a well-paid job, moving back to London would be impossible. Although, I was still contemplating the idea of heading back to Wellington where the school year started in January and I could apply for jobs for then.

The end of my trip was beginning to feel like the end of the season often does for us fans. A total fear of the nothingness to come in the months ahead, so I was determined to hang onto the happiness of the final few places in the way that I hang on to the last few games of the football season.

Crystal Palace...4 Dundee...3
Selhurst Park, 26/05/14
Julian Speroni Testimonial

Palace: Julian Speroni (Lewis Price 71); Peter Ramage (Neil Ashton 46), Brede Hangeland (Danny Butterfield 46), Damian Delaney (Matt Lawrence 46), Joel Ward (Morgan 46, Barrionuev 80); Wilfried Zaha (Fendley 46, E. Speroni 80), James McArthur (Jerome Boateng 46, Borsalino 72), Barry Bannan (Aki Riihilahti 46), Yannick Bolasie (Jake Gray 46, John Salako 60); Chung-Yong Lee (Sulley Kaikai 46, Alan Pardew 60), Dwight Gayle (Clinton Morrison 46, Pedercini 75).

Dundee: Gourlay (Julian Speroni 77), McGinn (A. Black 46), McPake, Gadzhalov (Konrad 46), Irvine (Kerr 46), Carreiro (Carranza 55, J. Black 83), McAlister (J. Black 61, Nemsadze 75), Adam (Colquhoun 46, Adam 75), Stewart (Ketsbaia 55), Tankulic (Sara 55), Wighton (Caballero 55).

Chapter 50 – Reunited – *Hong Kong & Munich, Cologne (Germany) 22nd June-5th July 2015*

My arrival in Hong Kong returned me to more familiar surroundings. European football shirts were everywhere: Bayern, Holland, Manchester United, Liverpool, Chelsea, Arsenal and you know what, if I looked hard enough, probably even Crystal Palace. However, I was pleased to see lots of evidence of support towards Hong Kong FC too. I might have been in Asia but it felt as though I was in the West. Football pitches and posters were everywhere and it was clear that this was a part of the world that loved our beautiful game.

As I came out of the tube to my hostel, the bright lights of the street made it seem like daytime, despite my evening arrival. In the room, I met a Uruguayan. Upon his discovery that I was English, he expressed a bold and immediate expectation that I'd know more about Louis Suarez than I did about the rest of his country. Unfortunately and embarrassingly, despite being able to make him incredibly jealous that I'd seen his nation's 2-1 victory over our nation in the World Cup, his assessment of English general ignorance and football addiction was correct. However, I was able to shock him with my knowledge about Gonzalo Sorondo, the former Palace defender and Uruguayan international.

The next day I was joined by Tom and Kresta, my friends from Singapore, which was a lovely mirror of the start of my year abroad. With them, I began to explore this crazy city. Eating great food and drinking craft beer at various roof-top venues and lively bars. We also ate the World's cheapest Michelin Star restaurant – a dim sum café in the main train station. Although, we possibly preferred the authentic local food at Lin Heung Tea House. The elderly ladies that brought food round on their trollies looked after us well.

My week in Hong Kong flew by quickly. Throughout it, I met various teachers out there who were having the time of their lives. Of course, speaking to Tom, who was teaching in Singapore, also prompted further seeds in my mind to move out there. I'd had an amazing experience living abroad and starting a life from scratch, with no friends, work or house. However, it had all felt a bit like a gap year. I still had an urge to actually live abroad with a long term 'real' job. I knew that I wanted to teach abroad. With this in mind, and a fear of returning home, I did various research into local international schools and the possibility of finding a job in Hong Kong. It wasn't that I'd instantly fallen in love with the place. It was simply an option that wasn't Egham, where I'd be returning to in England!

On one of our days, Kresta, Tom and I headed to the Ocean Park Theme Park, where as well as spotting many football shirts, including my own Palace top, we were 'thrilled' by the rickety old rides on the top of a steep hill, high above the water. Perhaps unfortunately reminding me of riding 'The Big

Dipper' at Blackpool Pleasure Beach and more poignantly, our 1-0 loss during a long, winless run in 2013 that followed my experience.

Soon enough, it was time to say goodbye to Tom and move on for another reunion. My friend Phill was due to get married in the following month and his stag do was being held in Cologne, Germany. My long haul flight was due to change over in Munich so I decided to have an extra night there to catch up with Max, who I'd met in New Zealand, and see the city.

During the flight from Hong Kong, as well as viewing various movies, I watched a compilation of '250 Great Goals'. It soon became apparent which competitions the producers held the rights to as I saw 'great goals' from the FA Cup, Champions League, U20s Copa America, random International friendlies and U21 internationals. Although the only goal that I'd seen live was a wonder strike by non-league Wrexham as the embarrassed Brentford in the 1st round of the FA Cup and criminally, Palace didn't feature once, I did enjoy seeing Zaha score for the England youth team. I also chuckled as poor old Matt Lawrence scored an own goal while playing for Gillingham.

Upon my arrival in Munich, Max walked me through the old city centre, which was as quiet as it was grand. He pointed out and gave a background to various landmarks, including the impressive Rathaus-Glockenspiel. When we strolled past the Gothic Town Hall, one of his comments particularly stuck with me.

"When Munich wins the Champions League, we all come here to party!"

Now, two things struck me about this. Firstly, how casually he spoke about the local side winning the Champions League. The German league and cup seemed to be dismissed as insignificant and unworthy of a party. Secondly, it was the word 'all' that hit me. Max is in no way a football fan but the biggest party in his town had been when Bayern won the Champions League. Everyone, even he, still mourned the loss to Chelsea in the 2012 final. I wondered if Croydon could hold such a party if we won another ZDS Cup, let alone a Champions League final.

When we met Max's friends in a central beer bar, I was instantly quizzed as to which EPL team I supported. In a strange way, I missed being able to confuse the room and declare that I don't support an 'EPL team' and introduce the blind to CPFC. However, the words 'Crystal Palace' are no longer greeted with blank faces and snide remarks.

"Oh cool!" was the enthusiastic response. A natural acceptance of my team to the big league. As the conversation continued, I reflected on an article that I'd read in the week, suggesting that the power of the Premier League meant that Palace were now one of the 50th biggest 'brands' in world football. Despite loving that and our continued resurgence as a club, part of me feels that it pulls me away from everything I've believed in since first catching the Palace Addiction as a kid.

After a bit of site-seeing, sausage eating and beer drinking (what else is there to do in Germany?) I set off for Cologne. There, I would see my some of my closest friends, who I hadn't seen for nearly a year. In the squares around the incredible cathedral, we drank kolsch beers and caught up with each other's stories. Three drunken days later, I stepped off a flight at Stansted, around midnight. It was cold, dark and raining. Welcome back to England. The Eagle had landed.

Chris Owen, member of the Hong Kong Eagles

The CPFC community in Hong Kong currently numbers just shy of 20 (accounted for). There have been reports of the odd sash or striped shirt spotted around the city or on outlying islands, but that's it in terms of known characters who we have on our Facebook group or Whatsapp chat.

Quite a few maintain their season tickets and travel back regularly to games, either coinciding with business trips or holidays. The age span is approximately 23 to 55 (some ages may have been massaged up or down!). The guys work in a cross section of jobs from banking, insurance, law and IT to teaching and design, and originate from all over South London and beyond - as well as HK and Jakarta. Although we are keen to grow the local fanbase, they don't seem to have found us in any great numbers yet.

We are well served for games here - the football network shows every single game live across its channels - better coverage than the UK! The only downside is that the analysis shows are in Cantonese and most of us are not sufficiently proficient to get much insight. However, the in-game commentary is in English.

Our pub of choice is now The Dog House in Wanchai, and has been for a couple of years. We were nomads in the early days of Premier League as we couldn't guarantee getting a landlord to give us a screen to ourselves. But over time we developed a good relationship with The Dog House and our loyalty is rewarded with CPFC games being shown on the big screen at the back of the bar every week.

Pre-Premier League it was nigh on impossible to see any games other than on feeds online (and not many Championship games get broadcasted), so for those who have been out here for a long time, these last four seasons have been a fantastic boost to connect back to watch Palace matches and meet a new group of mates.

Due to the time difference, kick off is usually 10 or 11 pm (for a 3pm game). We tend to meet an hour or so before for some casual grub and early bird beers. If Saturday is looking particularly clear a few of us will gather for the early game and some looseners in the area around The Dog House, which is not short of boozers! Depending on the result and spirits in the camp (celebratory sambucas have been few and far between in recent months), a group of us might head on for a couple of nightcaps before bidding our farewells until next week.

The 3-3 Liverpool game was a memorable one. We lucked out in Hong Kong because coincidentally that Tuesday was a public holiday, meaning a few of us didn't mind getting up at 3am to watch the match. We didn't meet up but the Whatsapp group was buzzing and eventually went into melt down when Gayley brought us level. I was giving my brother, who lives in Auckland, a blow by blow account over Whatsapp too as he was waking up to find out how we were getting on.

More recently a sizeable group made our way to London for the FA Cup final. We met up around Waterloo for breakfast beers and sat dotted around the stadium hoping to witness a bit of history. Most of us had a 24-36 hour turn around on flights to be back for work on Monday. That was a deflating 12 hours on the plane home!

I think we'd all agree it's been a great bonus to have access to Palace every week through the season. And we've all made a bunch of new mates we probably would never have met before. That's what Palace is all about. Win, lose or draw, we'll be back at The Dog House to share buckets of Heineken and spread the Palace gospel.

Chapter 51 – Same Old Palace – *Selhurst Park, 22nd August 2015*

Crystal Palace...2 Aston Villa...1
Selhurst Park, 22/08/15
Premier League

Palace: Alex McCarthy, Joel Ward, Scott Dann, Damian Delaney, Pape Souare, James McArthur, Yohan Cabaye (Mile Jedinak 82), Wilfried Zaha (Jordan Mutch 46), Jason Puncheon, Bakary Sako, Glenn Murray (Dwight Gayle 46).
Subs Not Used: Wayne Hennessey, Martin Kelly, Chung-Yong Lee, Patrick Bamford.

Aston Villa: Guzan, Bacuna, Richards, Clark, Amavi, Gueye, Westwood, Sanchez (Traore 69), Grealish, Agbonlahor, Gestede.
Subs Not Used: Bunn, Baker, Hutton, Veretout, Sinclair, Ayew.

When we worry about things in our personal life, we generally like to take control of them and fix them ourselves. In fact, we feel a huge amount of pressure to do so. If we don't take charge of our fate, our worries won't go away. No one will fix them for us. That's one of the appeals of football. Us fans can hand over our emotions and worries to eleven professionals who we trust to do their best for us. I'd spent much of the year fretting that Palace would be relegated, but through none of my own doing, my worries had been well and truly squashed.

Unfortunately, I hadn't done much to take charge of my own personal worries while I was away either. I'd looked at possibilities of teaching abroad here and there but ultimately, I'd treated my concerns – a lack of job, and girlfriend, and flat, and money – by ignoring them rather than tackling them. Amazingly, since I'd returned, I hadn't been left reaping the regret of my lack of actions. Like with most of my Palace worries over the last twenty years (Hillsborough, Wembley for two different play off finals, the Millennium, Stockport), everything had kind of fallen into place and worked out for the best.

On the opening day of the 2015/16 season, a game against Norwich City, my phone buzzed away in my pocket as I was at Phill's wedding. Since my cousin's wedding six years previously, which I'd missed to watch us host Plymouth Argyle on the opening day of that season, I'd obviously grown up a little and maybe even matured. Or maybe it was that I was simply more familiar with missing games? However, I never even considered missing this wedding for the match.

Then finally, a week later, I returned to my spiritual home as Palace took on Arsenal. The routine came rushing back like learning to ride a bike – meeting my Dad, a fry up in the morning, catching the train with my fellow eagles, stepping out of Selhurst Station and nipping into the Railway Club for a cheeky pint or two with my mates. From there, we strolled out into the August sunshine and optimistically joined the well-spirited crowd that was gathering and heading up the Holmesdale Road towards the ground. The whole experience is so much more sociable than a tiny group of dedicates turning up in the small hours, or watching a game alone in a hostel computer room. Although, part of me missed belonging to the rare and unexplainable cult of following Palace Down Under. Had Palace become too mainstream? Unlike most of my time supporting the club, the ground was packed, the bars were full and half time beers were certainly out of the question.

Perhaps even more incredibly, the confidence around SE25 was higher than I'd ever known it. Alan Pardew's name was sung with passion and belief as the club moved from success to success under him. We'd made the first signing that could genuinely be compared to Attilio Lombardo's arrival in South London in Yohan Cabaye, and we were dreaming of a European tour. Nobody, inside or outside of Selhurst Park was talking about relegation. But some things never change, Arsenal or Barnsley, Cabaye or David Wright, the sounds are the same.

"Selhurst Half-Time Super-Draw!"
"Daddy, can I have some chips?"
"Programmes! Get your match day programmes!"
"Wa'cha reckon today then?" "Gawd knows!"

There's nothing quite like ear-wigging conversations at football. No one ever agrees on anything – other than that the referee is, inevitably, a wanker.

Of course, as always, Palace made me feel really at home and welcomed back – by losing. Despite Joel Ward briefly giving us hope at 1-1.

However, it was the game a week later against Aston Villa that really helped me think that things had changed for me and Palace after a year away. For the first time, I was taking a girl I was dating to Palace. She loved it. Our pre-match meal with fellow eagles and friends, placing a bet on Jason Puncheon to score the opening goal, the drinking, the crowd, the aggression, the passion. I loved opening up my world to someone new.

Two days previously, I'd signed a contract to move into a flat with my friend Barlow. Originally, I'd wanted to move back to Battersea, where I'd lived before going away. However, desperate to re-find my identity in England, I'd decided to, finally, for the first time in my life, live in South London – Streatham. After not wanting to come back to England at all, South London had provided me with a spiritual home. I couldn't imagine being anywhere else now.

Waking up each morning and looking over South London from my balcony, seeing the Crystal Palace TV mast as I walk to the station. I grin and hum to myself. Growing up in the sleepy town of Ascot, I'd lacked an identity as a child and always latched onto Palace's, even trying to adopt a South London accent during my sixth form days. I mean, unless you own a race horse and have tea with the queen, what else can you identify with from Ascot? People live quiet, comfortable lives. Not the things that a teenager longs for! Often, people see me as a Palace fan first and James second. However, now, I was living the South London and Proud life. I'd even walked to Selhurst Park from my flat for a match, with a huge, ridiculous smile splashed across my face.

Indeed, I was not only living in South London, I was working there too. Just 30 hours after landing in England, I'd fallen into a teaching job. Helping me feel at home, half of the school's County Cup winning football team were signed up by the Palace youth academy, who supported the kids to stay on track with their education and behaviour in school. At first, I'd taken the job as I was limited on options, but I soon grew to love the place and while the dream of working abroad hasn't gone away, I'm currently very happy there, having been promoted onto the Leadership Team in my first year.

Of course, being able to nip up to Selhurst so easily for games helps my satisfaction too. Although, I've found it easier to decline the opportunity to head to an away game. However, unglamourous random trips to Middlesborough or Swansea remind me that the addiction hasn't completely gone away. Yet, I don't even judge myself for watching them on tele these days, such is the arm-chair fan that my year abroad and the ease of streaming matches has turned me into.

Back at Selhurst Park and the Villa game, it was the dramatic winner from our new signing, Bakery Sako, that really cemented that I moved from 'dating' to 'in a relationship' as Facebook would describe. Alongside me, she adopted my addiction and love by leaping into the air, jubilant at what the moment meant to me. Of course, for her, it could never be the same. She'd missed the journey. She'd not seen us losing at Preston and Huddersfield. As far as she knew, it was Yohan Cabaye, and Cup Finals, and last minute winners and beating Liverpool all the way. Ok, maybe beating Liverpool was all the way (even Trevor Francis managed that!)

The year abroad hadn't been completely fulfilling. I hadn't managed to teach in another country, but it had been far more successful than I'd ever imagined in so many other ways. I'd visited sixty two towns and cities over eleven countries, making dozens of friends along the way. Some, such as Richard and Joe, would develop into close friends, some I'd keep up regular contact with, others would simply flash up on my Facebook from time to time, and with a few of them, I'd never see or hear of them again outside of a small town in Asia somewhere. However, all of them helped to make my journey special.

Of course, none more so than the Crystal Palace Sydney Supporters Club. Despite living so far away, I'll always feel like I'm a member of that. Seeing a group of them come over for the weekend of the Cup Final added to the emotion of a roller coaster of a day. However, one thing that I had discovered was that while we stay in the Premier League, Palace will never be far away – wherever in the world I am. I'd watched us play in Malaysia, Thailand, Vietnam, Oz and New Zealand. No matter where I was, or what opportunities I was experiencing, I always found time for watching CPFC, however uncomfortable or preposterous it was. I guess, there really is no cure to the Palace Addiction.

I think you'll find, if you look out for it, the world really is red and blue. Or maybe that's just the lenses I wear...?

Appendix 1

	Club	Austrailian Location
1	Crystal Palace Hotel	Sydney
2	Liverpool Street	Sydney
3	Oxford Street	Sydney
4	Charlton Pool	Sydney Botantical Gardens
5	Preston Avenue	Sydney
6	York Street	Sydney
7	Rotherham Street	Brisbane
8	Ipswich	Brisbane
9	Everton Park	Brisbane
10	Brighton	Queensland
11	Mansfield	Queensland
12	Loftus Road (QPR)	Vacluse, Sydney
13	Newcastle	New South Wales
14	Torquay	New South Wales
15	Cardiff	New South Wales
16	Bradford Street	Sydney
17	Sheffield (Wednesday) Street	Paramatta, Sydney
18	Sheffield (United) Street	Paramatta, Sydney
19	Bolton Drive	Melbourne
20	Cheltenham	Melbourne
21	Blackburn	Melbourne
22	Doncaster	Melbourne
23	Newport	Melbourne
24	Southampton Drive	Melbourne
25	Tottenham	Melbourne
26	Bristol (City)	Great Ocean Road
27	Bristol (Rovers)	Great Ocean Road
28	Chesterfield	Great Ocean Road
29	Peterborough	Great Ocean Road
30	Chelsea Street	Sydney
31	Cambridge Avenue	Sydney
32	Derby Street	Sydney
33	Burton Street	North Sydney

A view from the top – Steve Browett, Co-owner of CPFC

What was your favourite match of the 2014/15 season?

Probably the Spurs game when we won in Alan Pardew's first home game. It was a great atmosphere and an important result for how the season would eventually pan out.

What was your favourite moment in the 2014/15 season?

Securing Pardew as manager as it was vital for the club's survival in the Premier League and longer term, progression as a club.

Who was your player of the season in 2014/15 season?

Jason Puncheon or Scott Dann. Both of them were exceptional as we stayed up for the second season in a row.

At Christmas, things didn't look great for us, but we ended up surviving quite comfortably. When did you believe we were safe?

West Ham away was the game that did it, but I felt confident we'd be ok fairly soon after Alan arrived.

Since taking over the club, has the rapid speed of our progress surprised even you as an owner?

Yes. Getting promoted in a season where we were tipped to go down was massive and a bit unexpected and after that, staying up in the Premier League is not what Palace normally do. With the club in administration, we bought it to ensure its survival so to have had such success too has been a real bonus.

Throughout the season, I followed the games in the middle of the night in Australia with our small but dedicated Sydney Supporters Club. How aware of different CPFC supporters clubs around the world are you?

Very much. I lived abroad for a year myself - in the days before the internet - and followed Palace from afar. I'm often in Hong Kong and have twice watched Palace recently in NYC at Legends with the NY Eagles.

Overall, after a season of so many highs and lows, how do you look back on the 2014/15 season?

I was very low when we lost our manager just before the start of the season. We had a difficult first half of the year but Neil Warnock did well to steady the ship and then of course, we had a great second half under a top manager.

Before the 2014/15 season started, what were your hopes/expectations?

I was confident looking forward to it with Tony in charge. Then with no manager on the eve of the season starting, I was very concerned. Staying up was the target and at the start of the season I'd have been happy with 17th.

Opponent	Score	Where I Watched it
GAK Graz (Pre season)	13 - 1	Stream in Battersea
Columbus Crew (Pre season)	2 - 2	Stream in Battersea
Philadelphia Union (Pre season)	1 - 0	-
Richmond Kickers (Pre season)	3 - 0	-
Brentford (Pre season)	2 - 3	Live
FC Augsburg (Pre season)	0 - 0	-
Arsenal	1 - 2	Cheers Bar, Sydney
West Ham United	1 - 3	The Royal Exhibition Hotel, Sydney
Walsall (League Cup)	3 - 0	-
Newcastle United	3 - 3	-
Burnley	0 - 0	25 minutes of the second half in Cheers Bar, Sydney
Everton	3 - 2	The final five minutes in Scruffy Murphys, Sydney
Newcastle United (League Cup)	2 - 3	The first half hour on a stream in Sydney
Leicester City	2 - 0	Second half in Cheers Bar, Sydney
Hull City	0 - 2	The Royal Exhibition Hotel, Sydney
Chelsea	1 - 2	Scruffy Murphys, Sydney
West Bromwich Albion	2 - 2	The Royal Exhibition Hotel, Sydney
Sunderland	1 - 3	Second half in an internet café in Surfurs Paradise
Manchester United	0 - 1	-
Liverpool	3 - 1	Second half in a restaurant in Melaka, Malaysia
Swansea City	1 - 1	-
Aston Villa	0 - 1	Brothel in Phuket, Thailand
Tottenham Hotspur	0 - 0	Pub in Koh Tao, Thailand
Stoke City	1 - 1	Pub in Chaing Mai, Thailand
Manchester City	0 - 3	Café in Hanoi, Vietnam
Southampton	1 - 3	Stream in Vacluse, Sydney
QPR	0 - 0	Stream in Vacluse, Sydney
Aston Villa	0 - 0	-

Dover Athletic (FA Cup)	4 – 0	Stream in Vacluse, Sydney
Tottenham Hotspur	2 – 1	Last half hour on a stream in Redfern, Sydney
Burnley	3 – 2	The Royal Exhibition Hotel, Sydney
Southampton (FA Cup)	3 – 2	-
Everton	0 – 1	The Royal Exhibition Hotel, Sydney
Leicester City	1 – 0	The Royal Exhibition Hotel, Sydney
Newcastle United	1 – 1	Cheers Bar, Sydney
Liverpool (FA Cup)	1 – 2	A stream in Newcastle, New South Wales
Arsenal	1 – 2	The Royal Exhibition Hotel, Sydney
West Ham United	3 – 1	The Royal Exhibition Hotel, Sydney
Southampton	0 – 1	Cheers Bar, Sydney
Queens Park Rangers	3 – 1	The Royal Exhibition Hotel, Sydney
Stoke City	2 – 1	The Royal Exhibition Hotel, Sydney
Manchester City	2 – 1	-
Sunderland	4 – 1	-
West Bromwich Albion	0 – 2	-
Hull City	0 – 2	-
Chelsea	0 – 1	-
Manchester United	1 – 2	A stream in Taupo, New Zealand
Liverpool	3 – 1	The Royal Exhibition Hotel, Sydney
Swansea City	1 – 0	Tony's flat, Sydney

James Howland

We All Follow The Palace,
Over Land and Sea!
(AND BRIGHTON!)
We All Follow the Palace,
On To Vic-Tor-Y!

16261638R00184

Printed in Poland
by Amazon Fulfillment
Poland Sp. z o.o., Wrocław